DEPRECIATION, INFLATION, AND THE TAXATION OF INCOME FROM CAPITAL

DEPRECIATION, INFLATION, AND THE TAXATION OF INCOME FROM CAPITAL

Edited by
Charles R. Hulten

With the Assistance of
Janice McCallum

*Publication of this volume was made possible
by financial support from the Ford Foundation*

An Urban Institute Book

  THE URBAN INSTITUTE PRESS · WASHINGTON, D.C.

THE URBAN INSTITUTE is a nonprofit policy research and educational organization established in Washington, D.C. in 1968. Its staff investigates interrelated social and economic problems of urban communities, and government policies affecting those communities and the people who live in them. The Institute disseminates significant findings of such research through the active publications program of its Press. The Institute has two goals for work in each of its research areas: to help shape thinking about societal problems and efforts to solve them, and to improve government decisions and performance by providing better information and analytic tools.

Through work that ranges from broad conceptual studies to administrative and technical assistance, Institute researchers contribute to the stock of knowledge available to public officials and to private individuals and groups concerned with formulating and implementing more efficient and effective government policy.

Conclusions or opinions expressed are those of the authors and do not necessarily reflect the views of other staff members, officers or trustees of the Institute, or of any organizations which provide financial support to the Institute.

PARTICIPANTS

Henry Aaron
The Brookings Institution

Valerie Amerkhail
Chase Econometrics

Lloyd Atkinson
Joint Economic Committee

Alan Auerbach
Harvard University

James Barth
National Science Foundation & George Washington University

Marc Bendick
The Urban Institute

Barry Bosworth
The Brookings Institution

David Bradford
Princeton University

E. Cary Brown
Massachusetts Institute of Technology

Dennis Cox
Office of Industrial Economics

Bruce Davie
House Ways and Means Committee

Frank DeLeeuw
Bureau of Economic Analysis

Thomas Dernburg
American University

W. Erwin Diewert
The University of British Columbia

Larry Dildine
Office of Tax Analysis

William Dinkelacker
Office of Management & Budget

Dennis Dugan
GAD Program Analysis Division

David Einhorn
Department of Housing and Urban Development

Robert Eisner
Northwestern University

Warren Farb
Department of Commerce

Jack Faucett
Jack Faucett Associates

Seymour Fiekowsky
Office of Tax Analysis

Don Fullerton
Princeton University

Harvey Galper
Office of Tax Analysis

Roger Gordon
Bell Laboratories

Jane Gravelle
Congressional Research Service

Allen Grommet
House Committee on the Budget

Robert E. Hall
Stanford University

Michael J. Harper
Bureau of Labor Statistics

Charles R. Hulten
The Urban Institute

George Idem
Congressional Budget Office

Dale W. Jorgenson
Harvard University
Arnold Katz
*Bureau of Economic
Analysis*
John W. Kendrick
*George Washington
University*
Kent Kunze
Bureau of Labor Statistics
Wilhelmina Leigh
National Urban League
James Lyday
*House Committee on
the Budget*
Jerome A. Mark
Bureau of Labor Statistics
Peter Mieszkowski
University of Houston
Richard Morgenstern
The Urban Institute
Dan Newlon
*National Science
Foundation*
Mieko Nishimizu
The World Bank
John R. Norsworthy
Bureau of Labor Statistics
Larry Ozanne
The Urban Institute
Rudolph Penner
*American Enterprise
Institute*
Janice Peskin
*Bureau of Economic
Analysis*
George Peterson
The Urban Institute

Joseph Riley
*Department of Housing
and Urban Development*
James Robertson
The Urban Institute
Elizabeth Roistacher
*Department of Housing
and Urban Development*
Jerry Silverstein
*Bureau of Economic
Analysis*
Larry Slifman
*Board of Governors of the
Federal Reserve System*
Charles Steindel
*Board of Governors of the
Federal Reserve System*
Emil Sunley
Department of Treasury
Paul J. Taubman
University of Pennsylvania
Eric Toder
*Office of Tax Analysis
Department of Energy*
Norman Ture
Norman B. Ture, Inc.
Kevin Villani
*Department of Housing
and Urban Development*
James Wetzler
*Joint Committee on
Taxation*
Frank C. Wykoff
Pomona College
Allan H. Young
*Bureau of Economic
Analysis*

CONTENTS

DEPRECIATION, INFLATION, AND THE TAXATION OF INCOME FROM CAPITAL

INTRODUCTION

Charles Hulten

Few areas of the U.S. Tax Code have been changed or revised more frequently than those sections relating to depreciable assets. Major revisions occurred in 1954 (accelerated depreciation), in 1962 (the Guidelines and the investment tax credit), and in 1971 (the Asset Depreciation Range system). Unfortunately, none of these changes anticipated the high rates of inflation of the 1970s, and the tax treatment of depreciable assets has once again surfaced as a major issue in the debate on tax reform. The basic question in this debate centers on the problem of designing a tax system which adequately corrects for the impact of inflation, provides neutral incentives for economic growth, and is administratively feasible. These matters were the subject of a one-day conference held by The Urban Institute on December 1, 1980.

Inflation creates an impact on the tax system in a variety of ways. Capital consumption allowances are, first of all, currently restricted to the original cost of the capital asset (gross of the investment tax credit). During inflationary periods, replacement cost exceeds original cost and depreciation deductions do not reflect the value of the capital used up in production (or, put differently, the real value of original cost depreciation deductions falls as the price level rises). The result is an upward bias in the effective tax rate on income from depreciable assets. This bias is reinforced by the taxation of inflation-induced capital gains, since a tax liability may be incurred even though no real gain has accrued.

On the other hand, inflation can lead to lower effective tax rates

1

because nominal interest payments are deductible for tax purposes. Nominal interest rates appear to move roughly point for point with the rate of inflation (Fisher's Law), so real pretax borrowing costs are not increased by inflation. The higher nominal interest rates, on the other hand, give rise to additional tax deductions and thus result in a downward bias in the effective tax rate on debt-financed depreciable assets. The relative importance of the upward and downward inflation biases is obviously an important issue in any effort to correct the tax system for the effects of inflation.

The 1970s were also characterized by a significant decline in the rate of productivity growth. A traditional policy prescription for slower economic growth has been to stimulate capital formation through increased tax incentives, and it is therefore not surprising that the recent productivity slowdown has led to widespread support for a reduction in effective tax rates. This may further complicate the problem of designing a business tax system to cope with the problem of inflation, since a proposed change in the system must also serve as a stimulus to investment spending. The problems of inflation and productivity are, of course, not entirely independent, since an inflation-induced increase in effective tax rates (because of original cost depreciation) may lead to reduced capital formation and thus to reduced productivity growth. If this is indeed the case, then a policy designed to compensate for inflation will also tend to stimulate growth. However, the link between inflation and productivity is problematic and, as noted above, inflation may have reduced effective tax rates instead of raising them.

While inflation and growth are the central issues in the current debate on tax reform, tax neutrality is also an important consideration in the design of new tax incentives. A nonneutral tax system may lead to an inefficient allocation of resources among assets or industries. Unfortunately, the current income tax system provides ample opportunities for tax-induced distortions in the allocation of resources (for example, the exclusion of income from owner-occupied housing, the partial coverage of the tax credit, and the potential divergence between tax and economic depreciation). Since inflation operates on the neutrality of the tax system through historical cost depreciation and the exclusion of interest paid (and via the taxation of capital gains), and since the misallocation of resources due to a nonneutral tax system may retard economic growth, neutrality must be considered jointly with the issues of inflation and growth.

A wide variety of policy proposals have been offered as a cure for the problems associated with inflation and slow productivity growth. They may be grouped under three general categories. The first category would lower effective income tax rates by accelerating depreciation write-off periods and increasing the rate of the investment tax credit. This category of tax incentive has been the traditional means of providing a stimulus to investment spending (the 1954, 1962, and 1971 tax reforms fall in this category), and the Conable-Jones and current administration proposals are nominally of this type. The second type of proposal would index depreciation allowances to the rate of inflation. This may be achieved by allowing the taxpayer to increase his remaining asset basis by an index of inflation, or through the Auerbach-Jorgenson first-year capital recovery allowance. Under the Auerbach-Jorgenson proposal, the taxpayer would receive an immediate deduction equal to the inflation adjusted present value of the true (economic) depreciation on his asset. Indexation in either form would involve a larger conceptual change in the tax code than the acceleration approach.

The third category of proposal would move toward a consumption tax by allowing taxpayers to immediately expense their investment expenditures. The switch from an income tax to a consumption tax is clearly the most radical of the tax proposals, although it can be partially achieved within the income tax framework by allowing a sufficiently large increase in the investment tax credit or an acceleration of depreciation allowances. At sufficiently low rates of inflation, the Conable-Jones-Reagan proposals achieve or exceed expensing and may therefore be regarded as belonging in part to this third category of proposal.

The papers in this volume are based on those presented at The Urban Institute's conference on depreciation analysis and policy, but include additional material as well. For the convenience of the reader, these papers have been organized into two parts. Those in part I deal with the general problems associated with the taxation of depreciable assets and include the papers by Bradford, Diewert, Hulten and Wykoff, and Brown. The papers in part II are more oriented to the specific policy proposals under discussion, or the analysis of the current tax treatment of depreciable assets. This part includes the papers by Sunley, Hall, Jorgenson and Sullivan, Bradford and Fullerton, Gravelle, and an edited version of the roundtable discussion held during the conference. Discussants' comments accompany those papers presented at the conference.

The various contributions can be briefly summarized. The paper by Bradford considers the problem of designing a neutral system of saving and investment incentives. An eight-fold classification of incentives is developed which includes as special cases the major policy options of (1) accelerating depreciation allowances (a "consumption tax rule" incentive, in Bradford's terminology), (2) instituting economic depreciation alone or in conjunction with partial expensing, and (3) manipulating the rate of the investment tax credit (a "direct grant type" incentive). Among the many results derived in this framework, Bradford shows that both economic depreciation and immediate expensing with no deduction of interest paid have desirable neutrality properties. A combination of depreciation and expensing can also be neutral, but a variable exclusion of interest from taxation is required (which depends on the marginal tax rate of the assets' owner). Failure to make this variable adjustment for interest exclusion will tend to drive real assets into the hands of the highest bracket tax-payers and interest-bearing assets into the hands of low bracket taxpayers.

Bradford also demonstrates that the traditional tax incentive devices—accelerated depreciation and the investment tax credit (ITC)—are not in general neutral. The neutrality condition for accelerated write-off periods is shown to depend on the rate of interest and the marginal tax rate, while the neutrality condition for the ITC depends on asset durability. Thus, unless the tax system is calibrated to allow for differences in these variables, the standard investment incentives are not consistent with Bradford's definition of neutrality. These results are obviously applicable to the ongoing debate over the use of accelerated depreciation and in-creased rates of the ITC as a general solution to the problems posed by in-flation.

Another important policy conclusion derived from the Bradford analy-sis is that no "front-end" adjustment (like Auerbach-Jorgenson or the in-vestment tax credit) will *perfectly* correct for inflation when tax rates vary across taxpayers, except immediate expensing. If one is prepared to aban-don the taxation of the return to savings (i.e., to move to a consumption tax), eliminating interest taxation plus immediate expensing will solve the problem of neutrality under inflation. The transition to such a system can be achieved by initially allowing partial expensing and partial interest tax-ation.

Tax neutrality is also the subject of the paper by Diewert. Here, though, the problem is to measure the efficiency loss associated with nonneutral tax systems. This is a familiar problem which has been dealt with exten-sively in the public finance literature. However, most treatments of the deadweight loss problem (e.g., the Harberger-type analysis) are essen-tially static in nature since they take the total stock of capital as exogenous (i.e., as determined independently of the tax system). In Diewert's proposed framework, the stock of capital is an endogenously determined variable which depends, in part, on tax policy.

The Diewert model is based on the Malinvaud framework which views capital and labor as producing output and, in addition, capital which is one year older. The latter is then viewed as an input to the following year's production, and production is thus a recursive process involving successive transfers of capital into the future. The total amount of capital used in each period is endogenous to the intertemporal optimization problem, and variations in tax parameters can influence the solution. Welfare loss in this framework is defined as the difference between the present value of the socially optimal production plan and the present value of the tax-distorted plan, valued at socially optimal prices. Diewert manipulates this framework to obtain an expression for the welfare loss which is essentially a dynamic "welfare triangle." He then applies his analysis to a stylized corporate income tax and concludes that the resulting welfare losses are potentially quite large.

The Diewert paper makes use of the theory of profit functions and is highly abstract in its style of presentation. The reader should bear this in mind when approaching this paper.

The Hulten-Wykoff paper deals with the theory and measurement of economic depreciation. It is of relevance to the current policy debate because of the widespread (but certainly not unanimous) view that tax depreciation should in principle correspond to true capital consumption costs. (As we have seen, this policy can be shown to have desirable efficiency features.) The difficulty with implementing this principle is that most assets are owner-utilized and therefore deteriorate in place. There is thus no observable dollar cost associated with actual capital consumption (as there is with labor and other current costs) and, consequently, no direct cost basis for tax deductions. This fact has led many observers to conclude that it is not feasible to base tax deductions on economic depreciation and to conclude that either arbitrary cost allocation or immediate expensing is necessary.

The Hulten-Wykoff paper challenges this view by showing that it is in fact possible to measure the rate of economic depreciation for a wide variety of assets. Rates of economic depreciation can be inferred from market data on used asset prices (there is a large literature on this subject, including previous research by Hulten and Wykoff) and from a variety of other sources. The main conclusion which emerges from the study of used asset prices is that the pattern of economic depreciation is approximately geometric (or declining balance, in the terminology of tax analysis) and can thus be summarized by a single rate. Rates of depreciation for assets without an active resale market are inferred using techniques similar to those used by the Bureau of Economic Analysis, and the average annual rate of economic depreciation is found to be 13.3 percent for equipment and 3.7 percent for plant. Detailed estimates for 32 types of structures and equipment are also shown (these estimates are used in the Jorgenson-Sullivan and Gravelle papers).

The main policy conclusion which emerges from this analysis is the feasibility of basing tax depreciation allowances on economic depreciation. If income (and not consumption) is to be the primary tax base, such a policy is desirable on neutrality grounds. Furthermore, the impossibility of measuring economic depreciation cannot be used as an argument for a consumption tax/immediate expensing policy.

The paper by E. Cary Brown explores the neutrality properties of the net investment tax credit. Where a standard investment tax credit is based on the gross cost of an asset, the net credit is based on the cost of the asset less the present value of depreciation deductions. When this present value is based on economic depreciation (as in the Auerbach-Jorgenson proposal), the net investment tax credit is shown to be neutral with respect to asset durability. The net credit could therefore be combined with the Auerbach-Jorgenson system to provide an extra degree of investment stimulus (the remarks in the Bradford paper about the Auerbach-Jorgenson system should be kept in mind, however).

The paper by Emil Sunley begins part II. This paper is a revised version of Sunley's introductory remarks which opened the conference. Sunley summarizes the general policy issues underlying the current debate over depreciation reform and describes and comments on the various reforms proposed in 1980: the 10-5-3 system, the Senate Finance Committee Bill, the Carter administration proposal, and the Auerbach-Jorgenson proposal.

The paper by Hall extends the well-known Hall-Jorgenson user cost framework to allow for the tax treatment of interest and capital gains in an inflationary economy. He argues that even without inflation, effective corporate (and total) tax rates on different equity-financed assets vary considerably, from an effective corporate rate of -2 percent on equipment to 37 percent on plant. Such variation implies the potential for large welfare losses. When investment is financed by borrowing from an untaxed individual, effective corporate tax rates become negative under Hall's assumption (-89 percent for equipment and -16 percent for plant). Thus, the tax becomes a substantial subsidy to those corporations with sufficient income from other sources to absorb the deduction. Under a 10 percent rate of inflation, the effective tax rates on equity financed equipment and plant are 44 percent and 51 percent, respectively. With debt finance, assuming that a modified Fisher's Law holds, the corresponding effective tax rates are a surprising −122 percent and −95 percent.

The basic message conveyed by these numbers is that if borrowers and lenders face widely different marginal tax rates (or, alternatively, if lenders accept negative real after-tax rates of return), variations in the degree of leverage can have a more powerful impact on effective tax rates than variations in the rate of inflation. Furthermore, the impact of inflation may depend on the degree of leverage: increasing effective tax rates when investment is financed with equity but lowering them to potentially absurd levels on debt financed investment (a point noted at the beginning of this introduction). One policy implication is that the case for granting business taxpayers relief from inflation (through accelerated depreciation or an increase in the ITC) is hard to make if inflation actually lowers effective tax rates.

The Jorgenson-Sullivan paper traces the history of effective corporate tax rates over the period 1946–1980. These tax rates are based on a model which simulates the capital consumption allowances actually claimed by taxpayers, and results are presented for 35 types of plant and equipment and 44 industries in selected years. The estimates of actual depreciation practices and the effective rates of the ITC are also presented. Jorgenson and Sullivan also analyze the effective tax rates implied by the Reagan administration proposal, and the Senate Finance Committee proposal. The Jorgenson-Sullivan paper thus provides a factual underpinning for the current policy debate.

The main finding of this paper is that although inflation increases effective tax rates, U.S. tax law results in effective tax rates which are well below the statutory tax rate, even at the very high currently anticipated rates of inflation. For the year 1980, Jorgenson and Sullivan report an effective tax rate of 19 percent for equipment and 35 percent for plant. These rates are consistent with the corresponding Hall rates calculated at zero and 10 percent expected rates of inflation for an equity financed investment. Jorgenson-Sullivan also find that the average effective corporate tax rate under current law (for plant and equipment combined) is 24 percent, and that this rate would fall to 13 percent under the Senate Finance Committee proposal, and that it would be negative under the Reagan administration proposal. Other interesting findings are (1) the current U.S.

tax law provides depreciation allowances for corporate investment that are in line with economic depreciation at currently anticipated rates of inflation, (2) that differences in effective tax rates among assets under current law are substantial even at the current high rate of anticipated inflation, (3) that these differences would increase as inflation falls, and (4) that the differences in effective tax rates among assets would widen under the Reagan proposal.

The paper by Bradford and Fullerton provides an analysis of the cost of capital approach to measuring effective tax rates used by Hall and by Jorgenson-Sullivan. While they generally welcome this approach as a useful analytical tool, they also point out that the resulting estimates are quite sensitive to assumptions made. First, tax rate estimates vary with the interest rate used in the calculations. Second, a net "subsidized" investment with a particular interest rate can show a subsidy rate that is arbitrarily high since the return on the project approaches zero in the denominator. Third, any effective tax rate results depend on the assumed relationship between inflation and nominal interest rates. Their conclusion is that much sensitivity analysis and specificity are required in studies that undertake to estimate effective tax rates.

The paper by Jane Gravelle presents an estimate of the welfare loss associated with the nonneutrality in the present U.S. tax law. Gravelle's method is a variant of the Harberger triangle analysis in which distortions are measured across asset types rather than industries. The uneven treatment of asset types under the current tax code is estimated to have resulted in a $2.5 billion welfare loss in 1978.

The roundtable discussion held at the end of the conference brought together economists from the universities and from the Washington policy community. This exchange of views provides an insight into the issues and questions surrounding the efforts to change depreciation policy.

Those papers in this volume which were presented at the December 1 conference (the Bradford, Hall, Hulten-Wykoff papers) are accompanied by the comments of the conference discussants. These comments reflect, to some extent, the papers as they stood at the time of the conference. Most of the papers were substantially revised, and the discussants' remarks should be interpreted with this in mind.

Finally, many thanks are due the people who assisted with the organization of the conference and the preparation of this volume. Special recognition is due Larry Dildine, Harvey Galper, and Emil Sunley (all of the U.S. Department of the Treasury). They were instrumental in helping to get the project under way and provided much encouragement and help thereafter. My colleague George Peterson also deserves special thanks for his support and advice. No amount of thanks, however, is adequate to express my gratitude to Janice McCallum and Jo West. They assisted in the administration of the conference and in the preparation of this volume, and contributed immeasurably to both projects.

PART ONE

ANALYSIS OF THE GENERAL ISSUES IN THE DESIGN OF BUSINESS TAX POLICY

ISSUES IN THE DESIGN OF SAVINGS AND INVESTMENT INCENTIVES

David F. Bradford

The view is widespread that the rate of accumulation of capital in recent years in the United States has been too low. This conclusion is based in part upon a comparison of the rate of net investment, especially of business fixed investment, relative to aggregate output both with its past value in the U.S. and with its value in the other advanced industrial countries. It is based as well upon symptoms that are presumptively traceable to a slow-down in capital formation, most especially the apparent cessation in the growth of labor productivity.

A deterioration in the rate of return to savers resulting from the interaction of inflation with an unindexed tax system is often cited among the reasons for this shift in performance of the U.S. economy. In particular, the failure of the tax rules to permit correct accounting for depreciation and capital gains, together with a not obviously explicable reluctance of businesses to use the LIFO (Last In First Out) inventory procedures per-

---

[The author is professor of economics and public affairs, Princeton University, and director of the research program in taxation of the National Bureau of Economic Research. Among the many individuals who helped in the development of these ideas, the author would like, in particular, to thank Alan Auerbach, E. Cary Brown, Dale Jorgenson, and Alvin Warren. Any opinions expressed are those of the author and not necessarily those of any of these individuals or institutions.]

mitted under the tax law, result in a burden of tax on the return from investment that increases with the rate of inflation. Furthermore, because the tax treatment of nominally denominated assets also ignores inflation, considerable if poorly understood stress is placed upon the financial structure of the economy in a period of rapid increase in the price level.

A consequence of this view, that there is a problem and that taxes have something to do with it, has been a movement to increase the incentive to save and invest by changing the rules. Somewhat oddly, there seems to be relatively little interest in approaching this by asking what steps would be necessary to correct for inflation. Nor has there yet appeared an explicit strategy of shifting taxation away from an income and toward a consumption base, a policy not necessarily related to inflation. Perhaps because of the perceived complexity of the former and unfamiliarity with the latter, policymakers and the interest groups actively involved with the issue have been attracted to ad hoc measures.

Most prominent and widely discussed among these have been proposals to allow taxpayers to write off the cost of acquisition of productive assets, for purposes of calculating income subject to tax, more rapidly than the economic definition of income would imply. Bills sponsored by House Ways and Means Committee members Conable and Jones (the "10-5-3 proposal"), by committee chairman Al Ullman, and by the Senate Finance Committee (the "2-4-7-10 proposal") would in various ways provide for a grouping of assets into categories, for which relatively rapid write-off for tax purposes would be allowed. Other changes in tax rules recently enacted or currently discussed with a similar objective of reducing the tax on capital income from present inflation-influenced levels are lower effective rates on long-term capital gains, exemption of a limited amount of dividends and savings account interest from individual income taxation, and relaxation of restrictions on tax deferred saving of the sort now allowed via employer sponsored pension programs, Individual Retirement Accounts (IRAs) and Keogh Plans.

These phenomena and policy choices raise issues of economic analysis, both theoretical and empirical, which have attracted an appropriate amount of professional attention. Perhaps the most important are whether the facts indeed warrant the conclusion that there should be more capital formation and whether, if so, rule changes of the sort under consideration are likely to call it forth. This paper dodges those difficult questions. It considers rather the problem of designing tax and related rules to promote capital formation.[1]

To put the matter somewhat more precisely, I take up in this paper the characteristics of and interactions among measures to effect savings and investment incentives (henceforth "S-I incentives") in the context of an income tax system that is inadequately indexed for inflation. Although the issues have been separately addressed many times, a treatment that is at once unified and reasonably simple is lacking.[2] Furthermore, existing analyses that may incorporate more realistic detail have failed to appreciate sufficiently what legal commentators call the "pressures" introduced to the tax system by inflation and by the present ad hoc measures to deal with it. These pressures are by and large created by the opportunity to make money by undertaking transactions which have offsetting effects on the balance sheet, but different tax consequences, a process I have referred to as "tax arbitrage." It is these opportunities for arbitrage profit and how the system eliminates them that I shall stress in the following pages.

Underlying the analysis in this paper is the view that rules which do not work well in a simple model world will also not work well in the complex real world. This is the justification for confining attention almost wholly to situations of no uncertainty, no borrowing and lending constraints, and uncomplicated financial relationships. There is no doubt that the extreme sorts of outcomes that emerge in simple models, such as conclusions that a taxpayer's wealth will consist all of one asset, or involve large borrowing, will often be prevented in actuality by information and other uncertainty-related costs. It is clear that a proper treatment of uncertainty is necessary to a full understanding of capital market equilibrium. However, arbitrage among relatively risk-free assets represents a significant subset of the transactions that must be dealt with by the tax system. The qualitative character of outcomes predicted by the certainty models is observed in the real world. Furthermore, the learning process is obviously still incomplete and cheap high-speed information handling is increasingly extending sophisticated tax arbitrage to a wider market. Thus problems now manifested in the "aggressive" behavior of a few taxpayers are quite likely to be seen more generally in the future.

In section I, I sketch out the criteria applicable to choice among savings and investment incentives and offer a classification of measures differing according to the transactions to which they apply and the way they work. Section II looks at the major elements of this structure in the context of stable prices, while section III takes up the difficult problems posed by inflation. There is a brief summing up in section IV.

I.   Background on Savings and Investment Incentives

First, I shall use the terms savings and investment more or less inter-changeably, but to the extent there is a distinction, investment refers to the acquisition of a real asset, while saving refers to the foregoing of consumption. Second, as to what I mean by savings and investment incentives, remember that the background for this discussion is an income tax system. An income tax, by definition, embodies a saving or investment *dis*incentive in that it creates a divergence between the rate of return on investment and the yield to the saver. Inflation may increase this tax wedge. Thus the incentives we are considering are relative to existing dis-incentives, whatever their merits.

It is important to be aware of a resulting ambiguity of the term savings or investment incentive as applied to the measures studied here. As I have stressed elsewhere [1980], in view of the government's budget constraint an incentive such as the investment tax credit may be bought at the price of higher tax rates than would otherwise be possible. The net effect may be an increase in the tax wedge applicable, at least for some savers.

CRITERIA FOR CHOICE AMONG SAVINGS AND INVESTMENT INCENTIVES

At the risk of banality, I would suggest that the criteria for choice among S-I incentive measures can be summarized by the familiar trinity of equity, efficiency, and simplicity.

Equity.   As usual, equity is the most difficult criterion to deal with. To start with, one of the objectives of currently considered S-I measures is to offset inequities that have been perpetrated by inflation, and thus concen-tration on the static characteristics of rules may miss part of the point. This is a particular aspect of the more general problem of distinguishing between transition and steady-state effects. It is regrettable that I shall have most to say about the better-understood steady state properties of S-I incentives.

As we shall see, there are essentially two sorts of available S-I incen-tives. The first—which I call C-tax measures—tend to equalize the rate of return received by savers at all levels of economic well-being. The second—which I call direct grant measures—tend to raise all rates of return received by savers, relative to the social rate of return, but do not alter the differentials among after-tax rates of return on savings characteristic of a graduated income tax. Even with a fixed structure of tax rates the difference in relative individual welfare involved is not a priori certain, as it has to do with the lifetime pattern of earnings and consumption, but it is plausible that the former class of incentives (basically deductions from the income tax base) is relatively more favorable to high bracket taxpayers than the latter (basically investment grants or credits). If desired, such differences could be offset by adjustments in marginal tax rates.

This would leave horizontal equity differences between the two approaches, and these are essentially the same as those involved in choosing between a consumption base and an income base for taxation. Relative to a consumption tax an income tax penalizes those who postpone consumption, whether because they simply prefer to do so, or because their labor earnings, gifts, transfers, etc., occur early in life.[3]

Efficiency. As Auerbach [1979b] has emphasized, we are dealing here with a problem in the economics of the second best. This means that, for example, a measure creating a divergence in the real rates of return on investment in machines of different durability may not be inferior to a measure, similar in most other respects, that causes these rates to be equalized. Our analysis of S-I incentives will simply point out the distortions they engender.

There are three margins of trade-off of particular interest. The first is that between present and future consumption. An income tax introduces a wedge between the trade-off available to individuals, through borrowing and lending or through real investment and production, and that available socially via the production process—the social rate of return on investment. It thus inherently involves an inefficiency, albeit a potentially second best one, since revenue must be raised somehow. When an income tax is assessed at different rates on different individuals, there is also a violation of exchange efficiency: different individuals have different marginal rates of substitution of present for future consumption. As has been mentioned, S-I incentives of the C-tax type ameliorate both sorts of wedges, while direct grant measures simply shift the distribution of private rates of return, after taxes, upward relative to the social rate of return.

The second margin is between investment in different forms or different sectors. This is a matter of production efficiency. If the real social rate of return is not the same in two activities, an opportunity exists to increase consumption in all periods by shifting resources from the low yield to the high yield activity. Such a situation commonly arises under an income tax with the weaknesses typical of actual tax accounting systems. Individuals have an incentive, for example, to push investment in owner-occupied housing to the point that the marginal social (and private) return equals the *after-tax* return in fully taxed industries. Similar inefficiencies are predicted by theory when S-I incentives are limited to particular classes of assets, for example, manufacturing equipment, or to particular industries. A particular case is the difference in social rate of return to capital of different durabilities that is predicted when an investment credit is not appropriately varied with the service life of the asset. At a more refined level of analysis, similar comments would apply to the risk characteristics of real investments.

A third significant margin, between different assets in the household's portfolio, also involves questions of risk bearing. Efficient allocation of risk will normally imply a certain division of each individual's portfolio among real asset types and among financial instruments such as bonds and shares. Equilibrium portfolios with taxes may be expected to diverge from efficiency, and S-I incentives often worsen the distortions characteristic of the existing income tax, typically in the direction of increasing debt-equity ratios in the aggregate and concentrating debt ownership relatively in low tax bracket hands (including life insurance and pension fund portfolios).[4]

The degree to which the S-I incentive displaces the existing income tax presents a further aspect of efficiency. It is reasonable to suppose that the basic outlines of the existing tax system will be maintained, with the relatively minor addition of S-I incentive features. It is also the case that the existing system has solved badly many problems of measuring income from capital, notably in the treatment of owner-occupied houses, accruing capital gains, and state and municipal bond interest, and in the absence of inflation adjustments. If the effect of the S-I incentive is to reduce reliance on these aspects of the income tax, it also diminishes the inefficiencies associates with such defects of income measurement.

Simplicity.   It is difficult to say very much in general about the potential tendency of S-I incentives to complicate further or to simplify compliance with and enforcement of the tax law. There is a certain risk that S-I incentives will bring with them hard-to-administer rules to prevent "abuse," as in the present rules disallowing deduction of interest traceable to the purchase or holding of tax exempt bonds, or will require inherently complex calculations, as in the case of some aspects of inflation adjustment.

One desirable characteristic that might be included under this heading is the degree to which an S-I incentive automatically adjusts to a changing rate of inflation. Arguments in favor of proposals, for example, for accelerated depreciation, often turn on their ability to offset the current rate of inflation. The measures typically will be inappropriate for other rates of inflation, implying the necessity for further rule adjustments when conditions change. Other S-I incentives may be more or less robust to varying inflation rates.

A CLASSIFICATION OF SAVINGS AND INVESTMENT INCENTIVES

As has been indicated, currently employed or discussed measures to encourage saving and investment can, with a little license, be placed in two broad categories, the class of consumption tax ("C-tax") rules and the class of direct grant rules. These rules in turn may be applicable to either real or financial assets, and they may apply to the purchase or sale of assets (a stock notion) or to the yield from assets (a flow notion). This generates an eight-way classification.

The usual approach to implementing a consumption tax base ("standard" C-tax treatment) is to permit the taxpayer to deduct from a conventional income tax base the net purchase of assets during the accounting period. Various S-I incentive measures have this character, notably including accelerated depreciation of real assets (the standard C-tax treatment would carry acceleration to the logical extreme of immediate expensing). Contributions by employers to a qualified pension plan on behalf of employees are subject to the standard C-tax treatment, since the procedure is equivalent to paying out the contributions in wages and allowing the employees to deduct the amounts saved in this form. Subsequent pension dissaving upon retirement is then included in the employees' income tax base. Similar rules apply to saving through Keogh Plans and IRAs, further examples of S-I incentives of the C-tax type.

A classical consumption tax, levied at a constant rate over time for a given taxpayer, is equivalent in its effect to exempting the yield from saving or investing from the income tax, and I refer to this as the "alternative" method of implementing a consumption tax. This approach is also used in S-I incentives, particularly in the deferral of tax on capital gains accruing in either real or financial assets and in the reduced rate of tax imposed on such gains upon realization. Reducing the rate of corporation income tax can also be viewed as belonging in this class of S-I incentives with respect to real assets. The exclusion of dividend and interest receipts (up to a limit) from individual income tax represents an application of the alternative consumption tax treatment to financial assets. One might also include here the exemption of state and municipal bond interest, although this is evidently not a measure designed to encourage saving and investment generally.

In addition to these two consumption tax approaches on the markets for real and financial assets, we can distinguish incentives having the character of a direct grant, which is not subject to tax or equivalent to a deduction from the income tax base. The prime example of this in the U.S. is the investment tax credit (ITC), which provides the investor (who has sufficient tax liability), in effect, a cash grant equal to a fraction of the cost of a real asset. Unlike the closely related techniques of accelerated depreciation or immediate expensing of investment outlays, the subsidy provided by the ITC is independent of the investor's marginal tax rate.

There is no program in the U.S. system obviously corresponding to this with respect to saving in the form of financial assets. In other countries, there exist direct subsidies to saving of a character similar to the U.S. investment tax credit: the public treasury supplements individual savings by direct grants, independent of the recipient's marginal tax rate.

For completeness, we may note the possibility in principle of S-I incentives of the yield exemption type analogous to the investment tax credit. Such measures would involve providing the owner of real or financial assets with an extra return not subject to income taxation. We would then have four approaches to the subsidy of each of the two asset types, real and financial, a total of eight hypothetical subsidy techniques. Table 1 displays the eight-way classification. Cells 6, 7 and 8 appear to be essentially empty in the U.S. today.

In the next section, we look at the way these different incentive measures work, and interact, under conditions of stable prices (or well-indexed income measurement rules, regardless of inflation).

II.   Savings and Investment Incentives in the Absence of Inflation

CONSUMPTION TAX INCENTIVES

To understand the way the different incentives work, how they differ, and how they interact, we are best served by considering their application in a context with a minimum of complication. Therefore, we focus on the case of an investment with a risk-free return. To start with, assume away also the graduated structure of tax rates.

It will be sufficient, furthermore, for most of our purposes to study the

TABLE 1

A CLASSIFICATION OF SAVINGS AND INVESTMENT INCENTIVES
IN AN INCOME TAX SYSTEM

		ASSET TYPE	
S-I INCENTIVE TYPE		Real	Financial
Consumption Tax Rules	Standard C-Tax Rules	(1) Accelerated Depreciation Expensing Research and Development	(2) Qualified Pension Saving
	Alternative C-Tax Rules	(3) Capital Gain Special Rules	(4) Capital Gain Special Rules
Direct Grant	Grant for Purchase of Assets	(5) Investment Tax Credit	(6) Savings Premium Programs (not U.S.)
	Supplement to Asset Yield (after taxes)	(7) No known examples	(8) No known examples

impact of the various rules on one particular sort of real investment opportunity, the exponentially decaying machine. This is the model made familiar by Jorgenson and colleagues.[5] A new machine costing one dollar produces at a rate of output valued at c, after allowing for payments to cooperating factors, and this is thus the rental rate a producer would be prepared to pay for the use of the machine. If the machine is of durability δ its rate of output declines at the constant relative rate δ; the smaller δ, the more durable the machine. The output rate of an s-year old machine is thus $ce^{-\delta s}$. Since an s-year old machine is just equivalent to $e^{-\delta s}$ new machines, economic depreciation takes place at rate $\delta e^{-\delta s}$. It is generally assumed that machines of different durabilities are in use at a given time, and their output rates will differ. When it is necessary to be explicit about this I write $c(\delta)$ for the output rate of a new machine of durability δ.

Simple wealth maximizing considerations will determine who will wish to own machines under various conditions. If the market rate of interest is given by i, a capitalist subject to a marginal tax rate m, will base his borrowing and lending on the after-tax interest rate, $(1 - m)i$. Such a taxpayer will be willing to offer for a new machine any amount up to the discounted (at rate $(1 - m)i$) sum of rental payments on the machine, net of taxes, plus depreciation allowances. This demand price for the real asset is a result of pure arbitrage considerations and has nothing to do with the capitalist's time preference or propensity to save. Since the supply price of a machine is 1, the elimination of arbitrage profit requires

$$1 = \int_0^\infty [(1 - m)c + m\delta]e^{-(\delta + (1-m)i)s}\, ds \quad . \tag{1}$$

Explicit integration leads from (1) to the familiar condition of equilibrium

$$i = c(\delta) - \delta \quad . \tag{2}$$

We may describe as the social rate of return, $r(\delta)$, on an asset of durability δ the internal rate of return on a unit of consumption foregone. That is,

$$1 \equiv \int_0^\infty c(\delta)e^{-(\delta + r(\delta))s}\, ds \quad . \tag{3}$$

Solving explicitly gives us

$$r(\delta) = c(\delta) - \delta \quad . \tag{4}$$

Conditions (2) and (4) tell us that in equilibrium with an income tax the social rate of return on investment in machines of different types is the same. The allocation is thus characterized by production efficiency.[6] While the common social rate of return in this equilibrium equals the interest rate, i, the savers receive a lower rate of return, $(1 - m)i = (1 - m)r$, whether they save in the form of financial or real assets. Note that as the marginal tax rate m does not appear in equilibrium condition (2), this analysis would continue to hold with different tax rates applicable to different capitalists.

Accelerated Depreciation. Consider now the way the accelerated depreciation for tax purposes influences the equilibrium outcome. There is no single interpretation to be given to this notion, but a natural approach in this context is to assume that in reckoning income tax the capitalist is allowed to treat the machine with actual durability parameter δ as though it were of durability δ^*. For example, since any likely measure of the average effective or expected lifetime of an asset of type δ will be inversely proportional to δ, allowing investors to assume δ* = 2δ could be taken to represent a halving of service lives for tax purposes.

If the taxation of interest is as before, the no-arbitrage equilibrium condition with accelerated depreciation is given by

$$1 = \int_0^\infty [(1 - m)ce^{-(\delta + (1-m)i)s} + m\delta^* e^{-(\delta^* + (1-m)i)s}] \, ds \quad , \tag{5}$$

which reduces to relationship (6) among rental rate, interest rate, and depreciation and tax parameters:

$$c = \left(\frac{(1 - m)i + \delta}{(1 - m)i + \delta^*}\right)(i + \delta^*) \quad . \tag{6}$$

We may verify by substitution that if tax and economic depreciation are the same (δ = δ*), condition (6) reduces to (2). Increasing δ* relative to δ reduces the equilibrium rental rate, given i, and results in the return to savers, (1 − m)i, being higher in relation to the social rate of return, c − δ.

If accelerated depreciation is carried to the extreme of instantaneous write-off, δ* = ∞, equilibrium condition (6) reduces to

$$c = (1 - m)i + \delta \quad . \tag{7}$$

This is the characteristic equilibrium condition for a flat rate income tax system in which real investment is given standard consumption tax treatment. Since c − δ is equated over all durabilities, this equilibrium is characterized by production efficiency, and since c − δ = (1 − m)i, the return to the saver, (1 − m)i, is just equated to the social yield on real investment. Note that in this equilibrium the market interest rate exceeds the social rate of return by the factor 1/(1 − m), so that the tax on interest just takes away the excess over the social return.

Returning to condition (6), we may inquire about the relationship between δ and δ* needed to assure that in equilibrium the social return, c(δ) − δ, is equated at some value r̄ for all asset types, a condition for production efficiency. If we let δ*(δ) stand for the depreciation rate allowed under the tax laws when the true depreciation rate is δ, a little algebra shows that production efficiency (c(δ) − δ = r̄) requires a particular relationship,

$$\delta^*(\delta) = \left(\frac{(1 - m)(i - \bar{r}) + m\delta}{\bar{r} - (1 - m)i}\right)i \quad . \tag{8}$$

It is assumed here that the rate of return to the saver, (1 − m)i, is below the social rate of return on investment, r̄.

Condition (8) may be more readily interpreted if we state the objective of the accelerated depreciation scheme to be obtaining a specified proportional difference, β, between the interest rate and the common social rate of return on investment, that is, to effect in equilibrium the relationship $\bar{r} = (1 - \beta)i$. With this substitution, (8) becomes (assuming β less than m)

$$\delta^*(\delta) = \left(\frac{(1 - m)\beta}{m - \beta} \right)i + \left(\frac{m}{m - \beta} \right)\delta \quad . \tag{9}$$

Increasing the degree of acceleration toward effectively eliminating the tax wedge between private and social return involves setting β closer to m. From (9), we see this does involve raising δ^* toward ∞, but (9) also tells us that to avoid inefficiency in the allocation of investment it is necessary to add a term, related to the interest rate, that itself tends to ∞.

To get some sort of feel for the inefficiency which might be engendered by failing to calibrate the tax depreciation appropriately to the interest rate and the applicable marginal tax rate, consider the particular case described in table 2.

The first column of table 2 shows the true depreciation rate of assets. The second shows the tax depreciation rate required to obtain the effect of a 50 percent relief from a 50 percent marginal tax rate, if the before-tax interest rate is 12 percent. Notable is the fact that the ratio of tax depreciation to true depreciation rate, near 2 for assets with an expected lifetime of two years, rises to 5 for assets with expected 50-year lives. Depreciation

TABLE 2

ILLUSTRATIVE ACCELERATION SCHEDULE AND EFFECTS OF USING
SIMPLE SCALING

Actual Depreciation Rate, (percentage)	Neutral Accelerated Depreciation, $\delta^*(\delta)$[a] (percentage)	Social Return $(c - \delta)$ When $\delta^* = 2.6\delta$[b] (percentage)
2	10	10.3
5	16	9.5
10	26	9.0
50	106	8.5

Assumptions: i = .12, m = .5, β = .25
a.   Calculated according to text expression (9).
b.   Derived from text expression (6).

of long-lived assets must be "more accelerated" than that of short-lived assets. Failing to calibrate the degree of acceleration in this way, by employing instead a simple proportional increase in depreciation rates, disadvantages more durable relative to less durable assets.

The third column of table 2 illustrates this by showing the social rate of return in equilibrium on assets of different durabilities when instead of the usual acceleration scheme a simple proportional shortening of lives is employed. In this example the proportionality factor is set to achieve the same incentive effect as the neutral pattern for assets with an expected life of 10 years. The result is a spread of roughly two percentage points, or 25 percent, between the equilibrium social return on the 2-year asset and that on the 50-year asset. This difference is the pure social gain that could be obtained at the margin by shifting investment from the least to the most durable assets in the table.

In assessing whether a given differential in rates of return or tax on rates of return is "large," it is well to keep in mind the proverbial power of compound interest. With 50 years of reinvestment at 10 percent, $1 accumulates to nearly $150; at 8 percent it accumulates to a little over $50. It thus may make sense to be concerned about differences in equilibrium rates of return that appear to be small.

Before leaving this exercise in calculating tax depreciation rates we should note that the assumption we have employed of a fixed interest rate involves a sort of self-contradiction. In view of the arbitrage potential, a fixed interest rate implies a fixed incentive to save, unless the tax rate declines. If the new equilibrium is to involve a larger amount of consumption foregone, it will presumably require a higher interest rate. Presumably also, the tax rate will need to be higher than otherwise to cover the revenue losses due to accelerated depreciation. If the tax depreciation rule is not well designed, it is possible that it would do no more than generate a higher interest rate, higher tax rate, and some deadweight loss.[7] Much the same can be said of any S-I incentive.

While exponential depreciation does not encompass all investment opportunities, we can learn several lessons from this analysis. We see that a mechanical compressing of the life of an asset for tax purposes will not in general generate an appropriate balancing of incentives across short- and long-lived assets, that the adjustment required to maintain efficient resource use may be moderately complicated to derive, and that it will in general depend upon the interest rate and the applicable marginal tax rate. However, the problem of designing a schedule of accelerated depreciation allowances is made to appear simpler in this case than it is when other possible patterns of the decline of asset value are taken into account. Each alternative requires, in principle, its own version of (9).

Arguably, this says nothing more than that in this sphere, as in others, there is a problem of choosing a sufficiently good approximation. A further oversimplification is not so easily dealt with. The marginal tax rate in the equilibrium condition, (6), and in the expression for a neutral acceleration schedule, (9), is not a constant. Taxpayers with different marginal tax rates will have different demand prices for the same real asset. Establishing equilibrium requires assuming constraints on arbitrage (for example, borrowing limits), or a mechanism that produces its own constraints. We shall return to this issue in the context of an alternative approach to the application of consumption tax rules to real investment.

Partial Expensing of Real Investment.   We know that taxation according to income properly measured, using economic depreciation, does not upset the aspect of production efficiency which we are studying, nor does taxation according to consumption principles, which involves immediate expensing of investment outlays. One suspects then that a "mixture" of the two approaches, appropriately designed, should share this virtue. As Harberger [1980] has recently argued, such is indeed the case.[8]

Specifically, consider the effect of allowing in this system the immediate expensing for tax purposes of a fraction α of the investment in the machine. This means that for given value of i, the demand price of the capitalist is increased by αm less the loss in value of depreciation allowances. If the basis for depreciation is reduced by just the amount expensed, elimination of arbitrage profits implies

$$1 = \int_0^\infty [(1 - m)c + m(1 - \alpha)\delta]e^{-(\delta+(1-m)i)s}\,ds + \alpha m \quad . \tag{10}$$

Again, explicit integration plus some algebra reduces (10) to

$$c - \delta = (1 - \alpha m)i \quad . \tag{11}$$

Thus, for the case of exponential depreciation (and this generalizes easily to all patterns of depreciation) equilibrium with a flat rate income tax allowing partial expensing of investment outlays, together with economic depreciation applied for tax purposes to the unexpensed basis, is characterized by production efficiency in the sense that the social rate of return to marginal investment in capital of all durabilities (in use) is the same, and given by $(1 - \alpha m)i$. In this equilibrium the interest rate exceeds the social rate of return:

$$i = \left(\frac{r}{1 - \alpha m} \right) , \tag{12}$$

while the rate of return received by the saver in either form is

$$(1 - m)i = \left(\frac{1 - m}{1 - \alpha m} \right) r . \tag{13}$$

The relationship holding when immediate expensing of all real investment is allowed is found by setting $\alpha = 1$, whereby $(1 - m)i = r$. The return to the saver equals the social return. This repeats the result above that immediate expensing of investment accomplishes the elimination of the tax "wedge" on the return to saving and thus effects consumption taxation, even though interest income is subject to tax (and interest outlays are allowed as a deduction).[9]

Note, though, that, as in the case of accelerated depreciation, the single marginal tax rate now enters the equilibrium condition. If the relationship between the interest rate, i, and the equilibrium rental rate, $c(\delta)$, is given by (11), the demand price for a unit machine of a taxpayer with marginal rate m', possibly different from m, will be given by

$$\frac{\delta + (1 - m')(1 + (m' - m)\alpha)i}{\delta + (1 - m')i} . \tag{14}$$

This demand price (obtained by evaluating the right-hand side of (10) for $m = m'$, given (11)), derived from pure arbitrage considerations, will be greater than the supply price, 1, if $m' > m$ and less if $m' < m$. This accords with intuition, most clearly for the case $\alpha = 1$. For we know that the application of consumption tax principles to the real investment amounts to exempting the yield from tax. Any taxpayer can then be assured the rate of return $r = c - \delta$. This will just equal the after-tax interest rate for the taxpayer with marginal rate m. For the taxpayer with rate $m' > m$, the after-tax return on lending or the cost of borrowing is less. Hence the situation presents an opportunity for arbitrage profit, with the high bracket taxpayer borrowing to finance the acquisition of machines, each time earning a pure profit at the expense of the tax system.

Although one must be cautious about a mechanical interpretation of this model, it is instructive to push it to an equilibrium. Such is permitted by the impossibility of holding negative quantities of the real asset (short sales of real assets seeming too far fetched). Tax arbitrage profits are eliminated when the marginal rate applicable to equilibrium condition (11) is m_{max}, the highest rate among taxpayers. At that point, all real assets are owned by top bracket taxpayers, while the portfolios of lower bracket households are entirely in loans. The yield on saving by the top bracket taxpayer is related to the social return according to (13) (with $m = m_{max}$) while taxpayers with lower rates obtain higher after-tax yields in the usual way. Those with a sufficiently low marginal rate (below αm_{max}) receive a return on saving in excess of r. When $\alpha = 1$, all taxpayers below the minimum tax bracket will have an after-tax interest rate in excess of the social rate of return on investment.

Adjusting the Treatment of Interest.   The phenomenon of lightly taxed assets migrating to the portfolios of high bracket taxpayers is not a new discovery. What seems yet to be recognized is the possibility of offsetting the effect through varying the rate of inclusion of interest receipts in (and deduction of interest outlays from) the income tax base. That is to say, a partial standard consumption tax treatment of real investment will be compatible with an appropriately partial alternative consumption tax treatment of borrowing and lending. The argument is general, not dependent on the exponential depreciation assumption, and is simply a matter of discovering the inclusion rate needed to foreclose arbitrage profit.

Because of the tax rebate, the taxpayer with marginal rate m can finance a fraction αm of the outlay on real assets by the tax reduction due to the immediate expensing of the fraction α. In a pure arbitrage transaction the remainder is financed by borrowing at interest rate i. If a fraction γ of interest payments is deductible from the tax base together with a fraction $(1 - \alpha)$ of δ, the decline in value of the asset during the period, the net of tax proceeds from rental will be $(1 - m)c + m(\gamma(1 - \alpha m)i + (1 - \alpha)\delta)$. This must cover the sum of interest payments and the actual loss in asset value to the holder. The former is simply $(1 - \alpha m)i$. The latter differs from δ because of the Treasury's claim on the value of the asset. A decline of δ in the market value of the asset implies a decline of $(1 - \alpha m)\delta$ in the value of the private owner's share. Thus the no arbitrage profit condition is given by

$$(1 - m)c + m(\gamma(1 - \alpha m)i + (1 - \alpha)\delta) = (1 - \alpha m)i + (1 - \alpha m)\delta \quad,$$

$$(15)$$

which reduces to

$$c = \left(\frac{(1 - \gamma m)(1 - \alpha m)}{1 - m} \right)i + \delta \quad .$$

$$(16)$$

The coefficient of i in (16) will be identically 1 if

$$\gamma = \frac{1 - \alpha}{1 - \alpha m} \quad . \tag{17}$$

When the proportion of interest allowed as a deduction is given by γ, defined in (17), taxpayers in all brackets are indifferent between lending and purchasing real assets. The equilibrium interest rate just equals $c - \delta$, the social rate of return on real investment, and the rate of return received by the saver is $(1 - \gamma m)i$. When $\alpha = 1$, the purchasers of real assets are allowed immediate expensing. The corresponding value of γ is zero: interest is not subject to tax. Both rules are precisely those of a consumption tax system with tax rates constant over time for each taxpayer, although graduated across taxpayers. When $\alpha = 0$, real assets are allowed only economic depreciation as a deduction in calculating the tax base, the principle of true income taxation. In this case, $\gamma = 1$; interest is taxed in full. Table 3 shows the values of γ for various combinations of write-off rate and marginal tax bracket.

The reader may verify that the demand price for a dollar's worth of exponentially depreciating real assets, given by the right-hand side of (10), is exactly one dollar, independent of the taxpayer's marginal rate, when the discount rate $(1 - m)i$ is replaced by $(1 - \gamma m)i$ and c is replaced by the equilibrium value $i + \delta$.

Cells 2 and 3. Thus far we have focused on the interactions between standard C-tax treatment of real investment (cell 1 of table 1) and alter-

TABLE 3

RATE OF INCLUSION OF INTEREST INCOME AND DEDUCTION OF INTEREST EXPENSE CORRESPONDING TO VARIOUS RATES OF EXPENSING REAL INVESTMENT (PERCENTAGE)

FRACTION OF REAL ASSET EXPENSED	MARGINAL TAX RATE				
	10	20	40	50	70
0%	100%	100%	100%	100%	100%
25	77	79	83	86	91
50	53	56	63	67	77
75	27	29	36	40	53
100	0	0	0	0	0

Note: Entries are calculated according to text expression (17) for γ, with α = fraction of real asset allowed as immediate deduction and m = investor's marginal tax rate.

native C-tax treatment of interest (cell 4 of table 1). The analysis of standard C-tax treatment of financial assets (cell 2 of table 1), typified by Keogh Plan saving is straightforward. As far as its interaction with the appropriate treatment of interest is concerned, the argument is basically the same as applied to real investment. The important difference is that there is now no possibility to equilibrate away tax arbitrage profits through a differential in the returns on the two forms of saving.

To illustrate, if saving in a pension plan could be used to secure a loan subject to conventional income tax rules, there would be a tax arbitrage profit obtainable through borrowing (to make the example particularly graphic, let it be from the pension fund itself) and depositing the funds, together with the tax refund due upon deducting the deposit, in the pension fund. This involves no change in consumption and no real change in portfolio. But the interest on the borrowing is deductible, while the interest on the offsetting "lending" is not taxed. Since the underlying asset is exactly the same, there is no possibility for this profit to be eliminated through yield differentials: the earnings of the fund *are* the interest paid on the borrowing.

Controlling this arbitrage profit. requires either direct limits on the arbitrage process or an offsetting change in the treatment of interest. (Another possibility is found in the endogenous adjustment of marginal rates over the life cycle; see Bradford [1980, pp. 47–49]). Current rules follow the first approach, setting ceilings on annual additions to tax-favored pension savings, restricting the pledging of pension wealth as loan collateral, prohibiting or penalizing withdrawal of funds before retirement, and so forth. While these rules no doubt inhibit arbitrage profit, they also tend to eliminate the incentive effect of the programs. An individual who has reached the ceiling confronts the usual $(1 - m)i$ yield on incremental savings, as does one sufficiently deterred by the restrictions on the pension asset to stop short of the statutory ceiling. Significantly lifting these restrictions on the standard C-tax treatment of financial assets calls for associated changes in the taxation of interest, along the lines discussed in connection with the standard C-tax treatment of real investment.

Discussion of cell (3) of table 1 requires a closer look at the rules for taxing sales of depreciable assets (importantly real estate) and certain tax favored activities, such as ship building and timber production. While there is no doubt an important story to be told here, it extends beyond my knowledge of the rules. However, we can readily see that there is a potential for "double-dipping," with assets subject to the incentive effects of both standard and alternative C-tax treatment. This would have the consequences of production inefficiency and portfolio distortion as a function of marginal tax brackets of the sort analyzed in connection with standard C-tax treatment of real investment with no change in the taxation of interest.

DIRECT GRANT INCENTIVES

We can move more quickly through the discussion of direct grant incentives since the basic analytical approach is now familiar. Furthermore, there is as a practical matter only one program in question, that of a direct subsidy to real investment expenditures. This happens to be administered through the tax system, in the form of the ITC. Two features distinguish it from a directly appropriated grant. First, the credit may only be applied to settlement of positive tax liability. This may mean the subsidy is not available to many firms at a given time. Certainly it introduces incentives for somewhat artificial financing arrangements and creates administrative complexity, an aspect of the ITC about which I have nothing new to say. Second, the subsidy is not reflected in the basis for depreciation. That is, while the cost of an asset to the taxpayer is the price net of tax credit, depreciation allowances are calculated as though the full price had been paid. This is nothing more than a mismeasurement of income, and the appropriate analysis is the same as that above in connection with accelerated depreciation.[10]

Zero arbitrage-profit equilibrium with an ITC correctly calibrated for durability, together with allowances for depreciation calculated on the basis of the purchase price of the asset net of tax credit, will be characterized by production efficiency in the sense we have been using, and neutrality with respect to the portfolios of wealth holders. The latter property, indeed, depends only on the use of economic depreciation (of the net of credit asset value) for tax purposes. We may see these conclusions easily in the exponential depreciation case, where the elimination of arbitrage profits requires

$$1 = \int_0^\infty [(1 - m)c + m(1 - k)\delta]e^{-(\delta + (1-m)i)s}\,ds + k \quad , \qquad (18)$$

where k is the fraction of the unit purchase price of the asset available as a credit against tax. Upon explicit integration and simplification, this condition reduces to

$$c - \delta = (1 - k)i - k\delta \quad . \qquad (19)$$

We see that, as m does not appear in the equilibrium condition, arbitrage profit opportunity is eliminated for individuals in all tax brackets by (19). However, to obtain equality of the social rate of return, $c - \delta$, over all asset types, δ, in use in equilibrium, a particular relationship, $k(\delta)$, between the credit rate and the durability of the asset is required. It follows from (19) that to obtain a given value, $\bar{r}$, of the social rate of return requires $k(\delta)$ to satisfy

$$k(\delta) = 1 - \left(\frac{\bar{r} + \delta}{i + \delta} \right) . \tag{20}$$

This relationship is illustrated in table 4. In the second column are shown the credit rates necessary to obtain a social rate of return of 9 percent where the associated interest rate is 12 percent, assumptions paralleling those of table 2. (The savers thus receive a rate of return of $(1 - m)12$ percent, depending upon individual marginal tax rates.) It will be seen that a considerable variation is required to implement a subsidy that does not distort the choice of asset lives. To give an idea of the effect of failing to take into account the need to calibrate the credit for durability, the third column of table 4 shows the social rate of return on assets of different lives when a flat rate credit of 13.6 percent is applied uniformly. This is the credit rate which induces a social yield of 9 percent for an asset with a 10-year expected life (still assuming an interest rate of 12 percent). Because of the bias toward short-lived assets this entails, invest-

TABLE 4

ILLUSTRATIVE NEUTRAL TAX CREDIT SCHEDULE
AND EQUILIBRIUM SOCIAL RATE OF RETURN
USING A FLAT RATE

Actual Depreciation Rate, δ (percentage)	Neutral ITC Rate,[a] $k(\delta)$ (percentage)	Social Return $(c - \delta))$ When $k(\delta) = .136$[b] (percentage)
2	21.4	10.1
5	17.6	9.7
10	13.6	9.0
50	4.8	3.5

a. Calculated according to text expression (20) for $\bar{r} = .09$, $i = .12$.
b. Calculated according to text expression (19) for $i = .12$, $k = .136$.

ment in less durable assets is driven to the point of very low social yield (it would go to zero for an asset with zero life) while the social rate of return on long-lived assets exceeds 9 percent (tending to 10.4 percent for a non-depreciating asset).

Certain general conclusions emerge from this discussion of direct grant incentives for the purchase of real assets. First, if economic depreciation of the net of credit cost of the asset is employed in calculating taxable income, we do not encounter differential effects on the demand price for assets as a function of the applicable marginal tax rate—effects which called for a change in the taxation of interest under the consumption tax approach to S-I incentives. A corollary is that increasing the rate of credit does not affect the relative taxation of the returns to saving as m varies across taxpayers. In the case of the consumption tax approach, as the level of incentive is increased, the rate of return on consumption foregone obtained by all savers tends toward equality with the social yield on investment. In the direct grant approach, as the subsidy level is increased the whole structure of individual rewards to saving goes up relative to the social return on investment, but there is no tendency toward equating the private yields of taxpayers in different marginal rate brackets.

Designing a credit structure to avoid production inefficiency may be difficult.[11] While in the particular case of exponential depreciation the formula is not particularly complex, it requires knowledge of both the target social rate of return and the interest rate that will call forth the private saving necessary to generate precisely that rate of return. Furthermore, a different formula applies to each pattern of depreciation.[12] In view of the difficulty tax authorities have in determining the facts about depreciation, a requirement that the credit rules be written with a detailed knowledge is a severe one.

Finally, we may note that the consumption tax approach to S-I incentives tends to substitute rules with few measurement problems for the income tax rules which are subject to many problems. The greater the C-tax type of incentive, the less important are the shortcomings of the income tax residual. The direct grant approach does not share this property.

III.   Savings and Investment Incentives with Inflation

BACKGROUND ON INFLATION AND TAXATION

The previous section considered the properties of various S-I incentive measures under conditions of stable prices. Inflation brings with it new problems of income measurement.[13] An ideal indexing system would solve those problems, and if we had such a system, the preceding analysis would be all that were needed. We do not, however, and the notion that an extra tax on the reward to saving is a consequence of inflation has motivated much of the recent movement to enact S-I incentives. In this section we consider, still in the simple model, the consequences of steady state inflation and the effectiveness of various measures to offset it.

To start with, let us review the way in which an unindexed tax system affects the equilibrium in the market for real assets, first in a flat rate tax system. With a steady rate of inflation π, the nominal flow of rentals obtained from a machine of age s is $ce^{(\pi-\delta)s}$, while under historic cost depreciation the allowance for tax purposes is $\delta e^{-\delta s}$. The no-arbitrage-profit condition becomes

$$1 = \int_0^\infty [(1-m)ce^{(\pi-\delta-(1-m)i)s} + m\delta e^{-(\delta+(1-m)i)s}]\,ds \quad . \tag{21}$$

Provided π is less than $\delta + (1-m)i$, this condition can be reduced to

$$c = \left(\frac{\delta + (1-m)i - \pi}{\delta + (1-m)i}\right)(i+\delta) \quad . \tag{22}$$

When $\pi = 0$ this reduces in turn to condition (2).

We can see from (22) that with historic cost depreciation and no indexing of interest inflation influences both the relative social yields from assets of different durabilities and the real return received after taxes by savers. The latter is given by $(1-m)i - \pi$, and thus whether it is increased or decreased by inflation depends upon whether the equilibrium interest rate increases by more or less than $1/(1-m)$ per point increase in inflation.[14] Letting $\hat{i}$ stand for the real interest rate, such an adjustment would imply

$$i = \hat{i} + \frac{\pi}{1-m} \quad . \tag{23}$$

An adjustment of this magnitude is apparently counter-factual in the U.S. recently. But we might ask whether it is likely even in our simple analytical model. Such an adjustment would imply no change in the equilibrium productivity, c, (also called the "gross rental rate") of assets at the two extremes of the durability spectrum.

This can be verified for the case of nondepreciating machines by substitution of (23) into (22) and evaluating at $\delta = 0$. The (infinite) rental rate of an instantaneously depreciating asset is inherently independent of both the discount rate and the inflation rate. For all other durabilities the equilibrium gross rental rate (and hence the social rate of return) would necessarily rise. If the law of diminishing returns applies independently to investments of different durabilities, this condition would imply a reduction in the capital stock in the aggregate. If the capital stock desired by private wealth holders is a declining function of the private rate of return, this is incompatible with the assumption, expressed in (23), of a constant value of $(1 - m)i - \pi$. In this sense there is a presumption that, absent correction of income measurement, inflation will lead to a decline in the real private rate of return, $(1 - m)i - \pi$, a decline in the overall capital stock, but an increase in the stock of the most and least durable forms of capital.[15]

All of the analysis thus far is based on the assumption of a single marginal income tax rate, m. We can see from (22) that with unadjusted depreciation, the demand price for investment goods will vary with the tax bracket of the investor. The rental rate in (22), which is the minimum required to cover taxes, depreciation, and interest, declines with m. If the rental rate and interest rate are such as to permit a taxpayer with marginal tax rate m to break even (on purchase of a machine of given durability), taxpayers in higher brackets will have an opportunity for pure arbitrage profit through borrowing to finance real investment while low bracket taxpayers will want to sell machines and lend. This is a situation similar to that just discussed. In that case equilibrium in the model required all real investment to be in the hands of top bracket taxpayers. While to elaborate on the details would require more space than merited, there does not seem to be any analogous way of achieving equilibrium in this case. Just how actual markets clear is not obvious, but it is safe to say that without correction of income measurement for tax purposes inflation generates distortions in the composition of both the real capital stock and individual portfolios.

Inflation Adjustment. Full inflation adjustment of the accounts would involve, first, converting all dollar amounts in the calculation of the tax to consistent units, that is, dollars of equal purchasing power. A natural choice of units is current dollars. Inflation adjustment thus calls for increasing the basis of assets sold in the calculation of capital gains and in the determination of depreciation allowances, as well as for similar changes in inventory accounting. These adjustments are conceptually straightforward.

Less obvious are the changes called for in the treatment of interest. In principle, the value of the lender's asset after the payment of interest is exactly what it was at the beginning of the period. Payments considered "interest" in the usual income tax rules are intended to have this character, and, by and large, they do when prices are stable. Thus, if a depositor withdraws the interest paid by a savings bank during a year, the nominal balance is constant. Regarding this interest as income is thus correct when there is no inflation, but when there is inflation it overstates the income of the depositor and understates that of the bank by the loss in purchasing power of the nominal balance over the year. Correcting the accounts calls for associating with interest payments a sum corresponding to the bank balance—presumably one would call it the "principal"—and allowing the creditor a deduction for the loss in purchasing power of the principal during the year, while assessing the debtor with additional income in equal amount.[16]

Following this procedure, the net of tax interest rate, that is, the discount rate applicable to nominal cash flows, becomes $(1 - m)i + m\pi$. In the case of steady inflation, this is equivalent to adjusting interest payments to reproduce the effect of taxing on the basis of the real interest rate, $i - \pi$. It may be readily verified that adjusting both the real and the financial sides of the accounts in this way restores the calculus of equilibrium to full equivalence to the no inflation case with the same real interest rate.

Because the adjustment of interest called for involves equal and opposite changes in the tax bases of debtors and creditors, precisely the same economic effect can be accomplished by a change in the interest rate in a flat rate tax world. To see this, note that with only depreciation allowances adjusted condition (21) becomes

$$1 = \int_0^\infty [(1 - m)c + m\delta]e^{(\pi - \delta - (1-m)i)s} \, ds \quad , \tag{24}$$

which reduces to

$$c = i + \delta - \frac{\pi}{1 - m} \quad . \tag{25}$$

Since (25) implies $c - \delta$ is the same for all δ we conclude that indexing real investment accounting will restore the property of production efficiency to capital market equilibrium. If, furthermore, the nominal interest adjusts according to (23), (24) implies in turn that

$$c = \hat{i} + \delta \quad , \tag{26}$$

which is to say the real rental rate and after-tax real interest rate are unaffected by inflation. Note again the large responsiveness of the interest rate to inflation required to obtain this outcome. The nominal rate must increase by enough to cover the inflation premium plus the tax due on that premium.

Unfortunately, if marginal tax rates vary across individuals, condition (25) tells us that portfolio distortion is still a problem. There will be opportunities for tax arbitrage profits, with high bracket taxpayers borrowing to buy real assets and low bracket taxpayers selling real assets to lend at interest. The result is pressure toward the sorting of portfolios along lines already discussed.

To sum up, it is possible by reasonably simple methods to correct for the effects of inflation on the tax base arising from real investment. Furthermore, this would be sufficient in a flat rate tax system, provided nominal interest rates were sufficiently flexible. However, with graduated rates, there will be portfolio biases unless the treatment of interest is adjusted as well. This is a much more difficult matter administratively. Current discussion of S-I incentives emphasizes their potential to offset inflation. One objection to this is obvious, that an incentive designed to offset one inflation rate will be inappropriate at another. Not so widely recognized is the fact that none of the measures under consideration addresses the need to simulate correction of interest transactions. Hence as we consider next the properties of S-I incentives under inflation, we know that this is one problem which they will not solve.

SAVINGS AND INVESTMENT INCENTIVES AND INFLATION

The way in which accelerated depreciation or the investment credit fits into this scheme requires no new analytical materials. From the discussion thus far, we know that these measures can not provide a general solution to the problems posed by inflation. The situation calls for a second-best analysis, to determine whether they could effect an improvement on equilibrium with existing rules.

The principal difficulty seems to be modeling the effect of inflation on the interest rate. It is tempting to deal with this by appealing to the observation that the interest rate moves roughly point-for-point with the inflation rate. However, consideration of the problem of setting depreciation allowances to maintain a fixed rate of return under this assumption simply draws attention to the paradox that it represents, namely, an inexplicably low nominal interest rate. For the adjustment required is a *cut* in depreciation allowances.

To see this, let δ^* be the depreciation rate allowed for tax purposes. The

zero arbitrage profit equilibrium condition, under the assumption of
Fisher's law, is then

$$1 = \int_0^\infty [(1 - m) c e^{(\pi - \delta - (1 - m) i) s} + m \delta^* e^{-(\delta^* + (1 - m) i) s}] \, ds. \qquad (27)$$

We can see that setting the tax depreciation allowance below the economic
level to the extent of the inflation rate, that is $\delta^* = \delta - \pi$ (making the tax
depreciation rate negative for the most durable assets), leads the equilibrium condition to reduce to

$$c = i + \delta^* \quad , \qquad (28)$$

and since, by assumption, $i = \hat{i} + \pi$, where $\hat{i}$ is the real interest rate, this
in turn implies

$$c = \hat{i} + \delta \quad . \qquad (29)$$

To rationalize Fisher's law thus calls for, in effect, taking into the tax base
the purely nominal capital gains on real assets, and under this condition,
real investment will be unaffected by inflation.

The difficulty is in explaining how the assumed relationship between
interest rate and inflation rate could characterize equilibrium without the
noted cut in depreciation allowances. My conjecture is that the apparent
validity of Fisher's law results from some combination of failing to account correctly for the riskiness of debt and incomplete adjustment of
markets.

The analysis above of equilibrium under C-tax treatment of real investment and graduated rates suggests we should anticipate an interest rate
adjustment close to that required to maintain the after-tax real return to
high bracket taxpayers. Jorgenson has also recommended working with
the assumption that the corporate tax rate, or a marginal tax rate of
roughly 50 percent, would dominate the arbitrage between the real capital
and lending markets. Whereas Fisher's law asserts a point-for-point
adjustment of nominal interest to inflation, this assumption involves a
$1/(1 - m)$ point increase in nominal interest rate per point increase in the
inflation rate. We know that indexing real investment returns will justify
this result and lead to efficient investment. In view of the difficulty of implementing indexation however, we may wish to consider acceleration as
an approximation if the rate of inflation is expected to be constant.

It turns out that for the exponential depreciation case this is relatively
simple. After integration and some algebra the zero-arbitrage-profit equilibrium condition (28), when combined with our interest rate assumption,
can be written as

$$c - \delta = \hat{i} + \left(\frac{1 - \Omega m}{1 - m} - 1 \right)\delta \quad , \tag{30}$$

where

$$\Omega = \left(\frac{(1 - m)i + \delta - \pi}{(1 - m)i + \delta^*} \right) \frac{\delta^*}{\delta} \quad .$$

In order that the equilibrium with inflation rate π be the same as that with zero inflation, tax depreciation, δ^*, should be set to render zero the coefficient of δ on the right-hand side of (30). This in turn requires setting δ^* as a simple multiple of δ according to the formula

$$\delta^* = \left(\frac{(1 - m)\hat{i} + \pi}{(1 - m)\hat{i}} \right)\delta \quad . \tag{31}$$

Note that under this interest rate adjustment assumption an *increase* in depreciation allowances is called for. The required adjustment is rather sensitive to the assumed real interest rate, $\hat{i}$. For example, for $m = .5$, $\hat{i} = .09$, and $\pi = .1$, (31) implies the tax depreciation rate should be about three times the economic rate; for $\hat{i} = .03$, tax depreciation should be at nearly *eight times* the economic rate. To get a feel for what this might mean in terms of service lives, we might interpret the "life" of an exponentially depreciating asset to be the point at which some specified fraction (e.g. 7/8) is exhausted. This would imply service lives inversely proportional to δ. Thus (31) would call for assets to be depreciated (on a declining balance basis) assuming lives roughly one third of those used in the absence of inflation for $\hat{i}$ assumed equal to 9 percent, one eighth for $\hat{i}$ assumed to be 3 percent.

Consumption Tax Rules and Inflation. One of the virtues of consumption tax rules is their indifference to inflation. A numerical example will make this clear. Take the case of an individual with a 50 percent marginal rate who wishes to save $100. Under the standard C-tax rules, he would nominally "save" $200, but would receive a tax rebate of $100 due to the resulting deduction, thereby foregoing just $100 in consumption. With stable prices and a 10 percent interest rate, the $200 would increase to $220 by the end of a year. The individual now has the option of "dissaving" $220, paying the associated tax of $110 and increasing consumption by $110, thus obtaining the full 10 percent return on postponed consumption. By the alternative C-tax rules of exempting the yield on saving, the 10 percent return is obtained directly.

Now suppose the situation is one of 100 percent per annum inflation. If the real interest rate is unchanged, $100 set aside in the first period will increase to $220 in the second period. The saver subject to the alternative C-tax rule of yield exemption obviously continues to receive a 10 percent real yield on consumption foregone. This is so because the $100 given up in the first period is equivalent to the $200 return of principal in the second period, while the $20 interest is equivalent to $10 of first period consumption. The same outcome obtains for the saver subject to standard C-tax treatment. The $200 "saving" involves foregoing $100 of consumption in the first period, while "dissaving" of the $440 accumulated by the second period is divided between $220 in taxes and $220 of increased consumption, exactly the same terms enjoyed by the conventional saver with exempt returns.

It is thus the case that the real effect of a flat rate C-tax system is independent of the rate of inflation. The same thing will hold for a graduated rate system in which the rate structure is corrected for inflation. This adjustment, the easy part of inflation indexing, is sometimes called in the tax policy jargon "type I indexing," and it is the only sort of tax correction that seems to have a significant political appeal. Absent type I indexing there is a tendency for inflation to subject the future dissaving corresponding to current saving to a higher rate of tax, and thereby inflation may interact even with C-tax rules.

We may easily verify the propositions about flat-rate C-tax rules under inflation for the case of exponential depreciation. With the interest rate adjusting point for point with the inflation rate, the no-arbitrage-profit condition with standard C-tax treatment of real investment and no inclusion or deduction of interest becomes

$$1 = \int_0^\infty (1 - m)ce^{(\pi - \delta - (\hat{i} + \pi))s}\,ds + m \quad , \tag{32}$$

which reduces, as expected, to

$$c - \delta = \hat{i} \quad . \tag{33}$$

While full application of C-tax rules is simultaneously an S-I incentive and a cure for inflation-induced measurement problems, partial application of C-tax rules, involving partial expensing of new investment and partial inclusion of interest income in the tax base, only partially solves these problems. The portion of the investment that is in effect taxed as income is subject to all of the difficulties due to defects in income measurement, including those associated with inflation. These include increased effective rates of taxation with inflation and pressure on portfolio composition, with high bracket taxpayers seeking to borrow from low bracket taxpayers to finance purchases of real assets. This suggests the continued importance of developing rules to measure income correctly or to impose a tax burden on investment equivalent to that resulting from correct income measurement.

THE AUERBACH-JORGENSON FIRST-YEAR WRITE-OFF SCHEME

In this connection it is appropriate to digress from the subject of S-I incentives to consider a suggestion put forward recently by Alan Auerbach and Dale Jorgenson [1980].[17] They address themselves to the notion that correcting depreciation allowances for inflation is too complex for practical administration. Under their proposal, as an alternative to current deduction of inflation-adjusted depreciation allowances, investors are allowed a single deduction at the time of acquisition of the asset equal to the present value of the appropriate stream of real depreciation deductions, where a real discount rate is applied in the calculation. This procedure is intended to accomplish the effect of indexing historical-cost based depreciation allowances for changes in the general price levels but to be simpler in implementation. Such complexity as there is is embodied in the derivation of tables by the tax authorities, specifying the allowance for each type of asset.

The characteristics of this scheme emerge immediately if we note that it involves eliminating the current depreciation allowances, as seen in the term $\delta e^{(\pi - \delta - (1-m)i)s}$ in the cash flow stream of expression (24) for the current-depreciation adjustment case and replacing them with a lump sum initial deduction of

$$\int_0^\infty \delta e^{(\tilde{\pi} - \delta - (1-m)\tilde{i})s} \, ds \quad , \tag{34}$$

where the tildes on π and i indicate the use of forecasted values of these variables. It follows immediately that the two schemes are wholly equivalent if the term $\tilde{\pi} - (1 - m)\tilde{i}$ is equal to $\pi - (1 - m)i$. The practical promise of the method, insofar as a reasonably exact substitute for inflation indexing is desired, depends upon determining the correct value of $\tilde{\pi} - (1 - m)\tilde{i}$.

This involves two difficulties. First is the necessity to employ a discount factor taking into account the individual tax bracket of the investor. Second is the necessity to incorporate the relationship between π and i into the adjustment. As we have seen this is problematical. The scheme works out precisely if the taxation of interest is also adjusted for inflation. Then the real after-tax interest rate for all taxpayers will be $(1 - m)\hat{i}$, and this replaces $-(\hat{\pi} - (1 - m)\tilde{i})$ in calculation of the first-year depreciation allowance. Since $\hat{i}$ is typically assumed constant, it is reasonably straightforward to adjust the allowance for differences in m, if m is known. Table 5 illustrates under the assumption $\hat{i} = .03$. To give an idea of the sensitivity of the scheme to the discount rate assumed, table 5 also shows the allowances for $\hat{i} = .09$.

For both corporate and individual taxpayers there may be a question about what marginal rate to employ in setting the first-year allowance. This difficulty also arises in the application of the adjustment of the interest deduction discussed above to coordinate with partial C-tax treatment of real investment. In that context, it may be acceptable to use the taxpayer's current marginal rate. In the Auerbach-Jorgenson scheme, however, more may well be riding on the rate chosen, because it affects the taxation of the entire asset purchase price and not just one year's yield. Thus problems caused by variations over the life cycle and variations which might be induced by the deduction itself (shifting the taxpayer to a lower bracket) may require resort to approximations.

While the discussion thus far incorporates the basic principle of the

TABLE 5

ILLUSTRATIVE FIRST-YEAR DEDUCTION UNDER THE
AUERBACH-JORGENSON APPROACH

Depreciation Rate, δ (percentage)	Marginal Tax Rate, m (percentage)				
	10	20	40	50	70
2	43	45	53	57	69
	(20)	(22)	(27)	(31)	(43)
5	65	68	74	77	85
	(38)	(41)	(48)	(53)	(65)
10	79	81	85	87	92
	(55)	(58)	(65)	(69)	(79)
50	95	95	97	97	98
	(86)	(87)	(90)	(92)	(95)

Note: Entries (in percentage) show the percentage first-year write-off equivalent to economic depreciation allowances, calculated according to the formula $\delta/(\delta + (1 - m)\hat{i})$, where $\hat{i}$, the real interest rate, is assumed $= .03$. Figures in parentheses show the allowance assuming $\hat{i} = .09$.

Auerbach-Jorgenson first-year allowance, their actual proposal does not discriminate according to the investor's marginal tax rate. Allowances are based instead on the present value of depreciation deductions using the same discount rate in all cases and thus are uniform for all taxpayers. One way to view this is as an approximation to the theoretical model. If the allowance corresponds to the ideal for a 50 percent marginal rate investor, for example, we see from table 5 the deduction will be "too large" for a lower bracket taxpayer, and "too small" for a higher bracket taxpayer. Correspondingly there will be a tendency for arbitrage to move the real assets toward low bracket portfolios, debt toward high bracket portfolios. Furthermore, if the allowances are "just right" for the 50 percent investor, they will not be correctly calibrated with respect to durability for the lower bracket investors, providing relatively too much incentive to purchase short-lived assets.

The first year allowances summarized in table 5 are predicated on the assumption of exponential depreciation. Other depreciation patterns would, strictly speaking, call for different allowances; otherwise some inefficiency in the composition of investment would be expected.[18] Much the same issue has already been discussed above in connection with investment credit. In the present state of knowledge about depreciation there is unlikely to be anything practical to be done about it.

Because under the Auerbach-Jorgenson scheme the full allowance for depreciation is taken in the first year, its real value is wholly insensitive to the rate of inflation.[19] As we have noted, if interest payments and receipts are adjusted for inflation, and if the correct value for the real interest rate is employed in the formula, the Auerbach-Jorgenson first-year allowance just duplicates the effect of indexing annual depreciation deductions. Otherwise, and in particular without correction of interest payments and receipts, the effect will not be identical. If the first-year allowances are based on an assumed real interest rate $\hat{i}$, but nominal interest is fully taxed and deductible, the no arbitrage-profit equilibrium condition is given by

$$c = \frac{\delta + (1 - m)i - \pi}{\delta + (1 - m)\hat{i}}(\hat{i} + \delta) \quad . \tag{35}$$

This equilibrium condition is to be compared with (25), the condition when depreciation is actually indexed but interest is not adjusted. Even with a single flat rate of tax, the two are not identical unless nominal interest adjusts according to (23). In addition, it should be stressed that under neither approach to insulating the accounting for income from real assets from inflation can the system reproduce the effect of adjusting interest payments and receipts when there are different marginal tax rates. This will always result in pressure for low bracket taxpayers to sell real assets to lend and high bracket taxpayers to borrow to buy real assets.

The Auerbach-Jorgenson first-year allowance is not, strictly, an S-I incentive measure. It is a procedure for approximating the indexation of depreciation allowances for inflation. It would, however, be a simple matter to combine the first-year depreciation allowance with a partial first-year expensing of investment or with an investment credit and thus realize any desired degree of S-I incentive. A flat credit on the difference between the cost of the new asset and the first-year allowance would maintain production efficiency. [20] In the case of partial expensing the entire deduction would be available in the first year, but it would consist of the desired fractional write-off of the investment, with the remaining fraction eligible for the Auerbach-Jorgenson allowance. As this approach represents simply a combination of two measures already discussed, it requires no fresh analysis.

IV. Summing Up

In this paper, I have suggested an eight-way classification of savings and investment incentives. Perhaps the most fundamental is the division into the class of consumption tax treatments and the class of direct grants. Roughly speaking, the former includes measures, such as accelerated depreciation and tax sheltered retirement savings plans, which increase deductions or reduce inclusions in the income tax, while the latter includes measures, primarily the investment credit, providing an incentive not directly related to the investor's income tax circumstances. The difference between the two classes is of importance primarily when tax rates vary in the population of savers and investors.

It proved possible for us to reach some fairly general conclusions about the way incentives of the two classes operate. As to the broad characteristics of the outcomes under the two approaches, we saw that increasing levels of consumption tax incentives tend to lead to a convergence of the returns received by savers toward the social rate of return on investment. At the same time, because the process has the effect of displacing the income taxation of the returns to saving, income measurement problems, including inflation correction, tend to diminish in importance. Consumption tax incentives can also be relatively simple to design. While this does not hold for accelerated depreciation, we saw that expensing immediately a specified fraction of investment outlay, together with a reduced inclusion of interest receipts, provides an incentive without distorting either investment choice (among assets of different durabilities) or portfolio composition (between debt and real asset ownership).

The direct grant approach via the investment tax credit, by contrast, leads to an increase, relative to the social return on investment, in the rates of return received by savers, but does not bring about their convergence. Provided the basis for depreciation of assets purchased is reduced by the amount of the credit (and provided the original depreciation rates are accurate), this approach also maintains neutrality with respect to portfolio composition. On the other hand, designing the credit to take correct account for differences in asset durability is relatively difficult. Furthermore, the direct grant approach does not share with the consumption tax approach to savings and investment incentives the tendency to displace imperfect income measurement rules as the amount of incentive is increased. In particular, it does not to the same degree reduce the sensitivity of the tax system to the rate of inflation.

A point that has been emphasized here is the interaction among the consumption tax incentives. In particular, it has been stressed that applying consumption tax incentives to real investment without implementing a corresponding exclusion of interest from tax (and corresponding reduction in interest deductibility) tends to drive real assets into the hands of the highest bracket taxpayers and to negate the potential of the consumption tax approach to bring about convergence of the yields on saving. What has not, to my knowledge, been recognized before is that there is an exact and relatively simple degree of interest inclusion appropriate for each level of write-off of real investment, a fact that would ease a gradual phasing in of a consumption-type base should this be the objective of policy.

Inflation upsets the measurement of the yield of both real and financial assets. S-I incentives are commonly viewed as instruments to offset these measurement problems. However none of them addresses the problem of correcting interest income. As a result it is difficult to reach clear conclusions about their relative properties, because it is difficult to model equilibrium in a graduated tax rate system. Without any correction for tax purposes, a change in the nominal interest rate of $1/(1 - m)$ points per point of inflation is necessary to maintain the after-tax yield of a lender (or after-tax cost of a borrower) with marginal tax rate m. Thus an interest rate change that just offsets inflation for one taxpayer will be too large or too small for most others.

Just where the change settles has a bearing on the predicted effect of measures, such as accelerated depreciation and the ITC, affecting the taxation of real assets. Theory predicts a concentration of real investment in the hands of relatively high bracket investors and relatively large changes in interest rates with inflation. To offset the resulting impact on the efficiency and quantity of real investment, accelerated depreciation or the ITC offer possible alternatives to indexing depreciation, but they do not correct the portfolio distortions. Furthermore, observed variation in interest rates does not seem large enough to be consistent with this view. Fully convincing analysis of the alternatives to indexing may have to await the sorting out of this puzzle.

REFERENCES

Aaron, Henry J. 1976. ed. *Inflation and the Income Tax.* Washington, D.C.: The Brookings Institution.

Auerbach, Alan J. 1979a. "Inflation and the Choice of Asset Life." *Journal of Political Economy* 87, no. 3 (June): 621–38.

_____. 1979b. "The Optimal Taxation of Heterogeneous Capital." *The Quarterly Journal of Economics* 93, no. 4 (November): 589–612.

_____. 1980. "Inflation and the Tax Treatment of Firm Behavior." NBER Working Paper no. 547. September, Cambridge, Mass.: National Bureau of Economic Research.

_____. 1981. "A Note on the Efficient Design of Investment Incentives." *The Economic Journal* 91, no. 361 (March).

_____., and Jorgenson, Dale. 1980. "Inflation-Proof Depreciation of Assets." *Harvard Business Review* (September-October).

Boskin, Michael J. 1978. "Taxation, Saving, and the Rate of Interest." *Journal of Political Economy* 86, no. 2, part 2 (April): S3-S28.

Bradford, David F. 1979. "The Case for a Personal Consumption Tax." In Joseph A. Pechman, ed. *What Should Be Taxed, Income or Expenditure?* Washington, D.C.: The Brookings Institution, pp. 75–113.

_____. 1980a. "The Economics of Tax Policy Toward Savings." In George M. von Furstenberg, ed. *The Government and Capital Formation.* Cambridge, Mass.: Ballinger, pp. 11–71.

_____. 1980b. "Tax Neutrality and the Investment Tax Credit." In Henry J. Aaron and Michael J. Boskin, eds. *The Economics of Taxation.* Washington, D.C.: The Brookings Institution, pp. 281-298.

_____., and Toder, Eric. 1976. "Consumption vs. Income Base Taxes: The Argument on Grounds of Equity and Simplicity." *Proceedings of the National Tax Association,* pp. 25-31.

Eisner, Robert. 1977. "Capital Shortage: Myth and Reality." *American Economic Review* 67, no. 1 (February): 110-15.

Fabricant, Solomon. 1978. "Accounting for Business Income Under Inflation: Current

Issues and Views in the United States." *The Review of Income and Wealth* 24, no. 1 (March): 1-24.

Feldstein, Martin S. 1976. "Inflation, Income Taxes and the Rate of Interest." *American Economic Review* 66, no. 4 (December): 809-820.

―――. 1977a. "Does the United States Save Too Little?" *American Economic Review* 67, no. 1 (February): 116-121.

―――. 1977b. "National Saving in the United States." In Eli Shapiro and William L. White, eds. *Capital for Productivity and Jobs.* Englewood Cliffs, N.J.: Prentice-Hall.

―――. 1980. "Inflation, Tax Rules and Investment: Some Econometric Evidence." NBER Working Paper 577. October, Cambridge, Mass.: National Bureau of Economic Research.

―――. 1981. "Adjusting Depreciation in an Inflationary Economy." *National Tax Journal* 34, no. 1 (March).

―――.; Green, Jerry; and Sheshinski, Eytan. 1978. "Inflation and Taxes in a Growing Economy with Debt and Equity Finance." *Journal of Political Economy* 86, no. 2, part 2 (April): S53-S70.

―――., and Summers, Lawrence. 1978. "Inflation, Tax Rules, and the Longer Term Interest Rate." *Brookings Papers on Economic Activity,* 1, pp. 61-109.

Gordon, Roger H. 1980. "Inflation, Taxation, and Corporate Behavior." NBER Working Paper 588. December, Cambridge, Mass.: National Bureau of Economic Research.

―――., and Malkiel, Burton G. 1980. "Taxation and Corporate Finance." NBER Working Paper 576. November, Cambridge, Mass.: National Bureau of Economic Research.

Hall, Robert, and Jorgenson, Dale. 1967. "Tax Policy and Investment Behavior." *American Economic Review* 57, no. 3 (June): 391-414.

Harberger, Arnold C. 1980. "Tax Neutrality in Investment Incentives." In Henry J. Aaron and Michael J. Boskin, eds. *The Economics of Taxation.* Washington, D.C.: The Brookings Institution, pp. 299-316.

Hendershott, Patric H., and Hu, Sheng-Cheng. 1980. "The Relative Impact of Various Proposals to Stimulate Business Incentives." In George M. von Furstenberg, ed. *The Government and Capital Formation.* Cambridge, Mass.: Ballinger, pp. 321-336.

Institute for Fiscal Studies. 1978. *The Structure and Reform of Direct Taxation, Report of a Committee Chaired by Professor J. E. Meade.* London: Allen and Unwin.

Jorgenson, Dale W. 1963. "Capital Theory and Investment Behavior." *American Economic Review* 53, no. 2 (May): 247-59.

King, Mervyn. 1980. "Savings and Taxation." NBER Working Paper 428, January. Cambridge, Mass.: National Bureau of Economic Research.

Malkiel, Burton G. 1979. "The Capital Formation Problem in the United States." *Journal of Finance* 34, no. 2 (May): 291-306.

Pechman, Joseph. 1980. "Tax Policies for the 1980's." *Tax Notes* 11, no. 25 (December 22): 1195-1208.

Samuelson, Paul A. 1964. "Tax Deductibility of Economic Depreciation to Insure Invariant Valuations." *Journal of Political Economy* 72 (December): 604-606.

Shoven, John B., and Bulow, Jeremy I. 1975. "Inflation Accounting and Nonfinancial Corporate Profits: Physical Assets." *Brookings Papers on Economic Activity,* 3, pp. 557-611.

―――. 1976. "Inflation Accounting and Nonfinancial Corporate Profits: Financial Assets and Liabilities." *Brookings Papers on Economic Activity,* 1, pp. 15-57.

Steuerle, Eugene. 1980. "Is Income from Capital Subject to Individual Income Taxation?" OTA Paper 42. October, Washington, D.C.: U.S. Treasury Department.

Stiglitz, Joseph E. 1980. "On the Almost Neutrality of Inflation: Notes on Taxation and The Welfare Costs of Inflation." NBER Working Paper 499. July. Cambridge, Mass.: National Bureau of Economic Research.

Discussion of David F. Bradford, "Issues in the Design of Savings and Investment Incentives"

Thomas Dernburg, Discussant

When I was on the staff of the Joint Economic Committee, we were greatly impressed by testimony such as that of Martin Feldstein, that original cost accounting causes overstatement of nominal profits during periods of inflation and that real after-tax rates of return on new investment therefore become decreasing functions of the inflation rate.

This conjured up images of a horrendous vicious circle in which rising inflation reduces investment and productivity which then comes back to haunt us with still more inflation in the future.

Congress takes such alarming scenarios very seriously, largely because expert witnesses and corporate lobbyists tell them to take them seriously.

In one of our Joint Economic Committee (JEC) reports we bemoaned the productivity slump and we proposed the indexing of depreciation allowances. None of the members of the committee dissented from this particular suggestion. Investment and productivity, like motherhood and the flag, are things everyone admires.

I have since come to realize that the analysis presented in our report was extremely naive. We did recognize that such indexing would have to use a general price deflator rather than a capital goods deflator so as not to lose relative price signals, and we recognized that any scheme to index corporate taxable income would have to be accompanied by the indexation of the individual income tax as well as interest income and capital gains.

Nearly all Hill staffers, other than the small minority that has some acquaintance with economics, view indexing schemes as equity adjustments and nothing more. In their opinion the corporate sector can take care of itself very nicely; thank you very much.

[The author is professor of economics, American University.]

Sermons by economists about the benefits of future productivity improvements are greeted with the usual derision accorded schemes that are perceived as trickling down proposals, which are viewed as devices designed to nourish sparrows by feeding horses.

We were also naive, because we did not realize that in combination with the investment tax credit, indexing depreciation would further contribute to the distortions in the tax system that currently favor short-lived assets; nor did we realize that because of the investment tax credit all machinery and equipment with a life of 15 years or less already enjoys a present value of 80 percent or more, despite inflation.

Calculations of effective tax rates and effective first-year capital recovery suggest that the business sector is not hurting nearly as badly from current tax practices as it likes to claim.

However, it is true that accelerating inflation has raised effective tax rates and that is what has brought about the flurry of new proposals to provide inflation offsets. The fact that productivity is in the dumps is probably incidental, but it does help support the argument for tax relief, at least in the eyes of impressionable politicians.

Of the proposals to provide inflation offsets, the 10-5-3 plan represented by Conable and Jones has received the most attention. Senator Long and Representative Ullman did bandy around the idea of a consumption VAT (value-added tax) that would have made first-year capital recovery automatic, but these proposals were never taken seriously.

The effect of the accelerated depreciation embodied in 10-5-3 would have been to raise the present value of depreciation to over 100 percent for all categories of machinery and equipment. It would therefore have greatly increased the distortions that now favor investment in machinery and equipment relative to investment in structures.

Moreover, the inflation offset, while substantial, is a one-time offset and does nothing to adjust depreciation in response to variable inflation rates.

Proposal 10-5-3 was opposed by the Treasury, largely because of the huge revenue losses that were implied by the bill. The plan seems now to have been shelved in favor of a Senate Finance Committee alternative known as 2-4-7-10. Although that plan which was developed by Senator Lloyd Bentsen's staff seems to be a great improvement over 10-5-3, it is of course being opposed by business, and Senator Bentsen himself has felt a great deal of political heat from the lobbyists who are not ready to give up on the 10-5-3 plan.

Frankly, I am not sure why we should bother with attempts to fine tune the taxation of business income. Part of our concern with the problem seems to arise from our preoccupation with individual assets. Accelerated depreciation implies an interest-free loan from the Treasury, and inflation produces a bias in favor of a short-lived asset where capital can be recovered quickly. We seem not always to be mindful of what Evsey Domar taught us a long time ago, namely, that when investment is viewed over time as a steadily growing stream, the sum total of all of the depreciation charges on all of the assets of different vintages tends to become a constant and large fraction of the value of the current year's investment.

For example, if assets lose value at a rate of 15 percent a year and investment outlays grow at a rate of 5 percent, the ratio of total depreciation to new investments will be about 80 percent. If that is the case, why not just have first-year capital recovery and be done with it? We can always make up for revenue losses by raising the statutory tax rate.

The difficulty, of course, is that it leaves us with a system that is far from neutral. It rewards rapidly growing firms and it creates a bias in favor of longer-lived assets. However, given our present situation, it is not clear why this is so awful.

If we do insist on letting ourselves be hooked by neutrality, then our best bet would seem to be the Auerbach-Jorgenson plan. Their system eliminates distortions caused by inflation without necessitating indexing, and it creates a neutral system of taxing business income that does not favor one class of assets over other classes. It does this by permitting firms to recover the present value of the sum of future economic depreciation during the year of acquisition.

Despite its enormous appeal, the Auerbach-Jorgenson plan has made very little headway on Capitol Hill. The first problem is that it would be applied only to new assets and would therefore be very expensive during the early years. The Congressional Research Service has estimated that the total cost of the plan in 1981 would be $56 billion, but since Auerbach and Jorgenson would also eliminate the ITC, the net cost would be reduced to about $36 billion—still a bigger chunk than the Treasury or the Congress are willing to swallow even during a period of recession.

To cut down the revenue loss there might be a gradual phase-in plan. Such a scheme would probably be chaotic, and it would very likely reduce capital spending during the phase-in period as firms wait to invest until the full benefits are made available.

Elimination of the investment tax credit is another obstacle to the Auerbach-Jorgenson plan. The credit is viewed by many legislators as the salvation of the enterprise system and their business constituents do nothing to disturb this conviction. Most proposals to change the ITC are not to reduce or abolish it but rather to extend it to structures and special tools and to make it refundable, so that the geriatrics of American industry such as the Chrysler Corporation can take advantage of it.

The most important problem that Auerbach and Jorgenson have is that people on the Hill simply do not understand what they are talking about. When Senator Stevenson asked me to explain present value to him, I knew we were in trouble. When my own immediate boss, Senator Riegle, asked me the same thing, I was relieved that he forgot the subject after being interrupted by a telephone call. I knew it was hopeless.

For his part, Dale Jorgenson struggled mightily all summer to educate every relevant congressional committee in sight, but he could not overcome the Hill's conviction that Harvard professors are enemies to communication.

As for desirable policy, I am struck by the fact that there seems to be an inverse confidence coefficient between politicians and economists. When economists admit that they are more confused and in a greater state of disarray than at any time since the early 1930s, the politicians suddenly, unanimously, and confidently agree that they have found a magic potion that will solve our problems willy-nilly.

The reverse is also true, as we learned during the early 1960s. The politicians' current view of the world is that the solution to the stagflation problem lies in substantial cuts in business taxes. This will work wonders for capital spending and restore productivity growth. Meanwhile, the job of slowing inflation is assigned to the Federal Reserve, which appears to be embarking on this objective with a zeal that is as unseemly as it is destructive.

The prescription of a policy mix which dangles a baleful monetary noose over a bottomless budgetary pit might have less to commend it than is generally supposed. Despite all efforts of economists to measure the effect of tax reduction on capital spending, the results still depend upon the elasticity of substitution between capital and labor, and we still cannot agree on the value of that elusive parameter.

Even under the most optimistic of assumptions, each dollar of revenue loss from reduction of business taxes always seems to generate less than its own value in new investment outlays. Therefore, it would appear to be cheaper for the government just to decide what capital goods we ought to have and to give these goods to business firms for nothing.

Sliding around a fixed production isoquant through relative price changes has its limitations, especially when substitution possibilities are meager. What we need is to get to a higher isoquant. To do this, we need to generate more demand, but we have become so intimidated by fear of inflation that we have created an environment in which real aggregate demand is virtually always deficient.

In my judgment, the monetary-fiscal mix in our economy is perverse and getting worse all of the time. With few exceptions, efforts to slow inflation have nearly always placed primary reliance on restrictive monetary policies. When monetary overkill leads to a recession, we pick up the pieces by resorting to fiscal measures including tax reduction and expenditure expansion. The fiscal measures support government and consumer spending. At the same time, the increase in the budget deficit combined with tight money causes increased competition for funds, raises interest rates, and has an adverse crowd-out effect on capital spending and home construction.

Therefore, we have a policy mix that is badly biased in a manner that creates the capacity and housing shortages that underwrite future inflation. Repetition of the sequence from one cycle to the next causes the bias to become worse over time.

Why not try to reverse this situation? Doing so is certainly not a novel idea. Indeed, when he was chairman of the Federal Reserve, G. William Miller attempted on several occasions to explain the idea to the congressional Banking and Budget Committees. Although the members nodded their heads in apparent comprehension and agreement, with this wisdom the mix is once again moving in the traditional direction.

Despite the poor performance of the economy, the Fed has announced that it will set its targets for growth of the money supply in 1981 at even less than in the current year. At the same time, President Ronald Reagan has determined to cut taxes and raise defense spending, and both political parties applaud this approach.

As long as we tolerate this mixed up mix without any net additional stimulus, it seems likely that we will continue to have huge deficits, further escalation of interest rates, prolongation of the productivity slump, and we will make very little headway against inflation.

I cannot imagine any tax reform that anyone sitting in this room can think of that could have much chance of altering such a sickening prognosis.

Discussion of David F. Bradford, "Issues in the Design of Savings and Investment Incentives"

Dale W. Jorgenson, Discussant

I will try as hard as I can to defend my reputation for an inability to communicate by cramming lots of material into a relatively few minutes.

First of all, I would like to try to provide a little bit of perspective on David Bradford's paper. At one level it would be possible to tackle this topic as, should we be worried about the connection between tax policy and productivity? That is, in fact, a subject for a panel discussion which will follow David's paper. I think this is a serious issue and should be addressed in all these papers.

On the one hand you have the extreme left-wing view, represented here by my distinguished colleague, Robert Eisner, which is that whatever is wrong with the current system, it should not be changed because we are collecting some taxes from capital income.

The alternative point of view, the extreme right—represented by the supply side economists such as Art Laffer, Jude Wanniski, and people like that—are also not very much concerned about the connection between productivity and business taxation. They are much more concerned about reducing taxation in general rather than focusing, as the Senate Finance Committee did, on specific provisions for capital recovery.

My position later this afternoon will be that productivity and tax policy do have a lot to do with each other, and we should worry seriously about the connection between tax policy and productivity. I think the published version of the story ought to discuss this issue.

The second question is, if we are going to worry about productivity, should we worry about it in the context of what you might call global tax reform, or should we think in terms of something more specific? I think that we can phrase that more precisely by saying, should we worry about replacing the income tax by a consumption tax, which is essentially the thrust of both the Bradford and the Hall papers, or should we think about working within the income tax system in order to achieve productive efficiency in the terms of the Bradford paper?

I think that it is interesting to discuss the possibility of converting to a consumption tax but not within the framework of this conference. I think that, as Bradford says, if you are going to go to a consumption tax, it really does not matter how you measure income. That is the great strength of a consumption tax. We are here to discuss the measurement of depreciation, which is important only in the context of an income tax. Within the context, there are a few things to say, and Bradford says quite a few useful things about it.

Let me insert parenthetically that I think Hulten and Wykoff deserve thanks from all of us, because it is possible at last to refute conclusively the views of, not the supply side economists, but many business tax lobbyists—some of whom will be prominent in the Reagan administration—that you cannot measure income and

[The author is professor of economics, Harvard University.]

therefore you ought not to worry about it. In other words, you ought to have business taxation without worrying about how to measure income. Hulten and Wykoff have made a major step forward by showing that it is possible to measure depreciation and therefore, to go on from there to measure income, that it is possible to discuss the question of an income tax.

Now we come to the point, which is, within an income tax, what do we do about capital recovery? That is, to my mind, the main issue before this conference. It is not perfectly reflected in the Hall and Bradford papers, but it is something which does play a role there. Is the issue whether the lifetimes are right or is inflation a problem for the income tax?

It is clear on the basis of the results of Hulten and Wykoff that inflation is the problem. The reason is that their depreciation rates, based on six years of careful research, are less accelerated than the rates currently used in the tax schedule. There is no need, in other words, to modify the rates in the tax schedule to make them more liberal or more generous on the basis of the Hulten and Wykoff results. On the contrary, if anything, there ought to be a move in the opposite direction.

Given the fact that we know much more precisely what economic depreciation rates are and we know that the lifetimes currently available to taxpayers are overly generous, what is the issue? The issue is that inflation based on historical cost depreciation has raised effective tax rates very substantially relative to the statutory rates on some assets, although for other assets it is considerably lower—not as low as Bob Hall's figures suggest, but still considerably lower. Therefore, there have become—there exist, and there will continue to exist in the tax code very substantial possibilities for taking a dollar's worth of investment from one class of assets, transferring it to another class of assets, and having additional GNP at no additional expense—in other words, a free lunch.

Then the question is, if inflation is the problem, how do you deal with it? Now we really get down to the trenches where the battle is joined, so to speak. The two basic approaches that have been discussed among practical men—not all of us are practical—are the approaches of indexing and acceleration. The acceleration approach is something that is very well exemplified by 10-5-3, by the 2-4-7-10 proposal that has come out of the staff of Senator Bentsen and the Joint Committee on Taxation staff, and by the position of the Treasury itself that depreciation ought to be geometric but at rates that are far in excess of the Hulten and Wykoff rates.

The indexing position is propounded by Alan Auerbach and myself. For those of you who have not yet had the opportunity to study our story at first hand, let me give you a reference so that you can consult a published original. It is in the *Harvard Business Review* for September-October 1980. The discussion in this paper incorporates a lot of material that we have presented in congressional testimony and in oral presentation before congressional staff members.

In any case, it seems to me that a paper like Bradford's or a paper like Robert Hall's ought to address the issue of how to deal with the impact of inflation on capital recovery within the income tax? Do you deal with it by indexing or do you deal with it by acceleration? The analytical methods that are presented by Bradford are perfectly appropriate for answering the question. I think that with a little bit of additional work the third section of the paper, which deals with inflation, can be focused on this specific issue.

Again, just to make sure that nobody misses the point that I am making: the problem is inflation and the question is whether a better attack on this problem is made by means of some kind of indexing scheme or by means of some kind of accelerated depreciation scheme within an income tax. Bradford has some very interesting suggestions about that. I think that on the basis of his results in the absence of inflation, which is dealt with in section II, the general conclusion one would reach is that acceleration is a nonstarter.

Of course, that is a very surprising conclusion to members of this audience, because every one of the major tax and analytical groups in Washington right now is attempting to deal with the problem of inflation from the standpoint of accelerated depreciation. Those are the proposals that have been advanced by the administration, have been put forth, first by the Joint Economic Committee and then by the Senate Finance Committee, that are being advocated by business lobbyists, and that are under serious discussion. Indexing, which is the economists' basic approach, is not represented.

The Bradford story says that there is no way to accelerate depreciation and to achieve productive efficiency at the same time. There is just no way to do it because it is just too complicated. That is a result which is outside the context of a discussion with inflation. If you put inflation into the problem, things become much more complicated.

What then is the case for indexing? As I say, Bradford does not deal with it at any great length, but let us indicate what the arguments are. [Ed. Note: These comments refer to the original Bradford paper and not the revised version published in this volume.] In his discussion of the first-year capital recovery system, Bradford's assumption that the tax rates are the same for all taxpayers, is the right one to use. There are two reasons for that. One is that the corporate tax, where a lot of the taxed assets that we are concerned about reside, is pretty much a flat-rate tax. There are, of course, special provisions for small corporations, but by and large the assets that are owned in the corporate sector are owned by people who are paying 46 percent rates. Second, given the nature of tax provisions of various kinds, we have the well-known result of Joe Pechman and others that after you get to the point where people have some property income, the effective tax rates for personal income tax purposes are essentially flat. There is no progressiveness in the actual tax structure. That is a very familiar conclusion. The conclusion is that we really do not have to worry a great deal about the fact that marginal tax rates may differ among investors. The flat-rate assumption is perfectly appropriate.

Should we worry about this issue that Bradford raises about offsetting effects of interest deductibility or the taxation of nominal capital gains? He only mentions one of those, but both of them are important. It seems to me that it is important to focus on the fact that depreciation is a big ticket item. It is there that the large discrepancies between an ideal system, or a completely indexed system and the actual system arise. The deductibility of interest is a second-order problem. In focusing on this problem, it is important to take into account also the fact that nominal capital gains at the individual levels, a point that is emphasized over and over again in Marty Feldstein's writing, are subject to taxation in an inflationary regime. This almost precisely offsets the tax deductibility of interest. The conclusion is that depreciation can be reformed by itself. You do not have to have a global approach to indexing in order to deal with the problem of capital cost recovery within an income tax.

That leaves us with the interesting question, which is posed in Emil Sunley's review. How in heaven's name do you make this appealing to the business community? They cannot even understand present value. I think that is really not true. It is true that some congressmen cannot understand present value. I am convinced of that. I am not convinced that business lobbyists, who inform these same congressmen, cannot understand present value. Business lobbyists understand present value perfectly well.

The first-year capital recovery system is based on the idea that you simply convert the economic depreciation that you would receive over the whole lifetime of an asset into its present value. In other words, you discount it back to the present and give that to the taxpayer as a first-year deduction. That would be something like 50 cents on the dollar for assets that are relatively long-lived and maybe 75 percent on assets that are relatively short-lived, maybe even 80 or 85 cents. At any rate, the present value of the depreciation is what is relevant. What Hulten and Wykoff have demonstrated, to my satisfaction at least, is that it is in fact possible to measure the economic depreciation that would underlie this part of the calculation. David Bradford is a good deal more skeptical about that in his paper, but I see no reason, after reviewing the Hulten-Wykoff results, that Bradford's attitude of skepticism should be maintained.

The second question is, can you measure the real rate of return? Is there such a thing as a real after-tax rate of return, and does it not vary substantially across taxpayers and also over time? The answer to both questions is no. The real rate of return after all taxes is something that is easy to measure. In the paper that Auerbach and I published in the *Harvard Business Review* we refer to yet another paper by Jorgenson and associates which deals with precisely this question of the measurement of the real rate of return after all taxes. That turns out to be something which is very close to constant over time, even though inflation rates have varied a lot over the post-War period, and the arguments I gave you earlier indicate that they are very similar across taxpayers even if they are at different levels of measured income.

The question is, how do you make the system more palatable? Is it just that the business community does not understand present value? Is that the problem? No. The problem is that this system would make an actual statutory rate of tax equal to the effective rate. It turns out that businessmen are already doing better on substantial portions of their assets, largely due to the investment tax credit. Therefore, if we want to induce the business community and their lobbyists to accept an indexing kind of scheme like this one, it is essential to sweeten the pot by lowering the effective tax rate.

There are a number of ways to lower effective tax rates. For example, you could lower the tax rate schedule. That is the whole thrust of the Kemp-Roth proposal. You could lower the corporate tax. The argument against that is that it creates rents. You have investors who were contemplating high rates and who are all of a sudden earning at rates that are in excess of what they contemplated. Therefore, there are windfalls. Of course, that is a no-no. Therefore, what we have to do is to figure out some way to continue to tax these investors on their assets in place and to tax new investments only.

Bradford's paper, if extended to deal with the problem of inflation in his analysis of the tax credit, would show that the most straightforward way of doing that is to have a tax credit that turns out to depend on the Hulten-Wykoff depreciation rate, on the real rate of return, and on nothing else. It does not turn out to depend on the marginal rate. That is something that could be combined with a first-year system in a practical form of this proposal. That would provide another solution to the problem, which I think David Bradford has very artfully posed in this paper, which is, how do we move from where we are, which is in an income tax, to the desired objective of both his paper and Bob Hall's—a consumption tax?

I think that you do it by combining the first-year capital recovery system with some kind of tax credit. I do not think that the issues which concern phasing it in are really serious, because the effective tax rates are higher for some assets and lower for others. I do not think there would be any net effect one way or another. My conclusion is that indexing is practical, that the measurements that are required in order to make it practical have been presented here by Hulten and Wykoff. We ought to get on with it and not continue to allow policymakers to engage in what I think is a cruel delusion—that it is somehow possible to deal with the problem posed by inflation in an income tax structure by means of accelerated depreciation.

ON MEASURING THE LOSS OF OUTPUT DUE TO NONNEUTRAL BUSINESS TAXATION

W. E. Diewert

I. Introduction

Many economists have asked the following question: under what conditions will a corporate tax (or more generally, a business tax) and depreciation policy be *neutral*? Many definitions of neutrality are possible.[1] We shall define a business tax system to be neutral if the production, employment, and investment decisions of a firm made in the absence of a business tax system would remain unchanged after the imposition of the tax system.

The above question is clearly an interesting one. However, what is somewhat surprising is that the existing literature on neutrality does not address the following more interesting question: given that a business taxation system is nonneutral, what is the *cost* to society of the nonneutral tax system? Obviously, if the costs are high, then we should direct our attention to reforming the nonneutral tax system in order to reduce the costs.

[The author is professor of economics, University of British Columbia. This research was funded in part by a Social Sciences and Humanities Research Council of Canada grant. The author thanks Charles Blackorby and Charles Hulten for helpful comments, and Janice McCallum for editorial assistance.]

A problem immediately arises: how should we measure the cost or excess burden of a given system of business taxation?

One approach would be to use Debreu's (1951, 1954) coefficient of resource utilization idea. Consider the initial observed equilibrium in the economy. In general, this equilibrium will not be Pareto optimal[2] due to the distortions induced by the existing tax system. Now remove the distortion and deflate the exogenous resources in the economy (i.e., land, the current stock of reproducible capital, mineral resources, etc.) by a proportionality factor until we reach an equilibrium where every consumer group has the same welfare as in the initial distorted equilibrium.[3] The resulting amount of resources that we can throw away (but still attain the same welfare as in the distorted economy) is a nice measure of the excess burden of the tax system in the distorted economy. The problem with this measure is that the informational requirements are very high: we require information not only on the technology of the economy but also on the preferences of each consumer group in the economy.

Due to the high informational requirements of the Debreu approach, we will not utilize it in the present paper. Instead, we will settle for a more partial equilibrium approach that has the advantage of having lighter informational requirements. We assume that there exists a set of producer prices for outputs and (noncapital) inputs that corresponds to some first or second best equilibrium of the economy. Relative to this set of "optimal" producer prices, we calculate the profit maximizing vector of outputs and inputs for the production sector under consideration. Capital stocks are endogenous variables chosen by the production sector so as to maximize the discounted present value of outputs minus variable inputs using the given producer prices.[4] We compare this optimal present value of net output with the present value of a tax distorted vector of outputs and variable (noncapital) inputs, where the outputs and inputs are valued at the "optimal" prices. The difference between the two present values is our suggested measure of the cost of the nonneutral tax system. Thus we are taking a productive efficiency approach to the evaluation of business tax policy.[5] The main advantage of our productive efficiency approach is that it only requires information on the technology of the economy. In fact, we will show how only local information on the technology is required in order to evaluate a quadratic approximation to the loss.

Our model of producer behavior is dynamic. In fact, we follow in the Malinvaud (1953) Dorfman, Samuelson and Solow (1958; chapter 12) tradition and assume that the sector has a one period technology which describes how current period capital stocks and inputs are transformed into current outputs and following period capital stocks. Section 2 explains our model of producer behavior in some detail. In particular, the comparative statics of changes in stock taxes turns out to be very important in section 4 when we evaluate the distortions inherent in the current system of business taxation.

In section 3, we show how the choice of an appropriate tax base for business taxation leads to a neutral corporate or business tax. Our result extends, for a more general technology, the earlier results of Brown (1948), Smith (1963), Hall and Jorgenson (1967), Sandmo (1974), King (1975), Boadway (1978, 1980), Schworm (1979), Hall (1980) and many others. We also show that the tax base appears to be the initial value of the economy's stock of reproducible capital plus pure profits plus discounted rents accruing to fixed factors. This tax base is not insignificant.

In section 4, we show how a somewhat stylized version of the current system of corporate taxation in most western countries can be transformed into the model of stock taxation developed in section 3. We obtain the usual two conditions for neutrality of the corporate tax that many authors have obtained in their models.

In section 5, we consider a very simple special case of the model presented in section 4, namely the one stock case with constant returns to scale. We calculate some approximate deadweight loss measures for this simple model. The surprising aspect about these rather rough and ready computations is that under what appear to be reasonable conditions, we can obtain gigantic losses. This is in contrast to much of the deadweight loss literature, where the losses are often rather small.[6]

Section 6 concludes with some limitations of our analysis and some directions for further research.

Before we develop our model in detail, it seems appropriate to indicate how our approach to modeling the loss of output induced by the current system of business taxation differs from Harberger's (1974, pp. 120–192) approach to modeling the loss of real income or utility induced by differential rates of corporate and noncorporate taxation.

Harberger's model has a consumer sector and two business sectors, a corporate and a noncorporate sector. The corporate income tax is higher than the noncorporate, and Harberger assumes that this difference in tax rates leads the corporate sector to discount investment at a rate of return which is higher than the noncorporate rate of return, where the difference in the discount rates equals the difference in the tax rates, so that after-tax rates of return are equalized. This difference in tax rates leads to a misallocation of resources. Harberger provides a quadratic approximation to the resulting loss of utility in the context of his general equilibrium model, assuming that the economy's total capital stock is fixed.

On the other hand, Stiglitz (1973, 1976) has argued that a properly designed corporate tax falls on pure profits and rents and is allocatively neutral. In this paper, we have taken the Stiglitz point of view, but we do not feel that Stiglitz is necessarily correct, and Harberger is necessarily incorrect. Who is correct is an empirical matter: do different sectors discount their future tax flows at different rates of return or not? If the answer is yes, then we require a Harberger sectoral approach to modeling the production sector, and the Stiglitz approach that we take in the present paper is inadequate.

However, our Stiglitz-like approach has some advantages over Harberger's approach. Harberger (1974, p. 132) himself recognized the chief weakness of his approach:

> The chief weakness of the model appears, at this writing, to be the assumption that the path of the capital stock through time is independent of the rate of corporate taxation.

Our approach makes the capital stock an endogenous variable which is affected by corporate tax policy.

Finally, we note that both the Harberger and Stiglitz models of corporate taxation are general equilibrium models, and they yield general equilibrium loss measures which consist of both losses of consumer's surplus, as well as losses of producer's surplus. Our loss measure consists only of the producer's surplus component, because we have modeled only producer behavior.

II. The Intertemporal Profit Maximization Model with Stock Taxes

The material in this section is taken from Diewert and Lewis (1981); the reader should consult this paper for further details on the model.

Denote the one period technology set of a firm by $S \equiv \{(x, s^0, s^1)\}$, where $x \equiv (x_1, x_2, \ldots, x_M)^T$ is an M dimensional vector of current period outputs (good m is an input if $x_m < 0$), $s^0 \equiv (s_1^0, \ldots, s_N^0)^T \geq 0_N{}^7$ is a nonnegative vector of beginning of the period stocks available to the firm, and $s^1 \equiv (s_1^1, \ldots, s_N^1)^T \geq 0_N$ denotes a nonnegative vector of end of the period stocks (which are available to the firm at the start of the next period).

The "stock" variables s^0 and s^1 are to be distinguished from the "flow" variable x on the following basis: well-defined market prices $p \equiv (p_1, \ldots p_M)^T \gg 0_M$ exist for the flow variable vector x, but no market prices necessarily exist for the stock variables. We assume that the stock variables consist of (i) inventories and goods in process, (ii) bolted-down pieces of capital equipment (as opposed to uninstalled pieces of capital equipment which appear as purchased inputs in the x vector), (iii) stocks of various grades of "tree" (or other renewable natural resources) on a plot of land that is owned or leased by the firm, or (iv) stocks of various grades of "ore" (or other nonrenewable natural resources) on a plot of land owned by the firm.

The sector under consideration could be a single firm or an aggregate of competitive firms or an entire economy. In the latter case, exports appear as outputs and imports appear as inputs in the x vector.

The technology set represents the set of "trade-offs" that the producer can make: given an initial stock vector s^0, the producer can produce more current net output x (or use less current input) at the cost of running down its internal stocks (i.e., less s^1 will be available at the start of next period). On the other hand, some components of s^1 could be increased by using more maintenance and repair variable inputs (which would appear as inputs in the x vector). Also increased utilization of the initial stocks s^0 will require increases in variable inputs (energy and maintenance labor) and lead to smaller end of the period stocks s^1. The point is that depreciation and utilization is endogenously determined within the model.[8]

For given beginning and end of period stock vectors s^0 and s^1, it makes sense for the producer to maximize profits. Thus for $p \gg 0_M$, $s^0 \geq 0_N$ and $s^1 \geq 0_N$, define the one period variable profit function[9] π as

$$\pi(p, s^0, s^1) \equiv \begin{cases} \sup_x \{p \cdot x: (x, s^0, s^1) \in S\} \text{ if there exists an x} \\ \qquad\qquad\qquad\text{such that } (x, s^0, s^1) \in S, \\ -\infty \text{ otherwise.} \end{cases} \tag{1}$$

Irrespective of the properties of S it can be shown that $\pi(p, s^0, s^1)$ is a convex and (positively) linearly homogeneous function in p. Moreover, if π is differentiable at (p, s^0, s^1) with respect to the components of p, then by a result due originally to Hotelling (1932, p. 594), we have

$$x(p, s^0, s^1) = \nabla_p \pi(p, s^0, s^1) \tag{2}$$

where $x(p, s^0, s^1)$ is the profit maximizing net output vector that is the solution to the profit maximization problem defined in the right hand side of (1) and $\nabla_p \pi(p, s^0, s^1) \equiv [\partial\pi/\partial p_1, \ldots, \partial\pi/\partial p_M]^T$ denotes the column vector of partial derivatives of π with respect to the components of p.

Throughout the paper we assume that S is a nonempty, closed set, an empirically harmless assumption. At times we shall place additional restrictions on S such as

S satisfies free disposal in the stock variables,[10]   (3)

S is a convex set,[11] and   (4)

S is a cone.[12]   (5)

If S satisfies (3), (4) and (5), then it can be shown that π satisfies (6), (7) and (8) below respectively:

$\pi(p, s^0, s^1)$ is nondecreasing in the components of s^0 and nonin-
creasing in the components of s^1,   (6)

$\pi(p, s^0, s^1)$ is a concave function[13] in (s^0, s^1) for fixed p, and   (7)

$\pi(p, s^0, s^1)$ is a (positively) linearly homogeneous function[14] in
(s^0, s^1) for fixed p.   (8)

We assume that the firm or sector has a T period horizon (where $T \geq 2$) and that its intertemporal profit maximization problem can be written in terms of the one period variable profit function π as follows:

$$\max_{s^1 \geq 0_N, \ldots, s^{T+1} \geq 0_N} \{ \pi(p^1, s^0, s^1) + (1 + r)^{-1} [\pi(p^2, s^1, s^2) - \tau^1 \cdot s^1]$$
$$+ (1 + r)^{-2} [\pi(p^3, s^2, s^3) - \tau^2 \cdot s^2] + \cdots$$
$$+ (1 + r)^{-(T-1)} [\pi(p^T, s^{T-1}, s^T)$$
$$- \tau^{T-1} \cdot s^{T-1}] + (1 + r)^{-T} [q^{T+1} \cdot s^T - \tau^T \cdot s^T] \}$$
$$\equiv V(\tau^1, \tau^2, \ldots, \tau^T, s^0, p^1, p^2, \ldots, p^T, q^{T+1}, r) \qquad (9)$$

where

π is the one period variable profit function defined by (1)

$p^t \gg 0_M$ is the vector of (variable) output and input prices that is expected to prevail during period t, $t = 1, 2, \ldots, T$

$s^0 \geq 0_N$ is the vector of initial stocks that the firm has at its disposal at the beginning of period 1

$s^t \geq 0_N$ is the vector of stocks that the firm has at its disposal at the end of period t (and the beginning of period $(t + 1)$ for $t = 1, 2, \ldots, T$ (note that $s \equiv (s^1, s^2, \ldots, s^T)$ is the vector of decision variables in the maximization problem (9))

$r > -1$ is the period t interest rate that the firm faces for $t = 1, 2, \ldots, T$

$\tau^t \equiv [\tau_1{}^t, \tau_2{}^t, \ldots, \tau_N{}^t]^T$ is the vector of stock tax (or subsidy) rates that the firm must pay on its holdings of stocks at the end of period t but the taxes are actually paid in period $t + 1$

$q^{T+1} \geq 0_N$ is the vector of scrap value prices that is expected to prevail during period $T + 1$ for the components of the firm's final period stock vector s^T, and

V is the firm's *value function*, which is defined to be the maximized (with respect to s) discounted stream of profits that the firm can earn over the period T horizon.

Note that V depends on five sets of variables: (i) the NT-dimensional vector of stock tax rates $\tau \equiv (\tau^1, \tau^2, \ldots, \tau^T)$, (ii) the N-dimensional vector of stocks s^0, (iii) the MT vector of expected variable input and output prices $p \equiv (p^1, p^2, \ldots, p^T)$, (iv) the N-dimensional vector of scrap value prices for the final period stocks q^{T+1}, and (v) the interest rate r. Define the $NT + N + MT + N + 1$ vector of exogenous variables as $z \equiv (\tau, s^0, p, q, r)$ and the NT vector of endogenous variables as $s \equiv (s^1, s^2, \ldots, s^T)$. Then the value function can be written as $V(z)$ and the solution to (9) as $s(z)$.

We now follow the standard Hicks (1946) Samuelson (1947) approach for obtaining comparative statics results. We assume that the solution $s^* \equiv (s^{1*}, \ldots, s^{T*})$ to (9) is unique and that

$$s^{t*} \gg 0_N \quad \text{for} \quad t = 1, 2, \ldots, T \tag{10}$$

so that we have an interior solution. We assume that s^* satisfies the first order conditions for the unconstrained maximization problem (9):

$$\nabla_{s^1} \pi(p^1, s^0, s^{1*}) + (1 + r)^{-1} \nabla_{s^1} \pi(p^2, s^{1*}, s^{2*}) = (1 + r)^{-1} \tau^1$$

$$(1 + r)^{-1} \nabla_{s^2} \pi(p^2, s^{1*}, s^{2*}) + (1 + r)^{-2} \nabla_{s^2} \pi(p^3, s^{2*}, s^{3*})$$

$$= (1 + r)^{-2} \tau^2, \tag{11}$$

.
.
.

$$(1 + r)^{-(T-2)} \nabla_{s^{T-1}} \pi(p^{T-1}, s^{T-2*}, s^{T-1*})$$
$$+ (1 + r)^{-(T-1)} \nabla_{s^{T-1}} \pi(p^T, s^{T-1*}, s^{T*}) = (1 + r)^{-(T-1)} \tau^{T-1},$$

$$(1 + r)^{-(T-1)} \nabla_{s^T} \pi(p^T, s^{T-1*}, s^{T*}) + (1 + r)^{-T} q^{T+1}$$
$$= (1 + r)^{-T} \tau^T \quad .$$

We further assume that the one period variable profit function is such that

$\pi(p^t, s^{t-1}s^t)$ is twice continuously differentiable in a neighborhood around

$$(p^t, s^{t-1*}, s^{t*}) \quad \text{for} \quad t = 1, 2, \ldots, T \quad . \tag{12}$$

Finally, we assume that the second order sufficient conditions for an unconstrained interior maximum hold: that is, we assume that the NT by NT matrix (call it A) of second order partial derivatives of the objective function (9) with respect to the components of s evaluated as s* is negative definite. (The matrix A can also be obtained by differentiating the first order conditions (11) with respect to the components of s).

Our last assumption implies that A^{-1} exists. Hence, we may apply the Implicit Function Theorem and conclude that a unique solution to (9), s(z), exists in a neighborhood of the vector of exogenous variables $z^* \equiv (\tau, s^0, p, q^{T+1}, r)$ with $s(z^*) = s^* \equiv (s^{1*}, s^{2*}, \ldots, s^{T*})$.

Using our differentiability assumption (12) and Hotelling's Lemma (2), the optimal period t variable output and input vector is

$$x^{t*} \equiv \nabla_p \pi(p^t, s^{t-1*}, s^{t*}) \quad , \quad t = 1, 2, \ldots, T \quad .$$

We can define the period t net supply functions in a neighborhood of $z^* \equiv (\tau, s^0, p, q^{T+1}, r)$ by

$$x^t(z) \equiv \nabla_p \pi(p^t, s^{t-1}(z), s^t(z)) \quad , \quad t = 1, 2, \ldots, T \tag{13}$$

where $s(z) \equiv (s^1(z), s^2(z), \ldots, s^T(z))$ is the NT-dimensional vector of optimal stock functions.

We can also define a vector of competitive imputed values or shadow prices for the initial stock vector s^0 by differentiating the value function with respect to the components of s^0, that is, define the initial shadow price vector w^{1*} as $w^{1*} \equiv \nabla_{s^0} V(z^*)$ and for z close to z^*, define

$$w^1(z) \equiv \nabla_{s^0} V(z) \tag{14}$$

$$= \nabla_{s^0} \pi(p^1, s^0, s^1(z)) \tag{15}$$

where (15) follows by differentiating the value function with respect to s^0 and then using the first order conditions (11) (except that the s^{t*} are replaced by $s^t(z)$ in (11)). (Note that in (15), $\nabla_{s^0} \pi(p^0, s^0, s^1(z))$ means differentiate π with respect to its second set of arguments only.) Note that if the free disposal assumption (3) is satisfied, using (6) yields $w^1(z) \geq 0_N$.

We now write the matrix A that is obtained by differentiating equation (11) with respect to the components of s in terms of T^2 N by N blocks, A_{rt}, r, t = 1, 2, \ldots, T. Assuming that $T \geq 2$ it can be verified that

$$A_{tt} \equiv (1 + r)^{-(t-1)} \nabla^2_{s^t s^t} \pi(p^t, s^{t-1*}, s^{t*})$$

$$+ (1 + r)^{-t} \nabla^2_{s^t s^t} \pi(p^{t+1}, s^{t*}, s^{t+1*})$$

$$\text{for} \quad t = 1, 2, \ldots, T - 1 \quad (16)$$

$$A_{TT} \equiv (1 + r)^{-(T-1)} \nabla^2_{s^T s^T} \pi(p^T, s^{T-1*}, s^{T*}) \quad , \quad (17)$$

$$A_{t,t+1} \equiv (1 + r)^{-t} \nabla^2_{s^t s^{t+1}} \pi(p^{t+1}, s^{t*}, s^{t+1*}),$$

$$t = 1, 2, \ldots, T - 1 \quad (18)$$

$$= [A_{t+1,t}]^T, \text{ the transpose of } A_{t+1,t}, \text{ and}$$

$$A_{r,t} \equiv 0_{N \times N} \quad \text{if} \quad |r - t| > 1 \quad . \quad (19)$$

Thus A is a block tridiagonal matrix. It is also negative definite and symmetric by our assumptions. Thus A^{-1} exists and A^{-1} is also negative definite and symmetric.

Define the NT by NT diagonal discount matrix D where the tth N by N block is the diagonal matrix $(1 + r)^{-t} I_N$ where I_N is the N by N identity matrix. Then differentiating the first order conditions (11) with respect to the components of s and τ yields the following expression for the NT by NT matrix of partial derivatives of the optimal stocks with respect to the components of τ, $\nabla_\tau s(z^*)$, evaluated at the initial equilibrium $z^* \equiv (\tau, s^0, p, q^{T+1}, r)$:

$$\nabla_\tau s(z^*) = A^{-1}D \quad . \quad (20)$$

Finally, we note how the value function V(z) changes as the components of τ change. Differentiating V with respect to τ at the initial equilibrium yields, using the first order conditions (11):

$$\nabla_\tau V(z^*) = -Ds^* \ll 0_{NT} \quad . \quad (21)$$

Thus $\partial V(z^*)/\partial \tau_n^t = -(1 + r)^{-t} s_n^{t*} < 0$ for $n = 1, 2, \ldots, T$; that is, as stock taxes increases, discounted optimal profit decreases.

For additional comparative statics results, see Diewert and Lewis (1981).

III. The Loss in Productive Efficiency Due to Stock Taxes

In this section, we shall show how taxes on a sector's capital stock variables impose a deadweight loss on society. In the following section, we indicate how the current system of U.S. business taxation can be regarded as a system that imposes taxes on capital stocks.

From the viewpoint of society, a reasonable objective function to maximize is the discounted net value of output that the production sector can produce. This is equal to the discounted value of consumption goods produced by the sector plus exports minus imports, labor services and intermediate input purchased, all valued at "optimal" producer prices (before commodity taxes if the good is an output but after if the good is an input into the sector).

Note that our objective function does not care about the stock variables per se: they are only useful to the extent that they help the sector to produce more net output. Thus our social valuation function S should be defined as the discounted net value of outputs and this is equal to the sector's private valuation function V defined by (9) in the previous section *plus* the (expected) discounted value of the stock taxes paid by the sector, that is

$$S(\tau, s^0, p, q^{T+1}, r) \equiv V(\tau, s^0, p, q^{T+1}, r)$$

$$+ \sum_{t=1}^{T} (1 + r)^{-t} \tau^t \cdot s^t (\tau, s^0, p, q^{T+1}, r) \quad . \quad (22)$$

The point is that the private valuation function V is equal to discounted net output minus discounted stock taxes, and thus in order to calculate S, it is necessary to add the discounted stock taxes back on to V. Note that the social and private objective functions will coincide only if the stock taxes $\tau \equiv (\tau^1, \tau^2, \ldots, \tau^T)$ are all zero.

In order to construct an approximate measure of the loss $S(\tau, s^0, p, q^{T+1}, r) - S(0_{NT}, s^0, p, q^{T+1}, r)$ in discounted net output induced by taxing the components of the capital stock vector $s \equiv (s^1, s^2, \ldots, s^T)$, we now calculate the vector of first order derivatives and the matrix of second order derivatives of the social valuation function S with respect to the components of the vector of stock tax rates τ, and we evaluate these derivatives at a socially optimally initial point where $\tau = 0_{NT}$; that is, where all of the stock taxes are zero initially:

$$\nabla_\tau S(\tau, s^0, p, q^{T+1}, r) = \nabla_\tau V(\tau, s^0, p, q^{T+1}, r) + Ds(\tau, s^0, p, q^{T+1}, r)$$
$$+ \nabla_\tau T_s(\tau, s^0, p, q^{T+1}, r)D\tau$$

where D is the diagonal discount matrix defined below (19)

$$= -Ds^* + Ds^* + D^T A^{-1} D\tau$$

letting $s^* \equiv s(\tau, s^0, p, q^{T+1}, r)$ and using (20) and (21)

$$= D^T A^{-1} D\tau \tag{23}$$

$$= 0_{NT} \quad \text{when} \quad \tau = 0_{NT} \quad . \tag{24}$$

Differentiating (23) with respect to the components of τ and evaluating the resulting matrix of second order partial derivatives at $\tau = 0_{NT}$ yields

$$\nabla_{\tau\tau}^2 S(0_{NT}, s^0, p, q^{T+1}, r) = D^T A^{-1} D \tag{25}$$

where the components of the negative definite symmetric matrix A are defined by (16)-(19). Thus a second order Taylor series approximation to the loss of discounted net output induced by a capital stock tax vector of size τ is

$$L(\tau) \equiv \tfrac{1}{2} \tau^T D^T A^{-1} D \tau \tag{26}$$
$$< 0 \quad \text{if} \quad \tau \neq 0_{NT}$$

where the inequality follows from the negative definiteness of the NT by NT matrix $D^T A^{-1} D$.

Our conclusion is that it is not a good idea to have a system of business taxation that imposes specific taxes (or subsidies) on the sector's stocks of reproducible capital. Such taxes will generally reduce (and can never increase) the discounted value of net output that the sector produces. To the second order, the loss of output grows quadratically as the tax-subsidy vector τ increases linearly.

If $\tau = 0_{NT}$, then $S(0_{NT}, s^0, p, q^{T+1}, r) = V(0_{NT}, s^0, p, q^{T+1}, r)$; i.e., the social and private valuation functions coincide.

We now ask the follow question: is it possible to impose a corporate or business tax on the sector that would not reduce the sector's optimal net discounted value of production but yet would raise a positive amount of revenue? The answer to this question is, of course, yes. Following in the footsteps of Brown (1948) and Smith (1963), we can impose a corporate or business profits tax on the sector at a rate of τ_c ($0 < \tau_c < 1$), where the tax base is taken to be the discounted value of net output. Under these conditions, the sector ends up solving the following maximization problem:

$$\max_{s^1, \ldots, s^T} (1 - \tau_c) \left\{ \sum_{t=1}^{T} (1 + r)^{t-1} \pi(p^t, s^{t-1}, s^t) \right.$$
$$\left. + (1 + r)^{-T} q^{T+1} \cdot s^T \right\} \tag{27}$$
$$= (1 - \tau_c) V(0_{NT}, s^0, p, q^{T+1}, r) \quad .$$

Under the above tax regime, the sector's investment decisions are unaffected by the business tax and there is no loss of discounted net output.

There are some subtle points about the above taxation scheme that merit further discussion. First, we are assuming if the sector is not the entire economy, then the sector's production of investment goods used by other sectors appears in the list of outputs while the sector's purchases of investment goods from other sectors appears in the list of inputs. This amounts to *immediate expensing* of the sector's purchases of capital equipment[15] or free depreciation or instantaneous deductibility of investment expenditures.[16] If the sector is the entire economy, then investment goods will not appear in the list of variable outputs and inputs (the M components of the x vector) except possibly as exports or imports or deliveries to the government sector. This is because production of capital goods by one firm delivered to another firm in the economy appears as an output and an input and the transaction nets to zero if immediate expensing of capital purchases is allowed for each firm.[17] Note that the expected net value of output to be produced in period t, $\pi(p^t, s^{t-1}, s^t)$, is simply expected period t cash flow when there is immediate expensing of investment purchases. A second point to note is that if the tax on cash flow is collected period by period, then in a period when there are heavy investment expenditures, cash flow with free depreciation could become negative. In this case, in order to preserve neutrality, the government must allow the sector to carry over the loss (properly discounted) until it can be deducted from positive cash flows in later periods.[18]

We conclude this section by calculating the *base* of a Brown-Smith (full loss offset with immediate investment expensing) cash flow business tax. First it is necessary to define a few additional variables. Recall that the stock solution to the sector's intertemporal profit maximization problem (9) was $s^* \equiv (s^{1*}, s^{2*}, \ldots, s^{T*})$. Thus the optimal period t expected variable profit or cash flow is $\pi(p^t, s^{t-1*}, s^*)$. We define the vectors of partial derivatives of the period t cash flow function with respect to the components of s^{t-1} and s^t as

$$w^t \equiv \nabla_{s^{t-1}} \pi(p^t, s^{t-1*}, s^{t*}); \qquad t = 1, 2, \ldots, T, \text{ and} \qquad (28)$$

$$q^t \equiv -\nabla_{s^t} \pi(p^t, s^{t-1*}, s^{t*}); \qquad t = 1, 2, \ldots, T \qquad (29)$$

Obviously, $w_n^t \equiv \partial\pi(p^t, s^{t-1*}, s^{t*})/\partial s_n^{t-1} \geq 0$ represents the marginal contribution to period t cash flow due to a marginal increase in s_n^{t-1}, the nth end of period $t - 1$ stock (or the nth beginning of period t stock). Hence w_n^t can be interpreted as the competitive payment out of period t cash flow paid to an owner of one unit of the nth stock who held the stock from period $t - 1$ to period t.[19] On the other hand, $-q_n^t \equiv \partial\pi(p^t, s^{t-1*}, s^{t*})/\partial s_n^t \leq 0$ represents the reduction to period t cash flow[20] if we increase next period's starting n^{th} stock by one unit (holding constant the starting period t stocks). Thus q_n^t can be interpreted as the opportunity cost of ordering one unit of the nth stock to be delivered next period: that is, we can interpret q_n^t as a period t investment price for the nth stock. Thus q^t is an implicit price vector for holding units of the stocks during period t until period t + 1. With stock taxes $\tau^t = 0_N$ for all t, the first order conditions (11) for the intertemporal profit maximization problem (9) can be re-written using (28) and (29) as

$$q^t = (1 + r)^{-1}w^{t+1}; \quad t = 1, 2, \ldots, T - 1 \text{ and} \tag{30}$$

$$q^T = (1 + r)^{-1}q^{T+1} \quad . \tag{31}$$

Thus if all expectations are realized, investors who buy units of stock n at price q_n^t during period t will be paid back $(1 + r)q_n^t = w_n^{t+1}$ during period t + 1.[21]

We may now define period t expected rents R^t. For $t = 1, 2, \ldots, T$, define

$$R^t \equiv \pi(p^t, s^{t-1*}, s^{t*}) - w^t \cdot s^{t-1*} + q^t \cdot s^{t*} \quad . \tag{32}$$

If the one period technology set S is subject to constant returns to scale (see (5)), then π will be linearly homogeneous in (s^{t-1}, s^t) (recall (8)), and by Euler's Theorem on homogeneous functions, $R^t = 0$ for all t.[22]

If the stock taxes τ_n^t are zero, using (11), (28), (29), and (32), we obtain the follow decomposition for the value function:

$$V(0_{NT}, s^0, p, q^{T+1}, r) \equiv \left\{ \sum_{t=1}^T (1 + r)^{-t+1} \pi(p^t, s^{t-1*}, s^{t*}) \right\}$$

$$+ (1 + r)^{-T}q^{T+1} \cdot s^{T*} = w^1 \cdot s^0 + \sum_{t=1}^T (1 + r)^{-t+1} R^t \quad . \tag{33}$$

Thus the tax base for a business tax on cash flow is equal to the real or im-puted value of the initial stocks plus discounted pure rents. This tax base is not insignificant, contrary to the opinion of some authors.[23]

Instead of assuming that the shareholders of the sector own the initial stocks, we could assume that the stocks are separately owned. In period 1, we could assume that the sector managers buy s^0 at a cost $w^1 \cdot s^0$. At the same time, they sell s^{1*}, in period 1 to capitalists for delivery in period 2 and gather $q^1 \cdot s^{1*}$ revenue in period 1 (hence they are borrowing $q^1 \cdot s^{1*}$ from capitalists during period 1). Then in period 2, they buy s^{1*} from the capitalists at a price $(1 + r)q^1 \cdot s^{1*} = w^2 \cdot s^{1*}$ (i.e., they repay the period 1 loan plus the interest on it) and they sell s^{2*} for delivery in period 3 and get $q^2 \cdot s^{2*}$ in revenue in period 2, etc. Thus our model can be thought of as generating a period by period borrowing requirement. This borrowing re-quirement is unaffected by the cash flow business tax.

IV. Modeling Economic Behavior with a Nonneutral Business Tax

In any given year, corporate or business taxable income is usually defined as that year's cash flow plus gross investment less deductions for the depreciation and interest costs of capital goods purchases. In this section, we attempt to make an approximate calculation of the deadweight loss that this type of tax policy generates for an entire economy.

Unfortunately, when we apply our model to an entire economy, gross investment does not appear in it, although we could define net investment in period t to be $s^{t*} - s^{t-1*}$. Also, economic depreciation does not appear explicitly in our model.

We suppose that the gross investment vector in period t, $i^t \equiv (i_1{}^t, i_2{}^t, \ldots, i_N{}^t)^T$, is defined to be a net investment vector $s^t - s^{t-1}$ plus an economic depreciation vector $\hat{\delta}^t s^{t-1}$; i.e.,

$$i^t \equiv s^t - s^{t-1} + \hat{\delta}^t s^{t-1} \quad , \qquad t = 1, 2, \ldots, T \tag{34}$$

where $\delta^t \equiv (\delta_1{}^t, \delta_2{}^t, \ldots, \delta_N{}^t)^T$ is a vector of period t economic depreciation rates on the starting capital stock vector s^{t-1} and $\hat{\delta}^t$ is a diagonal matrix with the elements of δ^t running down the main diagonal.

Recall that we defined $q^t \equiv - \nabla_{s^t} \pi(p^t, s^{t-1*}, s^{t*})$ to be a price vector for investment goods in period t. We suppose that individual firm managers treat these (expected) price vectors as constant vectors when they calculate their (expected) period t taxable income. Then expected period t taxable income T^t can be defined as period t cash flow plus period t gross investment minus any interest and depreciation deductions:

$$T^t(s^{t-1}, s^t) \equiv \pi(p^t, s^{t-1}, s^t) + q^t \cdot i^t - \beta^t \cdot s^t; \qquad t = 1, 2, \ldots, T \tag{35}$$

$$= \pi(p^t, s^{t-1}, s^t) + q^t \cdot [s^t - s^{t-1} + \hat{\delta}^t s^{t-1}] - \beta^t \cdot s^t$$

where the last equality follows using (34) and $\beta^t \equiv (\beta_1{}^t, \beta_2{}^t, \ldots, \beta_N{}^t)^T$ is a vector of period t depreciation and interest deductions associated with s^t.[24]

It is also useful to define a period t capital stock rental price vector ρ^t:

$$\rho^t \equiv q^t - (1 + r)^{-1} (I_N - \hat{\delta}^{t+1}) q^{t+1}; \qquad t = 1, 2, \ldots, T \tag{36}$$

$$= (1 + r)^{-1} \{ rq^t + \hat{\delta}^{t+1} q^{t+1} - (q^{t+1} - q^t) \} \quad . \tag{37}$$

Looking at the nth components of (36), we see that $\rho_n{}^t = q_n{}^t - (1 - \delta_n{}^{t+1}) q_n{}^{t+1}/(1 + r)$: that is, the cost of holding one unit of s_n from period t to period t + 1 is equal to the period t purchase price $q_n{}^t$ minus the discounted revenue received next period when the depreciated stock is sold. Equation (37) shows that $\rho_n{}^t$ can also be written as interest cost plus depreciation cost less any capital gains.

Finally, it is useful to define the difference between the interest and depreciation deduction for the nth stock in period t, $\beta_n{}^t$, and the corresponding user cost, $\rho_n{}^t$. Thus define

$$\gamma^t \equiv \beta^t - \rho^t \quad ; \quad t = 1, 2, \ldots, T - 1 \text{ and} \tag{38}$$
$$\gamma^T \equiv \beta^T - (\rho^T + (1 + r)^{-1} q^{T+1}) \quad .$$

We assume that firms try to maximize after-tax cash flow. In particular, we assume that the economy as a whole will end up trying to maximize the following objective function with respect to $s^1, s^2, \ldots, s^T$:[25]

$$\sum_{t=1}^{T} (1 + r)^{-t+1} \pi(p^t, s^{t-1}, s^t) + (1 + r)^{-T} q^{T+1} \cdot s^T$$

$$- \tau_c \left\{ \sum_{t=1}^{T} (1 + r)^{-t+1} \Upsilon(s^{t-1}, s^t) + (1 + r)^{-T} q^{T+1} \cdot s^T \right\}$$

$$= (1 - \tau_c) \left\{ \sum_{t=1}^{T} (1 + r)^{-t+1} \pi(p^t, s^{t-1}, s^t) + (1 + r)^{-T} q^{T+1} \cdot s^T \right\}$$

$$- \tau_c \left\{ \sum_{t=1}^{T} (1 + r)^{-t+1} [q^t \cdot (s^t - s^{t-1} + \hat{\delta}^t s^{t-1}) - \beta^t \cdot s^t] \right\}$$

using (35)

$$= (1 - \tau_c) \left\{ \sum_{t=1}^{T} (1 + r)^{-t+1} \pi(p^t, s^{t-1}, s^t) + (1 + r)^{-T} q^{T+1} \cdot s^T \right\}$$

$$- \tau_c \left\{ \sum_{t=1}^{T} (1 + r)^{-t} [rq^t + \hat{\delta}^{t+1} q^{t+1} - (q^{t+1} - q^t) - (1 + r)\beta^t] \right.$$
$$\left. - q^1 \cdot (I_N - \hat{\delta}^1) s^0 + (1 + r)^{-T} q^{T+1} \cdot s^T \right\}$$

using $\delta^{T+1} = 0_N$ and rearranging terms

$$= (1 - \tau_c) \left\{ \sum_{t=1}^{T} (1 + r)^{-t+1} \pi(p^t, s^{t-1}, s^t) + (1 + r)^{-T} q^{T+1} \cdot s^T \right\} \tag{39}$$

$$+ \tau_c \left\{ q^1 \cdot (I_N - \hat{\delta}^1) s^0 + \sum_{t=1}^{T} (1 + r)^{-t+1} \gamma^t \cdot s^t \right\}$$

where we have used (36) and (38). Since s^0 is fixed, maximizing (39) is equivalent to maximizing

$$\left\{ \sum_{t=1}^{T} (1 + r)^{-t+1} \pi(p^t, s^{t-1}, s^t) + (1 + r)^{-T} q^{T+1} \cdot s^T \right\}$$

$$- \sum_{t=1}^{T} (1 + r)^{-t} \tau^t \cdot s^t \tag{40}$$

where

$$\tau^t \equiv -(1 + r)\tau_c (1 - \tau_c)^{-1} \gamma^t \quad \text{for} \quad t = 1, 2, \ldots, T \quad . \tag{41}$$

Note that the objective function (40) is now exactly the same as the objective function in (9) if the stock tax vectors τ^t are defined by (41). Note that $\tau^t = 0_N$ if $\gamma^t = 0_N$, that is, if β^t (the period t depreciation and interest deduction vector) equals ρ^t (the period t economic user cost vector). Thus when $\beta^t = \rho^t$ for $t = 1, 2, \ldots, T$, the business tax leads to no loss of output and it is *equivalent* to the Brown-Smith immediate expensing full loss offset business tax discussed in the previous section. This kind of equivalence result has been obtained by many authors[26] in the context of somewhat simpler models.

In the case when $\rho^t \neq \beta^t$, we may use (41) and (26) in order to obtain a second order approximation to the loss of output induced by the nonneutral business tax. This is perhaps the main contribution of the present paper: we are able to go beyond the usual observation that the corporate tax is nonneutral unless the interest and depreciation deductibility provisions are equal to economic rentals in that we can evaluate the loss of output that is induced by the nonneutrality (to a second order approximation).

In the following section, we consider a very simple special case of loss formula defined by (26) and (41).

V.   The Case of One Stock with Constant Returns to Scale

In order to illustrate how the approximate loss formula (26) could be used, we consider the case where there is only one stock in the economy, and the one period technology set is subject to constant returns to scale, so that $\pi(p^t, s^{t-1}, s^t)$ is linearly homogeneous in its (scalar) arguments (s^{t-1}, s^t).[27] As a further simplification, we assume that the expected period t variable output and input price vector p^t is expected to equal the initial period's price vector p^1 times a constant inflation factor; that is, we assume

$$p^t = (1 + \Theta)^{t-1} p^1 \quad , \qquad t = 1, 2, \ldots \tag{42}$$

where $\Theta \geq 0$ is the constant expected inflation rate. As before r is the nominal interest rate and we now assume $r > \Theta$ so that the nominal interest rate is greater than the inflation rate.

We temporarily consider an infinite horizon version of the economy's intertemporal profit maximization model (9) with all stock taxes equal to zero. Using (42), the value function $V(s^0)$ regarded as a function of the initial stock s^0 can be defined as

$$V(s^0) \equiv \max_{s^1, s^2 \ldots} \left\{ \sum_{t=1}^{\infty} [(1 + \Theta)/(1 + r)]^{t-1} \pi(p^1, s^{t-1}, s^t) \right\} \quad (43)$$

We assume that $V(s^0) < \infty$ for all $s^0 \geq 0$. Because we have assumed that π is linearly homogeneous in its stock arguments, it is easy to show that $V(s^0)$ is linearly homogeneous in s^0; that is, for $s^0 \geq 0$ and $\lambda > 0$,

$$V(\lambda s^0) = \lambda(s^0) \quad . \quad (44)$$

It is also obvious that V will satisfy the following functional equation:

$$V(s^0) = \max_{s^1} \left\{ \pi(p^1, s^0, s^1) + [(1 + \Theta)/(1 + r)] V(s^1) \right\} \quad . \quad (45)$$

In general, the solution s^1 to (45) will depend on s^0. However, using our constant returns to scale assumption which implies (44), it is easy to show that $s^1 = (1 + \alpha)s^0$, where the growth rate α *does not depend on* s^0; that is, α is the solution to

$$\max_z \left\{ \pi(p^1, s^0, s^0(1 + z)) + [(1 + \Theta)/(1 + r)] V(s^0(1 + z)) \right\}$$
$$= \max_z \left\{ s^0 \pi(p^1, 1, (1 + z)) + [(1 + \Theta)/(1 + r)]s^0 V(1 + z) \right\}$$

using (44)

$$= s^0 \max_z \left\{ \pi(p^1, 1, (1 + z)) + [(1 + \Theta)/(1 + r)] V(1 + z) \right\} \quad . \quad (46)$$

Note that the maximization problem in (46) does not depend on s^0. Thus the period by period growth rate α for the capital stock will be the same for all periods under our assumptions.[28]

We may use equation (29) in order to define a period t price for the capital stock. In particular, define

$$q^{T+1} = -\partial \pi((1 + \Theta)^T p^1, s^{T*}, s^{T+1*})/\partial s^{T+1} \quad (47)$$

where $s^{T*} \equiv (1 + \alpha)^T s^0$ and $s^{T+1*} \equiv (1 + \alpha)^{T+1} s^0$. Using the period $T + 1$ "scrap value" price vector q^{T+1} defined by (47), we may return to our finite horizon model in order to evaluate the deadweight loss associated with a nonneutral business tax.

Our task now is to evaluate what are the elements of the A matrix defined by (16)-(19) above under our specialized assumptions model in this section. First, we note that the linear homogeneity of $\pi(p^1, s^0, s^1)$ in (s^0, s^1) implies that

$$\pi_{00}s^0 + \pi_{01}s^{1*} = 0 \tag{48}$$

$$\pi_{10}s^0 + \pi_{11}s^{1*} = 0$$

where $\pi_{ij} \equiv \partial^2\pi(p^1, s^0, s^{1*})/\partial s^i \partial s^j$ for $i, j = 0, 1$. Assumption (4) implies (7) which in turn implies that $\pi_{00} < 0$ and $\pi_{11} < 0^{29}$ and hence by (48), $\pi_{01} = \pi_{10} > 0$. Since $s^{1*} = (1 + \alpha)s^0$, (48) implies

$$-\pi_{00} = (1 + \alpha)\pi_{01} > 0 \tag{49}$$

$$-\pi_{11} = (1 + \alpha)^{-1}\pi_{01} > 0 \quad .$$

Using $p^t \equiv (1 + \Theta)^{t-1}p^1$, $s^* \equiv (1 + \alpha)^t s^0$ and the linear homogeneity of π in prices and in stocks, we can show that for $t = 1, 2, \ldots, T$:

$$\frac{\partial^2\pi}{\partial s^{t-1}\partial s^{t-1}}(p^t, s^{t-1*}, s^{t*}) = \frac{(1 + \Theta)^{t-1}}{(1 + \alpha)^{t-1}}\pi_{00}$$

$$= -(1 + \alpha)\frac{(1 + \Theta)^{t-1}}{(1 + \alpha)^{t-1}}\pi_{01} \tag{50}$$

$$\frac{\partial^2\pi}{\partial s^{t-1}\partial s^t}(p^t, s^{t-1*}, s^{t*}) = \frac{(1 + \Theta)^{t-1}}{(1 + \alpha)^{t-1}}\pi_{01}$$

$$\frac{\partial^2\pi}{\partial s^t\partial s^t}(p^t, s^{t-1*}, s^{t*}) = \frac{(1 + \Theta)^{t-1}}{(1 + \alpha)^{t-1}}\pi_{11}$$

$$= -(1 + \alpha)^{-1}\frac{(1 + \Theta)^{t-1}}{(1 + \alpha)^{t-1}}\pi_{01}$$

where we used (49) to establish the final equalities in (50).

Substitution of (50) into (16) to (19) yields the following expression for A:

$$A = -\pi_{01}(1 + \alpha)^{-1}\Phi B \Phi \tag{51}$$

where Φ is a diagonal T by T matrix with elements $1, \phi, \phi^2, \ldots, \phi^{T-1}$ running down the main diagonal where $\phi \equiv [(1 + \Theta)(1 + r)^{-1}(1 + \alpha)^{-1}]^{1/2}$ and B is a tridiagonal matrix with element $1 + \xi^2$ running down the main diagonal (except that the TTth element of B is 1), and $b_{t,t-1} = b_{t,t+1} \equiv -\xi$ where $\xi \equiv \phi(1 + \alpha) = (1 + \Theta)^{1/2}(1 + \alpha)^{1/2}/(1 + r)^{1/2} < 1$. Remember that α is the growth rate for the capital stock, Θ is the inflation rate and r is the nominal interest rate.

From (51), we can calculate A^{-1}:

$$A^{-1} = -\pi_{01}{}^{-1}(1 + \alpha)\,\Phi^{-1}\,B^{-1}\,\Phi^{-1}\quad. \tag{52}$$

Define the matrix C to equal the matrix B except that C has element 1 in row 1 and column 1 instead of $1 + \xi^2$; that is,

$$C \equiv \begin{bmatrix} 1, & -\xi, & 0, & 0, & \ldots, & 0, & 0, & 0 \\ -\xi, & 1 + \xi^2, & -\xi, & 0, & \ldots, & 0, & 0, & 0 \\ 0, & -\xi, & 1 + \xi^2, & -\xi, & \ldots, & 0, & 0, & 0 \\ \vdots & & & & & & & \vdots \\ 0, & 0, & 0, & 0, & \ldots, & -\xi, & 1 + \xi^2, & -\xi \\ 0, & 0, & 0, & 0, & \ldots, & 0, & -\xi, & 1 \end{bmatrix}. \tag{53}$$

The matrix C occurs in the econometrics literature. From Johnston (1972, p. 259), we find that

$$C^{-1} = (1 - \xi^2)\begin{bmatrix} 1, & \xi, & \xi^2, & \ldots, & \xi^{T-1} \\ \xi, & 1, & \xi, & \ldots, & \xi^{T-2} \\ \vdots & & & & \vdots \\ \xi^{T-1}, & \xi^{T-2}, & \xi^{T-3}, & \ldots, & 1 \end{bmatrix}. \tag{54}$$

Having calculated C^{-1}, it is rather easy to calculate B^{-1}; in general $B^{-1} \equiv [C + \xi^2 e_1 e_1{}^T]^{-1} = C^{-1} - \xi^2(1 + \xi^2 C_{11}{}^{-1})^{-1}C_{.1}{}^{-1}C_{1.}{}^{-1}$ where e_1 is a unit (column) vector with a 1 in the first component, $C_{11}{}^{-1}$ is the 1, 1 element of C^{-1}, $C_{.1}{}^{-1}$ is the first column of C^{-1} and $C_{1.}{}^{-1}$ is the first row of C^{-1}. With C^{-1} defined by (54), it turns out that

$$B^{-1} = C^{-1} - \frac{\xi^2(1 - \xi^2)^2}{1 + \xi^2(1 - \xi^2)}\begin{bmatrix} 1 \\ \xi \\ \vdots \\ \xi^{T-1} \end{bmatrix}[1, \xi, \ldots, \xi^{T-1}] \tag{55}$$

For simplicity, we suppose that the divergence between the user cost of capital and the interest depreciation deductibility provision for period t, γ^t, is a constant for all periods, that is,

$$\gamma^t \equiv \gamma, \qquad t = 1, 2, \ldots, T. \tag{56}$$

Now substitute (41), (56), (51) and (55) into the loss formula (26):

$$L(\Theta, \alpha, r, \gamma, \pi_{01}, \tau_c) \equiv \tfrac{1}{2}\, \tau \cdot DA^{-1}D\tau$$

$$= -\tfrac{1}{2}\, (1 + r)^2\, \tau_c^2\, (1 - \tau_c)^{-2}\gamma^2\, \pi_{01}^{-1}\, (1 + \alpha)1_T \cdot D\Phi^{-1}B^{-1}\Phi^{-1}D1_T \tag{57}$$

where

$\Theta \equiv$ one period inflation rate in output and input prices,
$\alpha \equiv$ one period growth rate of the capital stock,
$r \equiv$ one period nominal interest rate,
$\gamma \equiv$ difference between the user cost of capital and the deduction the tax system allows,
$\pi_{01} \equiv \partial^2\pi(p^1, s^0, s^{1*})/\partial s^0 \partial s^1 > 0$,
$\tau_c \equiv$ the business tax rate,
$1_T \equiv$ a vector of ones of size T,
$D \equiv$ a diagonal discount matrix with diagonal elements $[(1 + r)^{-1}, (1 + r)^{-2}, \ldots, (1 + r)^{-T}]$,
$\Phi \equiv$ a diagonal matrix with diagonal elements $[1, \phi, \phi^2, \ldots, \phi^{T-1}]$ where $\phi \equiv [(1 + \Theta)(1 + r)^{-1}(1 + \alpha)^{-1}]^{1/2}$.
$B^{-1} \equiv$ is defined by (54) and (55) and
$\xi \equiv (1 + \Theta)^{1/2}(1 + \alpha)^{1/2}/(1 + r)^{1/2}$.

If we set $\Theta = 0$ and ignore terms involving powers of α and r, we find that the loss defined by (57) is approximately equal to

$$L^* \equiv -\frac{\tau_c^2\gamma^2\, (1 + \alpha)(1 + r + \alpha)}{(1 - \tau_c)^2\, \pi_{01}\, (r - \alpha)} \tag{58}$$

It is convenient to express the loss as a fraction of the discounted value of output V^* that could be produced with a nondistortive business tax. If the inflation rate is $\Theta = 0$, then

$$V^* \equiv \sum_{t=1}^{\infty} (1 + r)^{-t+1}\, \pi(p^1, s^0(1 + \alpha)^{t-1}, s^0(1 + \alpha)^t) \tag{59}$$

$$= \pi(p^1, s^0, s^{1*})[1 + (1 + \alpha)(1 + r)^{-1} + (1 + \alpha)^2(1 + r)^{-2} + \ldots]$$

$$= \pi(p^1, s^0, s^{1*})(1 + r)(r - \alpha)^{-1} \quad .$$

Now define

$$\pi \equiv \pi(p^1, s^0, s^{1*}) > 0, \qquad \pi_0 \equiv \partial\pi(p^1, s^0, s^{1*})/\partial s^0 \equiv w^1 > 0$$
$$\text{and}$$
$$\pi_1 \equiv \partial\pi(p^1, s^0, s^{1*})/\partial s^1 \equiv -q^1 = -w^2/(1+r) = -w^1/(1+r) < 0$$

using the linear homogeneity of π in stocks. Thus,

$$-\pi_1 = \pi_0/(1+r) = q^1 = \text{period 1 investment good price.} \qquad (60)$$

Finally, define the inverse elasticity of substitution[30] between the starting and finishing capital stocks in the production of value added as

$$\sigma \equiv -\pi\,\pi_{01}/\pi_0\,\pi_1 > 0 \quad . \qquad (61)$$

The smaller is σ, the greater is the substitutability between the stocks, that is, the more like straight lines are the isoprofit lines of the form $\{(s^0, s^1): \pi(p^1, s^0, s^1) = k\}$.

Using (58) to (61), we may rewrite the loss L^* as a fraction of optimal discounted value added V^* as follows:

$$\frac{L^*}{V^*} = -\frac{\tau_c^2(\gamma/q_1)^2(1+\alpha)(1+r+\alpha)}{(1-\tau_c)^2(1+r)^2\sigma} \qquad (62)$$

If $\tau_c = \frac{1}{2}$ and r and α are close to zero, then L^*/V^* is approximately equal to $-(\gamma/q_1)^2/\sigma$. Thus if γ is large relative to q_1 or if σ is close to zero, the loss of output induced by the tax system could be huge. This is the most important implication of this paper, since much of the literature on the efficiency of the system of business taxation used in most western countries obtains very small deadweight losses.[31] Although there are many studies which indicate that γ/q_1 can be large,[32] unfortunately very little is known about the magnitude of σ, since very few models with endogenous variable depreciation rates have been estimated.[33]

VI. Conclusion

Our productive efficiency approach to the evaluation of business tax policy has provided a framework for calculating the loss of output that is due to the current inefficient system of business taxation that is in force in the U.S. and elsewhere. Some illustrative calculations presented in the previous section suggest that the loss of output could be very large. This is in contrast to Harberger's rather small losses. However, Harberger obtains small losses because he held aggregate capital stock fixed. In our model, reproducible capital stocks are directly influenced by the current nonneutral system of business taxation. Since capital stocks are large relative to output, and the tax distortions are also relatively large, there are potentially very large losses in our model depending on the various production elasticities. What is required at this stage is some econometric work on the structure of production in order to obtain estimates for these production elasticities. It may also be useful to develop alternative versions of the very general model presented in this paper that are perhaps less general but easier to implement econometrically.

There are a number of theoretical problems that should have been addressed in this paper but were not:

1. We have assumed that there is only a single business sector that faces a single business tax τ_c. Our model should be generalized to the case of many sectors, each of which faces a separate structure of taxation.[34]

2. Our model has implicitly assumed that the opportunity cost of labor is known and can be deducted from taxable income. For an unincorporated business, this assumption is not warranted.

3. We have not allowed for taxes on intermediate inputs. To deal with this problem, we would need to consider modeling several sectors simultaneously.

4. We have ignored the complications induced by variations in a firm's financial policies. On these complications, see Stiglitz (1973, 1976), King (1974, 1975), Boadway (1978, 1980), Auerbach (1979), and Atkinson and Stiglitz (1980).

5. We have also ignored any complications arising from noncompetitive behavior, uncertainty, and regulation.

Our overall conclusion is that immediate expensing with adequate loss carry over provisions should be seriously considered as an alternative to the current proposals for tax reform in the U.S.[35]

REFERENCES

Atkinson, A. B., and J. E. Stiglitz. 1980. *Lectures on Public Economics*. New York: Mc-Graw-Hill.

Auerbach, A. J. 1978. "Neutrality and the Corporate Tax." Discussion Paper 657, Harvard Institute of Economic Research, Harvard University, Cambridge, Mass., October.

Auerbach, A. J. 1979. "Wealth Maximization and the Cost of Capital." *Quarterly Journal of Economics* 93: 433–446.

Boadway, R. 1978. "Investment Incentives, Corporate Taxation, and Efficiency in the Allocation of Capital." *The Economic Journal* 88: 470–481.

———. 1980. "Corporate Taxation and Investment: A Synthesis of the Neoclassical Theory." *The Canadian Journal of Economics* 13: 250–267.

Boadway, R. W., N. Bruce, and J. M. Mintz 1981. "Corporate Taxation in Canada: Towards an Efficient System." Paper presented at the Canadian Tax Foundation Conference, March 4 and 5, Toronto, Canada.

Boiteux, M. 1951. "Le 'Revenu Distribuable' et les Pertes Economiques." *Econometrica* 19: 112–133.

Brown, E. C. 1948. "Business-Income Taxation and Investment Incentives." In L. Metzler et al. *Income, Employment, and Public Policy: Essays in Honor of Alvin H. Hansen.* New York: W. W. Norton.

Debreu, G. 1951. "The Coefficient of Resource Utilization." *Econometrica* 19: 273–292.

———. 1954. "A Classical Tax-Subsidy Problem." *Econometrica* 22: 14–22.

Diewert, W. E. 1973. "Functional Forms for Profit and Transformation Functions." *Journal of Economic Theory* 6: 284–316.

———. 1974. "Application of Duality Theory." pp. 106–171. In M. D. Intriligator and D. A. Kendrick. (eds.) *Frontiers of Quantitative Economics.* Vol. II. Amsterdam: North-Holland.

———. 1977. "Walras' Theory of Capital Formation and the Existence of a Temporary Equilibrium." pp. 73–126. In E. Schwodiauer (ed.) *Equilibrium and Disequilibrium in Economic Theory.* Dordrecht, Holland: D. Reidel Publishing Company.

———., and T. R. Lewis. 1981. "The Comparative Dynamics of Efficient Programs of Capital Accumulation and Resource Depletion." Resource Paper No. 59, Department of Economics, University of British Columbia. Vancouver, Canada.

Dorfman, R.; P. A. Samuelson; and R. M. Solow. 1958. *Linear Programming and Economic Analysis.* New York: McGraw-Hill.

Epstein, L. 1977. *Essays in the Economics of Uncertainty.* Unpublished Ph.D. Thesis, Department of Economics, University of British Columbia, Vancouver, Canada.

———., and M. Denny 1980. "Endogenous Capital Utilization in a Short-run Production Model: Theory and an Empirical Application." *Journal of Econometrics* 12: 189–207.

Gorman, W. M. 1968. "Measuring the Quantities of Fixed Factors." pp. 141–172. In J. N. Wolfe. (ed.) *Value, Capital and Growth: Papers in Honor of Sir John Hicks.* Chicago: Aldine.

Hall, R. E. 1980. "Tax Treatment of Depreciation, Capital Gains, and Interest in an Inflationary Economy." This volume.

———., and D. W. Jorgenson. 1967. "Tax Policy and Investment Behavior." *The American Economic Review* 57: 391–414.

———. 1971. "Application of the Theory of Optimum Capital Accumulation." In E. Fromm (ed.) *Tax Incentives and Capital Spending.* Washington, D.C.: Brookings Institution.

Harberger, A. C. 1964. "The Measurement of Waste." *The American Economic Review* 54: 58–76.

———. 1971. "Three Basic Postulates for Applied Welfare Economics: An Interpretive Essay." *The Journal of Economic Literature* 9: 785–797.

———. 1974. *Taxation and Welfare.* Boston: Little, Brown and Company.

Hicks, J. R. 1946. *Value and Capital.* second edition, Oxford: Clarendon Press.

Hotelling, H. 1932. "Edgeworth's Taxation Paradox and the Nature of Demand and Supply Functions." *Journal of Political Economy* 40: 577–616.

———. 1938. "The General Welfare in Relation to Problems of Taxation and of Railway and Utility Rates." *Econometrica* 6: 242–269.

Johnston, J. 1972. *Econometric Methods.* second edition, New York: McGraw-Hill.

King, M. A. 1974. "Taxation and the Cost of Capital." *The Review of Economic Studies* 41: 21-35.

_____. 1975. "Taxation, Corporate Financial Policy, and the Cost of Capital: A Comment." *Journal of Public Economics* 4: 271-279.

Lau, L. J. 1976. "A Characterization of the Normalized Restricted Profit Function." *Journal of Economic Theory* 12: 131-164.

Malinvaud, E. 1953. "Capital Accumulation and the Efficient Allocation of Resources." *Econometrica* 21: 233-268.

McFadden, D. 1978. "Cost, Revenue and Profit Functions." pp. 3-109. In M. Fuss and D. McFadden (eds.) *Production Economics: A Dual Approach to Theory and Applications.* Vol. 1, Amsterdam: North-Holland.

Samuelson, P. A. 1967. *Foundations of Economic Analysis.* Cambridge, Mass: Harvard University Press.

_____. 1953-4. "Prices of Factors and Goods in General Equilibrium." *The Review of Economic Studies* 21: 1-20.

_____. 1964. "Tax Deductibility of Economic Depreciation to Insure Invariant Valuations." *Journal of Political Economy* 72: 604-606.

Sandmo, A. 1974. "Investment Incentives and the Corporate Income Tax." *Journal of Political Economy* 82: 287-302.

Schworm, W. E. 1979. "Tax Policy, Capital Use, and Investment Incentives." *Journal of Public Economics* 12: 191-204.

Smith, V. L. 1963. "Tax Depreciation Policy and Investment Theory." *International Economic Review* 4: 80-91.

St. Hilaire, F., and J. Whalley 1981. "Recent Studies of Efficiency and Distributional Impacts of Taxes: Implications for Canadian Tax Reform Discussion." Paper presented at the Canadian Tax Foundation Conference, March 4 and 5, Toronto, Canada.

Stiglitz, J. E. 1973. "Taxation, Corporate Financial Policy, and the Cost of Capital." *Journal of Public Economics* 22: 1-34.

_____. 1976. "The Corporation Tax." *Journal of Public Economics* 5: 303-312.

THE MEASUREMENT OF ECONOMIC DEPRECIATION[1]

Charles R. Hulten and Frank C. Wykoff

I. Introduction

A reduction in business taxes, especially taxes on capital, is seen by many as the key to reversing the decline in the growth of U.S. labor productivity. One approach, which has received widespread support, is to liberalize tax depreciation deductions and to increase investment tax credits. While there is near consensus on the objective of stimulating capital formation, the most highly publicized proposal (by Representatives Conable and Jones) has attracted much critical attention.

The Conable-Jones bill (H.R. 4646) would abolish the current rules for tax depreciation, the Asset Depreciation Range System (ADR), and replace them with a greatly simplified system of depreciation allowances in which autos and light trucks would be depreciated over 3 years, other machinery and equipment over 5 years, and structures over 10 years. The straight-line, declining balance, and sum-of-the-years'-digits methods of depreciation currently allowed under ADR would be replaced with a single fixed method for each of the three Conable-Jones asset categories.[2]

[Charles R. Hulten is senior research associate, The Urban Institute. Frank C. Wykoff is professor of economics, Pomona College.]

Much of the criticism of this "10-5-3" proposal has focused on the ten-year life for structures, which is widely regarded as being far too short even for a growth-oriented liberalization of tax policy. A counter-proposal currently pending before the Senate Finance Committee would group equipment into four classes with lives of 2, 4, 7, and 10 years, depreciated with the declining balance method of depreciation. Structures would be depreciated over a 20-year period using the straight-line method. This system would alleviate some of the concern over the 10-year structure life, but it carries on an even more important problem with the Conable-Jones proposal: no factual basis is provided to justify the choice of lives, and there is thus no factual basis for choosing between 10-5-3 or 2-4-7-10, or perhaps 1-1-1. The choice of 10-5-3 or 2-4-7-10 lives are to be politically determined and are not systematically subject to revision in light of actual experience (except insofar as the whole system might be jettisoned). Unfortunately, differences in tax lives imply significant differences in tax liabilities among taxpayers, and one can reasonably expect intense tax-payer pressure to continually alter the politically determined parameters. Furthermore, a system of politically determined depreciation lives, without some factual basis, can lead to potentially serious distortions in the incentives to invest in various types of assets, and can therefore have an adverse impact on the rate and pattern of productivity growth.

Proponents of politically determined depreciation lives may, on the other hand, point to the failure of past efforts to base policy on actual depreciation practices. Both the reserve ratio test, established by Revenue Procedure 62-21 in 1962, and the ADR reporting system (ADRIS), established in 1971, proved to be administrative failures. These failures reflected, in part, a lack of consensus on the appropriate treatment of depreciable capital. While the failure of the Reserve Ratio Test and of ADRIS obviously does not imply that all possible efforts would also fail, they do raise the following fundamental question: can actual depreciation be measured with sufficient precision to be useful in the formulation of tax policy?

In our judgment, the answer to this question is yes: depreciation can be measured. We will show how depreciation can be estimated using an approach which relies on market price data, and we shall argue that this is a natural starting point for the analysis of depreciation. Market prices are, after all, the sine qua non of microeconomics, and to deny information contained in market prices is to deny much of the modern theory of microeconomics. In the special case of used asset markets, however, some economists believe that market prices are biased downward because the only assets which enter such markets are 'lemons,' that is, assets of inferior quality.[3] We will argue below (in section III) that the market for used business capital is frequently conducted between highly sophisticated specialists, and that there is thus no a priori reason to suppose that sellers systematically and persistently can dupe buyers with inferior goods. We will also suggest that the 'lemons' issue can itself be confronted with empirical evidence. Where the bias problem is present, it in principle can be measured, and the results then used to correct observed market prices.

The used market price approach to estimating depreciation is set forth in section III of this paper. In section IV this approach is compared to the methods used by the Bureau of Economic Analysis (BEA) in their numerous capital stock studies.[4] We find that the two approaches produce fairly similar results: the average BEA rate of depreciation for aggregate equipment is 14.1 percent, while the used market approach produces an aggregate rate of 13.3 percent; for aggregate nonresidential structures, the corresponding results are 6.0 percent and 3.7 percent. While both approaches may be wrong, it is certainly interesting that such widely differing methodologies produce reasonably similar results.

The comparison of the used market price and BEA methodologies highlights the fact that there is an important scientific reason for measuring economic depreciation quite apart from the analysis of tax policy. Economic analysis of growth and production, as well as the distribution of income, requires accurate estimates of capital stocks and of capital income. The estimation of capital stocks in turn requires an estimate of the quantity of capital used up in production, and the estimation of capital income requires an estimate of the corresponding loss in capital value. Thus, even if depreciation policy ignores economic depreciation, we must still try to measure economic depreciation for use in national income and wealth accounting.

Section V of this paper reviews other approaches to measuring economic depreciation and compares the results with those obtained by the BEA and used-market-price approaches. The results of this larger literature are by no means unanimous in support of one particular methodology or of one set of empirical results. However, there is a surprising degree of consistency in the various measured rates of depreciation for different types of assets. One finds almost no support for the proposition that economic depreciation cannot be measured with sufficient precision to be useful in policy analysis.

II.   Terms, Definitions, and Theoretical Framework

In our discussion of the measurement of economic depreciation, we will have frequent occasion to refer to the underlying theoretical structure of the problem. It is therefore useful to provide an overview of the theory of economic depreciation.[5] Depreciation theory involves distinguishing between the value of the stock of capital assets and the annual value of that asset's services, distinguishing between depreciation and inflation as sources of the change in asset value, and distinguishing between the depreciation in asset values and deterioration in an asset's physical productivity.

In theory, the price of a *new* asset is determined by the equilibrium between the cost of producing the asset and the value of the asset to the buyer. The value to the buyer may be related to the return obtained by renting the asset to subsequent users, or "renting" the asset to oneself. In the latter case, (i.e., when the asset is owner-utilized), the value of the capital services is usually called the quasi-rent or user cost. Under perfect foresight (i.e., perfect information about the future), the value of the asset is simply the present value of the rents or user costs.[6] In reality, other methods may be used in relating expected rents and user costs to asset values (e.g., the payback period approach).

Individual assets may or may not be resold after they are first put in place. If they are sold, the transaction price would reflect the remaining present value of the asset (adjusted perhaps for the risk of acquiring a defective asset). On the other hand, used assets which are not on the market also have a remaining present value. In principle, this remaining value is the same as the price of an identical market asset. (For this reason the in-place value of an asset can be called the 'shadow price'). There is an active controversy in the economic literature as to whether marketed used assets are really typical of the same type and vintage of unmarketed assets, or whether marketed assets are sold at a systematic risk discount. This problem, known as the 'lemons' problem, is discussed in detail below.

The central issue in depreciation theory is *how* the market (or shadow) prices of a collection of identical assets change with age. The older assets in the collection should be less valuable than the newer ones for two reasons: (1) the age of 'optimal' retirement from service is nearer for the older assets and (2) older assets may be less profitable because they either produce less output or because they require more input (i.e., maintenance) to operate. At any given point in time, an age-price profile of the collection of assets should be downward sloping. (A few types of assets, like wine, may improve with age, but they are a relatively insignificant component of the stock of depreciable capital). This decline in asset value with age is portrayed in figure 1. Figure 1 shows an age-price relationship in which the largest rate of price decline occurs in the early years of asset life. Had we drawn the age-price profile as a straight line, we would be portraying the case in which asset values decline in equal increments with age (an assumption popular in the accounting literature).

We define *economic depreciation* to be the decline in asset price (or shadow price) due to aging. In terms of figure 1, the value of a five-year old asset is represented by point *a* on curve AB, and the value of a six-year old asset by the point *b*. Economic depreciation is therefore equal to the difference (on the vertical axis) between *a* and *b*. The *rate* of economic depreciation is the elasticity of the curve AB between *a* and *b* or, equivalently, the percentage decline in asset price between these two points. The rate of depreciation usually varies with age, but in the special case in which AB has the geometric form, the rate of depreciation is constant. When AB is a straight line, economic depreciation is also said to be 'straight-line', but the *rate* of depreciation actually increases as the assets age.

FIGURE 1

Age-Price Profile for a Homogeneous Class of Assets

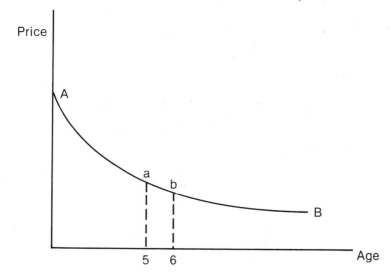

The curve AB is defined as the age-price profile of a collection of homogeneous assets at a *given* point in time. In the absence of inflation and obsolescence, AB would also trace out the price history of a single asset over time. In this special case, the *difference* in price between a five- and six-year old asset in 1979 would be the same as the *change* in the price of a given asset which is five years old in 1979 and six years old in 1980. If, however, inflation occurs between 1979 and 1980, this equivalence is no longer valid. The asset which is five years old in 1979 may actually be more valuable in 1980 because of inflation, even though it is one year older and has thus experienced an additional year's depreciation. The price history of this asset is clearly not equivalent to the movement along the curve AB from *a* to *b*.

Since inflation is a modern reality, it must be incorporated into our framework. This can be done by observing that inflation causes the prices of assets of all ages to increase.[7] In terms of the figure 1, the 1979 asset prices on line AB shift upward to line CD in 1980. The price of a five-year old asset in 1980 is now *c*, and a six-year old asset is *d*. The price history of the asset described in the preceding paragraph follows the curve ZZ, since the five-year old asset in 1979, located at *a*, is located at *d* when it is six years old in 1980. Fortunately, the movement along ZZ from *a* to *d* can be decomposed into two components: a movement along AB from *a* to *b*, and a shift in the curve from *b* to *d* (alternatively, we could think of this process as a shift from *a* to *c*, and a movement along CD from *c* to *d*).[8] The *ab* component of the total price change along ZZ is a pure aging effect, since it represents the change in asset price from one age to the next holding time constant. It therefore satisfies our previous definition of economic depreciation. The *bd* component represents the change in asset price due to inflation. The basic result, then, is that the change in asset price over time has two components, one due to depreciation and one due to inflation.

The depreciation-inflation distinction is central both to the theory and to the measurement of depreciation. Technological obsolescence is yet another important distinction. Assets built in one year frequently embody improvements in technology and design which make them superior to assets built in previous years. If we designate the year in which a cohort of assets is built as the *vintage* of these assets then we can frame this problem as the technological superiority of one vintage over another. Such technical superiority would normally make the assets of one vintage more valuable than those of another vintage. This, in turn, should drive a wedge

FIGURE 2

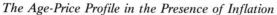

The Age-Price Profile in the Presence of Inflation

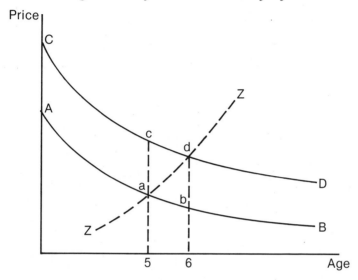

between the asset values of different vintages, and result in a price effect called obsolescence.

The price history of different vintages can be portrayed in the framework of figure 2. The price history of a given asset is represented in figure 2 by the curve ZZ. Figure 3 expands this diagram by adding the price history of assets built one year later. The resulting curves Z_0Z_0 and Z_1Z_1 thus portray the price histories of two successive vintages, and it is natural to look for the effect of obsolescence in the relationship between these two curves. Unfortunately, as shown in the seminal paper by Hall (1968), the trend effects of age, inflation, and obsolescence cannot be separately measured within the asset price framework of figure 3. He shows that the trend effect of obsolescence *is already* built both into the age-price profiles AB, CD, and EF, and into the distance between these profiles. This implies that the depreciation effect measured by the move from *a* to *b* in figure 2 combines pure depreciation with obsolescence and also that the inflation effect measured by the shift from *b* to *d* combines pure inflation and obsolescence.

Before concluding this section, a further distinction will prove useful in

FIGURE 3

Price-History Curves (ZZ) of Assets of Different Vintage

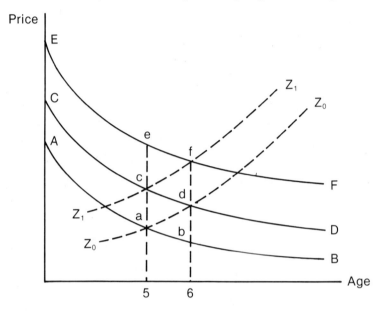

the following discussion of empirical results. We have dealt, so far, with the *value* of new and used assets, and defined economic depreciation as the decline in asset price associated with aging. Assets may also experience a decline in physical efficiency with age. A complete treatment of the relationship between declining physical efficiency (a quantity concept) and economic depreciation (a price concept) is beyond the scope of this paper.[9] It is sufficient for our purposes to note that the physical efficiency of a new asset can, in the absence of obsolescence, be assigned an efficiency index equal to one, and the efficiency index of a used asset can be defined as the marginal rate of substitution in production between that used asset and the new asset.[10] When obsolescence occurs, the efficiency index of new assets increases over time.

Figure 4 portrays three asset efficiency indexes associated with three possible efficiency decay processes. Curve I depicts geometric decay, in which the asset loses efficiency at a constant percentage rate (a melting block of dry ice or radioactive decay are two graphic examples), curve II depicts a straight-line decay process in which the asset loses efficiency in

FIGURE 4

Alternative Efficiency Profiles for Three Types of Processes: geometric decay (I), straight-line decay (II), and one-horse-shay decay (III).

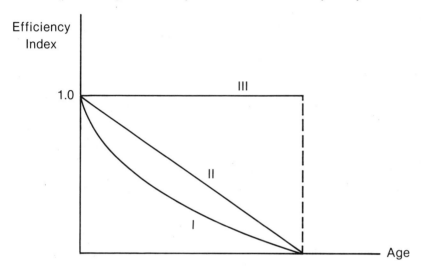

equal increments over its life. Curve III is the one-horse-shay pattern in which the asset retains its full efficiency until the moment it is retired from service (as in the case of a light bulb which burns with full brightness until it fails).

What is the relationship between the asset efficiency profiles of figure 4 and the shapes of the age-price profiles of the preceding figures? The answer is that, in most cases, the two profiles have different shapes. Only when the efficiency profile is geometric (curve I in figure 4) will the age-price profile (AB in figure 1) also be geometric, and vice versa. It cannot be overemphasized that this is the only case in which the efficiency profile and the age-price profiles have the same form. In all other cases, the two profiles differ. For example, straight-line decay (curve II in figure 4) implies a convex age-price profile (curve II' in figure 5). Conversely, a straight-line age-price profile (the dashed line in figure 5) implies a convex efficiency decay curve (i.e., one which is shaped like curve I in figure 4 but which is not geometric). Furthermore, the one-horse-shay efficiency profile (curve III in figure 4) does not lead to similar squared-off age-price profile, but rather to an average age-price profile like curve III' in figure 5.

FIGURE 5

The Age-Price Profiles Corresponding to the Efficiency Profiles of
figure 4: geometric decay (I'), straight-line decay (II'), and
one-horse-shay decay (III')

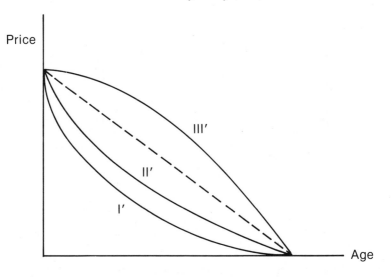

We have emphasized the general nonequivalence between the age-price profiles and asset efficiency profiles because it is probably the most misunderstood relationship in all of depreciation theory. Note, also, that asset efficiency profiles form the basis for calculations of physical capital stocks, whereas the corresponding age-price profiles form the basis for calculations of the capital income flows.

III. The Estimation of Economic Depreciation from Used Asset Prices

The analytical framework set out in the preceding sections will now be applied to the problem of estimating depreciation. In the first part of this section, we will describe an econometric model based on that framework. We will also report actual estimates of the rate of economic depreciation for 32 types of plant and equipment. These estimates are assessed in the second part of this section, with special attention given to the lemons problem.

A. THE ECONOMETRIC MODEL

Given a sufficient quantity of market price data, the age-price profiles AB and CD in figure 2 could be calculated directly. The average price of five-year old assets which were purchased in 1979 would be given, and the result plotted as point *a*. Point *b* would then be the average price of six-year old assets bought in 1979, etc. In this way, the whole curve AB would be traced out. The rate of depreciation could then be calculated directly as the percentage change between adjacent prices.

Such a procedure would, however, miss an essential point. Used market prices reflect only the value of assets which have survived long enough to be eligible for sampling. For example, the average market price of 10-year old cars represents the value of cars which have survived 10 years. Many cars of this vintage (i.e., cars put in service 10 years previously) have already been retired from service. The price of surviving assets does not, therefore, accurately measure the average experience of the vintage as a whole. This is unfortunate, since we are typically interested in evaluating policy as it pertains to a whole vintage of assets, or in measuring the amount of capital represented by the vintage.

In the terminology of econometrics, this problem is known as a 'censored sample bias.' This type of bias has been widely discussed in the context of labor supply schedules, where the part of the potential work force leaves the labor market, and where data is frequently 'capped' (meaning that incomes above a certain cutoff point are identified only as being larger than the cutoff amount). In the current context, the retirement of assets from service has the effect of censoring each vintage of assets.

We have corrected for censored sample bias in our analysis of used asset prices by multiplying each price by an estimate of the probability of survival. For example, the price of a five-year old asset is multiplied by the probability of having survived five years, that is, of not being retired in the first four years. If the assets which *were* retired in the first four years generated no net income at retirement (because removal and demolition costs just balanced scrap value), then the value of these retired assets to the original vintage is zero. The *average* price of assets in the fifth year of the vintage's existence is thus the price of surviving assets, multiplied by the probability of survival, plus the zero value of retired assets times the probability of retirement. The average price of assets in the vintage is therefore equal to the price of survivors multiplied by the probability of survival. The outcome of this analysis is that our procedure for dealing with censored sampled bias is equivalent to converting the price of surviving assets into an average price which takes into account both survivors and nonsurvivors.[11]

We applied this procedure to a diverse sample of used asset prices. For nonresidential structures, we used the sample collected by the Office of Industrial Economics, which is summarized in *Business Building Statistics.* For machinery and equipment, we used the machine tools sample collected by Beidleman, and we developed data on construction machinery, autos, and office equipment from a variety of sources, including the *Forke Brothers Bluebook, Ward Automotive Yearbooks, Kelly Bluebooks,* and auction reports from the General Services Administration. [12] The survival probabilities used to adjust this data were based on the Winfrey retirement distribution and *Bulletin F* mean asset lives. [13]

While the data samples contained a great quantity of information, there were not enough data to completely fill out the age-price profiles AB, CD, etc. of figure 2, for a reasonable number of years and asset ages. [14] Thus, it was necessary to estimate these age-price profiles econometrically. The prime consideration in selecting an econometric model is that the model be sufficiently flexible to avoid indirectly limiting the shape of AB. For example, if a linear regression model were selected, we would be assuming that the age-price profiles were all linear. In order to avoid this problem, we selected a highly flexible model which contains all the age-price profiles shown in figure 5 (geometric, linear, one-horse-shay) as special cases.

This model, the Box-Cox power transformation, involves jointly estimating the parameters which determine specific functional forms within the Box-Cox class, and the parameters which determine the slope(s) and intercept of the equation. [15] Unlike the standard regression model, the Box-Cox model assigns two parameters to each regressor. Letting q_i represent the market transaction price of an asset of age s_i in year t_i, we apply the Box-Cox model to the used asset pricing problem in the following way:

$$q_i^* = \alpha + \beta s_i^* + \gamma t_i^* + u_i \qquad i = 1, \ldots, N \tag{1}$$

where

$$q_i^* = \frac{q_i^{\theta_1} - 1}{\theta_1} \quad , \qquad s_i^* = \frac{s_i^{\theta_2} - 1}{\theta_2} \quad , \qquad t_i^* = \frac{t_i^{\theta_3} - 1}{\theta_3} \tag{2}$$

and where the subscript i indexes observations from 1 through N, and the u_i are N independent random disturbance terms which are assumed to be normally distributed with zero mean and constant variance σ^2. [16] The unknown parameters $\theta = (\theta_1, \theta_2, \theta_3)$ determine the functional form within the Box-Cox power family, whereas the unknown parameters (α, β, γ) determine the intercept and slope(s) of the transformed model.

To see the degree of flexibility associated with the Box-Cox model, it is useful to compare equations (1) and (2) to the age-price profiles of figure 5. When $\theta = (0, 1, 1)$, the Box-Cox model has the semi-log form, and is equivalent to the geometric curve I′ of figure 5.[17] When $\theta = (1, 1, 1)$, the Box-Cox model is linear, and is equivalent to the dotted straight line in figure 5. When $\theta = (1, 3, 1)$, curve III′ is reproduced. Note, also, that the time variable t allows for shifts in the age-price profile. In terms of figure 2, the time variable allows for the profile to shift from AB to CD.

The Box-Cox model was applied to our various samples, and the parameters were estimated using maximum likelihood methods. We then used the asymptotic likelihood ratio test to determine which case, the geometric, linear, or one-horse-shay fit the data best. We found that, in general, none of these alternatives is statistically acceptable. However, we also found that the age-price profiles estimated using the Box-Cox model were very close, on average, to being geometric in form. In other words, when we plotted the age-price profiles implied by the Box-Cox parameter estimates, they looked very much like the curve I′ in figure 5.

The approximately geometric form of the age-price profiles for assets ranging from buildings to machine tools to construction equipment is the most significant finding of our research. It is particularly important when one recalls that the geometric form is the only pattern for which the associated rate of depreciation is constant. Geometric age-price profiles imply that each class of assets in our sample can be approximately characterized by a single constant rate of depreciation (although the actual average rates of depreciation vary among asset classes).

In order to find the constant rate of depreciation associated with each asset class, we estimated the geometric curve which most nearly fit the corresponding Box-Cox age-price profile. We did this by regressing the logarithm of the Box-Cox fitted prices (i.e., the estimated values of q_i in (1)) on age, s, and year, t. The coefficient of age in this regression is the predicted average percentage change in asset price for a one-year change in age. Since this percentage corresponds to the definition of economic depreciation given in section II, the coefficient of age can be interpreted as the average geometric rate of depreciation associated with each asset class.[18] We also calculated the R^2 statistic for each of these regressions and found that the geometric approximation provided very close fits to the underlying Box-Cox age-price profiles.

The analysis, as outlined, left us with summary rates of depreciation for a large and diverse variety of assets. The list of assets studied, however, did not come close to providing a comprehensive characterization of depreciable assets used in business. What is needed for policy analysis and capital stock estimation is a summary rate of depreciation for each of the

22 types of producers' durable equipment and 10 types of nonresidential structures defined in the *U.S. National Income and Product Accounts* (NIPA). For those NIPA asset classes that contained our asset types, we used an average of our depreciation rates. For example, we averaged the rates of depreciation for the four types of machine tools in our study to obtain an average rate for the NIPA classes 'metal working machinery' and 'general industrial equipment.' Using this approach, we derived depreciation rates for 8 of the 32 NIPA assets categories: tractors, construction machinery, metalworking machinery, general industrial equipment, trucks, autos, industrial buildings, and commercial buildings. Although only a quarter of the asset categories are accounted for by this approach, these categories included 55 percent of 1977 NIPA investment expenditures on producers' durable equipment and 42 percent of 1977 NIPA investment in nonresidential structures. [19]

Depreciation rates for the remaining 24 NIPA asset classes were derived by exploiting the fact that all of the assets in our sample seemed to have approximately geometric age-price profiles. Since assets as diverse as buildings and machine tools seemed to have the geometric form, we thought it reasonable to impose this form on the asset categories for which we had no direct information. The geometric form implies a constant rate of depreciation, δ, for these classes. Furthermore, the rate of depreciation can (by definition) be written:

$$\delta \equiv \frac{R}{T} \tag{3}$$

where T is mean asset life and R is called the declining balance rate, (i.e., when R equals two, (3) defines the double-declining balance form of depreciation).

The problem now is to impute a value for δ for each NIPA asset class. This was done by observing that the BEA capital stock studies contain estimates of T for each of the 32 asset categories in question. We estimated the average R for the four equipment categories for which information was available using $R = \delta T$. The resulting value for R was 1.65. The average value for the two types of structures was found to be 0.91. We then estimated the depreciation rate for the remaining equipment categories using the relationship $\delta = (1.65)/T$; the remaining structure categories were estimated using $\delta = (0.91)/T$.

Table 1 sets out the results of these calculations. The average rate of depreciation for equipment was found to be 13.3 percent. The average

TABLE 1

ASSET CLASSES AND RATES OF ECONOMIC DEPRECIATION
(ANNUAL PERCENTAGE RATES OF DECLINE)

Producer Durable Equipment

1. Furniture and fixtures	.1100
2. Fabricated metal products	.0917
3. Engines and turbines	.0786
4. Tractors	.1633
5. Agricultural machinery (except tractors)	.0971
6. Construction machinery (except tractors)	.1722
7. Mining and oilfield machinery	.1650
8. Metalworking machinery	.1225
9. Special industry machinery (not elsewhere classified)	.1031
10. General industrial equipment	.1225
11. Office, computing, and accounting machinery	.2729
12. Service industry machinery	.1650
13. Electrical transmission, distribution, and industrial apparatus	.1179
14. Communications equipment	.1179
15. Electrical equipment (not elsewhere classified)	.1179
16. Trucks, buses, and truck trailers	.2537
17. Autos	.3333
18. Aircraft	.1833
19. Ships and boats	.0750
20. Railroad equipment	.0660
21. Instruments	.1473
22. Other	.1473

Private Nonresidental Structures

1. Industrial	.0361
2. Commercial	.0247
3. Religious	.0188
4. Educational	.0188
5. Hospital and institutional	.0233
6. Other	.0454
7. Public utilities	.0316
8. Farm	.0237
9. Mining exploration, shafts, and wells	.0563
10. Other	.0290

SOURCE: The Hulten and Wykoff studies of economic depreciation.

rate for structures was found to be 3.7 percent.[20] Autos had the largest depreciation rate (33 percent), with office equipment and trucks following (25 and 27 percent respectively). Other equipment categories had depreciation rates ranging from 6.6 percent to 18.3 percent, a not unreasonable range of rates. The depreciation rates for structures were considerably lower, ranging from 1.9 percent to 5.6 percent.

We wish to emphasize, at this point, that the numbers shown in table 1 are in no way intended to be definitive estimates of depreciation. There is a great deal of room for further research, particularly in the areas of (1) improved estimates of the retirement process (and thus of the survival probabilities used to weight the data); (2) larger and more detailed samples of those assets included in our statistical analysis; (3) extension of the list of assets for which used assets prices can be analyzed; and (4) improvements in the method for inferring the depreciation rates for assets for which no market information exists. We offer table 1 as an example of what can be achieved with the used asset price approach and as a basis of comparison with existing methodologies and results.

B. THE LEMONS PROBLEM

The depreciation rates shown in table 1 are derived (directly or indirectly) from information on the price of used capital assets. If these estimates are to be of any use in policy analysis or capital stock estimation, the market oriented estimates must also be applicable to those assets which are never sold. This raises the issue of whether a systematic difference exists between assets which find their way into used markets and those which are held until retirement by their original owners. Proponents of the lemons argument would say that a substantial difference does indeed exist.[21]

The lemons argument may be explained in the following way. Suppose that a certain type of machine is produced so that some units are defective and will subsequently require a great deal of maintenance, while others will require only a nominal amount of maintenance. Suppose, furthermore, that the two types of machines (lemons and pearls, respectively) are outwardly identical so that neither buyer nor seller initially knows which is which. Of course, once the machine is put in place, the owner is able to tell which sort of machine he has. If the machine is a lemon, the owner may wish to sell it in the used machine market, since prospective buyers cannot (by hypothesis) distinguish lemons from pearls.

The outcome of the Lemons Model is that lemons dominate the used machine market. This occurs through the following process: owners of pearls will tend to hold on to their high quality machines rather than risk replacement with new or used lemons. Owners of lemons, on the other hand, have an incentive to get rid of their machines with the hope of duping an unaware buyer. As a result, lemons will begin to appear on the used machine market with a much greater proportion than their share in the new machine market. If the owners of pearls must sell, then they have a strong incentive to go outside the organized used machine market to trade with an acquaintance with whom their credibility is established and who will accept the statement that the machine is a pearl. In this way, the original owner of the pearl can extract the maximum price for the machine. The result is that buyers increasingly assume that marketed used machines are lemons and thus offer reduced prices as a hedge against the increased probability of acquiring a lemon. Lower average used market prices act as a further disincentive to the sale of used pearls, and ultimately an equilibrium is reached in which only lemons are sold in used markets.

Asymmetric market information is, of course, the essence of this result. Sellers, with more information about asset quality than buyers, exploit this informational advantage and offer only lemons. Buyers soon come to realize that the appropriate strategy is to assume that they are buying a lemon, and offer only lemon prices. If, on the other hand, buyers and sellers have the same information, then the lemons dominance does not hold. Under equal information, lemons and pearls will receive their true separate value in used asset markets, and there is no advantage (in equilibrium) to selling a lemon or to withholding a pearl.

The Lemons Model is thought by some to characterize the market for used business assets. Were this contention true, then the market-oriented depreciation rates of table 1 would not be representative of all vintage assets. Now, while it is plausible to assume a priori that the owner will know more about his asset than a prospective buyer, this assumption fails to take into account the nature of prospective buyers. Buyers of used business assets are typically specialists at buying and refurbishing used assets for resale (often under warranty). Many used-asset buyers acquire and then resell used equipment as a routine and ancillary part of their enterprise, (i.e., construction contractors and commercial real estate investors). In both cases, buyers of used business assets are likely to have both the incentive and expertise to identify unprofitable assets (those whose prices do not reflect their in-place value).

We have now seen that the viability of the lemons argument depends on the assumption of asymmetric information. In fact, the extent to which the Lemons Model applies to the market for used business assets is ultimately an empirical issue. It is, in principle, possible to compare marketed and unmarketed assets of a given type to see what difference, if any, really exists. If a given asset is truly a lemon, then there must be some observable manifestation of this fact such as increased maintenance costs or increased breakdown rates. If such manifestations do not appear, then one would be inclined to be skeptical of the Lemons Model. Where differences do exist, their importance can be evaluated and then perhaps used to correct the observed market prices.

One piece of evidence which tends to reject the importance of the Lemons Model is found in the market for heavy construction machinery. Construction machinery (e.g., D-7 tractors) are frequently sold after the completion of a given contracted project and are then repurchased when new work is begun. There is little reason to believe that the assets in this market are lemons. Indeed, the routine sale and resale of equipment in a comparatively active auction market would seem to be testimony to the fact that lemons are not a practical problem. Our analysis of this particular market shows that the age-price profiles of construction equipment are very nearly geometric, just like the profiles of the other assets in our Box-Cox analysis. This point is significant, because proponents of the Lemons Model have argued that the age-price profiles can *appear* to be geometric because (a) used asset prices reflect lemons dominance; (b) lemons are heavily discounted relative to typical used assets still in place, and thus (c) the price of used marketed assets is seen to fall rapidly in the early years of asset life, which gives rise to the apparent geometric age-price profile. The construction equipment market serves as a counter-example to this line of reasoning.[22]

Before leaving this section, we shall consider one further criticism of the used market approach to measuring depreciation. Taubman and Rasche (1971) and Feldstein and Rothschild (1974) both note that the price of used assets depends on taxes, interest rates, and other variables which are subject to change over time. When such changes occur, asset prices will also change, and there is no a priori reason to believe that the rate of depreciation (i.e., the rate of change of the asset price) remains constant.[23] In order to evaluate this possibility, we took one of our largest samples (office buildings) and applied the Box-Cox analysis to individual years in that sample (i.e., we calculated Box-Cox estimates separately for 1951, 1954, etc.). We then applied a statistical test to see if the parameter estimates changed from year to year, an implication of the variability of asset prices. We found almost no statistical evidence that parameters changed significantly over time, and we therefore concluded that this instability issue did not appear to pose a major problem for our analysis. [24]

IV.   The Bureau of Economic Analysis Methodology[25]

The capital stock studies of the U.S. Bureau of Economic Analysis provide a natural basis for evaluating our depreciation estimates which were obtained from the used market price approach. BEA capital stock estimates have been widely used by economists, and, since 1976, BEA has presented a revised version of the *U.S. National Income and Product Accounts* which substitutes their estimate of economic depreciation for the alternative tax based estimate used in the main version of the NIPA, (i.e., "economic" depreciation is substituted for the depreciation allowances claimed by taxpayers). [26]

The BEA provides estimates of gross and net capital stocks for a variety of assets and sectors. Since our intent is to compare our approach with that of BEA, we will restrict our attention to the 32 categories of producers' durable equipment and nonresidential structures which appear in table 1. We will also restrict our comparison to the calculation of net (rather than gross) capital stocks. (The gross stock concept is meaningful only if efficiency change follows the one-horse-shay pattern of curve III in figure 4. Since our used market price results have rejected the one-horse-shay pattern, we omit gross stocks from our comparisons).

The BEA uses a capital stock methodology which focuses on physical quantities rather than prices and income, and their approach therefore refers to the quantity framework of figure 4 rather than to the price framework of figure 5. However, in the case of geometric depreciation (and only in this case), the rate of (price) depreciation is the same as the rate of change of physical capital used up in production (i.e., the rate of "physical depreciation" or replacement)). The geometric price depreciation rates of table 1 can thus be reinterpreted as rates of physical depreciation and compared to BEA physical depreciation rates.

The BEA procedure for imputing physical depreciation is based on the Winfrey retirement studies and on *Bulletin F* asset lives. (Recall that we also used these sources in our calculation of our survival probabilities). [27] The actual imputation procedure is rather complicated, but an illustrative example will be useful. Suppose that $300 of a particular type of asset was produced in 1975. BEA procedures would assign to that vintage of assets a *mean useful life,* (say 5 years), and a retirement pattern (say one-third of the vintage retired at the mean life and one-third in the years immediately preceding and following the mean life). Three subcohorts are then created from the original $300 asset investment: a $100 subcohort with a four-year life, a $100 subcohort with a five-year life, and a $100 subcohort with a six-year life. The first subcohort is depreciated using the straight-line form and a four-year life; the five- and six-year subcohorts are depreciated using straight line with five and six years lives. Total depreciation attributable to this whole vintage cohort is therefore $61.67 in each of the first four years ($25 + $20 + $16.67), $36.67 in the fifth year, and $16.67 in the sixth and last year of the cohort's existence. The original $300 is added to the perpetual inventory of cumulative gross investment, and the depreciation deductions are added to the inventory of accumulated depreciation. The net capital stock is the difference between the two inventories.

As noted, the actual mean useful asset lives for plant and equipment are based on the allowable IRS tax lives published in the 1942 edition of *Bulletin F.* The *Bulletin F* lives are shortened by 15 percent to reflect the belief that the original lives were probably too long. Alternative estimates based on the original lives and on 25 percent shorter lives are also calculated. The retirement distribution used by BEA for plant and equipment is a truncated form of the 1935 Winfrey S-3 distribution. The S-3 distribution is a bell shaped distribution which has been truncated so that no retirement occurs before 45 percent of mean useful life and retirement is completed at 155 percent of useful life. The subcohorts defined by the S-3 distribution are "depreciated" using the straight-line form, although alternative estimates using the double declining-balance form are also calculated. An adjustment for accidential damage is added to the "depreciation" estimates.

The combined effects of straight-line depreciation and S-3 retirement can lead to potential confusion about the actual form of BEA depreciation. While each subcohort is depreciated using the straight-line form, retirement is also occurring, and the depreciation of the cohort as a whole is accelerated relative to straight-line. Figure 6 depicts a BEA efficiency profile based on our analysis of their procedures which is conceptually analogous to the curves shown in figure 4. In figure 6, a $100 cohort of assets is assigned a 10-year mean useful life, and retired according to the truncated S-3 distribution. For the first 4½ years, the depreciation of the cohort as a whole follows the straight-line pattern. This is reflected in figure 6 by a linear decline in the value of assets remaining in the cohort.

FIGURE 6

Depreciation Profile for an Investment Cohort
under BEA Capital Stock Methodology

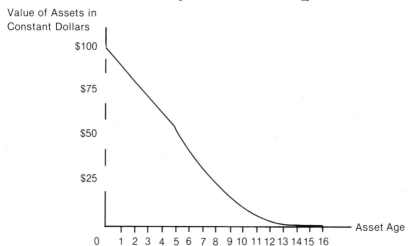

After 4 ½ years, the retirement process begins and the value falls off more rapidly than straight-line, and then begins to level off, and at 15½ years the cohort is fully depreciated. The depreciation pattern between 4½ and 15½ years is thus closer to the geometric (or constant rate) pattern than it is to the straight-line pattern. It would therefore be incorrect to say that the BEA procedures imply straight-line depreciation for each annual investment cohort taken *as a whole.*

The *actual* rates of depreciation implicit in the BEA methodology can be calculated using BEA data on gross investment. The starting point for this calculation is the BEA perpetual inventory method, which can be represented by the following equation:

$$K_t = I_t - D_t + K_{t-1} \quad , \tag{4}$$

where D_t is total physical depreciation (or loss of efficiency, in the terminology of section II) occurring on all assets in year t, I_t is total gross investment, and K_t is the stock of capital. Defining the one-period rate of physical depreciation to be

$$\delta = \frac{D_t}{K_{t-1}} \tag{5}$$

equation (4) can be written

$$K_t = I_t + (1 - \delta_t) K_{t-1} \quad . \tag{6}$$

The parameter δ_t is the rate of physical depreciation of the capital stock and combines the effects of retirement from service and the in-place loss of efficiency. The special case of geometric depreciation occurs when $\delta_t = \delta$, that is, when the rate of depreciation is constant over time.

Equation (6) can be rearranged to a yield a relationship which is useful in comparing BEA procedures to used market estimates of depreciation:

$$\delta_t = -\frac{K_t - K_{t-1} - I_t}{K_{t-1}} \tag{7}$$

We have used equation (7) to obtain the values of δ_t implied by the BEA estimates of net capital stock and the underlying gross investment series. The average annual results for aggregate plant and equipment reported in table 2, and the results for the 32 asset classification are given in Appendix table A.1, for a 26-year period ending in 1974. Inspection of this table reveals that for equipment, the BEA δ_t figures display a high degree of constancy. This observation is confirmed by a linear regression of δ_t on time, that is,

$$\delta_t = \delta + \beta t + \epsilon_t \quad . \tag{8}$$

When corrected for first-order autocorrelation, only 5 of the 20 equipment coefficients of time were statistically significant at the 95 percent level. This implies that the hypothesis that δ_t is constant cannot be rejected for a majority of PDE classes. The situation is different for nonresidential structures. Here, the coefficient of time was significant in 8 of the 10 classes, indicating that the rate of depreciation cannot be treated as being constant.

The relative constancy of the implicit BEA rates of depreciation for equipment may be somewhat surprising, in view of the widely held belief that BEA uses the straight-line depreciation method. Inspection of figure 6, however, shows that approximately two-thirds of a vintage cohort's life is spent in the convex (nearly geometric) portion of the depreciation profile. Given a more or less constant growth in total gross investment, this means that approximately two-thirds of all unretired investment is being depreciated with a nearly constant rate of depreciation. For short-lived assets (equipment), abnormally large or small variations in the quantity of gross investment will pass rapidly through the linear range of figure 6 into the geometric range and will not exert a prolonged departure from the constant rate. With longer-lived assets (plant), the effects of large swings in gross investment are more pronounced, since the aberration occurs on the linear segment for a longer period of time. This effect may explain the greater variability in the rate of depreciation of structures.

The depreciation rates of table 2 were aggregated to the level of total plant and total equipment by applying equation (7) to the aggregate capital stock series.[28] As noted in the introduction, the aggregate BEA equipment rate is 14.1 percent while the used asset price rate for equipment is 13.3 percent. In view of the vast difference in the two methodologies, these rates are remarkably close. Indeed, in only 5 of the 22 equipment classes is the divergence in rates across methods more than 30 percent: tractors, construction machinery, autos, aircraft and railroad equipment. The first three of these categories were studied directly in our statistical samples, and therefore represent our best information. That three of the five equipment classes in our direct Box-Cox analysis should differ significantly from the BEA rates is somewhat unfortunate, but, in our judgment, for at least one of these classes (autos) the BEA estimates are suspect. Autos are the one class of equipment which BEA values directly, rather than employing the methodology underlying figure 6. The BEA autos' rate of 12.6 percent is far below the rates of depreciation usually found in the numerous studies of the auto market (and certainly does not conform to the intuition of those who drive airport rental cars with any degree of frequency).

The BEA aggregate structures rate is 6.0 percent, and the used asset price is 3.7 percent. A 6.0 percent depreciation rate for buildings and other structures seems (to us) to be somewhat high, but we do not have direct evidence to support this intuition.

The aggregate capital stock estimates corresponding to our table 1 rates of depreciation are shown in table 3. These stocks were calculated for the 32 asset categories of table 1 using BEA investment data to arrive at the aggregate figures for plant and equipment. The stock of aggregate equipment is $451.9 billion in 1974, compared to $434.7 billion using the BEA approach. These two estimates are obviously quite close. The structures comparison, on the other hand, is quite different. Our estimate of aggregate nonresidential structures is $696.0 billion in 1974, while the BEA figure is $530.3 billion. The used asset price approach thus leads to an estimate (in 1974) which is 31 percent larger than the corresponding BEA estimate. This difference could significantly alter the estimates of the differential return to various types of capital.[29]

TABLE 2
COMPARISON OF DEPRECIATION RATES BY ASSET CLASS

ASSET CLASS	AVERAGE IMPLICIT BEA RATES	TABLE 1 RATES	PERCENTAGE DIFFERENCE BEA/TABLE 1 RATES
A. Producers' Durable Equipment			
Furniture and fixtures	.1267	.1100	15.18
Fabricated metal products	.1012	.0917	10.36
Engines and turbines	.0888	.0786	12.98
Tractors	.2542	.1633	55.66
Agricultural machinery	.1094	.0971	12.67
Construction machinery	.2316	.1722	34.49
Mining and oilfield machinery	.1924	.1650	16.61
Metalworking machinery	.1278	.1225	4.33
Special industry machinery	.1161	.1031	12.61
General industrial machinery	.1320	.1225	7.76
Office, computing, and accounting machinery	.2569	.2729	−5.86
Service industry machinery	.1860	.1650	12.73
Electrical and communication equipment	.1251	.1179	6.11
Trucks, buses, and truck trailers	.2301	.2537	−9.30
Autos	.1263	.3333	−62.11
Aircraft	.0755	.1833	−58.81
Ships and boats	.0947	.0750	26.27
Railroad equipment	.1697	.0660	157.12
Instruments	.1659	.1473	12.63
Other	.1695	.1473	15.07
B. Nonresidential Structures			
Industrial	.0721	.0361	99.72
Commercial	.0518	.0247	109.72
Religious	.0355	.0188	88.83
Educational	.0352	.0188	87.23
Hospitals and institutional	.0340	.0233	45.92
Other	.0600	.0454	32.16
Public utilities	.0588	.0316	86.08
Farm	.0466	.0237	96.62
Mining exploration, shafts and wells	.1174	.0563	108.53
Other	.0638	.0290	120.00

SOURCE: See text.

TABLE 3

COMPARISON OF AGGREGATE NET CAPITAL STOCKS
(BILLIONS OF 1972 DOLLARS)

Year	TOTAL			EQUIPMENT			PLANT		
	Used Asset Price	BEA	Percentage Difference	Used Asset Price	BEA	Percentage Difference	Used Asset Price	BEA	Percentage Difference
1949	451.8	350.0	28.86	168.4	151.4	11.21	283.4	198.5	42.8
1950	469.4	367.5	27.62	177.2	162.1	9.36	292.2	205.4	42.2
1951	488.0	385.9	26.46	186.5	172.7	8.00	301.5	213.2	41.4
1952	503.1	401.1	25.43	193.1	180.5	6.96	310.1	220.5	40.6
1953	521.5	418.3	24.67	201.5	189.1	6.55	320.0	229.2	39.6
1954	537.0	432.6	24.13	206.5	194.1	6.41	330.4	238.5	38.5
1955	557.3	451.3	23.49	213.9	201.7	6.06	343.4	249.6	37.6
1956	579.8	472.2	22.79	221.9	209.4	5.97	357.9	262.8	36.2
1957	601.9	492.3	22.26	229.8	216.9	5.93	372.1	275.3	35.1
1958	615.0	504.4	22.19	230.8	217.9	5.88	384.2	285.3	34.7
1959	631.8	517.0	22.21	235.1	221.5	6.12	396.7	295.4	34.3
1960	651.6	533.0	22.25	240.3	225.9	6.40	411.2	307.1	33.9
1961	669.8	547.1	22.43	243.7	228.5	6.68	426.1	318.7	33.7
1962	692.1	565.3	22.43	250.1	233.9	6.90	442.1	331.4	33.4
1963	715.7	584.5	22.45	258.2	241.2	7.06	457.5	343.3	33.3
1964	745.0	609.5	22.23	270.5	252.4	7.17	474.5	357.1	32.9
1965	785.8	645.9	21.66	288.5	269.7	6.98	497.3	376.2	32.2
1966	832.8	689.2	20.84	310.9	292.0	6.45	521.9	397.1	31.4
1967	872.8	725.6	20.29	328.4	310.2	5.88	544.4	414.5	31.0
1968	914.4	763.2	19.81	347.2	329.4	5.40	567.3	433.8	30.8
1969	958.2	802.5	19.40	367.5	349.9	5.02	590.7	452.6	30.5
1970	993.4	833.7	19.16	381.0	364.4	4.57	612.4	469.3	30.5
1971	1023.8	859.5	19.12	391.3	375.4	4.22	632.5	484.1	30.7
1972	1060.2	889.8	19.15	407.0	390.4	4.25	653.2	499.4	30.8
1973	1106.3	929.5	19.02	431.6	414.3	4.16	674.8	515.2	31.0
1974	1148.9	965.1	19.04	451.9	434.7	3.95	696.0	530.3	31.2

V.   Review of Other Studies of Depreciation

The preceding sections have presented, and compared, two approaches to measuring depreciation. In this section, we will provide an additional perspective on the problem by giving an overview of other depreciation studies. We group these studies into two categories: studies which base their estimates of depreciation on price data (like the model of section III), and studies which base their estimates on nonprice information (like the BEA methodology of section IV). We shall review the former in part A of this section, and the latter in part B. Rather than aiming at a comprehensive literature review, we will try to indicate general directions of the relevant research.

A.   PRICE-ORIENTED STUDIES OF DEPRECIATION

Our study of used asset prices is by no means the first effort in this direction: the use of asset prices to study depreciation goes back at least as far as Terborgh (1954). The largest number of used price studies have dealt with automobiles: Ackerman (1973), Cagan (1971), Chow (1957, 1960), Ohta and Griliches (1976), Ramm (1970), and Wykoff (1970). Tractors have been studied by Griliches (1960), pickup trucks by Hall (1971), machine tools by Beidleman (1976), ships by Lee (1978), and residential housing by Chinloy (1977), and Malpezzi, Ozanne, and Thibodeau (1980). The statistical methods used in these studies vary greatly and include the analysis of variance model, the hedonic price model, and various linear and polynomial regression models. Many studies use dealers' price lists or insurance data sources rather than market transaction prices. Furthermore, none of these studies adjust for censored sample bias. However, even though methods do vary across studies, the general conclusion which emerges is that the age-price patterns of various assets have a convex shape (as in curve I' in figure 5). Some studies, particularly those of automobiles, found that depreciation was even more rapid than implied by the constant depreciation rate pattern of the geometric form.

We have summarized the rates of depreciation reported in the various studies in table 4. A comparison of the columns of table 4 shows reasonably close agreement between our auto estimate of table 1 and the estimates of the five other studies of the used auto market. Our estimate is at the top of the depreciation ranges of these studies, but it must be remembered that we have corrected for censored sample bias, and this has the effect of increasing the average estimated rate of depreciation. For this reason, we interpret our truck results as being basically consistent with the

TABLE 4

A COMPARISON OF RESULTS FROM VARIOUS STUDIES
OF USED ASSET PRICES

Study	Approximate Range of Depreciation Rates	Table 1 Rates	Implicit BEA Rates
Auto:			
Ackerman (1973)	28%–34%	33%	13%
Cagan (1971)	21%–30%		
Chow (1957, 1960)	19%–30%		
Ohta-Griliches (1976)	25%–33%		
Ramm (1970)	25%–30%		
Wykoff (1970)	17%–27%		
Pickup trucks:			
Hall (1971)	17%	25%	23%
Tractors:			
Griliches (1960)	11%–12%	10%	11%
Machine tools:			
Beidleman (1976)	4%–21%	12%	13%
Ships:			
Lee (1978)	12%–15%	7%	9%

study by Hall but our estimates are not in agreement with the Griliches study, nor is our estimate for 'ships and boats' in agreement with Lee's studies (the Lee study, however, refers to the Japanese fishing fleet and may therefore not correspond well to the NIPA 'ships and boats' category).

The general agreement with the geometric (or near-geometric) form of the age-price profiles, along with the rough consistency among depreciation rates in table 4, has led us to the following conclusion: used asset prices do contain systematic information about the pattern and rate of depreciation of capital assets which can be helpful in policy analysis and useful in capital stock measurement.

A second major component of the price-oriented literature on depreciation deals with rental prices rather than asset prices. The basic rental price approach is to estimate age-rent profiles instead of age-price profiles. The estimated age-rent profiles are potentially interesting because they relate directly to the asset efficiency profiles of figure 4. This relationship arises from the equilibrium relationship between rents and asset efficiency indexes, which (in the absence of obsolescence) takes the following form:

$$\Phi(s) = c(s)/c(0) \tag{9}$$

where $\Phi(s)$ is the relative asset efficiency index of an s year old asset, and
$c(0)$ and $c(s)$, the rental prices (or quasi-rents) of new and s year old
assets.[30] The curves in figure 4 are plots of the function $\Phi(s)$. Equation (9)
indicates that the figure 4 curves can be inferred from data on relative rental prices.

Suppose, for example, that assets have the one-horse-shay form of asset
efficiency. In this case, the Φ function takes the following form:

$$\Phi(0) = 1, \quad \Phi(1) = 1, \quad \Phi(2) = 1, \quad \dots ,$$
$$\Phi(T) = 1, \quad \Phi(T + 1) = 0 \quad , \dots \tag{10}$$

that is, the asset retains full efficiency until it is retired at age T, and has
zero efficiency thereafter. From (9), this form of the efficiency function
implies that the rental prices are equal for all assets up to age T. When
depreciation occurs at a constant (geometric) rate δ, then the function
takes the following form:

$$\Phi(s) = (1 - \delta)^s = c(0)/c(s) \tag{11}$$

equation (11) implies that the age-rent profile is also geometric. In
general, the age-rent profile can assume any of the forms consistent with
the form of the Φ function, and the function can be estimated from rental
data by normalizing the rental price of a new asset to equal one (again,
this assumes no obsolescence). Given this normalization, $\Phi(s) = c(s)$.

The advantage of the rental price approach is that it sidesteps the issue
of lemon-dominated used asset markets. Firms engaged in the leasing
business would seem to have no incentive to provide their clients with
lemons, since the lessor typically maintains the assets and the lessee usually has the option of not renewing the lease. On the other hand, rental
prices are subject to another important source of sampling bias. This
sampling bias is over and above the censored sample bias associated with
the retirement process (which applies to both asset and rental prices). This
additional source of bias in rental prices arises because leasing firms
generally have an inventory of unrented assets (which, in buildings, takes
the form of a nonzero vacancy rate). The charges on assets which are actually rented must include the cost of idle assets (vacancies), and rental
charges are therefore not representative of the typical asset available for
leasing.

Firms typically deal with the idle asset (vacancies) problem by offering
discounts on long-term leases. A recent inquiry to a leasing firm un-
covered the following pricing schedule for a portable computer terminal:

TABLE 5

Length of Lease	Annual Rental Cost
2	$996
3	$775
4	$678
5	$612

This leasing rates schedule indicates a considerable incentive for lessees to undertake long-term contracts. From the standpoint of lessees, discounts for long-term contracts compensate for the decreased flexibility implied by the long-term commitment as well as for the implicit requirement to use the asset when it is older (and potentially more obsolete) in the later years of the contract.

The econometric problem with the availability of long-term leases is that there is, by the terms of the lease, no variation in rentals with age. In view of equation (10), this leasing practice implies that an analysis of rents would be biased in favor of the one-horse-shay hypothesis. Thus, even if asset efficiencies followed the geometric pattern of equation (12), a market dominated by long-term leases would give the impression that (11) is the correct form.

The well-known Taubman and Rasche study of office building rentals found a one-horse-shay pattern of asset efficiency, and in assessing their results the remarks of the preceding paragraph should be borne in mind. While, of course, a potential for bias does not necessarily mean that it exists, one must realize that office space is frequently rented under long-term lease agreements. In this context, the study of Malpezzi, Ozanne, and Thibodeau of residential rentals is extemely interesting. Residential units (apartments and houses) are typically rented with leases of one year duration or less, and Malpezzi, Ozanne, Thibodeau found the age-rent profile for this type of asset to be geometric. This finding, along with our analysis, suggests to us that (a) the rental price and asset price approaches are inherently consistent, and (b) that the one-horse-shay pattern found by Taubman and Rasche may have been the result of long-term lease bias.

The above observations are particularly important since the Taubman and Rasche "one-horse-shay" finding could be interpreted as implying the existence of a lemons bias in the used asset approach.[31] If depreciation were, in fact, one-horse-shay, then the geometric age-price profiles could reflect price profiles of lemons only (i.e., the rapid fall in price during the early years of asset life could be due to the fact that only lemons are entering the used asset markets). If, however, it is the Taubman-Rasche result which is biased (and we believe it to be biased upward), then their result obviously cannot be adduced as evidence in favor of the lemons argument. One should note, however, that regardless of the true form of the depreciation pattern, the central conclusion of this paper, that economic depreciation can be measured, still holds.

B. NONPRICE STUDIES OF DEPRECIATION

The nonprice studies of depreciation employ a wide variety of approaches. It is consequently difficult to provide an integrated and comprehensive picture of this part of the literature on the measurement of depreciation. Instead, we shall describe three of the main nonmarket approaches: the retirement approach, the investment approach, and the polynomial-benchmark approach.

The BEA methodology described in section III is a good illustration of the retirement approach. A retirement distribution is estimated either directly, such as in the Winfrey studies, or indirectly through the analysis of book values or through analysis of changes in the stock of physical assets, such as would have been possible with data from the ADR information system. The estimated retirement distribution is then used to allocate each year's investment flow into subcohorts which are each identified by their date of retirement. A method of in-place depreciation is then selected (usually by assumption) and applied to each subcohort separately. The straight-line and declining balance form are typically assumed. The Faucett capital stock studies are another interesting example of this approach.[32]

The investment approach was developed by Robert Coen (1975, 1980). Coen's procedure was to find which form of depreciation (one-horse-shay, geometric, straight-line, sum-of-the-years'-digits) best explained the investment flows in two-digit manufacturing industries within the context of a neoclassical investment model.[33] Coen (1980) found that for *equipment*, 14 of the industries had depreciation patterns which were more accelerated than straight-line (11 were geometric with a truncation at the end of the service life, and 3 were sum-of-the-years'-digits). The remaining seven industries had straight-line depreciation patterns, and none had one-horse-shay patterns. For *structures*, Coen found that 14 industries had geometric patterns, 5 had straight-line patterns, and only 2 had one-horse-shay patterns.

The weight of Coen's study is evidently on the side of the geometric and near-geometric forms of depreciation. Coen's results are thus consistent with the results obtained from the used asset price approach, and are basically inconsistent with the results of the Taubman-Rasche study of office buildings. (However, we should note that most manufacturing structures are factories rather than the type of structures studies by Taubman and Rasche: office buildings).

The third nonprice approach we shall summarize, the polynomial-benchmark approach, is based on the perpetual inventory model of equation (6). This equation states that the capital stock in year t is equal to the real gross investment in that year, plus the undepreciated remainder of the preceding year's stock: $K_t = I_t + (1 - \delta_t)K_{t-1}$. A similar expression holds for the preceding year's stock, $K_{t-1} = I_{t-1} + (1 - \delta_{t-1})K_{t-2}$. By assuming geometric depreciation (i.e., that δ's are the same in all equations), and by repeatedly substituting for the preceding year's capital stock, we obtain

$$K_t = I_t + (1 - \delta)I_{t-1} + (1 - \delta)^2 I_{t-2} + \cdots$$
$$+ (1 - \delta)^{s-1} I_{t-s+1} + (1 - \delta)^s K_{t-s} \quad . \qquad (12)$$

This expression defines a polynomial in $(1 - \delta)$. Given estimates of the benchmarks K_t and K_{t-s}, and of the investment series I_{t-k}, equation (12) can frequently be solved for a unique value of $1 - \delta$.

Nishimizu has applied the poloynomial-benchmark approach to data from the Japanese National Wealth Survey. The results for equipment are shown in table 6. (Structures are omitted because the different nature of construction in Japan makes comparison with the U.S. meaningless). With three exceptions—agriculture, construction, and real estate—the Japanese machinery depreciation rates are quite similar to the U.S. machinery rates reported in table 1. The Japanese ships and boats figures are, however, much larger than the U.S. figure. In the other transportation equipment category, the Japanese depreciation rates tend to be quite a bit lower than the U.S. rates but are higher in one industry. The Japanese tools and fixture category has no counterpart in table 1.

It is difficult to draw conclusions from a comparison of tables 1 and 6 because of the potential differences in the composition of the capital stocks of the two countries, and because 22 categories are compared with 4. There does appear to be sufficient similarity between the two sets of results to warrant further investigation of the polynomial-benchmark method as a source of valuable information.[34] Note, that this approach also has been applied to tenant-occupied and owner-occupied housing by Leigh (1977), using data from the Census of Housing. Leigh obtains results which are generally consistent with the results of other studies (see Leigh, p. 233, Chinloy (1977), and Malpezzi, Ozanne, Thibodeau (1980)).

TABLE 6

Implicit Rates of Equipment Replacement from Nishimizu's
Study of Japanese Corporate Industries, 1955–1960s:
An Application of the Polynomial-Benchmark Method

	ASSET			
Industry Asset	Machinery	Ships and Boats	Other Transportation	Tools and Fixtures
1. Agriculture forestry, and fishery	0.0533	0.6854	0.0892	0.0646
2. Mining	0.0748	0.2274	0.2075	0.2055
3. Manufacturing	0.1328	0.5122	0.0530	0.1269
4. Construction	0.3387	0.6854	0.1939	0.5305
5. Electricity, gas, and water	0.1911	NS	0.4324	0.2370
6. Transportation and communication	0.1819	0.5511	0.1944	0.2513
7. Wholesale and retail trade	0.2506	0.4835	0.0306	0.1329
8. Finance and insurance	0.1782	NS	0.1328	0.0827
9. Real estate	0.0381	NS	0.0689	0.0488
10. Services	NS	0.1095	0.2396	0.1343

Source: Nishimizu (1974).
Note: NS indicates "no solution" using the polynomial benchmark technique.

VI. Summary

We return, in conclusion, to the starting point of our remarks. A major policy initiative is currently under way which would result in a system for nearly total political determination of tax depreciation periods. We believe that politically determined depreciation lives make sense only if true depreciation cannot be measured. We have argued against the proposed system by showing that depreciation can indeed be measured using a variety of approaches. We have also shown that many of these studies obtain the result that depreciation is accelerated relative to straight-line and can be reasonably well approximated by geometric (or declining balance) depreciation. This last conclusion is by no means unanimously supported, but it is sufficiently well established that it should serve as the working hypothesis for the vast amount of research which still remains to be done.

APPENDIX TABLE A.1

BEA DEPRECIATION RATES BY ASSET CLASS
ANNUAL PERCENTAGE DECLINE

	Furniture and Fixtures	Fabricated Metal Products	Engines and Turbines	Tractors	Agricultural Machinery	Construction Machinery
1949	12.92	9.26	9.38	23.15	10.24	21.02
1950	12.82	9.28	9.66	23.59	10.03	20.27
1951	12.51	9.39	9.01	23.34	9.93	20.58
1952	12.33	9.43	9.14	23.86	9.92	23.68
1953	12.25	9.43	8.88	24.38	9.94	24.13
1954	12.37	9.48	8.99	25.08	10.10	24.42
1955	13.06	9.44	8.39	26.71	10.32	24.99
1956	12.92	9.57	8.45	26.76	10.46	25.21
1957	12.73	9.75	8.54	26.27	10.70	24.18
1958	12.66	9.78	8.37	26.84	11.10	23.91
1959	12.63	9.85	8.48	27.04	11.18	24.32
1960	12.58	10.00	8.49	25.68	11.27	23.89
1961	12.58	10.19	8.45	26.62	11.42	23.58
1962	12.69	10.37	8.56	26.66	11.59	23.35
1963	12.74	10.65	8.73	26.73	11.78	24.40
1964	12.77	10.86	8.90	26.44	11.77	24.38
1965	12.83	11.00	9.04	25.51	11.80	23.74
1966	12.81	10.99	9.14	25.18	11.71	22.67
1967	12.60	10.84	9.21	23.82	11.55	21.92
1968	12.54	10.76	9.20	23.98	11.34	21.90
1969	12.50	10.69	9.08	24.09	11.27	22.13
1970	12.41	10.63	8.95	25.02	11.19	22.28
1971	12.41	10.55	8.84	25.37	11.00	22.54
1972	12.57	10.52	8.78	26.28	11.06	22.95
1973	12.72	10.56	8.72	26.67	11.13	23.20
1974	12.73	10.51	8.72	25.98	10.94	22.71

SOURCE: See text.

APPENDIX TABLE A.1 (continued)

BEA DEPRECIATION RATES BY ASSET CLASS
ANNUAL PERCENTAGE DECLINE

	Mining and Oilfield Machinery	Metalworking Machinery	Special Industry Machinery	General Industrial Machinery	Office, Computing, and Accounting Machinery	Service Industry Machinery
1949	18.30	11.29	11.03	12.44	22.83	16.49
1950	18.85	13.22	10.92	12.39	23.20	16.70
1951	19.23	14.60	10.95	12.92	24.32	16.79
1952	19.07	14.37	10.97	13.08	24.67	17.71
1953	18.84	14.21	11.20	13.31	25.28	18.47
1954	18.82	13.73	11.21	13.41	25.66	18.70
1955	19.38	12.98	11.41	13.48	25.65	19.16
1956	19.17	13.53	11.65	13.56	26.01	19.28
1957	18.93	13.21	11.71	13.47	25.84	19.17
1958	18.53	12.73	11.72	13.30	25.09	18.79
1959	19.13	12.76	11.89	13.42	24.99	18.91
1960	19.72	12.94	12.08	13.51	25.62	19.05
1961	19.86	12.82	12.06	13.51	25.79	19.04
1962	20.23	12.83	12.17	13.57	26.11	19.25
1963	20.72	12.93	12.11	13.63	27.45	19.22
1964	20.52	12.92	12.20	13.60	27.20	19.40
1965	20.13	13.00	12.23	13.41	27.14	19.49
1966	19.46	12.89	12.00	13.25	27.58	19.28
1967	18.57	12.44	11.69	12.91	26.17	18.81
1968	18.74	11.99	9.39	12.82	25.46	18.62
1969	18.93	11.91	13.37	12.90	25.62	18.55
1970	19.45	11.74	11.48	12.88	25.39	18.35
1971	19.33	11.54	11.44	12.88	25.24	18.37
1972	19.09	11.70	11.56	13.03	26.27	18.66
1973	19.23	11.89	11.70	13.23	26.84	18.66
1974	18.61	12.01	11.69	13.35	26.55	18.58

SOURCE: See text.

APPENDIX TABLE A.1 (continued)

BEA DEPRECIATION RATES BY ASSET CLASS
ANNUAL PERCENTAGE DECLINE

	Electrical and Communications Equipment	Trucks, Buses, and Truck Trailers	Autos	Aircraft	Ships and Boats	Railroad Equipment
1949	11.83	20.21	19.31	22.80	8.14	8.11
1950	11.97	20.51	17.82	24.76	7.58	7.58
1951	12.10	21.05	14.14	27.19	10.75	7.51
1952	12.33	20.73	12.16	30.89	8.22	7.25
1953	12.32	21.68	15.24	28.92	8.58	7.09
1954	12.30	23.11	15.20	28.02	8.73	6.93
1955	12.25	23.60	11.65	18.67	8.72	7.03
1956	12.42	22.79	14.03	23.49	9.67	7.17
1957	12.46	23.50	13.10	21.84	9.66	7.26
1958	12.30	23.40	12.08	17.28	9.14	7.15
1959	12.54	24.51	11.84	21.60	9.42	5.56
1960	12.77	24.56	12.41	19.21	9.58	9.19
1961	12.78	24.64	12.33	19.38	9.64	7.61
1962	12.78	25.18	11.57	19.39	10.16	7.74
1963	12.72	24.62	11.56	19.72	10.37	7.93
1964	12.77	23.83	13.41	21.78	10.41	8.09
1965	12.80	23.88	11.75	21.65	10.50	8.13
1966	12.80	23.53	9.15	23.60	10.78	8.05
1967	12.61	22.26	10.90	20.89	10.77	7.83
1968	12.58	22.94	10.77	20.53	10.33	7.67
1969	12.62	23.28	13.16	17.12	9.67	7.75
1970	12.61	22.45	11.10	17.86	9.39	7.63
1971	12.55	22.81	9.16	16.61	9.21	7.64
1972	12.54	23.69	12.78	16.89	9.16	7.61
1973	12.75	23.32	10.54	20.11	9.01	7.64
1974	12.87	22.21	11.22	19.74	8.65	7.67

SOURCE: See text.

APPENDIX TABLE A.1 (continued)

BEA DEPRECIATION RATES BY ASSET CLASS
ANNUAL PERCENTAGE DECLINE

	Instruments	Other PDE	Industrial Construction	Commercial Construction	Religious Buildings	Educational Buildings
1949	14.91	16.38	7.85	6.23	4.17	3.87
1950	14.94	16.34	7.74	6.17	4.10	3.82
1951	15.24	16.24	7.25	6.07	4.00	3.77
1952	15.56	16.54	7.05	5.98	3.89	3.71
1953	15.82	16.83	6.96	6.02	3.86	3.70
1954	15.85	17.09	6.93	5.95	3.84	3.67
1955	16.57	17.49	9.15	5.88	3.77	3.57
1956	16.83	17.48	7.05	5.66	3.70	3.57
1957	16.98	17.46	6.92	5.41	3.61	4.47
1958	16.91	17.53	6.72	5.27	3.54	3.47
1959	17.32	17.50	6.99	5.23	3.47	3.42
1960	17.53	17.35	7.29	5.07	3.44	3.41
1961	17.56	17.14	7.58	4.93	3.39	3.40
1962	17.60	17.00	7.67	4.87	3.34	3.39
1963	17.85	16.87	7.53	4.75	3.31	3.37
1964	17.81	16.76	7.20	4.69	3.29	3.35
1965	17.83	16.65	7.29	4.85	3.29	3.34
1966	16.95	16.70	7.19	4.62	3.26	3.35
1967	16.37	15.77	7.00	4.59	3.24	3.34
1968	16.21	16.72	6.94	4.62	3.25	3.32
1969	16.31	16.96	6.99	4.48	3.25	3.30
1970	16.37	17.06	6.72	4.45	3.27	3.28
1971	16.55	17.30	6.49	4.46	3.29	3.81
1972	16.62	17.45	6.54	4.48	3.33	3.33
1973	16.65	17.43	6.62	4.47	3.38	3.34
1974	16.72	17.15	6.71	4.45	3.42	3.37

SOURCE: See text.

APPENDIX TABLE A.1 (continued)

BEA DEPRECIATION RATES BY ASSET CLASS
ANNUAL PERCENTAGE DECLINE

	Hospitals and Institutional Buildings	Other Nonfarm Buildings	Public Utilities	Farm Buildings	Mining, Exploration, Shafts, and Wells	All Other Private Construction
1949	3.96	7.16	6.17	5.40	11.62	8.52
1950	3.99	7.01	6.07	5.20	11.57	8.50
1951	3.84	6.91	5.99	5.03	11.46	8.09
1952	3.69	6.75	5.93	4.90	11.29	8.08
1953	3.61	6.68	5.88	4.76	11.17	7.98
1954	3.57	6.59	5.80	4.67	11.09	7.70
1955	3.55	6.38	5.75	4.60	11.04	7.49
1956	3.50	6.33	5.76	4.56	10.97	7.10
1957	3.54	6.24	5.73	4.52	10.91	7.00
1958	3.49	6.20	5.70	4.50	10.91	6.68
1959	3.43	6.09	5.69	4.51	11.10	6.42
1960	3.40	5.98	5.71	4.46	11.22	6.31
1961	3.38	5.79	5.72	4.45	11.42	5.92
1962	3.36	5.66	5.76	4.46	11.67	5.77
1963	3.29	5.58	5.81	4.44	11.81	5.64
1964	3.27	5.48	5.86	4.43	12.03	5.50
1965	3.20	5.47	5.91	4.45	12.15	5.43
1966	3.15	5.36	5.94	4.46	12.21	5.30
1967	3.11	5.28	5.95	4.48	12.25	5.17
1968	3.11	5.13	5.96	4.47	12.31	5.15
1969	3.12	5.23	5.93	4.49	12.38	5.14
1970	3.10	5.31	5.93	4.52	12.39	5.10
1971	3.08	5.40	5.91	4.54	12.40	5.01
1972	3.07	5.51	5.92	4.56	12.55	4.93
1973	3.05	5.62	5.91	4.63	12.58	4.92
1974	3.01	5.70	5.92	4.66	12.65	4.97

SOURCE: See text.

APPENDIX TABLE A.2

Capital Stocks by Asset Type

(Based on depreciation rates of table 1)

	Furniture and Fixtures	Fabricated Metal Products	Engines and Turbines	Tractors	Agricultural Machinery	Construction Machinery
1949	8202.21	5887.07	3583.05	6067.21	10838.18	6394.41
1950	8599.96	6245.22	4051.42	6733.44	11820.80	6381.30
1951	9160.97	6743.54	4286.98	7316.87	12658.00	6428.44
1952	9611.26	7350.15	4696.02	7735.02	13375.91	6724.46
1953	9970.02	7965.15	5023.91	7957.89	13817.11	6881.51
1954	10439.32	8604.74	5603.03	7751.37	14111.46	6785.51
1955	11188.00	9054.69	5998.64	8048.57	14450.24	6974.05
1956	11951.32	9500.37	6306.14	8190.24	14528.12	7332.12
1957	12504.67	10090.19	6721.48	8082.77	14514.44	7382.53
1958	12991.16	10522.92	7127.17	8138.86	14992.09	7420.25
1959	13468.13	10765.97	7402.98	8403.78	15358.36	7684.49
1960	13900.64	10948.73	7628.10	8051.44	15481.06	7736.22
1961	14212.57	11042.73	7758.53	7922.64	15538.85	7638.04
1962	14577.18	11033.11	7802.71	7899.88	15637.03	7619.77
1963	15107.69	11156.37	7842.42	8121.83	16003.67	8070.65
1964	15783.85	11455.34	7868.01	8646.53	16374.72	8801.88
1965	16626.62	11972.88	7915.58	9199.55	16999.73	9655.20
1966	17678.70	12639.97	8066.42	10191.27	17754.06	10515.57
1967	18580.04	13198.88	8444.40	10693.03	18590.14	11124.79
1968	19364.23	13721.55	8942.67	11134.86	19170.04	11820.10
1969	20281.17	14275.28	9460.77	11277.54	19934.63	12559.68
1970	20975.24	14830.24	9946.16	11505.92	20837.97	13126.90
1971	21399.96	15262.30	10339.39	11507.00	21339.61	13573.45
1972	21973.97	15666.75	10703.71	11937.91	22237.53	14337.10
1973	23066.83	16249.11	11055.40	13018.45	24124.27	15512.25
1974	24341.48	16822.07	11441.45	14474.53	26325.80	16305.04

Source: See text.

APPENDIX TABLE A.2 (continued)

CAPITAL STOCKS BY ASSET TYPE

(BASED ON DEPRECIATION RATES OF TABLE 1)

	Mining and Oilfield Machinery	Metal-working Machinery	Special Industry Machinery	General Industrial Machinery	Office, Computing, and Accounting Machinery	Service Industry Machinery
1949	3611.24	13489.62	16965.99	15099.01	2293.57	5192.30
1950	3681.39	13930.14	17956.80	15080.38	2459.66	5620.57
1951	3887.96	14976.70	18991.45	15308.04	2658.42	5791.18
1952	4066.45	15897.05	19604.44	15400.80	2820.93	6025.63
1953	4147.48	17201.66	20287.22	15789.20	3012.10	6433.40
1954	4136.15	18554.46	20576.61	16119.03	3132.10	6716.89
1955	4340.68	19040.54	21190.16	16754.45	3324.35	7131.60
1956	4533.47	20141.07	21977.45	17492.03	3623.13	7656.89
1957	4647.45	20898.79	22523.58	18144.25	4106.38	8160.50
1958	4448.62	20529.69	22669.40	18262.58	4440.75	8366.02
1959	4296.60	20243.80	22932.18	18473.42	4682.87	8537.63
1960	4227.66	20249.94	23523.87	18908.42	5032.91	8719.92
1961	4092.09	19919.32	23876.56	19174.14	5174.43	8827.13
1962	3973.90	19732.20	24426.89	19600.31	5250.33	9004.66
1963	4034.21	19901.01	24855.48	20365.27	5796.51	9136.89
1964	4174.56	20122.13	25692.88	21497.53	6401.65	9414.30
1965	4388.76	20917.17	27311.94	22863.08	7139.64	9956.94
1966	4601.61	22143.82	29061.08	24562.35	8576.23	10668.05
1967	4530.35	23842.20	30229.88	25633.46	9751.78	11235.82
1968	4474.84	24948.53	31403.18	26467.36	10564.52	11824.91
1969	4442.49	25924.34	32488.51	27580.11	11813.46	12527.80
1970	4629.48	26494.61	33387.95	28460.55	12805.57	13058.71
1971	4886.62	26078.02	33835.65	28922.13	13288.93	13538.02
1972	5140.32	25929.46	34503.19	29437.17	13999.38	14429.26
1973	5688.17	26303.10	35836.92	30473.12	14974.95	15491.42
1974	6215.62	27203.97	37228.13	32223.16	15094.29	16672.34

SOURCE: See text.

APPENDIX TABLE A.2 (continued)

CAPITAL STOCKS BY ASSET TYPE

(BASED ON DEPRECIATION RATES OF TABLE 1)

	Electrical and Communications Equipment	Trucks, Buses, and Truck Trailers	Autos	Aircraft	Ships and Boats	Railroad Equipment
1949	13587.46	11846.07	5305.51	2402.06	13922.14	17927.51
1950	14893.50	12862.72	6809.18	2107.76	13237.98	18386.30
1951	16447.55	13834.45	6384.68	1864.41	13560.13	19327.80
1952	18488.39	13395.65	5326.67	1869.66	13322.13	19970.17
1953	20583.61	13036.17	6081.29	1850.95	13172.97	20373.14
1954	22304.80	12727.90	6179.40	1892.67	12690.99	20006.51
1955	24012.06	13339.83	6563.80	1748.75	12167.17	19793.08
1956	26182.04	13576.51	5840.09	1978.20	11854.63	19903.74
1957	28475.18	13545.15	5648.59	2339.60	11739.53	20383.09
1958	29645.95	12954.75	4203.91	2369.75	11540.07	19806.81
1959	31079.70	12847.13	4365.75	3054.37	11281.56	19362.56
1960	33238.40	12737.81	4654.64	3483.51	10996.45	19249.63
1961	35630.59	12756.23	4568.25	3884.98	10649.71	18775.15
1962	38274.75	13713.97	5174.65	4162.86	10410.98	18722.99
1963	40620.15	14711.74	5358.94	4018.81	10142.16	18759.27
1964	43284.04	15606.37	5941.81	4346.16	9960.50	19348.16
1965	46650.85	17347.03	7220.40	4636.51	9885.46	20311.18
1966	50789.71	19541.09	7010.84	5989.64	9890.05	21576.65
1967	54281.61	20345.52	6733.13	7764.74	9948.30	22419.59
1968	57671.81	22127.86	7671.98	10512.46	10160.18	22637.89
1969	61738.30	24886.02	8808.91	11476.53	10380.16	23430.79
1970	65971.35	25731.44	7331.90	11762.88	10558.65	23760.36
1971	69136.33	27107.37	7782.18	10611.74	10643.75	24172.18
1972	71046.16	30801.23	9288.38	10069.61	10977.47	24409.81
1973	73735.82	35519.96	10802.56	10682.85	11677.16	24770.77
1974	76559.37	37670.55	10524.07	10116.68	12373.37	25512.90

SOURCE: See text.

APPENDIX TABLE A.2 (continued)

CAPITAL STOCKS BY ASSET TYPE

(BASED ON DEPRECIATION RATES OF TABLE 1)

	Instruments	Other PDE	Industrial Construction	Commercial Construction	Religious Buildings	Educational Buildings
1949	2697.76	3100.33	58833.42	62111.38	9610.67	7587.51
1950	3060.38	3307.65	59800.54	63609.23	10300.99	8070.87
1951	3447.59	3414.44	61767.74	64870.08	10955.33	8566.14
1952	3852.76	3535.49	63815.92	65394.79	11478.37	9046.09
1953	4246.25	3658.71	65617.17	67080.54	12120.58	9651.03
1954	4431.77	3770.78	67124.39	69599.65	12999.71	10457.59
1955	4775.97	3990.35	70698.20	73555.54	14035.32	11117.98
1956	5144.47	4201.57	73740.99	78257.72	15135.45	11862.97
1957	5486.69	4406.68	76967.94	82205.75	16262.91	12589.94
1958	5621.50	4678.57	78244.40	86288.27	17401.17	13313.25
1959	5837.45	5032.42	79220.78	90944.95	18666.02	13941.96
1960	6118.60	5442.15	81592.91	95922.61	20031.10	14640.85
1961	6366.33	5902.52	83967.40	101524.32	21343.52	15390.61
1962	6624.57	6426.08	86367.18	107763.67	22670.26	16238.26
1963	7186.77	7022.52	88517.32	113375.91	23871.06	17034.98
1964	8101.16	7674.10	91278.85	119374.52	25012.28	17831.73
1965	9188.86	8339.70	96197.68	127206.97	26413.05	18634.49
1966	10501.34	9131.27	102783.95	134347.96	27622.49	19676.16
1967	11594.49	9470.23	107804.45	140863.56	28608.18	20723.25
1968	12606.62	9930.27	112407.71	148256.23	29541.35	21835.65
1969	13753.67	10462.54	117094.79	156219.31	30190.97	22680.14
1970	14948.75	10899.41	120460.67	163483.69	30669.38	23226.75
1971	16377.80	11453.92	121841.04	171831.64	30946.80	23781.09
1972	17946.35	12190.76	122166.57	181290.40	31209.00	24302.01
1973	19568.85	13016.06	123472.36	191163.52	31367.27	24611.13
1974	21372.36	13452.80	125526.01	200112.79	31571.56	24714.44

SOURCE: See text.

APPENDIX TABLE A.2 (continued)

Capital Stocks by Asset Type

(Based on Depreciation Rates of Table 1)

	Hospitals and Institutional Buildings	Other Nonfarm Buildings	Public Utilities	Farm Buildings	Mining, Exploration, Shafts, and Wells	All Other Private Construction
1949	5504.79	10909.92	100041.87	22103.84	23775.78	6710.40
1950	6108.52	11223.61	103149.55	23169.98	25156.20	6744.80
1951	6752.20	11554.06	106225.02	24117.85	26748.91	6663.20
1952	7313.87	11784.50	109486.31	25128.26	28427.94	6614.97
1953	7719.46	12058.49	113132.54	25949.72	30183.45	6630.13
1954	8169.59	12536.03	116181.56	26703.71	32045.12	6653.86
1955	8594.24	12692.90	118638.22	27363.83	34060.98	6742.90
1956	8977.00	12950.64	122141.25	28050.31	36074.35	6758.35
1957	9621.83	13203.68	125719.59	28623.52	37731.36	6875.36
1958	10401.64	13720.23	128723.85	29171.14	38851.09	6975.97
1959	11119.28	14412.33	131171.18	30088.78	40042.77	7109.67
1960	11887.21	15340.01	133637.17	30814.68	40864.36	7366.49
1961	12908.23	16154.58	135651.23	31551.37	41587.70	7562.86
1962	14254.47	16981.16	137582.66	32412.60	42508.31	7784.54
1963	15597.34	17894.22	139930.05	33202.42	43177.09	8041.79
1964	17303.92	18707.82	142688.26	33951.53	44102.22	8329.58
1965	19072.74	20017.48	146243.31	34763.88	45068.27	8709.02
1966	20749.35	21266.69	150721.02	35617.97	45905.93	9150.46
1967	22151.89	22360.18	155754.23	36659.83	46568.42	9510.09
1968	23789.75	22195.03	161784.40	37450.99	47117.62	9995.30
1969	25880.45	22144.37	167673.01	38176.40	47683.90	10625.44
1970	28119.43	22038.02	174042.55	38970.62	47976.29	11387.30
1971	30473.25	21895.49	179949.80	39682.02	47899.23	12110.07
1972	32935.22	21815.44	186568.39	40173.55	48034.50	12699.88
1973	35050.83	21818.02	192950.83	41157.44	47975.16	13176.58
1974	37012.15	21688.48	199277.58	42414.01	47827.16	13666.46

Source: See text.

REFERENCES

Ackerlof, George. 1970. "The Market for Lemons." *Quarterly Journal of Economics* no. 3 (August): 488–500.

Ackerman, Susan Rose. 1973. "Used Cars as a Depreciating Asset." *Western Economic Journal.* 11 (December): 463–474.

Amemiya, Takeshi. 1973. "Regression Analysis When the Dependent Variable is Truncated Normal." *Econometrica* 41, no. 6 (November): 997–1016.

Beidleman, Carl R. 1976. "Economic Depreciation in a Capital Goods Industry." *National Tax Journal* 29, no. 4 (December): 379–390.

Box, G. E. P., and Cox, D. R. 1964. "An Analysis of Transformations." *Journal of the Royal Statistical Society, Series B* 26, no. 2: 211–243.

Cagan, Philip. 1971. "Measuring Quality Changes and the Purchasing Power of Money: An Exploratory Study of Automobiles." In Zvi Griliches, ed. *Price Indexes and Quality Change,* Cambridge, Mass: Harvard University Press.

Chinloy, Peter. 1977. "Hendonic Price and Depreciation Indexes for Residential Housing: A Longitudinal Approach." *Journal of Urban Economics:* 469–482.

Chow, Gregory, C. 1957. *The Demand for Automobiles in the United States.* Amsterdam: North Holland.

––––––– "Statistical Demand Functions for Automobiles and Their Use for Forecasting." 1960. In Arnold Harberger, ed. *The Demand for Durable Goods.* Chicago: University of Chicago Press.

Coen, Robert. 1975. "Investment Behavior, the Measurement of Depreciation and Tax Policy." *American Economic Review* 65 (March): 59–74.

––––––. 1980. "Depreciation, Profits, and Rates of Return in Manufacturing Industries." In Dan Usher, ed. *The Measurement of Capital.* National Bureau of Economic Research, Studies in Income and Wealth, Vol. 45. Chicago: 121–152.

Eisner, Robert. 1972. "Components of Capital Expenditures: Replacement and Modernization." *Review of Economics and Statistics* 54 (August): 297–305.

Faucett, Jack G. 1973. *Development of Capital Stock Series by Industry Sector.* U.S. Office of Emergency Preparedness. Washington, D.C.

Feldstein, M. S., and Foot, D. K. 1971. "The Other Half of Gross Investment: Replacement and Modernization Expenditures." *Review of Economics and Statistics* 56, no. 2 (February): 49–58.

––––––– and Rothschild, Michael. 1974. "Towards an Economic Theory of Replacement Investment." *Econometrica* 42 (May): 393–423.

Griliches, Zvi. 1960. "The Demand for a Durable Input: U.S. Farm Tractors, 1921–57." In Arnold Harberger, ed. *The Demand for Durable Goods.* Chicago: University of Chicago Press.

Hall, Robert. 1968. "Technical Change and Capital from the Point of View of the Dual." *Review of Economics and Statistics* 35 (January): 35–46.

––––––. 1971. "The Measurement of Quality Change from Vintage Price Data." In Zvi Griliches, ed. *Price Indexes and Quality Change.* Cambridge, Mass: Harvard University Press.

––––––– and Jorgenson, Dale W. 1967. "Tax Policy and Investment Behavior." *American Economic Review* 57 (June): 391–414.

Hausman, Jerry A., and Wise, David A. 1977. "Social Experimentation, Truncated Distributions, and Efficient Estimation." *Econometica* 45 (May): 919–938.

Heal, Geoffrey, 1967. "Do Bad Products Drive out Good?" *Quarterly Journal of Economics* 90 (August): 449–502.

Heckman, James J. 1976. "The Common Structure of Statistical Models of Truncation, Sample Selection. Limited Dependent Variables and a Simple Estimator for Such Models." *Annals of Economic and Social Measurement* 1976. 5 (Fall): 474–492.

Hotelling, Harold S. 1925. "A General Mathematical Theory of Depreciation." *Journal of the American Statistical Society* 20 (September): 340-353.

Hulten, Charles R., and Wykoff, Frank C. 1975. "Empirical Evidence of Economic Depreciation of Structures." In U.S. Treasury, *Conference on Tax Research 1975:* 105-158.

_____., and _____. 1978. "On the Feasibility of Equating Tax to Economic *Depreciation.*" 1978 Compendium on Tax Research. U.S. Department of the Treasury, Office of Tax Analysis: 89-120.

_____., and _____. 1979. *Economic Depreciation of the U.S. Capital Stock.* Report submitted to U.S. Department of Treasury, Office of Tax Analysis. Washington, D.C.

_____., and _____. 1981. "The Estimation of Economic Depreciation Using Vintage Asset Prices: An Application of the Box-Cox Power Transformation." *Journal of Econometrics,* forthcoming.

Jorgenson, Dale W. 1971. "Econometric Studies of Investment Behavior: A Survey." *Journal of Economic Literature* 9 (December): 1111-1147.

_____. 1973. "The Economic Theory of Replacement and Depreciation." In W. Sellekaerts, ed. *Econometrics and Economic Theory,* New York: MacMillan.

Lee, Bun Song. 1978. "Measurement of Capital Depreciation Within the Japanese Fishing Fleet." *Review of Economics and Statistics* (May): 255-337.

Leigh, Wilhelmina. 1977. *An Analysis of the Growth of the Stock of Housing in the United States,* 1950-1970. Doctoral Dissertation, The Johns Hopkins University.

Malpezzi, Stephen; Ozanne, Larry; and Thibodeau, Thomas. 1980. "Characteristic Prices of Housing in Fifty-Nine Metropolitan Areas." *Working Paper 1367-1,* The Urban Institute, Washington, D.C.

Marston, Anson; Winfrey, Robley; and Hempstead, John C. 1953. *Engineering Valuation and Depreciation.* Ames, Iowa: McGraw-Hill.

Musgrave, John C. 1976. "Fixed Nonresidential Business and Residential Capital in the United States, 1925-75." *Survey of Current Business* 56 (April): 46-52.

Nishimizu, Mieko. 1974. *Total Factor Productivity Analysis: A Disaggregated Study of the Post-War Japanese Economy.* Doctoral Dissertation, The Johns Hopkins University.

Ohta, Makoto, and Griliches, Zvi. 1976. "Automobile Prices Revisted: Extensions of the Hedonic Price Hypothesis." National Bureau of Economic Research, Studies in Income and Wealth, Vol. 40: 325-390.

Ramm, Wolfhard. 1970. "Measuring the Services of Household Durables" The Case of Automobiles." *Proceedings of the Business and Economic Statistics Section of the American Statistical Association,* Washington, D.C.: 149-158.

Taubman, Paul, and Rasche, Robert. 1969. "Economic and Tax Depreciation of Office Buildings." *National Tax Journal* 22 (September): 334-346.

_____, and _____. 1971. "Subsidies, Economic Lives and Complete Resource Misallocation." *American Economic Review* 61 (December): 938-945.

Terborgh, George. 1954. *Realistic Depreciation Policy.* Machinery and Allied Products Institute.

Tobin, James. 1958. "Estimation of Relationships for Limited Dependent Variables." Econometrica 26: 24-26.

U.S. Department of Commerce, Bureau of Business Economics. 1966. *The National Income and Product Accounts of the United States, 1929-1965, A Supplement to the Survey of Current Business,* Washington, D.C.

U.S. Department of Commerce, Bureau of Economic Analysis. *Survey of Current Business.* Washington, D.C. (selected issues).

U.S. Treasury, Bureau of Internal Revenue. 1942. *Income Tax Depreciation and Obsolescence Estimated Useful Lives and Depreciation Rates.* Bulletin "F" revised (January).

U.S. Treasury, Office of Industrial Economics. 1975. *Business Building Statistics,* Washington, D.C. (August).

Winfrey, R. 1935. *Statistical Analyses of Industrial Property Retirements.* Iowa: Engineering Experiment Station, Bulletin 125.

Wykoff, Frank C. 1970. "Capital Depreciation in the Postwar Period: Automobilies." *Review of Economics and Statistics* 52 (May): 168-176.

Young, Allan H. 1975. "New Estimates of Capital Consumption Allowances Revision of GNP in the Benchmark." *Survey of Current Business* 55 (October): 14-16, 35.

_____., and Musgrave, John C. 1980. "Estimation of Capital Stock in the United States." In Dan Usher, ed. *The Measurement of Capital.* Vol. 45. National Bureau of Economic Research, Studies in Income and Wealth, Chicago: 23-82.

Discussion of Charles R. Hulten and Frank C. Wykoff, "The Measurement of Economic Depreciation"

Frank DeLeeuw, Discussant

I will comment on three topics—tax benefits, lemons, and scrappage. What the three have in common is that they all bear on how to interpret the age-price profiles which are the centerpiece of the Hulten-Wykoff analysis.

As you have just heard, the Hulten-Wykoff interpretation of these profiles is that, after adjustment for retirements, their rates of decline measure rates of depreciation, which in turn reflect (although they are not the same thing as) declines in efficiency with age. The interpretation suggested in these comments is that age-price profiles may reflect not only depreciation but other phenomena as well. If they do, then it is necessary to correct in some way for these other influences before drawing conclusions about depreciation rates.

Before turning to the three topics, however, let me say that I think the series of Hulten-Wykoff papers are major contributions. My comments amount to proposals for modifying their analysis and testing some alternative assumptions but certainly not displacing their basic framework. I think we are all in their debt for the painstaking and ingenious econometric work that they have done.

I. Tax benefits.

I would expect age-price profiles to reflect not only depreciation of capital goods but also the time-pattern of tax advantages to owners of capital goods.

Let me use the investment tax credit as an example. Bear in mind that there is a cap on the investment tax credit for used capital goods, so that at least for big com-

---

[The author is chief statistician, the Bureau of Economic Analysis.]

panies the credit is much larger for new than for used equipment. The investment tax credit is therefore a benefit which should add much more to the present discounted value of a new capital good than to the present discounted value of a used capital good. Since it is present discounted values that are assumed to underlie age-price profiles, it seems to me that the investment tax credit should cause a steeper decline of age-price profiles in the first year than is due to depreciation alone.

For structures there is no investment tax credit. Indeed, even for equipment there is more to consider than just the tax credit. Nevertheless, it is true for structures as well as for equipment that tax benefits favor new over used structures. George Peterson has carefully studied those advantages and their consequences.

Now Hulten and Wykoff do report, in a technical paper referenced in their conference paper, on a test for whether changes in tax laws affect age-price profiles. However, the test is restricted to office buildings over a period during all of which there was substantial tax advantage for new structures as compared to used structures. There were tax changes during the period, but they were changes which I suspect would tend to shift the entire age-price profile rather than alter its slope— and the tests were for changes in slope. I hope that the tests are deficient; for if careful tests revealed that provisions such as the investment tax credit had no effect on age-price profiles, then I would be forced to have doubts about the entire Hulten-Wykoff approach.

If tax benefits are a problem in interpreting age-price profiles, what can be done to correct for their impact? Let me offer two suggestions.

One possibility is to adjust the price observations for the effect of tax benefits. For the investment tax credit, for instance, one could subtract 10 percent, or 7 percent, or some appropriate percent from the price of a new asset and fit the age-price curves to the modified observations. For structures, it is much harder to make such corrections, but it is possible. What is required is a typical stream of tax benefits and the present value of that stream every year. Present values can then be subtracted from actual prices before fitting age-price curves.

Another possible solution to the problem is to refit the curve leaving out data that may be highly "contaminated." For example, in the case of the investment tax credit, one could simply fit curves omitting the new price observations but including all other observations. It would be of interest to know how much this omission changed estimates of depreciation rates, at least for a few types of equipment. This approach is possible only when benefits in one or two years are very large relative to benefits in other years.

II.   Lemons.

What I mean by the "lemons" argument is the proposition that defective capital goods are represented more heavily in used markets than they are in new markets. As Hulten has explained, if this is the case it will depress the nonnew portions of the age-price profile.

Hulten and Wykoff argue that this phenomenon depends upon an asymmetry of information between buyers and sellers. It seems to me that asymmetry of information is *one* possible cause of a lemons problem but not the only one. Suppose that a producer finds that a new capital good he has bought is defective; that is, it will not do what he had planned for it to do. Obviously, he then has to change his plans in some way. One change he can make is to sell the capital good and buy another one. Another is to resign himself to lower production then he had planned. There are other options as well.

It seems to me that as long as selling the good is an important option, you have a lemons problem. It seems to me that that is so, even if buyers and sellers have exactly the same information. I cannot see that asymmetry of information is a necessary condition for this source of the "lemons" phenomenon.

Nevertheless, like Hulten and Wykoff, I do not really know whether the lemons problem is important or not. It depends crucially on whether defective capital goods are an important proportion of new production; and we do not really have information to make a judgment.

Since it may be important, however, it is worth asking what can be done about it. One simple correction it seems to me, is to omit new price observations before fitting age-price curves—exactly the same remedy as one suggested for the investment tax credit problem. The reason this omission ought to help is that the lemons phenomenon, if it exists, should depress *all* used prices, but not—at least according to any argument I am aware of—one-year used prices relative to two-year used prices or three-year used prices. It is only the new prices that are out of line.

Because of the lemons possibility as well as the investment tax credit, therefore, I think it would be extremely instructive to see some of the equipment results with new-price observations omitted.

Another option for dealing with the lemons problem, as Hulten pointed out, is to use rent data rather than price data. Since Taubman was a pioneer in using rent data, I will leave discussion of that approach to him.

III.   Scrappage.

It is a contribution of the Hulten-Wykoff approach to recognize that prices of surviving capital goods may not be representative of prices of retired or scrapped capital goods. Because of this problem, as Hulten noted, price observations have been corrected for the effect of retirements before fitting age-price curves. The correction is equivalent to assuming a zero scrappage value for all equipment and structures that are retired from the stock.

For equipment, I do not have any strong feeling about whether or not that is an accurate assumption. For structures, however, I feel that the correction goes much too far. One important reason for retiring structures is that land use patterns change—for example, an area that used to be suitable for low-rise stores now becomes profitable for high-rise office buildings, and the store owners are bought out by office builders. In such a case, the scrappage value—that is the sale price of a structure that is about to be demolished—could easily be as great as or even greater than the present discounted value of the structure in its old use.

Therefore, for structures I would not be surprised if estimates based on uncorrected age-price profiles (which are presented in the Hulten-Wykoff technical papers) would be more accurate than the ones based on corrected data, which are the ones presented in their conference paper. Estimates based on uncorrected profiles, incidentally, lead to depreciation rates for structures substantially lower than the ones reported in their conference paper.

Let me sum up by repeating, first of all, that the Hulten-Wykoff work represents an important contribution. I feel, however, that tax benefits, lemons, and scrappage raise questions about the specific estimates they have produced so far. What I would like to see is some reestimation—by no means a major job—modifying some of their assumptions and procedures in ways I have suggested. I believe that a little work along these lines would bring us much closer to a consensus view about economic depreciation rates.

Discussion of Charles R. Hulten and Frank C. Wykoff, "The Measurement of Economic Depreciation"

Paul Taubman, Discussant

Having received the paper with only one day to prepare my comments, I do not feel bound to stick only to the paper itself. I will speak about a broader set of issues.

A crucial issue in tax policy is the proper treatment of depreciable assets. The main issues are the life of the asset, the pattern of depreciation rates, and the treatment of inflation. Since the solution of the inflation problem involves different sorts of questions, I will ignore the issue except to note that the use of adjustments to depreciation charges which are not related to the differential burden across industries of inflation are not the way to provide equitable relief.

While it is always possible to find a multitude of lives and depreciation patterns that have the same present discounted value of deductions, it is usual to separate the aspects into what is the useful life and what is the pattern of depreciation rates. Considered separately, the equitable and efficient solution is that firms should use actual lives and actual depreciation patterns.

The reserve ratio tests let firms claim whatever lives they wanted and then tested whether the lives are actually used. Simulation studies done by Pollock have shown that, except for one technical and correctable flaw, the method did what it was supposed to do.

The stories I have heard from Treasury people involved with this issue is that the only problem with the reserve ratio test was that it clearly revealed that many businesses had lives much longer than businessmen were claiming.

I do not believe that anyone disputes that in determining costs, depreciation should be allowed. Nor does anyone argue that, if the information were clearly known, the actual annual loss in value should be used.

We have only limited evidence on the subject of what is true depreciation, so there is a question of how Congress should set rules. There is, however, a separate

---

[The author is professor of economics, University of Pennsylvania.]

issue of whether business capital should be subsidized and, if so, if some sort of accelerated depreciation should be used.

Let us consider briefly the second issue. There are several reasons why the U.S. should subsidize investments. Tax policy may restrict total saving and cause investments to be less than optimal and interest rates higher than in an economy with no taxes on savings. Savings may also be restricted by such considerations as people being short-sighted with respect to future generations, the pay-as-you-go feature of Social Security taxes, et cetera. It is also possible that the annualized cost of plant and equipment is too high because of other tax laws or because of excess private over social riskiness.

These reasons may justify a subsidy to investment or they may justify a change in the tax treatment of savings, but they hardly justify a haphazard approach.

Plans which call for an arbitrary 10-year life of buildings give the most benefit to those firms with the longest life of buildings and those which are heavily business intensive. Offhand, I do not know what these industries are. I suspect most congressmen do not.

Thus, if we really were to impose such a tax scheme, what we are basically arguing for is that we want essentially nonplanned affairs.

Let us turn to the content of the paper and to the depreciation patterns that they found.

Techniques have come a long way since Terborgh graphed the rate of change in prices of seven or eight used assets in 1954. Hulten and Wykoff are to be commended for their innovative use of Box-Cox techniques to try and estimate true depreciation rates.

In the paper that we have here today and in the technical paper, which they recently finished, they concentrate on several issues which include the propositions that the depreciation rates can be estimated from used market price quotations, that it is desirable from an econometrician's viewpoint to have geometric depreciation, that depreciation is geometric, that their results are buttressed by being in accord with those of the Bureau of Economic Analysis (BEA), and that some work that Bob Rasche and I did a decade ago on buildings is wrong. Let me consider each of these points.

The rough correspondence between BEA numbers and Hulten-Wykoff's is irrelevant. BEA uses a procedure, which Chuck Hulten described to you, which is arbitrary in many ways. There is no evidence that the Winfrey retirement pattern applies to each asset type. BEA does not know what economic lives are, and BEA applies straight-line depreciation. Thus, the numbers are not useful as a guide to what is reasonable.

I find concern for the labors of econometricians most touching and amusing. I thought econometricians liked tough estimation problems. That is an easy way to get publications.

Moreover, the quality of the data is of much greater concern than whether the depreciation pattern in geometric or not. To illustrate this, about 10 days ago I saw a BEA press release on the new plant and equipment figures. For the most recent year the investment series was raised by more than 50 percent. I guess this is going to reduce sharply the productivity problem, the saving rate problem, and the investment-is-only-for-the-environment problem, but it will also give huge headaches to econometricians.

Hulten and Wykoff's estimates clearly show that the estimates are close to geometric for a large number of assets. They argue that this is not due to a lemons problem, since businessmen are informed buyers and since the tractor market is one wherein sales occur because of the ebb and flow of the market. I think they are probably right on lemons for most assets.

However, I do not trust their results for all assets, particularly buildings. While I realize that I am not unbiased, having obtained different results on the same topic, I do not have that much of an investment to protect, since I mostly work in a different field these days.

I agree that Bob Rasche and I in our well-known piece had to estimate the age and income size from very few data points, but I think the fact that we used very few data points is one of the ways that we get around the long-term lease problem that was raised. As I recall that piece, we had data for the first 10 years, 10 to 25 years, 25 to 50 years, and above 50 years. When you use the average rents in those particular classifications, the problems associated with long-term leases just vanish.

The problem was that we had few data points with which to establish the shape of the profile. I would think that getting more data on rents would certainly be quite valuable because of the types of issues that Frank DeLeeuw raised as to the interpretation and use of the price data.

I might add that, in terms of the survival problem in buildings, there is another issue that has to be considered. That is that some buildings disappear because of fires, and some of those fires are accidental.

There are two other ways in which one might want to judge our results versus theirs. I think their results taken at face value would have some strange implications. In the mid 1960s, when inflationary expectations were less than 1 percent per year, it was possible to get from insurance companies 30-year mortgages on office and apartment buildings with zero down payment. If true depreciation were something like 2.5 percent per year, as comes out of one of the tables that they have, the insurance companies were running tremendous risks of bankruptcy, because there would be no buildup in the value of the asset in terms of payments of the mortgage and at the same time the building would be running down in terms of value.

If, as Bob Rasche and I found, depreciation at the beginning is no more than .5 of 1 percent per year, these companies were not running a very great risk.

There is, however, another very clear implication from the two findings. If the buildings' owners are allowed to depreciate assets so that they reduce ordinary taxes in the early years of the buildings' life, they would save on ordinary income taxes then. Moreover, the market value of the asset will exceed the remaining book value even in a noninflationary period. Since capital gains are taxed at a favorable rate, owners will sell assets when tax depreciation begins to exceed true depreciation.

This, incidentally, is a reason why you do not have to worry too much about lemons in the buildings market. Many of the transactions are dominated by tax considerations.

Hulten and Wykoff's depreciation rates for buildings are smaller than those currently in use. I would be willing to support them on an interim basis and expect to see investors engaging in capital gains sales 6 to 10 years later. At that point, I would then argue for further steps to tighten up the laws.

I think that the used market price mechanism is a valuable way to get at true depreciation rates and that it should be encouraged. I also think they can be improved, in that more data including actual information on retirements are necessary.

I think a rational tax policy is crucial, in that too short lives and too quick depreciation is not the way to go, even if stimulation is needed.

THE "NET" VERSUS THE "GROSS" INVESTMENT TAX CREDIT

E. Cary Brown

The standard analysis of an infinite stream of revenues, c, exponentially decaying at rate δ, gives a present value (equal to or greater than a cost of q) of

$$q \leq V(0) = \int_0^\infty ce^{-(\delta+r)t}\, dt = \frac{c}{\delta + r}$$

where

$$\frac{c}{q} = \delta + r = \text{Rental value of capital.}$$

With a tax, u, assuming the pretax interest rate remains unchanged (though this assumption does not affect the result)

$$\frac{c}{q} = [(1 - u)r + \delta]\frac{(1 - uz)}{(1 - u)} \quad,$$

where z = present value of depreciation as a percentage of initial capital. For a series with exponential decay

$$z = \frac{\delta}{(1 - u)r + \delta} \quad.$$

[The author is professor of economics, Massachusetts Institute of Technology.]

Substituting in expression (1) above, gives

$$\frac{c}{q} = \delta + r,$$

or the rental cost of capital is unchanged by the tax when economic depreciation is charged. A *gross* investment credit at rate k changes the expression to

$$\frac{c}{q} = \frac{[(1 - u)r + \delta](1 - k - uz)}{1 - u} = r + \delta - \frac{k[r(1 - u) + \delta]}{1 - u}$$

Note that

$$\frac{d\frac{c}{q}}{dk} = -\frac{r(1 - u) + \delta}{1 - u} \quad ,$$

hence it depends on δ—hence it is not neutral with respect to asset life.

If, however, the credit (k) were applied to net investment—cost less the present value of depreciation $(q - z)$—the result is

$$\frac{c}{q} = [(1 - u)r + \delta]\frac{1 - k + z(k - u)}{1 - u} \quad .$$

If economic depreciation is used

$$\frac{c}{q} = \frac{[(1 - u)r + \delta]\left[1 - k + (k - u)\left(\dfrac{\delta}{(1 - u)r + \delta}\right)\right]}{1 - u} = \delta + r(1 - k)$$

There is thus no variation in rental price with respect to depreciation rate.

$$\frac{d\frac{c}{q}}{dk} = -r \quad ,$$

and is neutral with respect to δ. Since δ is a proxy for length of life of an asset, this procedure does not have a systematic bias by durability of asset.

PART II

ANALYSIS OF CURRENT LAW AND TAX REFORM PROPOSALS

ACCELERATION OF TAX DEPRECIATION: BASIC ISSUES AND MAJOR ALTERNATIVES

Emil M. Sunley

Revision of tax depreciation is probably the key tax policy issue to be addressed by the Reagan administration and the ninety-seventh Congress. Although there is general agreement that tax depreciation should be liberalized, there is considerable disagreement on just how this should be done. The disagreement is due in part to the lack of agreement about the goals of depreciation policy. In the context of an income tax, depreciation policy should relate to the measurement of income. That is, in order to have an income tax, there first must be rules for measuring income. Then one decides at what rates to tax that income. Obviously no one knows how to measure income with precision, particularly in a world with inflation. This may suggest that the tax depreciation rules should err on the liberal side.

Not everyone agrees that depreciation policy should relate to the measurement of income. Some tax policy experts want to move away from the income tax toward the consumption tax. For these people, the goal of depreciation policy is to move toward expensing of investments. The consumption tax advocates, however, often seem to forget that in a world with the expensing of capital investments one would not permit a deduction for interest on borrowed money.

[The author is deputy assistant secretary for tax policy, U.S. Treasury Department.]

Form of Business Tax Cut

There has been a political consensus that the centerpiece of the business portion of the next tax bill should be acceleration of tax depreciation. There clearly, however, are three other possible ways of providing a general business tax reduction: (1) reduce corporate tax rates, (2) integrate corporate and individual income taxes, and (3) increase the investment tax credit. In the long run, all business tax reductions can reduce the level of taxes on capital income, and, per dollar of tax reduction, they are likely to have about the same effect on the level of investment and the size of the capital stock. In the short run, however, increasing the investment tax credit or accelerating tax depreciation is likely to have a greater effect on investment per dollar of revenue loss. The tax relief is tied directly to placing new investment in service.[1] As a result, capital losses are imposed on owners of existing assets, and these losses generally are not recognized for tax purposes. In contrast, corporate rate reductions or integration result in tax losses with respect to income earned on the existing capital stock. These revenue losses provide little incentive to increase investment.

It is often alleged that accelerated tax depreciation has more bang for the buck than the investment tax credit, or vice versa. I believe that the bang-for-the-buck argument gives very little support for favoring accelerated depreciation or the investment tax credit. This is true when the bucks are correctly measured, that is, measured in terms of the present value of the future revenue losses.

For any acceleration of tax depreciation, one can determine the increase in the investment tax credit which, for a given discount rate, will leave businesses indifferent, at least on economic grounds, between the two tax changes.[2] If the government has the same discount rate, the present value of the future revenue losses will also be the same, so the government too should be indifferent. In the short run, however, acceleration of depreciation will involve larger revenue losses.[3]

Given the greater concern over the size of the budget deficit in the current fiscal year as opposed to budget deficits in future years, the investment tax credit is to be preferred to an acceleration of tax depreciation providing in present value terms the same amount of stimulus. Also, on tax policy grounds, the investment tax credit is preferable since the credit would keep investment incentives separate from the measurement of income.

Nevertheless, 1981 is going to be the year for accelerating tax depreciation. That is what business wants, in part, because an acceleration of tax depreciation is not as visible as an increase in the investment tax credit. Also, Congress, particularly the Ways and Means Committee, is tired of pushing the investment tax credit up and down.

10-5-3 Proposal

The business community has strongly endorsed the 10-5-3 proposal for accelerating tax depreciation. This proposal would greatly shorten the period over which most capital expenditures can be written off. It would permit nonresidential buildings to be written off over 10 years, most machinery and equipment over 5 years, and a limited amount of expenditures for cars and light trucks over 3 years.[4] Taxpayers would write off their investments over these shortened periods using, in effect, the double declining balance method of depreciation with a switch to the sum-of-the-years'-digits method. Taxpayers would be permitted to "bank" allowable depreciation deductions and to use them in a subsequent tax year. The 10-5-3 proposal would be phased in over 5 years. The investment tax credit would be liberalized by allowing the full 10 percent credit for equipment depreciated over 5 years and a 6 percent credit for the 3-year class of cars and light trucks.

The Carter administration was strongly opposed to the 10-5-3 formula for accelerating tax depreciation because (1) it costs too much, (2) its phase-in would add complexity and provide an incentive to delay investment, and (3) it favors long-lived assets, particularly buildings and public utility property, and thus distorts investment.

Given the phase-in of the 10-5-3 proposal, the first year revenue cost of the proposal is less than $5 billion. The cost rises rapidly to more than $50 billion by the fifth year. Even taking into account feedback effects, the revenue losses from 10-5-3 cannot fit into any conceivable future budget unless federal spending is drastically cut.

If enacted, the 10-5-3 proposal would provide an incentive to delay investment. Congress, in effect, would be telling businesses that if you wait until next year your capital recovery would be more favorable than this year. If you wait two years, the capital recovery will be even more favorable. And if you wait five years, nirvana.

The major concern of the Carter administration was that the 10-5-3 proposal is simply tilted too much toward long-lived assets. Unfortunately, when all businesses are permitted to use the same useful life for machinery and equipment, all businesses do not get the same tax reduction or the same incentive to invest. This is so because all machinery and equipment does not have the same annual depreciation or capital cost. The arbitrary capital cost recovery permitted under the 10-5-3 proposal may approximate the rate of actual depreciation for some industries. But for other industries it would provide allowances for capital recovery that would exceed actual depreciation, possibly many times over. To the extent that the 10-5-3 proposal would distort investment toward long-lived assets, it would reduce the effective capital stock. Improving the allocation of investment would increase the effective capital stock. It would be equivalent to increasing the level of investment, but it would not have the disadvantage of having to give up current consumption to do so.

Senate Finance Committee Bill

On September 10, 1980, the Senate Finance Committee reported out the Tax Reduction Act of 1980, containing its version of liberalized depreciation, commonly known as 2-4-7-10 proposal or the Bentsen bill. The Finance Committee bill is responsive to the three major concerns of the Carter administration. First, the cost of the finance bill is significantly less, particularly in the out years, than the 10-5-3 approach. Second, there is no phase-in so businesses would have no incentive to delay investment. Third, the finance bill does not tilt as much toward long-lived assets as the 10-5-3 approach.

Under the Finance Committee bill, machinery and equipment, except public utility property, would be placed in one of four asset classes, having tax lives of 2, 4, 7, and 10 years. These asset classes would be open-ended accounts. To compute each year's depreciation deduction, taxpayers would elect a declining balance method of depreciation—200 percent, 150 percent, or 100 percent. Sales or other dispositions of personal property subject to this system of depreciation would not generally result in immediate recognition of gain (including recapture of prior depreciation allowances or loss). Instead, the proceeds from dispositions would reduce the account balance on which future allowances would be computed. However, if the account balance is reduced to zero, additional proceeds would be treated as ordinary income.

The bill classifies assets into the four new asset classes based on their ADR guideline period.[5] Taxpayers, however, would be able to elect to place property in the asset class having the next longer recovery period than the recovery period otherwise allowed. Also, taxpayers would be able to elect to expense each year up to $25,000 of new or used personal property used in the taxpayer's trade of business and placed in service during the taxable year. Taxpayers electing this option would have to forego the investment tax credit.

Public utility machinery and equipment would continue under the ADR system, but the ADR range would be increased from 20 to 30 percent. Thus public utility machinery and equipment would be treated much less generously than other machinery and equipment.

The tax credit for machinery and equipment in the 7-year or the 10-year asset classes would remain at 10 percent. Only a 6 percent investment credit would be allowed for machinery and equipment in the 4-year asset class, and a 2.5 percent investment credit for the 2-year asset class. These reductions in the investment tax credit ensure that the combination of the investment credit plus fast write-offs would not result in capital recovery more favorable than expensing.

Finally, the committee bill would provide an optional system for depreciating new real property. If taxpayers forego component depreciation, they would be able to depreciate structures over the period of 20 years using the straight-line method of depreciation (or 15 years in the case of low-income rental housing). Owner-occupied business structures could be depreciated over 15 years using the 150 percent declining balance method, but any gain on the sale of the building would be taxed as ordinary income to the extent of any prior depreciation.

Though the description of the basic features of the Senate Finance Committee bill makes it seem considerably more complicated than the 10-5-3 proposal, the finance bill does in fact contain the kernel of significant simplification; namely, open-ended accounts. Stated simply, when open-ended accounts are used, each year's investments are added to the account. The allowable depreciation is computed by multiplying the adjusted basis of the account by the depreciation rate. The allowable depreciation is then subtracted from the account. Any proceeds from the sale of existing assets are also subtracted from the account.

If open-ended accounts are used, taxpayers are no longer required to maintain vintage accounts for each year's investment. The complex section 1245 recapture rules are not needed. Instead, the seller of used equipment subtracts the proceeds from his asset account and the purchaser adds the purchase price to his asset account. Thus, the sale of used property reduces future depreciation for the seller and increases future depreciation for the purchaser by the same amount.

Although open-ended accounts are the key to significant simplification of tax depreciation, the Finance Committee bill contains a number of tax-payer elections that makes its depreciation system more complicated than the ADR system of depreciation.[6] First, small businesses would have to decide whether to forego the investment tax credit and expense up to $25,000 of investment each year or to use the four asset classes. Expensing generally would not be advantageous, but owners of small businesses would often need professional tax advice to know whether or not to elect expensing. Second, taxpayers would have to select the declining balance rate to apply to each asset class. Third, taxpayers would have to decide whether to place assets in the next longer asset class. It would generally be advantageous for taxpayers to place assets in the shortest asset class allowable and to use the double declining balance rate, but this would not always be so. Taxpayers with investment credits or foreign tax credits about to expire or with substantial net long-term capital gains would be better off postponing depreciation. Whether or not to postpone depreciation deductions, however, would depend not only on the current year's tax situation but also on projections of tax situations in future years. Elections of this sort would not be easy for taxpayers to make and ex post many tax-payers would make the wrong election.[7]

Compared to 10-5-3, the Finance Committee bill would not tilt as much toward long-lived assets. The bill, however, if enacted would result in considerable variations across industries. This variation would be due to (1) the compression of the myriad ADR lifetimes into four classes, (2) the reduction in the investment credit for the two-year and four-year asset classes, and (3) the smaller reduction in lifetimes for utility property.

One measure of the variation across industries is the percentage change in the present value of the tax savings from depreciation plus the investment tax credits.[8] Using this measure, among the relatively small gainers would be electronics (4.0 percent), motor vehicles (4.8 percent), and communications (3.0 percent). Petroleum refining (16.2 percent), water transportation (14.3 percent), and ferrous metals (13.1 percent) would be among the larger gainers. The reasons for this variation are best illustrated by looking at two industries in more detail.

Overall, the steel industry would be among the most favored industries. The reason for this is that most steel industry investment (75 percent) is in a machinery and equipment category that would enjoy (1) a relatively large reduction in lifetime and (2) no reduction in the investment credit. Steel thus benefits from the fact that its ADR guideline is in the upper end of the range of those lifetimes that would be collapsed into the seven-year class.

The auto industry would benefit relatively little from the Senate Finance Committee bill. Assets used in the manufacture of motor vehicles fall mainly into two ADR classes—(1) machinery and equipment and (2) special tools. Both of these classes happen to fall at the lower end of the range of lifetimes that would be collapsed into an asset class under the Finance Committee bill. As a result, the tax life for machinery and equipment would be reduced only from 9.5 to 7 years and for special tools from 3 to 2 years. The latter class also would suffer a 25 percent reduction in the investment tax credit.

The Carter Administration Proposal

In August of 1980 President Carter proposed a new liberalized and simplified depreciation system—constant rate depreciation—and a more generous investment tax credit. Under President Carter's proposal, the depreciation for equipment would be up to 40 percent greater than the most favorable depreciation permitted under present law. The rate would be adjusted to ensure that the allowable depreciation plus the investment credit would not provide benefits that are greater than immediate expensing. The investment credit would be 10 percent for all new equipment with a life of more than one year. Like the Senate Finance Committee bill, President Carter proposed that taxpayers would not need to establish separate accounts for each year. Instead, all assets purchased—new or used—would be added to one open-ended account for each class. The number of asset classes would be reduced to 30 (compared to 130 classes under the ADR system). Most taxpayers would use only two accounts for machinery and equipment, one for common assets (vehicles and office furniture) and the other for equipment classified by industry (such as agriculture, construction, utilities, and various categories of manufacturing). A single depreciation rate for each class would replace the need to choose useful life and methods. The constant rate depreciation system would apply to industrial and commercial real estate. A separate account would be established for each building.

Compared to the Finance Committee bill, President Carter's proposal would provide about the same amount of acceleration of tax depreciation.[9] The Carter proposal would cost less in the earlier years than the Senate Finance Committee bill, but more in the later years. A part of the explanation for this is that for short-lived assets the Carter proposal would increase the investment tax credit to 10 percent and not accelerate depreciation much. In contrast, the Senate Finance Committee bill would accelerate depreciation for short-lived assets and offset this by actually cutting back on the investment tax credit. The combination of more depreciation and less investment credit in the Finance Committee bill costs more in the early years and less in the later years. Also, the Finance Committee bill would permit taxpayers to elect to expense up to $25,000 of investment each year. This feature has a high short-run revenue cost.

Both the Senate Finance Committee bill and the Carter proposal would require open-ended accounts—the key to significant simplification. The Finance Committee bill would be considerably more complex because of the elections that taxpayers are permitted to make. Under the Carter proposal, taxpayers would be required to place assets into a particular open-ended account, and only one rate of depreciation would be used in computing the allowable depreciation on that account.

Finally, the Carter proposal would be more evenhanded across industries since the 130 ADR classes would not be compressed into just 4 asset classes (excluding public utility property). Although this proposal would maintain 30 classes, most taxpayers would only use 2 classes. The number of classes, however, is not the source of complexity in a depreciation proposal. Complexity comes from vintage accounts and taxpayer elections requiring complicated calculations to determine what maximizes the tax savings from capital recovery.

The First Year Capital Recovery System

The most novel approach to revision of tax depreciation is that suggested by Auerbach and Jorgenson.[10] Under their proposal, taxpayers would deduct the present value of economic depreciation as an expense in the year an asset is acquired. The Auerbach-Jorgenson proposal would make capital recovery invariant to the rate of inflation since the deduction for capital recovery would be taken the same year that the asset is acquired.

The Auerbach-Jorgenson approach has received some interest on Capitol Hill, but it has not been endorsed by either the business community or the Carter administration. Though I find the Auerbach-Jorgenson approach quite intriguing, there are four problems with it. First, the revenue cost of the proposal is bunched in the first year, and there is no way to phase in the proposal without favoring certain industries or providing incentives for delaying investment. Second, it is not clear that one wants to, in effect, index depreciation for inflation if other aspects of the tax system are not also indexed. The third problem with the Auerbach-Jorgenson approach is that smaller, relatively unsophisticated businesses will not understand why when $100 is paid for a machine only $80 can be deducted. Fourth, as originally presented by Auerbach and Jorgenson, the first-year capital recovery system would replace not only the ADR system of depreciation but also the investment tax credit. In present value terms, the Auerbach-Jorgenson proposal would not increase the present value of the tax savings from capital recovery, given moderate rates of inflation. Although this fourth problem is not inherent in the Auerbach-Jorgenson approach, it is unlikely that the business community will sign on to this approach unless it is liberalized to provide a greater tax savings than that permitted under current law.

An Evenhanded or Neutral Incentive

The Carter administration, as indicated previously, criticized the 10-5-3 proposal as tilting too much toward long-lived assets, particularly public utilities and real estate. Given the tax shelter potentials of the 10-5-3 proposal, the Finance Committee agreed that all machinery and equipment should not be depreciated over the same period and that buildings should not be treated as generously as under the 10-5-3 proposal.

There has, however, been little discussion as to just what would be an evenhanded or neutral depreciation change with respect to short- and long-lived assets. The Senate Finance Committee bill was fashioned so that the combination of accelerated depreciation and the investment tax credit would not be better than expensing. This required a reduction in the investment tax credit for the machinery and equipment in the two-year and four-year asset classes.

Although there are a number of possible measures of the economic impact of depreciation and investment tax credit changes, at Treasury four alternative measures have been used:

The percentage increase in the present value of the tax savings from depreciation plus the investment tax credit.

The percentage reduction in the rental cost of capital.

The percentage increase in the after-tax rate of return.

The effective tax rate on capital income.

Of these four measures, the first is clearly the easiest to compute. Although an equal percentage increase in the present value of tax savings from capital recovery may have some intuitive appeal as a criterion for neutrality, economic theory gives no underpinning for this measure. The other three measures can only be computed if assumptions are made regarding the taxpayer's marginal tax rate, the rate of return or discount rate, and actual or economic depreciation. The best estimates of economic depreciation are those of Hulten and Wykoff; namely, that economic depreciation is approximated by 165 percent declining balance depreciation, assuming the tax life is the mean asset life used by BEA.[11]

On theoretical grounds, a proportionate reduction in the rental cost of capital is probably not evenhanded between long-lived and short-lived assets. In the short run, it will tend to favor short-lived assets because these assets experience more depreciation per unit of rental cost than long-lived assets. If the price of a 1-year asset and a 5-year asset and a 50-year asset are all reduced by the same proportionate amount, businesses will purchase relatively more of the 1-year asset and relatively less of the 50-year asset.

Economic theory suggests that investment occurs at the margin until after-tax rates of return of alternative investment are equalized. Therefore, any incentive which increases the after-tax rate of return more for some investments will induce a shift toward those investments with the higher after-tax rates of return. This suggests that a neutral depreciation or investment tax credit should increase proportionately the after-tax rate of return of long- and short-lived assets.

An increase in the after-tax rate of return on all assets would increase the demand for capital services. As the quantity of capital increases, the marginal product of capital falls and the after-tax rate of return also falls. If one assumes that in the long run the equilibrium after-tax rate of return remains unchanged, then one can compute the effective tax rate on short-lived and long-lived assets.

The percentage increase in the after-tax rate of return is a measure of the initial impact of a change in depreciation. The effective tax rate is a long-run measure after investment has occurred and rates of return have been restored. I would conclude that these are the best two criteria for judging evenhandedness or neutrality. But, as indicated above, the one difficulty with these measures is that they require estimates of actual or economic depreciation.

Real Estate

In 1969 when Congress cut back on accelerated depreciation for real estate, Congress favored residential rental real estate over commercial or industrial real estate. Times have changed. All the major depreciation proposals under consideration do not apply to residential rental real estate. Instead Congress is likely to increase the capital recovery permitted on commercial and industrial real estate relative to that permitted on residential real estate.

Although the Carter administration was quite critical of the 10-5-3 proposal as being too generous for real estate, some have suggested that current law discriminates against real estate. Real estate, except a qualified rehabilitation, is denied the investment tax credit. Also, in times of rapid inflation, depreciation based on historic costs may be less and less realistic, particularly for long-lived assets. Economists ought to provide some guidance to the administration and Congress regarding the appropriate amount of acceleration of real estate compared to machinery and equipment.

Conclusion

I have no doubt posed more questions than I have answered. The papers at this conference should help us answer some of the crucial questions of depreciation policy.

What should be the goal of depreciation policy?

If we want to increase investment incentives, how do we do it in an evenhanded or neutral manner?

Can we measure economic depreciation in order to tell whether tax depreciation provides a neutral incentive for investment?

Does current law favor or discriminate against real estate? In making this determination does it matter that real estate investments are typically more leveraged than investments in machinery and equipment?

Are there trade-offs between simplicity and fairness?

What impact will depreciation proposals have on equipment leasing? How many companies will be made nontaxable?

TAX TREATMENT OF DEPRECIATION, CAPITAL GAINS, AND INTEREST IN AN INFLATIONARY ECONOMY

Robert E. Hall

Introduction

Inflation complicates the measurement of capital income for tax purposes. Tax laws are written in terms of the U.S. dollar, not an abstract currency of constant purchasing power. Though my assignment is to discuss the definition and tax treatment of depreciation, I find I cannot write sensibly without bringing in the measurement and taxation of capital gains and interest as well. Depreciation, after all, is the supposed decline in value of assets as time goes by, yet current dollar prices of most assets today are rising, not falling. Nonetheless, depreciation is a genuine economic phenomenon requiring recognition by the tax laws. But capital gains and inflation-swollen nominal interest rates have their own, closely related issues for taxation.

This paper examines the taxation of the two most significant types of transactions between corporations and savers in the United States. In the

[The author is professor of economics, Department of Economics, and senior fellow of the Hoover Institution, Stanford University. The author thanks Alan Auerbach and Dale Jorgenson for helpful comments at an early stage in this work and Don Fullerton for extremely helpful discussion of the first draft. All opinions expressed are the author's alone.]

first, an individual places savings in the hands of a corporation for the purpose of investment through the purchase of an equity share. The returns are taxed twice, once under the corporate income tax and again under the personal income tax when the individual receives dividends and capital gains. In line with the evidence on the typical owner of common stocks, the individual is assumed to be in the 40 percent marginal bracket for ordinary income. In the second type of transaction, the savings are made available through the purchase of corporate debt. Because interest payments are deductible under the corporate income tax, the corporate tax actually subsidizes the return to investment financed in this way. I further assume that the debt is held by an individual in such a way as to face low marginal rates under the personal income tax. Pension funds are an example of the mode of ownership of debt that I have in mind.

Even without inflation, the taxation of these transactions differs strikingly. The effective corporate rate on equity-financed investments in the more favorably-treated assets, equipment and intangibles, is roughly zero with stable prices. Equity-financed investment in plant, which receives no investment credit and limited benefit from fast depreciation, is taxed at an effective rate of 37 percent under the corporate tax. When the second round of taxation under the personal tax is added, total effective rates in the absence of inflation are 26 percent for equipment, 28 percent for intangibles, and 55 percent for plant. On the other hand, debt-financed investments in all three assets are heavily subsidized even under price stability—effective corporate tax rates are –89 percent for equipment, –85 percent for intangibles, and –16 percent for plant.

Under 10 percent annual inflation, the situation worsens dramatically. Taxation of equity-financed investment rises because of the adverse effect of historical-cost depreciation, while the subsidy of debt-financed investment rises because of the deductibility of the full nominal interest rate, including its inflation premium. Effective taxation of the earnings of equity-financed investment in equipment, plant, and intangibles under the combination of corporate and personal taxes with 10 percent inflation are 60, 65, and 28 percent respectively. Because the great bulk of corporate investment is financed from equity (mainly in the form of reinvestment of retained earnings), the high current rates of taxation of the returns to plant and equipment represent a worrisome disincentive. By contrast, incentives to invest in debt-financed assets are now absurdly excessive—effective tax rates at 10 percent inflation are –122 percent for equipment, –95 percent for plant, and –298 percent for intangibles.

Reform of depreciation rules is one way to solve the problem of excessive taxation of equity-financed investment under inflation. Indexing depreciation in one way or another and permitting depreciation at economic rates would reduce the effective rates of taxation of equity-financed equipment to 17 percent and of plant to 46 percent. Further, these would remain the effective tax rates if inflation subsides or worsens. Another, less desirable reform is to adopt depreciation schedules based on historical cost which are sufficiently rapid to overcome inflation. Something like the "10-5-3" proposal would reduce effective tax rates to 19 and 42 percent for equipment and structures at 10 percent inflation. But under this approach, depreciation lifetimes need to be changed every time the inflation rate changes. If inflation dropped to zero under the 10-5-3 system, the corporate income tax would wind up paying a 48 percent subsidy to the earnings of equipment. Adoption of 10-5-3 would make sense only if coupled with a policy of stabilizing inflation at 10 percent per year, something hardly anybody favors.

Reforming depreciation will not solve the problem of subsidies to debt-financed investment. Neither significantly shorter lifetimes for depreciation purposes nor the adoption of replacement-cost depreciation would alter the basic pattern of heavy incentives for leveraged investments. As long as an important segment of taxpayers face zero or low marginal tax rates under the personal income tax, deductibility of interest payments under the corporate income tax will create a subsidy for investments financed by borrowing from those taxpayers. We need to abolish the deductibility of interest and reduce the effective rate of taxation to a sensible level for all investments, independent of the method of financing. The tax system proposed by Alan Auerbach and Dale Jorgenson, where a first-year allowance takes the place of the stream of deductions associated with an investment, provides a convenient way to do this. The most desirable reform, in my view, is immediate expensing of all investment (as is done for intangibles today) and elimination of all deductions for interest and depreciation. With this approach, the corporate income tax would become a tax on gross cash flow less investment. The administration of such a tax would be far simpler and it would eliminate the current absurd heavy taxation of unleveraged plant and equipment and distortion in favor of debt-financed investment.

Definitions, Assumptions, and Analytic Technique

The analysis of capital taxation presented here appeared first in Hall and Jorgenson (1967); related aspects of the theory of depreciation appear in Hall (1968). The starting point is to consider the price of a capital good as a function of time, t, and age, a: $p(a, t)$. The price of new capital goods is established by their producers and is $p(0, t)$. Markets for used capital goods determine prices $p(a, t)$. As time passes, the price of a particular capital good changes. The total change can be decomposed into depreciation, $d(a, t)$, defined as the rate of decline of the price as age, a, increases, and capital gains, $f(a, t)$, defined as the rate of growth of the prices as time, t, increases (technically, these are the partial derivatives of p with respect to a and t). The pattern of depreciation can be inferred by comparing the prices of identical capital goods of different ages at the same time, as in Hall (1971) and Hulten and Wykoff (1981).

A central concept for what follows is the *rental price of capital goods*. Conceptually, it is the price charged by the owner to a renter who assumes responsibility for all operating and maintenance expenses. In the absence of taxes, the rental price bears a simple relation to the asset price: rental is the interest cost of the asset plus depreciation less capital gains:

$$c = np(a, t) + d(a, t) - f(a, t)$$

Here n is the firm's nominal cost of funds—the dollar compensation per year required by the stockholders and bondholders for each dollar tied up in the capital good. In a competitive rental market, this formula will describe the observed rental rate, where the owners are capturing their costs and no more. Further, as noted by Jorgenson (1963), the same expression appears in the analysis of the investment decision of a firm which chooses to own its capital. Such a firm should establish an internal rental price at this level and then push investment to the point where the marginal revenue product of capital equals its rental price.

Nothing will be lost in the ensuing discussion under the convenient simplifying assumption that both depreciation and inflation take place at smooth exponential rates, d and f, respectively, in which case the price of a capital good of age a at time t is

$$p(a, t) = p_0 e^{ft-da}$$

and depreciation and capital gains are simply proportional to the price:

$$d(a, t) = dp(a, t)$$

$$f(a, t) = fp(a, t)$$

This gives a simple expression for the rent,

$$c = (n + d - f)p$$

Generally, it will be convenient to deal with the rental-price ratio,

$$c/p = n + d - f.$$

For example, if the interest rate is 14 percent, depreciation is 10 percent per year, and capital goods prices are rising 11 percent per year, the rent is $.14 + .10 - .11 = .13$ dollars per dollar's worth of capital per year.

Taxation complicates the relation between capital goods prices, interest rates, and the rental price. First, I will assume that the gross earnings of capital are taxed at a rate u. This is the statutory marginal tax rate, currently 46 percent for most corporations.

Second, the law may impose taxation on the capital gains earned by a capital good. Under current U.S. law, capital gains are taxed only at realization, and, for individuals, at reduced rates. Taxation at realization is effectively a turnover tax; capital goods held until they are retired escape taxation for capital gains altogether. I will assume that capital goods are held long enough to make the capital gains tax irrelevant. I will not attempt to deal with the anomalies in depreciation rules that may make it attractive to realize capital gains on real estate. All investment decisions studied in this paper are of the "buy and hold" type.

Third, the law provides for deductions for depreciation. Investors may deduct the dollar amount of the original cost of a capital good according to a schedule defined in the law. For almost all assets, the schedule understates the number of years over which the decline in value actually takes place—lifetimes for tax purposes are shorter than true lifetimes. On the other hand, after the first year, the permissible depreciation deduction is depressed by the use of historical rather than market prices. Depreciation for tax purposes sums to the original purchase price, while actual depreciation sums to a much larger number at current rates of inflation. This feature of the tax system has been emphasized in most discussions of the harmful effect of inflation on the incentives to invest (which have concentrated on the case of equity financing); the implications of deductibility of interest are shown in this paper to be even more important for debt-financed investment.

Finally, the current tax law provides a tax credit for investment in equipment at a rate of 10 percent. Its effect is essentially to reduce the price of equipment by 10 percent and so reduce its rental price in proportion. However, the effect of the credit is somewhat stronger because the cost basis for depreciation is not reduced by the amount of the credit.

To quantify these various provisions, it will be convenient to let $V(x)$ be the present value at real discount rate r of a stream of income that starts this year at \$1 and grows in nominal terms at annual rate x. The growth rate x should include the influence (if any) of inflation on the stream. Plainly, $V(x) = 1/(r - x + f)$, where f is the expected rate of inflation.

The strategy of this analysis rests on the principle that market forces will equate the price of a new capital good to the present discounted value of its future rental earnings less the present value of taxes plus the present value of deductions and credits. This is a condition of long-run equilibrium and will only hold after enough time has passed for investment to drive the rental price of capital to the market-clearing level. If capital goods prices are rising at rate f, then rental prices will be rising at the same rate. The rate of growth of the earnings of a particular capital good is $f - d$, so the present value of all its earnings is $cV(f - d)$, where c is the current rental price. In case the law is reformed so that some fraction, g, of capital gains is taxed on an accrual basis, I will include the term $ugfpV(f - d)$ as the present value of capital gains taxes. I assume that the law provides for an exponential pattern of depreciation (so-called declining balance depreciation, but without any switchover to other formulas) at a rate d'. Further, to evaluate reforms that would index depreciation to replacement cost, I let f' be the rate of growth of depreciation deductions permitted to account for inflation ($f' = 0$ for the current historical cost basis and $f' = f$ for fully indexed depreciation). Thus the present value of depreciation deductions is $ud'pV(f' - d')$. Finally, I let k be the rate of the investment tax credit, which adds a term kp to the value of earnings and tax effects but also reduces the amount of capital tied up in the investment by a factor of $1 - k$.

The relation between the price of a new capital good and the various components of its returns, after taxes, is

$$p = (1 - u)cV(f - d) - ugf(1 - k)pV(f - d) + ud'pV(f' - d') + kp$$

Inserting the formula for V( ) and solving for the rental-price ratio, c/p, gives

$$c/p = \frac{(1 - k)}{1 - u}r + \frac{ug(1 - k)}{1 - u}f + \frac{1 - k}{1 - u}d$$
$$- u\frac{(r + d)}{(1 - u)(r + f - f' + d')}d'$$

Most of the rest of the paper is devoted to manipulation of this formula. Rising inflation brings about very different shifts in the rental-price ratio for assets with different tax treatments.

The rental formula tells us the equilibrium rental earnings of capital given the real after-tax interest rate, r, the rate of inflation, f, and the various parameters of the tax system. It can be put to use to compute the effective rate of taxation of capital income under the U.S. tax system. Here it is essential to distinguish between the tax rate imposed by the system in a given state of the economy and the effect of taxes on the general equilibrium of the economy. The apparatus of this paper can only do the first.

The conceptual basis for the measurement of tax rates is the following. Consider an economy in which corporations and households are in financial equilibrium. Corporations have equated the real, after-tax yields of all investments and borrowing opportunities to a common value, r. Each household has equated the real, after-tax yields for all of its opportunities to a common value, h. The household rate, h, differs from the corporate rate, r, because of the taxation of income flows between corporations and individuals. Different households have different values of h. The analysis of how the economy reaches this kind of equilibrium, and, indeed, whether it truly is in equilibrium, is the subject of much current controversy in finance theory but is not the subject of this paper.

In this setup, suppose first that a household provides one dollar of its wealth to a corporation through the purchase of equity, and the corporation invests in one or another productive asset. This asset earns the equilibrium after-tax return, r. It incurs corporate income taxes, y_c, in the amount

$$y_c = c/p - d - r \quad ;$$

this says that taxes are the only source of discrepancy between the earnings of capital net of depreciation, $c/p - d$, and the after-tax return, r. I define the effective corporate income tax rate in this case as $y_c/(c/p - d)$.

Corporate equity income is taxed again when it is paid to the household. I will assume that half of the income is paid as dividends and half as capital gains. The effective rate of personal taxation is an equally weighted average of the marginal tax rate for ordinary income and the rate for capital gains (here I ignore the extra taxation of capital gains arising from the taxation of nominal rather than real gains; the practical effect of this feature of the tax law is surprisingly small at current rates of inflation). Net of taxes, the household earns its return h. Thus the total tax from both corporate and personal taxes is

$$y = c/p - d - h \quad .$$

I define the total effective tax rate as $y/(c/p - d)$.

Now suppose that a household provides one dollar of its wealth to a corporation through the purchase of debt. The amount of the corporate income tax paid is drastically reduced because the corporations' interest payments are deductible. Further, when inflation has put a premium into nominal interest rates, this premium is deductible. On the other hand, the full nominal interest rate is taxable under the personal income tax. For a taxpayer whose marginal rate under the personal income tax equals the marginal corporate rate, the deduction and taxation of the inflation premium wash out. But the interesting and relevant case is where the individual has a much lower marginal tax rate than does the corporation. In this case, the corporate income tax provides an astonishingly large subsidy. The analytical details and computations are provided together in a later section of the paper.

The tax rates on debt and equity measure the amount of tax incurred when a household forgoes a dollar's worth of consumption and all of the resources are put into a productive asset. They are the relevant rates for appraising the distorting effect of taxation on the savings-consumption choice. Under inflation, effective tax rates on equity have risen, thanks mainly to historical-cost depreciation. But effective rates on debt owned by taxpayers with low marginal tax rates have fallen to extremely negative levels. The tax system as a whole functions to tax investments financed by equity in order to subsidize those financed by debt. This inefficiency clearly needs reform.

Taxation of Equity-Financed Capital under Current Laws

The relevant features of current tax laws for corporations are as follows:

1. Accrued capital gains are never taxed. Because the rational corporation avoids realizing capital gains, I will assume that all gains escape taxation.

2. Depreciation is on the basis of historical cost, so the parameter f′ is zero. I will use actual depreciation rates of 10 percent per year for equipment and 3 percent per year for structures (d = 0.1 and 0.03, respectively). I assume that allowable depreciation rates for tax purposes are half again the economic rate for equipment and twice the economic rate for structures (d′ = 0.15 and 0.06, respectively). For intangible investments, I assume actual depreciation at a rate of 10 percent per year, while the law permits expensing (d = 0.1 and d′ = infinity).

3. An investment tax credit at a rate of 10 percent is provided for equipment only.

Table 1 presents results on the effective taxation of three equity-financed investments under current tax laws at two rates of inflation: zero and 10 percent. I have taken the real after-tax yield and borrowing cost, r, as 4 percent to approximate the measured after-tax earnings of capital. The effective tax rates in the table are quite sensitive to the assumption about r—for lower values, the negative rates are even more negative and the positive ones are even more positive.

The low-inflation rows of table 1 show serious problems in the taxation of capital even without inflation. The corporate income tax subsidizes the return to equipment slightly—the subsidy arises from the combination of depreciation rates in excess of economic depreciation and the investment credit. Intangible investments escape tax or subsidy. Plant, however, is taxed at an effective rate of 37 percent, not too far below the statutory rate of 46 percent. The only factor depressing the effective rate of taxation of plant below the statutory rate is depreciation at 6 percent instead of the

TABLE 1

RENTS AND EFFECTIVE TAX RATES UNDER EXISTING TAX LAWS FOR
INVESTMENT FINANCED BY SELLING EQUITY TO A TAXPAYER IN THE
40 PERCENT BRACKET

ASSET	IN-FLATION	RENTAL ($ PER $ OF CAP-ITAL PER YEAR)	EFFECTIVE TAX RATE (PERCENTAGE)		ASSUMPTIONS		
			Cor-porate	Total	d	d'	k
Equipment	low	0.139	−2	26	.10	.15	.1
	high	0.172	44	60			
Plant	low	0.094	37	55	.03	.06	0
	high	0.112	51	65			
Intangibles	low	0.140	0	28	.10	*	0
	high	0.140	0	28			

NOTE- * means infinite depreciation—expensing of investment.
Low inflation is zero rate.
High inflation is 10 percent rate.
Marginal tax rates are 46 percent for corporate and 28 percent for personal (average of 40 percent on ordinary income and 16 percent on capital gains).

economic rate of 3 percent, and the extra three percentage points are not too important. If inflation were to end today and all the existing provisions for the taxation of capital were to remain, all of the revenue from the corporate income tax would come from the taxation of plant and none from intangibles or equipment. The tax would seriously distort investment decisions away from plant.

Total taxation of the return to capital under both taxes with zero inflation is 26 and 28 percent for equipment and intangibles, and 55 percent for plant. The latter figure represents a serious wedge in consumption-investment decisions.

The high-inflation rows of table 1 show that taxation of capital becomes even more perverse when prices are rising at a 10 percent annual rate. Effective tax rates under the corporate tax are 44 percent on equipment and 51 percent on plant—the adverse effect of historical-cost depreciation is responsible for the rise. Corporate investments in intangibles still escape taxation—instant write-off means that inflation has no depressing effect on the value of depreciation. Total effective tax rates under the corporate and personal taxes are clearly worrisome: 60 percent for equipment and 65 percent for plant. Only intangibles are taxed at reasonable total rates under 10 percent inflation.

Depreciation Reform

By now it is widely known that the central problem with the depreciation provisions of the U.S. tax law is the use of historical rather than replacement cost as the basis for depreciation. Martin Feldstein (1979) has proposed the enlargement of depreciation deductions in line with the movements of official indexes of replacement costs. Alan Auerbach and Dale Jorgenson (1980) have proposed a reform in which the stream of deductions at replacement cost is restated as a first-year deduction with the same present value. The two proposals are economically equivalent; the choice between them is a matter of administrative convenience and political judgment about the transitory decline in revenue accompanying the shift to the first-year recovery system. This decline has no economic significance to the federal government—the present value of revenue is the same under the two proposals. I find Auerbach and Jorgenson's proposal much preferable on administrative grounds. In any case, the economic analysis given here treats the two proposals as equivalent and refers to them as indexed depreciation. In terms of the earlier formula for the rental price of capital, indexed depreciation has the rate of inflation embodied in depreciation rules, f ′, equal to the actual rate of inflation, f. Furthermore, because indexing accomplishes more effectively what the government has been trying to do rather crudely by permitting faster depreciation, it seems appropriate to examine the joint effects of indexing depreciation and using economic depreciation rates. For this reason, I will use d ′ = d in the analysis as well.

As table 2 shows, indexing makes the effective corporate tax rate independent of the rate of inflation. For plant, the rate is exactly the statutory rate of 46 percent; for equipment, it is rather less, 17 percent, because of the investment tax credit. Were inflation to come to an end under current tax provisions, tax rates would be lower for both plant and equipment than they would be with indexed economic depreciation.

Table 2 shows only the effective corporate rates under indexing. The total effective rates including the personal tax would be 40 percent for equipment and 61 percent for plant. Again, taxation at such a high rate for plant creates a very significant wedge. Depreciation reform alone would not solve the problem of excessive taxation of capital income, especially income from plant.

Accelerated Depreciation

There is considerable political impetus behind a number of proposals to raise the present value of depreciation deductions by further reducing lifetimes for tax purposes instead of indexing. Were we confident of the

TABLE 2

EFFECTS OF INDEXED ECONOMIC DEPRECIATION

ASSET	INFLATION	RENTAL		EFFECTIVE CORPORATE TAX RATE	
		Current	Indexed	Current	Indexed
Equipment	low	0.139	0.148	−2	17
	high	0.172	0.148	44	17
Plant	low	0.094	0.104	37	46
	high	0.112	0.104	51	46

NOTE: Assumptions are the same as in table 1.

continuation of inflation at a stable rate close to the current rate, then downward adjustment of lifetimes would be just as good as indexing depreciation to restore economically appropriate tax treatment of depreciation. But as a believer in the feasibility and desirability of ending inflation, I am reluctant to see a change made that will further contribute to the distortionary treatment of certain types of investment when inflation is controlled.

Table 3 indicates implications for rental and effective tax rates of a sharp acceleration of depreciation allowances. The depreciation rates are chosen to resemble the Conable-Jones 10-5-3 proposal—declining-balance depreciation rates of 33 percent per year for equipment (to approximate a 5-year lifetime) and 15 percent per year for buildings (to approximate a 10-year lifetime). Needless to say, accelerated depreciation on this scale would dramatically lower effective tax rates. At current rates of inflation, effective corporate tax rates would be almost exactly the same as with indexed economic depreciation—19 percent for equipment and 42 percent for plant. Again, the tax system would be biased in favor of equipment because of the investment credit, but the acceleration of depreciation would accomplish its task of offsetting the adverse consequences of inflation.

Table 3 shows that ending inflation would bring a substantial subsidy to income from equipment, if accelerated depreciation and all the other features of the tax system assumed in the table remained. The effective

TABLE 3

IMPLICATIONS OF ACCELERATED DEPRECIATION AT ZERO
AND TEN PERCENT INFLATION

ASSET	INFLATION	RENTAL		EFFECTIVE CORPORATE TAX RATE	
		Current	Accelerated Depreciation	Current	Accelerated Depreciation
Equipment	low	0.139	0.127	−2	−48
	high	0.172	0.150	44	19
Plant	low	0.094	0.083	37	24
	high	0.112	0.099	51	42

NOTE: Assumptions are the same as in table 1.

corporate rate would be -48 percent, and even after positive taxation under the personal tax, the total effective rate would be -7 percent. There is no good economic case for subsidizing the return to equipment in this way. If accelerated depreciation is adopted to offset the adverse effects of inflation, then it should be removed once inflation is brought under control.

Effective Tax Rates When Investment is Financed by Borrowing from an Untaxed Individual

The calculations presented so far apply to the bulk of investment by U.S. corporations, because most investment is financed from retained earnings, which amounts to the sale of equity to stockholders. But about 20 percent of the earnings of capital are paid out as interest, and a large fraction of this flows to individuals and institutions with zero or low tax rates. As this section will demonstrate, inflation has dramatically influenced the taxation of this type of investment, so that it is now heavily subsidized. Much of the worst distortions in the current tax system for capital income arise from the deductibility of full nominal interest payments under the corporate income tax, when the corresponding interest receipts escape taxation altogether or are taxed at low rates.

In this section I consider the case of a corporation in exactly the same equilibrium considered earlier, which finances a \$1 increment in capital by selling a bond to an untaxed individual. Recall that the firm has a real, after-tax return of r. Let the nominal interest rate on the bond be n. Because the full amount of the nominal interest is deductible, the equilibrium condition relating r and n is

$$r = (1 - u)n - f \quad .$$

Solving for the nominal interest rate gives

$$n = (r + f)/(1 - u) \quad .$$

In the earlier case, the corporation paid taxes of $c/p - d - r$. It still pays this amount, but it receives a deduction for n. Net taxes are $c/p - d - r - un = c/p - d - (n - f)$. The effective corporate tax rate is this amount divided by $c/p - d$. No individual income tax is paid, so the effective corporate rate is the effective total rate as well.

TABLE 4

RENTS AND EFFECTIVE TAX RATES UNDER EXISTING TAX LAWS FOR
INVESTMENT FINANCED BY SELLING DEBT TO AN UNTAXED INDIVIDUAL

ASSET	INFLATION	RENTAL ($ PER $ OF CAPITAL PER YEAR)	EFFECTIVE TAX RATE (PER-CENTAGE)	ASSUMPTIONS		
				d	d '	k
Equipment	low	0.139	−89	.10	.15	.1
	high	0.172	−122			
Plant	low	0.094	−16	.03	.06	0
	high	0.112	−95			
Intangibles	low	0.140	−85	.10	*	0
	high	0.140	−298			

NOTE: The assumptions are the same as in table 1.

Table 4 shows the effective tax rates derived from these calculations. In all cases, tax rates are negative and subsidies are being paid. Even without inflation, equipment and intangibles are subsidized at rates in excess of 80 percent. Recall that both had effective corporate rates of close to zero even when the return to the individual was not deductible to the corporation. The rate of interest paid on the debt is nearly twice the after-tax return earned by the corporation (4 percent), so permitting its deduction amounts to a subsidy of close to 100 percent. Even in the case of plant, which is heavily taxed under zero inflation with equity financing, effective taxation is negative with debt financing.

Inflation worsens the inefficient subsidies. At 10 percent inflation, equipment is subsidized at 122 percent, plant at 95 percent, and intangibles at an outrageous 298 percent. The last figure has the following interpretation: for each dollar received as interest by the untaxed lender to a corporation investing in intangibles, 75 cents is paid by the taxpayers as a subsidy through the corporate income tax and 25 cents is the earnings of the investment itself.

The computations overstate the magnitude of the subsidy to debt-financed investments for two reasons. First, not every owner of a corporate bond is literally untaxed. Many bonds are held by pension funds on behalf of present and future retirees who will be paying some income tax on the retirement benefits when they are eventually paid. Still, the typical marginal income tax rate of the retired is far below the statutory corporate marginal rate of 46 percent, so a substantial element of subsidy is involved in any loan from a retirement fund to a corporation.

Second, nominal interest rates have consistently been far below the level predicted by the equilibrium condition. With zero inflation and 4 percent after-tax return to corporations, bond rates should be around 8 percent. In fact, they were close to 4 percent in the 1950s, the most recent experience with zero inflation. With current inflation of 10 percent and the same 4 percent after-tax real return to corporations, nominal corporate bond rates should be around 25 percent. Again, actual rates have been about half this level. Bond-financed investments have indeed been heavily subsidized, but half of the subsidy has come from the lender, not the federal government. Even so, the government subsidy through the corporate income tax has been substantial. The tax treatment of interest and the disparity between the corporate marginal rate of 46 percent and the much lower rate imposed on lenders creates a major inefficiency.

Low levels of bond interest rates in the U.S. seem to stem from a general reluctance on the part of corporations to make leveraged investments. The equilibrium condition fails because firms do not pursue debt financing anywhere near as aggressively as the conditions calls for. But certain types of investment are typically leveraged at rates of close to 100 percent. These include highly fungible assets like airplanes, office buildings, and apartments. These investments are thus very substantially subsidized by the combination of favorable tax treatment and low nominal interest rates. When a pension fund finances an apartment complex with a 14 percent mortgage, much of the return comes from the value of the interest deduction to the owners of the complex (whether corporate or individual) and the failure to recapture much of the return through taxation of the interest receipts.

Moves to reduce the excessive current taxation of equity-financed investment are likely to worsen the inefficient subsidy of leveraged investment. Accelerated or indexed depreciation will only further raise the tax incentive to invest in those types of assets where leverage is customary and only worsen our over-supply of these assets.

How to Avoid Subsidizing Leveraged Investments

Consider the following provisions of a revised tax law: (1) indexed depreciation at the economic rate ($f' = f$ and $d' = d$); (2) no investment credit (k = 0); (3) taxation of accrued capital gains (g = 1). Then the taxes imposed upon capital (not counting interest deduction) are

$$c/p - d - r = \frac{u}{1 - u} (r + f)$$

This is exactly the amount of the interest deduction, so the effective corporate income tax rate is zero under accrual taxation of capital gains. Thus one solution to the problem of current heavy subsidies of debt-financed investment is to abolish the investment credit, use indexed economic depreciation, and fully tax accrued capital gains. Together these would raise effective tax rates to zero.

A solution to the subsidy of leveraged investment based on accrual taxation of capital gains is both undesirable and impractical. It is inappropriate for equity-financed investment or investment financed by selling debt to taxpayers. It is administratively impractical because it rests on asset valuations not obtained from actual market transactions. There seems little potential role for capital gains taxation under the corporate income tax.

An alternative approach seems much more promising based on Auerbach and Jorgenson's proposed streamlining of the corporate income tax with a first-year capital recovery allowance extended to cover interest deductions for leveraged investments as well as depreciation. In this way the corporate income tax could be reformed to impose the same effective tax rate at all rates of inflation, all rates of depreciation, and all degrees of leverage. Auerbach and Jorgenson's original proposal accomplishes the first two but not the third.

If depreciation deductions and the investment credit are eliminated and a first-year allowance, a, is introduced, the equilibrium relation between the real rental rate and its determinants becomes

$$c/p = \frac{1 - ua}{1 - u} (r + d)$$

The effective corporate tax rate is

$$v = \frac{u(1 - a) (r + d)}{(1 - ua)r + u(1 - a)d}$$

The formula for the allowance, a, that equates the effective tax rate, v, for all assets is

$$a = \frac{(u - v)r + u(1 - v)d}{u(1 - v)(r + d)}$$

If the effective rate is to be equal to the statutory rate ($u = v$), then this formula simplifies to

$$a = \frac{d}{r + d}$$

which is simply the present value of indexed economic depreciation. To achieve an effective rate of taxation which is comparable to current rates with some leveraging of investment, an effective rate somewhat below the statutory rate would be appropriate. For example, to achieve an effective rate of 35 percent for equipment with $d = 0.1$, use $a = 0.82$, as against a $= 0.71$ for economic depreciation and an effective rate of 46 percent. For structures with $d = 0.03$, use $a = 0.64$ instead of $a = 0.43$. In other words, denial of interest deductions ought to be coupled with a somewhat more generous first-year allowance than the one proposed by Auerbach and Jorgenson, else an actual increase in capital taxation will occur.

This proposal would eliminate the highly inefficient subsidy currently paid for leveraged investments. An even simpler proposal is to grant a first-year allowance in the full amount of the investment, in which case the corporate income tax would be a tax on gross cash flow less investment. Plant and equipment would be treated in the same way as intangibles. Of course, the effective rate of taxation under this proposal is zero; the corporate income tax would be a tax on pure rents earned by the corporation. In the steady state, the contribution of such a tax to total federal revenue would be small.

Though this is a paper about corporate taxation, I cannot help mentioning that no comparable reform of the provisions of the personal income tax for the treatment of capital is possible. Denial of interest deductions for investment is meaningless as long as interest earnings are taxed. All of the absurd subsidies identified in this paper are available to the individual investor who finances a business investment by borrowing from an untaxed individual. Permitting expensing of investment without eliminating deductibility of interest would only further increase the subsidy. The necessary reform is the abolition of the taxation of interest and other earnings of capital. This step is justifiable only if the consumption financed by capital income can be taxed with a suitable consumption tax.

To summarize, two items should be high on the tax reform agenda, improvement of depreciation through some kind of recognition of current replacement cost or its equivalent, and elimination of interest deductions together with a compensating increase in first-year allowances or tax credit. As it stands, we impose much too high taxes on the bulk of corporate income and use part of the proceeds to subsidize leveraged investments.

REFERENCES

Auerbach, Alan J., and Dale W. Jorgenson. 1980. "Inflation-Proof Depreciation of Assets." *Harvard Business Review* (September–October): 113–118.

Feldstein, Martin. 1979. "Adjusting Depreciation in an Inflationary Economy: Indexing versus Acceleration." Discussion Paper no. 731, December, Harvard Institute for Economic Research (processed).

Hall, Robert E. 1968. "Technical Change and Capital from the Point of View of the Dual." *Review of Economic Studies* 35 (January): 35–46.

_____. 1971. "The Measurement of Quality Change from Vintage Price Data." In Zvi Griliches. ed. *Price Indexes and Quality Change.* Harvard University Press, pp. 240–71.

_____., and Dale W. Jorgenson. "Tax Policy and Investment Behavior." 1967. *American Economic Review* 57 (June): 391–414.

Jorgenson, Dale W. 1963. "Capital Theory and Investment Behavior." *American Economic Review Papers and Proceedings* 53 (May): 247–259.

Hulten, Charles R., and Frank C. Wykoff. 1981. "The Estimation of Economic Depreciation Using Vintage Asset Prices: An Application of the Box-Cox Power Transformation." *Journal of Econometrics,* forthcoming.

Discussion of Robert E. Hall, "Tax Treatment of Depreciation, Capital Gains, and Interest in an Inflationary Economy"

John Kendrick, Discussant

Before commenting on Professor Hall's paper I would like to make a few general remarks on the theme of this session, taking off from part II of the Hulten-Wykoff paper. When we speak of the *physical* efficiency or productivity of fixed capital I interpret this as a relationship between the real gross capital stock in use (valued by prices of the capital goods in a base period, or what it would have cost to produce the goods at base period prices and technology) and the physical volume of output produced, or the potential output at full utilization, valued at base-period prices. The relationship is obviously not purely physical, in that relative prices and the economic lives of capital goods are economic variables. But we can even dispense with relative prices in looking at one capital good, a machine, producing one output. Here I believe that the one-horse-shay analogy is applicable. Given adequate maintenance and repair, the machine should continue to have much the same output-producing capacity throughout its economic life. As it ages, the physical efficiency may decline a little, if more down-time for maintenance and repair is required. For an aggregation of capital goods, I would expect that aggregate output at full capacity would closely parallel the movements of the real gross capital stock, in the absence of technological change. With capital cost-reducing innovations the output would rise in relation to the real stock, indicating an increase in capital productivity.

In current value terms the picture is quite different. From the revenues derived from output sales must be deducted the labor compensation, intermediate purchases, and other operating costs to obtain the net capital income before interest

---

[The author is professor of economics, The George Washington University.]

and depreciation. Given technological progress, the net income produced by a given capital good declines primarily because productivity advances increase costs in relation to prices of the outputs. To this may be added some possible increases in repair and maintenance costs as particular capital goods age. Hulten and Wykoff's efficiency index reflects these phenomena and is thus based on an economic rather than a physical efficiency concept.

Likewise, the value of capital goods is an economic concept, reflecting the estimated present values of the expected future net income streams on the demand side, and the supply schedules, reflecting production costs in the case of new capital goods. In equilibrium, the two are equal. As all authors agree, economic depreciation is the decline in the value of fixed capital goods as they age. The decline reflects both the decline in net income over the remaining lifetime of the goods, as affected by physical and technological forces, and the shortening of the future income expected from the capital goods as they age.

To me, the capital stock, net of depreciation, is meaningful only in terms of current values, not in constant dollars. For there is no physical counterpart of depreciation, which is a purely economic concept. The physical realities are numbers of capital goods at the beginning of accounting periods, additions through new investment and subtractions through retirements, which give the numbers at the end of the period. Thus, it is the real gross stocks and associated inputs that are relevant in productivity studies which are concerned with physical output-input relationships.

From an economic viewpoint, however, depreciation estimates are very important in deriving estimates of (net) national income as an approximation to the income which can be spent for consumption while maintaining capital intact. The latter phrase I interpret as referring to the net income producing capacity of capital—not the physical output-producing capacity. In this connection, the work of Hulten and Wykoff is very positive in providing the basis for improved depreciation estimates. But it must be recognized that at best depreciation formulas are stylized and the estimates conventional approximates to the economic reality—if only because they are based on past experience and cannot currently reflect accurately the future lifetime experiences of capital goods.

For this reason, I would like to see the national income and product accounts feature gross national income as the key aggregate on the factor cost side, together with corporate income gross of depreciation (and interest). As Jorgenson has pointed out, this also provides symmetry with labor compensation, which is likewise gross of depreciation—on human capital. The Ruggleses have made an intriguing suggestion that in addition to the deduction of interest paid on debt-financed capital, an imputed estimate of implicit interest on equity-financed capital should also be deducted from gross business income—in which case "pure profits" would tend to average around zero over a period of years. If net national income is to be shown as a subtotal, much more thought and statistical work needs to be given to the problem of measuring depreciation of human capital as a measure of the allowances needed to maintain the stock of human capital intact. I attempted such measures in my *Formation and Stocks of Total Capital* (National Bureau of Economic Research, 1976).

Finally, I agree with Hall that "true" economic lives should be used in calculating depreciation for tax purposes as well as for economic accounts, in order to avoid distorting investment decisions. If stimuli for investment are needed, they can be provided more directly than by jiggering depreciation rates. But I also believe that indexing of depreciation to replacement costs is desirable for both purposes.

To come to Professor Hall's paper, he has provided us with a clear exposition of the formula for the rental price of capital goods and its ratio to the asset price, in terms of which he analyzes the effect of the tax system, and possible tax modifications, on rents and on effective tax rates.

One might question some of the assumptions behind his analysis, such as the leverage ratios of 0.2 for corporations and 1.0 for individual investors, and the real interest rate of 4 percent. Nevertheless, I am inclined to accept the broad contours and conclusions of his analysis with respect to tax effects under low and high (10 percent) inflation—in particular, under high inflation, with respect to corporations "the heavy taxation of plant and equipment and heavy subsidy of leveraged investment and intangibles," and with respect to persons, the "even higher rates of capital subsidy" including buildings and equipment.

The subsidies on leveraged building investments by corporations and all tangible investments of individuals seem unnecessary. But a case can be made in favor of subsidizing intangible investments—primarily business research and development expenditures—in view of the externalities involved. Mansfield estimates that the social rate of return on innovations resulting from research and development average more than twice the private rates. However, the most disturbing of Hall's conclusions is the high effective tax rate on income from corporate investments in plant and equipment under high inflation. This must have contributed to the decline in rates of return from the mid-1960s to date, and the deceleration in growth of capital per worker, which contributed significantly to the productivity slowdown.

A case might also be made for certain tax sheltered investments, namely, oil and gas drilling partnerships, depending on the urgency with which one views the need to achieve greater energy interdependence. Although I would not generally defend tax-created distortions of investment incentives, I would not categorically oppose political intrusions into the operation of market forces in all cases.

In considering possible reforms of the tax system, Hall points out that indexing of depreciation at 10 percent inflation depresses effective tax rates on all assets to negative levels, given the assumed leverage ratios and current depreciation rates in excess of actual economic rates. He does agree with Martin Feldstein that when corporate and personal tax rates are combined, the deductibility of interest is offset by excessive taxation of nominal interest receipts by individuals. But he maintains that his analysis still correctly indicates the distortion of investment choices occasioned by the tax system.

Hall also points out that accelerated depreciation, modeled after the Jones-Conable 10-5-3 proposal, would also produce or accentuate negative tax rates except for a modest positive rate on income from corporate structures, given 10 percent inflation. But he likes acceleration even less than indexing, since it would contribute further to distortions at lower inflation rates (if such are achieved).

The first proposal Hall makes to avoid subsidizing leveraged investments, he concedes is impractical, since it involves accrual taxation of capital gains. His alternative proposal, extending Auerbach and Jorgenson's proposed first-year capital recovery allowance, is to include a deduction for the present value of interest as well as of depreciation, less the present value of accrued capital gains. It seems to me that this would also present difficult administrative problems.

More attractive is the proposal he mentions for basing the corporate income tax on gross cash flow less investment. The revenue from the tax would be greatly reduced, of course, and there would be phase-in problems. Also, as Hall points out, this would not eliminate the distortions arising from the provisions of the personal income tax. But could not personal investments in real income producing property not be subjected to the same treatment as corporate income—as if the individual investor were a corporation, required to report transfers of funds between his personal and real investment accounts?

Hall's ultimate solution is the abolition of the taxation of interest and other capital income, with replacement of income taxes by a comprehensive consumption tax. This appeals to me the most, less because the present system "subsidizes certain kinds of investment at outrageous rates," than because it subjects saving to double taxation—once on the income out of which saving is made, and again on the income from the investments into which savings flow (with some exceptions). There are problems, of course, with direct consumption taxes, or value added taxes, particularly with respect to building in at least rough progressivity. But if a progressive personal income tax is retained, with exemption of saving, this imposes horrendous accounting problems for individuals in estimating the allocation of their income between consumption and saving and for the IRS in verifying the allocations. Possibly a combination of an income tax, with exemptions of specific types of saving up to certain amounts, and a value added tax would be more workable.

These are the kinds of issues that the panel on policy initiatives to stimulate productivity will be grappling with this afternoon. But I hope they will not confine themselves to tax policy to stimulate saving and investment, even if the latter is construed broadly to include intangible investments in research and development, education, training, health, safety, and mobility. After all, there are many causes of productivity advance, and a program to promote productivity must be multi-faceted and include public investment polices, economic and social regulations, antitrust rules, labor policies, and policies to promote technology over and above the research and development effect. Elsewhere, I have presented and discussed around 100 policy options for promoting productivity (in *Agenda for Business and Higher Education*, American Council on Education, 1980).

INFLATION AND CORPORATE CAPITAL RECOVERY

Dale W. Jorgenson and Martin A. Sullivan

I. Introduction

The objective of this paper is to analyze the impact of inflation on capital recovery under the U.S. corporate income tax. Corporate tax payments depend on the statutory corporate tax rate. They also depend on capital consumption allowances, expensing of investments, investment tax credits, and the deductibility of interest. We refer to the tax rate actually paid as the effective tax rate. The common feature of tax systems leading to an efficient allocation of capital is that they result in the same effective tax rate for all assets.

One approach to the efficient allocation of capital among assets is to permit taxpayers to deduct the decline in the value of their assets with age in arriving at taxable income. The decline in the value of an asset with age

[Dale Jorgenson is Frederic Eaton Abbe Professor of Economics at Harvard University and Martin Sullivan is a senior at Harvard College. The authors are indebted to the American Council on Life Insurance for financial support of this research. We are grateful to Andrew Abel, Alan Auerbach, David Bradford, Cary Brown, Pat Corcoran, Dennis Cox, Lawrence Dildine, Barbara Fraumeni, Donald Fullerton, Jane Gravelle, Charles Hulten, Peter Merrill, John Musgrave, Leonard Sahling, Jerry Silverstein, William Sutton, James Wetzler, Kenneth Wertz, Frank Wykoff, and Allan Young for valuable advice and assistance. Any remaining deficiencies in this paper are the sole responsibilities of the authors.]

is called economic depreciation. Economic depreciation can be measured by observing the profile of prices corresponding to assets of different ages at a given point of time. A system of capital recovery enabling taxpayers to deduct economic depreciation would lead to income as a base for taxation and to an effective tax rate equal to the statutory rate for all assets.

An alternative approach to the efficient allocation of capital among assets is to allow taxpayers to deduct the actual cost of acquisition of assets in arriving at taxable income. In this approach the acquisition of assets would be treated in precisely the same way as other business expenses. However, income from capital in the form of interest, dividends, or retained earnings would not be deducted from income for tax purposes. This would have the effects of shifting the base for taxation from income to consumption and reducing the effective income tax rate to zero.

Deducting economic depreciation and expensing the cost of acquisition of assets could be combined without sacrificing efficiency. For example, a certain proportion of the net acquisition cost of assets could be expensed, while the remainder could be recovered through capital consumption allowances equal to economic depreciation. Combinations of these systems could lead to any effective tax rate between zero and the statutory tax rate. Although there are many ways to design a tax system that would lead to the same effective tax rate for all assets, the level of the effective tax rate can differ widely between the alternative systems.

To analyze the impact of inflation on the U.S. corporate income tax we first determine the effective tax rate for each type of asset for each year of the postwar period 1946-1980. Throughout this period the system of capital recovery has been based on the historical cost of an asset. Cost of acquisition provides the basis for the investment tax credit as an offset to tax liability. Historical cost also provides the basis for capital consumption allowances as a deduction from income for tax purposes. Finally, interest payments are also treated as a deduction from income under U.S. law.

Our most surprising finding is that for currently anticipated rates of inflation, which are among the highest of the postwar period, U.S. tax law results in effective corporate tax rates that are well below the statutory rate. This is due to the liberalization of capital consumption allowances during the postwar period and, most importantly, to the introduction of the investment tax credit. We also find that an increase in the rate of inflation for any given set of tax provisions results in higher effective tax rates on all corporate assets, while a decrease results in lower effective tax rates.

Our second major finding is that differences in effective tax rates among assets under the U.S. corporate income tax are very substantial.

Transfers of investment from lightly taxed assets to heavily taxed assets would result in large gains in future output with no sacrifice of consumption either now or in the future. Under current law the differences in effective tax rates among assets would increase with a decrease in the rate of inflation, thereby further reducing the efficiency of capital allocation.

We next consider the likely impact of two specific proposals for more rapid capital recovery:

1. The Reagan administration proposal, introduced by Congressmen Conable and Jones in 1979 and advanced in somewhat different form by President Reagan in 1981.

2. The Senate Finance Committee proposal, originally introduced by Senator Bentsen in 1980 and reintroduced by Senator Long in 1981.

The Reagan administration and Senate Finance Committee proposals involve accelerated capital recovery rather than economic depreciation or expensing of acquisition costs. More rapid recovery of the cost of acquiring assets would be permitted by substituting more generous formulas and shorter lifetimes for those employed under current law. In addition, the rate of the investment tax credit would be increased. The objective of these proposals is to reduce effective tax rates on all assets.

In addition to the two proposals listed above for revising tax provisions for capital recovery, we consider expensing the costs of acquisition of assets and deducting economic depreciation as potential approaches to capital recovery under the U.S. corporate income tax. For current law and for each of the two proposed changes, we determine the effective tax rate for each type of asset. Under economic depreciation the effective rate for all assets would be equal to the statutory tax rate, while under expensing the effective tax rate on all assets would be equal to zero.

We find that the U.S. corporate income tax provides capital consumption allowances for corporate investment as a whole that are in line with economic depreciation at currently anticipated rates of inflation. At these inflation rates the Reagan administration proposal would provide capital consumption allowances 33.6 percent in excess of economic depreciation. The Senate Finance Committee proposal would result in an excess of 27.5 percent.

At current rates of inflation the effective tax rate on new corporate investment under present law is 24 percent or a little over half the statutory rate of 46 percent, due mainly to the impact of the investment tax credit. The Senate Finance Committee proposals would reduce the effective tax rate on corporate investment to 13 percent or a little over one-fourth the statutory rate. Finally, the Reagan administration proposal would result in a negative effective tax rate for corporate investment.

Under the Reagan administration proposal the combination of very short asset lifetimes for tax purposes and an increase in the investment tax credit for some assets would imply that the corporate income tax would be replaced by a corporate income subsidy for depreciable assets. Tax deductions and credits for these assets would be available to "shelter" income from nondepreciable assets such as land, inventories, and financial claims. The negative effective tax rate under the Reagan proposal would rise to 46 percent at rates of inflation anticipated in 1966 and to 58 percent at rates of inflation anticipated in 1960.

The second issue we consider in analyzing the impact of inflation on capital recovery under present law and alternative proposals is differences in effective tax rates among assets. Under present U.S. tax law the difference between effective tax rates on equipment and structures is 16 percent at currently anticipated rates of inflation. Under the Reagan administration proposal this difference would widen to 36 percent. The gap for the Senate Finance Committee proposal would be 23 percent.

We conclude that differences in effective tax rates among assets under present U.S. tax law are substantial, even at the very high anticipated rates of inflation prevailing currently. These differences would increase with a decrease in the rate of inflation, reducing efficiency in the allocation of capital. The differences in effective rates would widen significantly under the Senate Finance Committee proposal and would widen even further under the Reagan administration proposal. Just as under present law, these gaps would increase with a decrease in the rate of inflation.

In closing, we outline an approach to the reform of capital recovery under the U.S. corporate income tax that would deal effectively with the problem of inflation. The first step would be to replace existing capital recovery allowances for tax purposes by a first year allowance, as proposed by Auerbach and Jorgenson (1980). The first year allowance would provide taxpayers with a deduction from income equal to the present value of economic depreciation on an asset over its lifetime.

The second step in reform of capital recovery would be to provide an investment tax credit proportional to the difference between the cost of acquisition of an asset and the first year allowance, as proposed by Brown (1981). By varying the proportion of the investment tax credit between zero and the statutory corporate tax rate, it would be possible to produce any effective tax rate between the statutory rate and zero. Since the first year allowance and the investment tax credit would be taken in the same year an asset is acquired, the resulting first year capital recovery system would make corporate capital recovery completely independent of the rate of inflation.

II. Theoretical Framework

To analyze the impact of inflation on capital recovery under U.S. tax law we begin by modeling the provisions of the law over the postwar period 1946–1980 and under changes in tax law proposed by the Reagan administration and the Senate Finance Committee. For simplicity we limit ourselves to the provisions of the corporate income tax. We introduce the characteristic features of the tax law into the annualized cost or rental value of each type of asset. For this purpose we employ the concept of rental value introduced by Jorgenson (1963, 1965) and further developed by Hall and Jorgenson (1967).[1]

Under U.S. tax law the rental price of capital services depends on the statutory tax rate, which we denote by u, the depreciation formula giving capital consumption allowances at time s on one dollar's worth of investment at time t, denoted by $D(s - t)$, and the rate of the investment tax credit, denoted k.[2] We can determine the values of these tax parameters for each type of assets for each year during the period 1946–1980 and for each of the proposed changes in tax law. Using the rental price of capital services, we can determine the effective tax rate corresponding to each set of tax parameters.

The rental price of capital services is defined, implicitly, by the equality between the cost of acquisition of an asset at time t, say q(t), and the present value of future rentals after taxes. In the absence of taxation this equality can be written

$$q(t) = \int_t^\infty e^{-(r+\pi)(s-t)}\, e^{-\delta(s-t)}\, c(s)\, ds \quad .$$

In this formula the rental price of capital services at time s, c(s), is multiplied by the quantity of capital services at time s, $e^{-\delta(s-t)}$.

We assume that the quantity of capital services resulting from the acquisition of one unit of the capital asset at time t declines exponentially at the rate of economic depreciation δ. Hulten and Wykoff (1981a) have shown that exponential or geometric decline in the quantity of capital services provides a satisfactory approximation to actual patterns of decline.[3] The rental value at time s, $e^{-\delta(s-t)}$ c(s), is discounted by the factor

$e^{-(r+\pi)\,(s-t)}$, where $\pi = \dot{q}/q$ is the rate of inflation in the price of assets and r is the rate of return corrected for inflation.

Differentiating both sides of the identity between the cost of acquisition of an asset and the present value of future rentals, we obtain

$$c = q(r + \delta) \quad .$$

The rental price is the product of the acquisition price and the sum of the rate of return corrected for inflation and the rate of depreciation. We can solve this expression for the rate of return, obtaining

$$r = \frac{c}{q} - \delta \quad .$$

For productive efficiency in the allocation of capital, the addition to wealth generated by one dollar's worth of an asset must be the same for all assets. This addition to wealth is measured by the rate of return before correction for inflation, $r + \pi$.

In the presence of taxation the cost of acquisition of an asset is reduced by an offset to tax liability for the investment tax credit and by deductions from taxable income for capital consumption allowances. The acquisition cost after taxes is equal to the present value of future rentals after taxes. The investment tax credit, $kq(t)$, is a direct offset to tax liability and is not discounted. We can view capital consumption allowances as an offset to the cost of acquisition of an asset by introducing the present value of capital consumption allowances, say z:

$$z = \int_t^\infty e^{-[r(1-u)\,+\,\pi]\,(s-t)}\,D(t - s)\,ds$$

where $r\,(1 - u) + \pi$ is the after-tax discount rate.

Given the definition of the present value of capital consumption allowances, we can express the cost of acquisition of an asset at time t, net of the investment tax credit and the present value of tax deductions for capital consumption, as the present value of future rentals after taxes:

$$(1 - k - uz)\,q(t) = \int_t^\infty e^{-[r(1-u)\,+\,\pi]\,(s-t)}\,e^{-\delta(s-t)}\,(1 - u)\,c(s)\,ds \quad .$$

Our final step in modeling the provisions for capital recovery under U.S. tax law is to determine the rental price of capital services as a function of the cost of acquisition of an asset $q(t)$, the rate of return r, and the tax parameters—k, u, and z. For this purpose we differentiate both sides of the equality between the cost of acquisition of an asset after taxes and the present value of future rentals after taxes, obtaining

$$c = \frac{1 - k - uz}{1 - u} q \, [r(1 - u) + \delta] \quad .$$

Efficiency in the allocation of capital requires that the addition to wealth generated by the acquisition of one dollar's worth of an asset, net of depreciation, is the same for all assets. This addition to wealth is measured by the social rate of return before correction for inflation, say $\rho + \pi$, where

$$\rho = \frac{c}{q} - \delta \quad .$$

Maximization of private wealth requires that the addition to wealth generated by the acquisition of one dollar's worth of an asset, net of both depreciation and taxes, is the same for all assets. This addition to wealth is measured by the private rate of return before correction for inflation $r(1 - u) + \pi$.

To summarize the impact of U.S. tax law on capital recovery on the efficiency of capital allocation, we employ the effective tax rate, say e. Reducing the social rate of return by the effective tax rate results in the private rate of return after taxes:

$$(1 - e) \rho = (1 - u) r \quad .$$

We can express the effective tax rate as a function of the private rate of return, the statutory tax rate, the investment tax credit, and the present value of capital consumption allowances:

$$e = 1 - \left(\frac{(1 - u) r}{\dfrac{1 - k - uz}{1 - u} [(1 - u) r + \delta] - \delta} \right) \quad .$$

Maximization of private wealth results in an efficient allocation of capital only if the effective tax rate is the same for all assets. [4]

If capital consumption allowances were equal to economic depreciation, the present value of these allowances would be given by

$$z = \int_t^\infty e^{-r(1-u)(t-s)} \delta \, e^{-\delta(t-s)} \, ds$$

$$= \frac{\delta}{r(1 - u) + \delta} \quad .$$

If the investment tax credit were equal to zero, the effective tax rate for all assets would be equal to the statutory tax rate. Alternatively, if the acquisition of assets could be immediately expensed, the present value of capital consumption allowances would be equal to unity. Again, setting the investment tax credit equal to zero, the effective tax rate for all assets would be equal to zero. Expensing a proportion of the cost of acquisition of assets and recovering the remainder through economic depreciation could lead to any effective tax rate between zero and the statutory rate.[5]

III.   Empirical Implementation

The measurement of effective tax rates under U.S. tax law requires data on economic depreciation, the after-tax rate of return, capital consumption allowances for tax purposes, and the investment tax credit. Hulten and Wykoff (1981b) have estimated rates of economic depreciation for all types of assets employed in the U.S. national income and product accounts. These rates of economic depreciation are based on an analysis of data on the prices of assets of different ages. Economic depreciation is measured by the decline in the value of an asset with age.

In table 1 we present a list of the assets employed in the U.S. national accounts, the corresponding economic depreciation rates estimated by Hulten and Wykoff, and the percentage of each asset in total corporate investment in 1978. The first 20 categories of assets are classified as producers' durable equipment, the next 14 are classified as nonresidential structures, and the last is residential structures. Economic depreciation rates for equipment range from 33.33 percent per year for automobiles to 6.60 percent per year for railroad equipment. Rates for structures range from 5.63 percent per year for mining, exploration, shafts, and wells to 1.30 percent per year for residential structures.

Hulten and Wykoff (1981b) have compared their estimates of rates of economic depreciation by type of asset with estimates employed since 1976 in the U.S. national income and product accounts.[6] We present average economic depreciation rates employed in the national accounts in table 1. The depreciation rates for producers' durable equipment obtained by Hulten and Wykoff are similar in the aggregate to those employed in the U.S. national accounts but differ for specific types of equipment. The economic depreciation rates for nonresidential structures estimated by Hulten and Wykoff are much lower than those employed in the U.S. national accounts. Estimates employed in the national accounts are based on

TABLE 1

ASSET CATEGORIES AND DEPRECIATION RATES

Asset Category	Hulten-Wykoff[a] Depreciation Rate	BEA[a] Depreciation Rate	Percentage[b] of 1978 Corporate Investment
1 Furniture and fixtures	11.00	12.67	2.7
2 Fabricated metal products	9.17	10.12	1.7
3 Engines and turbines	7.86	8.88	0.7
4 Tractors	16.33	25.42	1.5
5 Agricultural machinery	9.71	10.94	0.2
6 Construction machinery	17.22	23.16	3.3
7 Mining and oilfield machinery	16.50	19.24	1.2
8 Metalworking machinery	12.25	12.78	3.5
9 Special industry machinery	10.31	11.61	2.9
10 General industrial equipment	12.25	13.20	4.1
11 Office, computing, and accounting machinery	27.29	25.69	4.7
12 Service industry machinery	16.50	18.60	1.8
13 Electrical machinery	11.79	12.51	10.4
14 Trucks, buses, and trailors	25.37	23.01	11.9
15 Autos	33.33	12.63	4.8
16 Aircraft	18.33	7.55	1.7
17 Ships and boats	7.50	8.37	0.8
18 Railroad equipment	6.60	16.97	1.7
19 Instruments	15.00	16.59	4.5
20 Other equipment	15.00	16.95	1.5
21 Industrial buildings	3.61	7.21	6.3
22 Commercial buildings	2.47	5.18	7.3
23 Religious buildings	1.88	3.55	0.0
24 Educational buildings	1.88	3.52	0.0
25 Hospital buildings	2.33	3.40	0.1
26 Other nonfarm buildings	4.54	6.00	0.4
27 Railroads	1.76	4.88	0.5
28 Telephone and telegraph facilities	3.33	6.35	2.8
29 Electric light and power	3.00	5.81	7.1
30 Gas	3.00	5.93	1.1
31 Other public utilities	4.50	7.75	0.3
32 Farm	2.37	5.88	0.1
33 Mining, exploration, shafts and wells	5.63	11.74	6.1
34 Other nonbuilding facilities	2.90	6.38	0.5
35 Residential	1.30	2.71	1.7

a. Bureau of Economic Analysis (BEA) rates are estimated by Hulten and Wykoff (1981b) to be those implicit in the National Income and Product Accounts. Both sets of rates are found in table 2 of their study, except categories 27, 28, 29, 30, 31, and 35. These were derived for this study by applying Hulten-Wykoff methodology to data disaggregated by type of asset.

b. Investment data for 34 nonresidential assets for farm, manufacturing, and nonfarm, nonmanufacturing sectors in current dollars from 1832 to 1978 were made available by John Musgrave of the Bureau of Economic Analysis. To derive corporate investment, the proportions of investment in each category of assets by corporations (also supplied by John Musgrave) were employed. Corporate residential investment was provided by Jerry Silverstein of the Bureau of Economic Analysis.

studies of useful lives for tax purposes summarized in *Bulletin F* (1942), issued by the Internal Revenue Service, and on data on retirement of assets collected by Marston, Winfrey, and Hempstead (1953).

The first step in the estimation of effective tax rates under U.S. tax law is to measure the offset to the cost of acquisition of assets provided by capital consumption allowances. To measure this offset we require present values of these allowances over the lifetime of each asset. Capital consumption allowances for tax purposes depend on accounting formulas for allocating the historical cost of an asset over its lifetime. They also depend on useful lifetimes and salvage values for assets permitted for tax purposes. Although lifetimes, salvage values, and accounting formulas are provided by statute or by regulations, considerable discretion is permitted to individual taxpayers in the calculation of capital consumption allowances.

To summarize practices permitted by the Internal Revenue Service in calculating capital consumption allowances for tax purposes, we have developed a detailed simulation model for the generation of the capital consumption allowances actually claimed by corporations. This model incorporates information about lifetimes and salvage values of assets and accounting formulas permitted for tax purposes. In table 2 we present two sets of lifetimes by type of asset—*Bulletin F* lifetimes, introduced by the Internal Revenue Service in 1942, and Guideline lifetimes from the Asset Depreciation Range System introduced in 1971.

Considerable survey evidence is available about the accounting formulas actually employed by taxpayers in calculating corporate capital consumption allowances. We can combine this information with scattered evidence on lifetimes used for tax purposes and on the salvage values of assets. Finally, we can simulate the values of capital consumption allowances claimed for tax purposes on the basis of data on investment by type of asset. We have adjusted our estimates of accounting formulas, lifetimes, and salvage values employed for tax purposes to fit historical data on capital consumption allowances; additional details are given in the appendix to this paper. We present simulated capital consumption allowances and estimates of these allowances based on *Statistics of Income* in table 3.[7] We also present simulated and actual values of the percentage of capital consumption allowance calculated on the basis of straight-line accounting formulas.

The results of our simulation of capital consumption allowances actually claimed by U.S. corporations over the period 1946 to 1978 are presented in table 4. Since these data include capital consumption allowances

TABLE 2

ASSET LIFETIMES FOR TAX PURPOSES

Asset Category	Bulletin F Lifetime	Guideline ADR Midpoint Lifetime
1 Furniture and fixtures	17.6	10.0
2 Fabricated metal products	21.2	12.5
3 Engines and turbines	24.7	15.6
4 Tractors	9.4	4.3
5 Agricultural machinery	20.0	10.0
6 Construction machinery	10.6	9.9
7 Mining and oilfield machinery	11.8	9.6
8 Metalworking machinery	18.8	12.7
9 Special industry machinery	18.8	12.7
10 General industrial equipment	16.5	12.3
11 Office, computing, and accounting machinery	9.4	10.0
12 Service industry machinery	11.8	10.3
13 Electrical machinery	16.5	12.4
14 Trucks, buses, and truck trailers	10.6	5.6
15 Autos	11.8	3.0
16 Aircraft	10.6	6.3
17 Ships and boats	25.9	18.0
18 Railroad equipment	29.4	15.0
19 Instruments	12.9	10.6
20 Other equipment	12.9	10.2
21 Industrial buildings	31.8	28.8
22 Commercial buildings	42.3	47.6
23 Religious buildings	56.5	48.0
24 Educational buildings	56.5	48.0
25 Hospital buildings	56.5	48.0
26 Other nonfarm buildings	36.5	30.9
27 Railroads	60.0	30.0
28 Telephone and telegraph facilities	31.8	27.0
29 Electric light and power	35.3	27.0
30 Gas	35.3	24.0
31 Other public utilities	30.6	22.0
32 Farm	44.7	25.0
33 Mining, exploration, shafts, and wells	18.8	6.8
34 Other nonbuilding facilities	36.5	28.2
35 Residential	40.0	40.0

a. *Bulletin F* lifetimes are obtained from the capital stock study by the Bureau of Economic Analysis (1976).

b. Guideline ADR midpoint lifetimes were calculated in three stages: (1) Where possible, Guideline lives were applied directly to asset categories, (2) Using industry investment in each category, industry-specific lifetimes were weighted to obtain average asset lifetimes, (3) Investment not covered otherwise was assigned 65 percent of *Bulletin F* lifetimes, which the Treasury estimated to be equivalent to Guideline lifetimes on average.

TABLE 3

SIMULATED CORPORATE CAPITAL CONSUMPTION ALLOWANCES, 1946–1978

| | CORPORATE CAPITAL CONSUMPTION ALLOWANCES | | | PROPORTION OF DEPRECIATION USING STRAIGHT-LINE | |
| | | | Difference | | |
Year	Simulated	Actual[a]	(1)-(2)	Simulated	Actual[b]
1946	4.82	4.59	0.23	0.97	
1947	5.53	5.68	−0.14	0.95	
1948	6.49	6.82	−0.33	0.94	
1949	7.43	7.77	−0.34	0.94	
1950	8.37	8.50	−0.13	0.93	
1951	9.67	9.81	−0.14	0.93	
1952	11.24	11.10	0.14	0.93	
1953	12.92	12.79	0.13	0.92	
1954	14.84	14.50	0.34	0.89	0.89
1955	17.03	17.21	−0.19	0.82	0.81
1956	19.10	18.90	0.20	0.74	0.74
1957	20.97	20.90	0.07	0.68	0.70
1958	22.35	22.23	0.12	0.63	0.61
1959	23.64	23.62	0.02	0.58	0.58
1960	25.05	25.25	−0.20	0.54	0.53
1961	26.38	26.61	−0.23	0.50	0.50
1962	30.50	30.44	0.06	0.48	
1963	32.48	32.44	0.04	0.45	
1964	34.72	34.57	0.15	0.42	
1965	37.83	37.41	0.42	0.39	
1966	41.25	40.61	0.64	0.36	
1967	44.54	44.12	0.42	0.34	
1968	48.53	48.09	0.44	0.32	
1969	52.99	52.99	0.00	0.30	
1970	56.64	56.61	0.02	0.28	
1971	60.33	60.89	−0.55	0.27	
1972	66.15	67.88	−1.73	0.25	
1973	74.08	73.75	0.34	0.24	
1974	82.31	81.61	0.70	0.22	
1975	89.66	89.22	0.43	0.21	
1976	97.20	97.12	0.08	0.20	
1977	107.73	109.29	−1.56	0.19	
1978	122.26	119.81	2.46	0.17	

a.   Corporate capital consumption allowances based on *Statistics of Income* for corporations were prepared by Jerry Silverstein of the Bureau of Economic Analysis for this study.

b.   Proportions of corporate capital consumption allowances using the straight-line method are reported for the years 1954–1961 in the *Statistics of Income: Corporation Income Tax Returns,* 1959–1960, p. 7, table E, and 1961–1962, p. 6, table E.

TABLE 4

TAX PARAMETERS EMPLOYED IN SIMULATION OF CORPORATE CAPITAL
CONSUMPTION ALLOWANCES

Year	Average Equipment Lifetime	Average Structures Lifetime	Proportion Of New Investment Using Accelerated Methods	Equipment Salvage Value as Proportion of Original Cost
1930	11.80	25.67	0.00	0.08
1931	11.02	25.34	0.00	0.08
1932	11.07	24.14	0.00	0.08
1933	10.88	22.93	0.00	0.08
1934	15.72	33.18	0.00	0.10
1935	15.30	31.71	0.00	0.10
1936	15.71	32.27	0.00	0.10
1937	15.98	30.77	0.00	0.10
1938	15.00	30.13	0.00	0.10
1939	13.77	28.62	0.00	0.10
1940	14.32	28.67	0.00	0.10
1941	14.42	28.53	0.00	0.10
1942	15.65	28.68	0.00	0.10
1943	15.36	28.04	0.08	0.09
1944	14.81	27.34	0.08	0.09
1945	13.63	27.23	0.08	0.09
1946	13.16	28.14	0.08	0.09
1947	13.80	27.93	0.08	0.09
1948	13.64	28.12	0.08	0.09
1949	13.56	28.21	0.08	0.09
1950	13.11	27.80	0.08	0.09
1951	13.69	27.50	0.08	0.09
1952	13.72	27.09	0.09	0.09
1953	13.56	27.25	0.09	0.09
1954	13.32	27.18	0.30	0.06
1955	13.00	27.06	0.52	0.06
1956	13.33	27.59	0.52	0.06
1957	13.36	27.29	0.57	0.06
1958	12.99	27.47	0.65	0.06
1959	12.60	27.45	0.69	0.06
1960	12.65	27.38	0.70	0.06
1961	12.32	27.24	0.71	0.06
1962	11.73	27.27	0.71	0.05
1963	11.54	27.55	0.72	0.04
1964	11.44	27.48	0.72	0.03
1965	11.23	27.80	0.73	0.03
1966	11.09	27.59	0.73	0.03
1967	11.02	27.57	0.74	0.03
1968	10.43	27.39	0.75	0.03
1969	10.33	27.85	0.77	0.03
1970	10.39	27.55	0.78	0.03
1971	9.66	28.09	0.80	0.01
1972	8.51	28.06	0.81	0.01
1973	8.40	27.83	0.82	0.01
1974	8.57	27.00	0.83	0.01
1975	8.71	25.23	0.84	0.01
1976	8.43	24.75	0.84	0.01
1977	7.78	24.58	0.85	0.01
1978	7.64	24.72	0.85	0.01

on assets acquired in earlier years, we have developed estimates of life-times and salvage values for assets and relative proportions of newly ac-quired assets depreciated by straight-line and accelerated methods back to 1930. We have assumed that depreciation practices before 1930 are the same as those that prevailed in that year. Our results include estimates of lifetimes used for tax purposes for all 35 types of assets listed in table 1. The results also include simulated percentages of capital consumption al-lowances calculated on the basis of accelerated methods. Finally, we pres-ent simulated salvage values as a proportion of the acquisition cost of equipment. Salvage values for structures are simulated at 1 percent of ac-quisition cost throughout the period.

Comparing the average lifetimes presented in table 4 with the statutory lifetimes presented in table 2, we observe that lifetimes used for structures have declined steadily over the postwar period. At the end of this period the lifetimes are closely comparable to those employed during the 1930s. By contrast the lifetimes used for equipment have declined dramatically over the postwar period after rising during the 1930s. Although acceler-ated methods for calculating capital consumption allowances were used before 1954, the proportion of assets treated by these methods jumped from 9 percent in 1953 to 30 percent in 1954 and 52 percent in 1955. Since that time the proportion of assets depreciated by accelerated methods has risen steadily to a level of 85 percent in 1978. Salvage values as a propor-tion of cost of acquisition of equipment rose from 8 percent in 1933 to 10 percent in 1934. Since that time this ratio has declined steadily, reaching the level of 1 percent in 1978.

Our simulation model of capital consumption provides estimates of life-times and salvage values of assets and accounting formulas employed by taxpayers for each year and for each of the 35 types of assets listed in table 1. To proceed with the calculation of present values of capital con-sumption allowances for new assets acquired in each year, we require ap-propriate discount factors to be applied to the capital consumption allow-ances permitted under U.S. law. The discount factors depend on after-tax rates of return, not adjusted for inflation, since capital consumption al-lowances were based on historical cost. If capital consumption allowances were based on replacement cost, the inflation in capital consumption al-lowances would precisely offset the inflation in the after-tax rate of return.

Since tax deductions for capital consumption are an obligation of the U.S. government, we have constructed discount factors for these allow-ances on the basis of yields on U.S. government securities. These yields have precisely the characteristics appropriate to the discounting of government obligations. Second, since tax deductions are calculated at historical cost of acquisition of assets, the discount factors should not be corrected for inflation. Yields on government obligations embody anticipations about inflation that are current at the time an investment is made. We present yields on government securities by maturity in table 5.

We have estimated present values of capital consumption allowances for tax purposes for each of the 35 types of assets presented in table 1. We have weighted these present values by actual investment by type of asset in table 6. The first column of this table gives the present value for capital consumption allowances for tax purposes under U.S. tax law for an investment of one dollar in each year of the postwar period 1946-1980. Table 6 also provides data for investment in equipment and structures separately. We can compare the present value of capital consumption allowances on assets acquired in each year with the present values of economic depreciation on these assets.

The first two columns in table 6 give the present values of capital consumption allowances for tax purposes and economic depreciation for all corporate investment. Capital consumption for tax purposes has exceeded economic depreciation in every year by amounts ranging from 39 percent in 1946 at the beginning of the postwar period to 9 percent in 1980 at the end of the period. We present similar comparisons for investment in equipment and structures in table 6. We find that the present value of capital consumption allowances has exceeded economic depreciation on equipment by amounts ranging from 5 to 18 percent. The present value of capital consumption allowances has exceeded economic depreciation on structures by amounts ranging from 107 percent at the beginning of the period to 25 percent in 1980.

We have compared present values of capital consumption allowances for tax purposes and economic depreciation in table 6. This comparison provides the appropriate measure of the impact of inflation on capital consumption allowances for new investment. A different perspective on the impact of inflation is provided by a comparison between capital consumption allowances claimed for tax purposes at historical and at replacement cost. We present such a comparison, based on our simulation model for generating capital consumption allowances, in table 7. For this purpose we employ simulated values of lifetimes and salvage values and relative proportions of assets depreciated by accelerated methods for all 35 types of assets listed in table 1.

Since the rate of inflation in the prices of assets has been positive throughout the postwar period, except for 1958 and 1961, capital con-

TABLE 5

Yields on U.S. Government Securities by Maturity, 1950–1980[a]

Year	1 yr.	2 yr.	3 yr.	4 yr.	5 yr.	7 yr.	10 yr.	20 yr.	30 yr.
1950	1.28	1.37	1.42	1.47	1.54	1.77	2.11	2.39	2.39
1951	1.70	1.83	1.90	1.96	2.03	2.18	2.41	2.60	2.60
1952	1.87	2.03	2.14	2.22	2.26	2.30	2.47	2.68	2.68
1953	2.13	2.32	2.42	2.50	2.57	2.61	2.78	2.92	3.25
1954	1.03	1.24	1.46	1.70	1.89	2.11	2.43	2.57	2.76
1955	1.97	2.27	2.42	2.51	2.58	2.64	2.72	2.83	2.95
1956	2.89	3.03	3.10	3.12	3.13	3.10	3.08	3.07	3.10
1957	3.48	3.58	3.63	3.64	3.63	3.59	3.54	3.45	3.44
1958	2.17	2.50	2.75	2.89	2.98	3.10	3.27	3.45	3.48
1959	3.80	4.10	4.21	4.26	4.26	4.23	4.13	4.12	4.08
1960	3.55	3.78	3.97	4.08	4.13	4.13	4.13	4.13	4.12
1961	2.89	3.23	3.46	3.61	3.69	3.75	3.84	3.90	3.94
1962	3.05	3.28	3.47	3.61	3.71	3.81	3.96	4.02	4.06
1963	3.29	3.45	3.61	3.72	3.80	3.83	3.98	4.06	4.07
1964	3.80	3.94	4.01	4.05	4.08	4.12	4.17	4.18	4.19
1965	4.07	4.11	4.15	4.17	4.20	4.22	4.25	4.23	4.22
1966	5.12	5.19	5.20	5.18	5.14	5.03	4.86	4.72	4.69
1967	4.77	4.87	4.94	4.98	5.00	5.00	4.97	4.93	4.90
1968	5.54	5.56	5.57	5.57	5.56	5.58	5.48	5.40	5.35
1969	6.95	6.90	6.85	6.78	6.73	6.63	6.46	6.25	6.17
1970	7.05	7.22	7.33	7.41	7.43	7.30	7.21	6.79	6.73
1971	4.89	5.22	5.56	5.78	5.96	6.14	6.11	6.01	6.00
1972	4.88	5.29	5.59	5.77	5.90	6.07	6.23	5.82	5.80
1973	7.24	6.85	6.78	6.78	6.76	6.74	6.73	6.97	6.99
1974	8.23	7.83	7.75	7.74	7.73	7.66	7.31	7.93	7.98
1975	6.65	7.18	7.36	7.47	7.61	7.72	7.42	8.04	8.21
1976	5.92	6.50	6.82	7.04	7.20	7.46	7.53	7.86	7.94
1977	5.94	6.30	6.55	6.77	6.91	7.11	7.36	7.62	7.68
1978	8.20	8.22	8.21	8.22	8.23	8.28	8.33	8.42	8.42
1979	10.54	9.99	9.57	9.47	9.40	9.37	9.34	9.24	9.20
1980	11.61	11.38	11.10	11.11	11.15	11.12	11.16	11.09	11.03

a. *Source:* Salomon Brothers, *Analytical Handbook of Yields and Yield Ratios.* These yields are used to construct discount factors for calculating the present value of depreciation allowances.

sumption allowances at historical cost have always fallen short of capital consumption at replacement cost. Historical cost capital consumption declined from 73 percent of replacement cost in 1946 to a postwar low of 66 percent in 1948. As inflation slowed during the 1950s and early 1960s, historical cost capital consumption rose relative to replacement cost, reaching a peak of 90 percent in 1965. The increase in the rate of inflation in the late 1960s and early 1970s resulted in a sizeable decline in the historical cost capital consumption relative to replacement cost capital consumption, reaching a trough of 72 percent in 1975.

We have compared capital consumption allowances for tax purposes at historical and at replacement cost in table 7. We can provide an analogous comparison between economic depreciation at historical and at replacement cost. The results are given for each year of the period 1946-1978 in table 8. At the beginning of the postwar period historical cost depreciation was 76 percent of replacement cost depreciation. As a consequence of the rapid inflation in the prices of assets during the period 1946-1948, the ratio of historical cost depreciation to replacement cost depreciation fell to 70 percent of 1948. This ratio began to rise gradually after 1948 as the rate of inflation declined, reaching a peak during the period 1964-1966 of 90 percent. This peak resulted from relatively low rates of inflation in asset prices during the period 1958-1964.

Rates of inflation in asset prices began to increase after 1964; by 1966 the ratio of historical cost depreciation to replacement cost depreciation began to decrease and fell to the postwar low of 69 percent during the period 1975-1978. Comparing economic depreciation at historical and replacement cost in table 8 with capital consumption allowances in table 7, we find that the impact of inflation was very similar. High rates of inflation result in a cumulative divergence between historical and replacement cost capital consumption allowances. The pattern of divergence for economic depreciation is nearly identical.

The next step in our analysis of the impact of inflation on capital recovery under the U.S. corporate income tax is to compare the allowances claimed by U.S. corporations with economic depreciation at replacement cost. We find that capital consumption allowances were below economic depreciation from the beginning of the postwar period until 1962. The reduction in asset lifetimes allowed for tax purposes and the introduction of new accounting formulas for accelerated capital recovery in 1954 did not overcome the impact of rapid inflation during the early years of the postwar period. In 1962 the Depreciation Guidelines were introduced, making shorter lifetimes applicable to existing assets. As a consequence,

TABLE 6

PRESENT VALUES OF CORPORATE CAPITAL CONSUMPTION ALLOWANCES FOR TAX PURPOSES AND ECONOMIC DEPRECIATION ON NEW INVESTMENT, 1946–1980

YEAR	TOTAL[a]			EQUIPMENT			STRUCTURES		
	Tax	Economic	Ratio (1)/(2)	Tax	Economic	Ratio (1)/(2)	Tax	Economic	Ratio (1)/(2)
1946	0.767	0.551	1.39	0.795	0.697	1.14	0.730	0.358	2.04
1947	0.769	0.569	1.35	0.789	0.687	1.15	0.732	0.359	2.04
1948	0.769	0.567	1.36	0.791	0.691	1.14	0.732	0.356	2.06
1949	0.768	0.564	1.36	0.792	0.697	1.14	0.731	0.354	2.07
1950	0.773	0.579	1.34	0.795	0.706	1.13	0.734	0.357	2.06
1951	0.756	0.568	1.33	0.778	0.689	1.13	0.719	0.362	1.99
1952	0.752	0.565	1.33	0.774	0.685	1.13	0.716	0.367	1.95
1953	0.730	0.566	1.29	0.762	0.691	1.10	0.678	0.363	1.87
1954	0.784	0.568	1.38	0.817	0.694	1.18	0.730	0.364	2.00
1955	0.785	0.575	1.36	0.817	0.700	1.17	0.730	0.364	2.01
1956	0.768	0.563	1.37	0.802	0.688	1.16	0.713	0.359	1.99
1957	0.754	0.564	1.34	0.788	0.687	1.15	0.696	0.357	1.95
1958	0.761	0.553	1.38	0.802	0.685	1.17	0.698	0.350	1.99
1959	0.739	0.572	1.29	0.780	0.697	1.12	0.664	0.349	1.91
1960	0.738	0.567	1.30	0.780	0.693	1.13	0.663	0.346	1.92

1961	0.749	0.561	1.34	0.793	0.694	1.14	0.676	0.341	1.98
1962	0.756	0.566	1.34	0.806	0.698	1.15	0.671	0.338	1.98
1963	0.762	0.565	1.35	0.815	0.697	1.17	0.668	0.334	2.00
1964	0.764	0.568	1.34	0.819	0.696	1.18	0.663	0.334	1.98
1965	0.762	0.568	1.34	0.819	0.697	1.18	0.659	0.336	1.96
1966	0.745	0.572	1.30	0.803	0.696	1.15	0.636	0.339	1.88
1967	0.740	0.571	1.29	0.800	0.696	1.15	0.627	0.340	1.84
1968	0.732	0.575	1.27	0.797	0.703	1.13	0.609	0.333	1.83
1969	0.702	0.570	1.23	0.774	0.702	1.10	0.572	0.331	1.73
1970	0.667	0.561	1.19	0.756	0.695	1.09	0.516	0.332	1.56
1971	0.710	0.564	1.26	0.808	0.702	1.15	0.542	0.328	1.65
1972	0.728	0.568	1.28	0.827	0.706	1.17	0.552	0.323	1.71
1973	0.705	0.572	1.23	0.816	0.709	1.15	0.506	0.324	1.56
1974	0.688	0.577	1.19	0.799	0.707	1.13	0.484	0.336	1.44
1975	0.692	0.579	1.19	0.794	0.703	1.13	0.503	0.351	1.43
1976	0.705	0.590	1.20	0.801	0.710	1.13	0.518	0.353	1.47
1977	0.726	0.598	1.21	0.819	0.716	1.14	0.532	0.352	1.51
1978	0.699	0.593	1.18	0.802	0.720	1.11	0.504	0.351	1.44
1979	0.679	0.593	1.15	0.783	0.720	1.09	0.481	0.351	1.37
1980	0.645	0.593	1.09	0.753	0.720	1.05	0.438	0.351	1.25

a. The present value of capital consumption allowances is represented as a proportion of the original cost of the asset. Total is a weighted average for all 35 categories of investment. Equipment is a weighted average on 20 types of equipment. Structures is a weighted average on 15 types of structures.

TABLE 7

THE EFFECT OF INFLATION ON CORPORATE CAPITAL CONSUMPTION ALLOWANCES
FOR TAX PURPOSES, 1946–1978

Year	SIMULATED CORPORATE CAPITAL CONSUMPTION ALLOWANCES		Ratio (1)/(2)	Percentage Change of Investment Price Deflator[b]
	Historical Cost	Replacement[a] Cost		
1946	4.82	6.57	0.73	11.3
1947	5.53	8.22	0.67	18.4
1948	6.49	9.78	0.66	9.6
1949	7.43	10.72	0.69	2.2
1950	8.37	11.70	0.72	3.1
1951	9.67	14.09	0.69	7.6
1952	11.24	15.73	0.71	2.1
1953	12.92	17.26	0.75	1.3
1954	14.84	19.08	0.78	0.8
1955	17.03	21.14	0.81	2.2
1956	19.10	24.45	0.78	5.5
1957	20.97	26.97	0.78	3.8
1958	22.35	28.05	0.80	−0.1
1959	23.64	29.23	0.81	1.2
1960	25.05	30.34	0.83	0.5
1961	26.38	31.08	0.85	−0.4
1962	30.50	35.27	0.86	0.5
1963	32.48	36.90	0.88	0.2
1964	34.72	38.98	0.89	0.8
1965	37.83	42.12	0.90	1.5
1966	41.25	46.23	0.89	3.3
1967	44.54	50.34	0.88	3.3
1968	48.53	55.44	0.88	4.3
1969	52.99	61.48	0.86	5.8
1970	56.64	67.07	0.84	4.8
1971	60.33	72.84	0.83	5.2
1972	66.15	79.57	0.83	4.3
1973	74.08	88.93	0.83	6.0
1974	82.31	105.48	0.78	10.7
1975	89.66	123.92	0.72	12.8
1976	97.20	133.65	0.73	5.6
1977	107.73	145.66	0.74	7.7
1978	122.26	164.38	0.74	9.2

a.   Capital consumption allowances at replacement cost were calculated by multiplying the allowances for all assets by the ratio of the price deflator in each year to the price deflator in the year the asset was acquired.

b.   Implicit price deflators corresponding to our 35 categories of investment were taken from the National Income and Product Accounts.

TABLE 8

THE EFFECT OF INFLATION ON CORPORATE ECONOMIC DEPRECIATION, 1946-1978

Year	CORPORATE ECONOMIC DEPRECIATION			Percentage Change of Investment Price Deflator[c]
	Historical Cost[a]	Replacement Cost[b]	Ratio (1)/(2)	
1946	5.47	7.24	0.76	11.3
1947	6.47	9.18	0.70	18.4
1948	7.71	11.03	0.70	9.6
1949	8.81	12.09	0.73	2.2
1950	9.81	13.09	0.75	3.1
1951	10.91	15.24	0.72	7.6
1952	11.93	16.21	0.74	2.1
1953	12.97	16.99	0.76	1.3
1954	14.04	17.84	0.79	0.8
1955	15.17	18.88	0.80	2.2
1956	16.48	21.36	0.77	5.5
1957	17.94	23.31	0.77	3.8
1958	19.11	24.14	0.79	−0.1
1959	20.26	25.17	0.80	1.2
1960	21.68	26.28	0.82	0.5
1961	22.93	26.94	0.85	−0.4
1962	24.10	27.73	0.87	0.5
1963	25.46	28.79	0.88	0.2
1964	27.21	30.46	0.89	0.8
1965	29.61	32.92	0.90	1.5
1966	32.61	36.44	0.89	3.3
1967	35.68	40.21	0.89	3.3
1968	38.98	44.45	0.88	4.3
1969	42.68	49.62	0.86	5.8
1970	45.89	54.59	0.84	4.8
1971	49.11	59.77	0.82	5.2
1972	53.04	64.82	0.82	4.3
1973	58.43	71.74	0.81	6.0
1974	64.27	84.81	0.76	10.7
1975	69.78	100.06	0.70	12.8
1976	75.48	108.99	0.69	5.6
1977	82.97	119.63	0.69	7.7
1978	92.75	135.05	0.69	9.2

a. Economic depreciation at historical cost is calculated by applying Hulten-Wykoff depreciation rates to historical cost of acquisition of assets.

b. Economic depreciation at replacement cost is calculated by multiplying depreciation at historical cost for all assets by the ratio of the price deflator for each year to the price deflator in the year the asset was acquired.

c. Implicit price deflators used correspond to our 35 categories of investment. Price deflators were taken from the National Income and Product Accounts.

capital consumption allowances for tax purposes overtook economic depreciation at replacement cost in 1962; the excess of capital consumption allowances over economic depreciation rose to 14 percent in 1965. With increased rates of inflation beginning in 1965, the ratio of capital consumption allowances to economic depreciation began to decline but remained above unity through 1973. In 1971 the Asset Depreciation Range System was introduced, further shortening lifetimes for tax purposes. Beginning in 1974 very high rates of inflation resulted in economic depreciation in excess of capital consumption allowances for tax purposes.

Our overall conclusion is that the present value of capital consumption allowances, based on expectations of inflation current at the time of investment, have exceeded the present value of economic depreciation throughout the postwar period, as indicated in table 6. This is the reverse of the relationship between capital consumption allowances actually claimed by U.S. corporations and economic depreciation at replacement cost in table 9 for the years 1946–1961 and 1974–1978. The difference is accounted for by the fact that increases in the rate of inflation have been entirely unanticipated.

Throughout the postwar period anticipated future inflation rates have been close to current rates of inflation, as indicated by the term structure of interest rates on U.S. government securities given in table 5. Actual inflation rates have risen steadily since 1965, thereby exceeding the rates of inflation that were anticipated. As a consequence, the present value of capital consumption allowances at currently anticipated rates of inflation has exceeded the present value of economic depreciation. Actual capital consumption allowances claimed by U.S. corporations have fallen short of economic depreciation at replacement cost, except for the period 1962–1973.

The final step in our analysis of the impact of inflation on capital recovery under U.S. tax law is to incorporate the offset to the cost of acquisition of assets provided by the investment tax credit. The investment tax credit was first adopted in 1962. It originally applied to equipment and certain special purpose structures. Under the Long amendment the credit was subtracted from the cost of acquisition of assets in establishing the historical cost employed in calculating capital consumption allowances for tax purposes. This amendment was repealed in 1964. The investment tax credit was suspended briefly in 1967–1978, abolished in 1969, and reinstituted in 1971. During the period from 1962 to 1974 the definition of special purpose structures was gradually broadened.

In 1975 the investment tax credit was made permanent; the statutory

TABLE 9

CORPORATE CAPITAL CONSUMPTION ALLOWANCES FOR TAX PURPOSES AND
ECONOMIC DEPRECIATION, 1946–1978

Year	Actual Corporate Capital Consumption Allowances[a]	Replacement Cost Corporate Economic Depreciation[b]	Ratio (1)/(2)
1946	4.59	7.24	0.63
1947	5.68	9.18	0.62
1948	6.82	11.03	0.62
1949	7.77	12.09	0.64
1950	8.50	13.09	0.65
1951	9.81	15.24	0.64
1952	11.10	16.21	0.68
1953	12.79	16.99	0.75
1954	14.50	17.84	0.81
1955	17.21	18.88	0.91
1956	18.90	21.36	0.88
1957	20.90	23.31	0.90
1958	22.23	24.14	0.92
1959	23.62	25.17	0.94
1960	25.25	26.28	0.96
1961	26.61	26.94	0.99
1962	30.44	27.73	1.10
1963	32.44	28.79	1.13
1964	34.57	30.46	1.13
1965	37.41	32.92	1.14
1966	40.61	36.44	1.11
1967	44.12	40.21	1.10
1968	48.09	44.45	1.08
1969	52.99	49.62	1.07
1970	56.61	54.59	1.04
1971	60.89	59.77	1.02
1972	67.88	64.82	1.05
1973	73.75	71.74	1.03
1974	81.61	84.81	0.96
1975	89.22	100.06	0.89
1976	97.12	108.99	0.89
1977	109.29	119.63	0.91
1978	119.81	135.05	0.89

a. Corporate capital consumption allowances based on *Statistics of Income* for corporations were prepared by Jerry Silverstein of the Bureau of Economic Analysis for this study.

b. Economic depreciation at replacement cost is calculated by multiplying depreciation at historical cost for all assets by the ratio of the price deflator in each year to the price deflator in the year the asset was acquired.

rate was raised from 7 to 10 percent for most assets and from 4 to 10 percent for public utility assets. The credit was made applicable to a large proportion of structures as well as equipment. As much as 57 percent of the cost of acquisition of structures in 1975 was covered by the investment tax credit. Effective rates of the investment tax credit for all of the investment for equipment and structures separately are given in table 10 for the period 1962 to 1980. These rates are based on estimates of effective rates for each of the 34 types of assets presented in table 1. The effective rates

TABLE 10

EFFECTIVE RATES OF THE INVESTMENT TAX CREDIT, 1962–1980

	INVESTMENT TAX CREDIT[a]		
Year	Total	Equipment	Structures
1962	0.034	0.054	0.000
1963	0.036	0.055	0.002
1964	0.037	0.055	0.005
1965	0.037	0.056	0.003
1966	0.030	0.043	0.004
1967	0.033	0.046	0.009
1968	0.038	0.054	0.009
1969	0.011	0.015	0.002
1970	0.000	0.000	0.000
1971	0.028	0.040	0.007
1972	0.037	0.053	0.009
1973	0.037	0.052	0.009
1974	0.038	0.053	0.011
1975	0.062	0.074	0.040
1976	0.070	0.081	0.049
1977	0.069	0.079	0.048
1978	0.067	0.078	0.044
1979	0.067	0.078	0.044
1980	0.067	0.078	0.044

a.   Effective rates of the investment tax credit are averages of effective rates calculated separately for each category of investment, based on methods developed independently by Corcoran (1979) and Jeremias (1979). Estimates of the amount of property covered by the investment credit are derived from *Statistics of Income*. The applicable statutory credit rates are weighted by these amounts in each category. Public utility property before 1975 and shorter-lived assets are eligible for only a fraction of the full rate. Effective rates are also less than the statutory rate due to considerable carryover. In certain years the credit was available only part of the year.

by type of asset are weighted by actual investment in each type of asset in each year to obtain averages for equipment and structures.

IV.   Capital Recovery During the Postwar Period

The objective of our analysis of capital recovery under U.S. tax law during the postwar period 1946–1980 is to estimate effective tax rates for equipment and structures acquired by U.S. corporations during this period. We recall from the discussion of section I that the investment tax credit is a direct offset against tax liability, while capital consumption allowances are a deduction from taxable income. The effective tax rate for an asset depends on the statutory tax rate, the effective rate of the investment tax credit, the present value of capital consumption allowances for tax purposes, the rate of economic depreciation, and the rate of return after taxes, corrected for inflation.

We present effective tax rates for all corporate investment for each year in the postwar period 1946–1980 in table 11. We also present effective tax rates for structures and for equipment separately. If capital consumption allowances were equal to economic depreciation and the investment tax credit were equal to zero for all assets, the effective tax rate would be the same for all assets and equal to the statutory rate. We present the statutory rate in table 11 as a basis for comparison with the effective tax rates under U.S. tax law. We find that the effective tax rate was below the statutory rate in every year. The ratio of the effective tax rate to the statutory rate is given in the final column of table 11.

We find that the ratio of the effective tax rate on corporate investment to the statutory rate fluctuated between 68 and 80 percent over the period from 1946 to 1961. When the investment tax credit was first adopted in 1962, the ratio of the effective tax rate to the statutory rate dropped to 55 percent in that year from 76 percent in 1961. When the investment tax credit was repealed in 1969 and 1970, the effective tax rate climbed to 78 percent of the statutory rate in 1969 and to 87 percent of the statutory rate in 1970. Reinstitution of the investment tax credit in 1971 reduced the effective tax rate to 60 percent of the statutory rate in that year and 48 percent in the following year. Liberalization of the investment tax credit in 1975 reduced the effective tax rate to 43 percent of the statutory rate. The effective tax rate fell to 12.8 percent in 1977 as the rate of inflation decreased and rose to 24.3 percent in 1980 as the rate of inflation increased.

Our first conclusion is that the effective tax rate under U.S. tax law has

TABLE 11

EFFECTIVE CORPORATE TAX RATES, 1946–1980

| Year | EFFECTIVE CORPORATE TAX RATE[a] | | | Statutory Tax Rate | Ratio (1)/(4) |
	Total	Equipment	Structures		
1946	0.258	0.301	0.202	0.380	0.680
1947	0.265	0.301	0.201	0.380	0.697
1948	0.264	0.302	0.200	0.380	0.696
1949	0.266	0.307	0.200	0.380	0.699
1950	0.303	0.346	0.226	0.420	0.720
1951	0.389	0.436	0.310	0.510	0.762
1952	0.398	0.445	0.322	0.520	0.766
1953	0.418	0.460	0.348	0.520	0.803
1954	0.366	0.400	0.312	0.520	0.704
1955	0.370	0.405	0.311	0.520	0.712
1956	0.379	0.411	0.325	0.520	0.728
1957	0.394	0.429	0.335	0.520	0.758
1958	0.377	0.408	0.330	0.520	0.725
1959	0.412	0.444	0.355	0.520	0.792
1960	0.411	0.442	0.356	0.520	0.790
1961	0.397	0.428	0.346	0.520	0.764
1962	0.285	0.250	0.345	0.520	0.548
1963	0.265	0.219	0.344	0.520	0.509
1964	0.237	0.189	0.324	0.500	0.474
1965	0.213	0.160	0.309	0.480	0.444
1966	0.274	0.247	0.324	0.480	0.570
1967	0.269	0.240	0.323	0.480	0.560
1968	0.259	0.221	0.330	0.480	0.539
1969	0.372	0.378	0.361	0.480	0.776
1970	0.416	0.429	0.394	0.480	0.867
1971	0.289	0.244	0.367	0.480	0.603
1972	0.229	0.157	0.357	0.480	0.478
1973	0.257	0.188	0.383	0.480	0.536
1974	0.281	0.221	0.394	0.480	0.586
1975	0.206	0.131	0.345	0.480	0.430
1976	0.161	0.081	0.320	0.480	0.336
1977	0.128	0.041	0.308	0.480	0.266
1978	0.180	0.099	0.335	0.480	0.376
1979	0.192	0.121	0.327	0.460	0.418
1980	0.243	0.185	0.352	0.460	0.528

a. Effective tax rates are weighted averages of effective tax rates calculated for each category of investment. An after-tax rate of return corrected for inflation of .0606 is used. This is equal to the average rate of return after corporate taxes in the 1946–1978 period, based on the results of Christensen and Jorgenson (1978). Present values of capital consumption allowances for tax purposes and economic depreciation correspond to those of table 6. Effective rates of the investment tax credit correspond to those of table 10.

been below the statutory tax rate throughout the postwar period 1946–1980. The effect of inflation under any given set of tax provisions for capital recovery is to increase the effective tax rate. This occurs through an increase in the discount rates applied to future capital consumption allowances, as indicated in table 5. However, tax provisions have been revised at frequent intervals with major revisions in 1954, 1962, 1970, and 1975. The impact of these revisions has been to reduce effective tax rates very dramatically, especially in 1962 with the adoption of the investment tax credit and the Depreciation Guidelines and, in 1975, with the liberalization of the investment tax credit.

Since the effective tax rate increases with the rate of inflation, a decrease in the rate of inflation to levels below those prevailing since 1973 would reduce the effective tax rate substantially. The decrease in the rates of inflation in the prices of assets from 12.8 percent in 1975 to 5.6 in 1976 and 7.7 in 1977 brought the effective tax rate down to a level of 16.1 percent in 1976 and 12.8 percent in 1977. These tax rates can be compared with the statutory rate of 48 percent in both years. The increases in the rate of inflation in 1978, 1979, and 1980 brought effective tax rates up to 18.0 percent in 1978, 19.2 percent in 1979, and 24.3 percent in 1980.

Our second conclusion is that the U.S. corporate income tax imposes significantly different effective tax rates on different assets, resulting in serious misallocations of capital. Effective tax rates for equipment and structures have been substantially different through the postwar period. Until 1962, effective tax rates for structures were below those of equipment by 8 to 12 percent. After the introduction of the investment tax credit in 1962, the effective tax rate on equipment fell below that of structures by 10 percent in that year. After the liberalization of the investment tax credit in 1975 the gap between effective tax rates for equipment and structures rose to 21 percent in that year and reached a maximum of 27 percent in 1977. Differences in tax rates among assets increase with a decrease in the rate of inflation, resulting in greater misallocations of capital.

Differences in effective tax rates among assets result in differences in social rates of return on these assets. The gap between social rates of return on equipment and structures creates the opportunity for gains in future output at no sacrifice of consumption either now or in the future. For any given asset the social rate of return ρ, corrected for inflation and for taxes paid at the effective tax rate e, is equal to the private rate of return r, corrected for inflation and for taxes paid at the statutory rate u:

$$(1 - e)\,\rho = (1 - u)\,r \quad .$$

We can denote effective tax rates on equipment and structures by e_E and e_S; the corresponding difference in social rates of return, say ρ_E and ρ_S is given by

$$\rho_S - \rho_E = \left(\frac{1}{1 - e_S} - \frac{1}{1 - e_E} \right)(1 - u)\, r \quad .$$

Considering the effective tax rates in 1977 of 4.1 percent for equipment and 30.8 percent for structures, we find that the difference in social rates of return is 2.44 percent. This implies that the social rate of return to the transfer of one dollar's worth of investment from equipment to structures in 1977 would have been 2.44 percent per year. This can be compared with the private rate of return of 6.06 percent per year for the postwar period as a whole. To gain perspective on the gap between social rates of return that existed in 1977 we can consider the value of an investment at this rate of return in 1946. By 1956 this investment, corrected for inflation, would have been worth $1.27. By 1966 the investment would have been worth $1.62. By 1976 the investment would have been worth $2.06 and by 1981 the investment would have been worth $2.33. The returns of $.27 by 1956, $.62 by 1966, $1.06 by 1976, and $1.33 by 1981 for each dollar's worth of investment correspond to costless increases in the national wealth that would be available for consumption or additional investment.

In table 12 we present estimates of effective tax rates for the 35 types of assets listed in table 1. We give these effective tax rates for six business cycle peak year during this period—1953, 1957, 1960, 1966, 1973, and 1979. The discount rates applied to future capital consumption allowances have increased steadily from peak to peak throughout the postwar period. For each type of assets we present the present value of capital consumption allowances for tax purposes, the effective rate of the investment tax credit, and the effective tax rate. Differences in effective tax rates are much greater among the 35 types of assets given in table 12 than between equipment and structures given in table 11.

The gap among effective tax rates for different assets in 1953 was a maximum for autos with an effective tax rate of 58 percent and a rate of 29 percent for mining and exploration structures, shafts and wells. The gap of 29 percent equals the maximum gap between equipment and structures for the postwar period. The gap between effective tax rates for these two assets was also a maximum for 1957 at 26 percent and for 1960 at 25 percent. By 1966 the maximum effective tax rate for any asset had shifted to hospital buildings at 39 percent. The gap between effective tax rates for hospitals and for mining and exploration structures, shafts and wells was

TABLE 12

EFFECTIVE CORPORATE TAX RATE BY TYPE OF ASSET, SELECTED YEARS: 1953, 1957

	1953			1957		
Asset	Present Value	ITC	Effective Tax Rate	Present Value	ITC	Effective Tax Rate
1	0.751	0.00	0.43	0.776	0.00	0.41
2	0.720	0.00	0.43	0.748	0.00	0.41
3	0.691	0.00	0.43	0.721	0.00	0.41
4	0.825	0.00	0.41	0.846	0.00	0.38
5	0.730	0.00	0.43	0.756	0.00	0.41
6	0.813	0.00	0.44	0.836	0.00	0.41
7	0.801	0.00	0.44	0.825	0.00	0.41
8	0.740	0.00	0.46	0.766	0.00	0.43
9	0.740	0.00	0.43	0.766	0.00	0.41
10	0.760	0.00	0.44	0.785	0.00	0.41
11	0.825	0.00	0.51	0.846	0.00	0.48
12	0.801	0.00	0.44	0.825	0.00	0.41
13	0.760	0.00	0.43	0.785	0.00	0.41
14	0.813	0.00	0.51	0.836	0.00	0.48
15	0.801	0.00	0.58	0.825	0.00	0.55
16	0.813	0.00	0.45	0.836	0.00	0.42
17	0.681	0.00	0.44	0.714	0.00	0.41
18	0.650	0.00	0.44	0.689	0.00	0.41
19	0.791	0.00	0.44	0.815	0.00	0.41
20	0.791	0.00	0.44	0.815	0.00	0.41
21	0.683	0.00	0.35	0.703	0.00	0.34
22	0.600	0.00	0.38	0.633	0.00	0.36
23	0.519	0.00	0.41	0.557	0.00	0.39
24	0.519	0.00	0.41	0.557	0.00	0.39
25	0.519	0.00	0.42	0.557	0.00	0.40
26	0.639	0.00	0.41	0.671	0.00	0.38
27	0.502	0.00	0.41	0.540	0.00	0.39
28	0.683	0.00	0.35	0.703	0.00	0.33
29	0.650	0.00	0.36	0.680	0.00	0.34
30	0.650	0.00	0.36	0.680	0.00	0.34
31	0.694	0.00	0.37	0.711	0.00	0.35
32	0.586	0.00	0.38	0.619	0.00	0.36
33	0.805	0.00	0.29	0.802	0.00	0.29
34	0.639	0.00	0.37	0.671	0.00	0.35
35	0.616	0.00	0.34	0.647	0.00	0.32

TABLE 12　(continued)

EFFECTIVE CORPORATE TAX RATE BY TYPE OF ASSET,
SELECTED YEARS: 1960, 1966

	1960			1966		
Asset	Present Value	ITC	Effective Tax Rate	Present Value	ITC	Effective Tax Rate
1	0.763	0.00	0.42	0.797	0.05	0.20
2	0.732	0.00	0.42	0.770	0.04	0.26
3	0.704	0.00	0.42	0.740	0.03	0.29
4	0.841	0.00	0.39	0.822	0.02	0.33
5	0.742	0.00	0.42	0.790	0.05	0.20
6	0.829	0.00	0.42	0.809	0.05	0.24
7	0.817	0.00	0.42	0.820	0.05	0.20
8	0.751	0.00	0.45	0.767	0.05	0.26
9	0.751	0.00	0.42	0.773	0.05	0.23
10	0.772	0.00	0.43	0.803	0.05	0.21
11	0.841	0.00	0.49	0.814	0.05	0.29
12	0.817	0.00	0.42	0.815	0.05	0.22
13	0.772	0.00	0.42	0.784	0.04	0.25
14	0.829	0.00	0.49	0.865	0.03	0.28
15	0.817	0.00	0.56	0.890	0.02	0.31
16	0.829	0.00	0.43	0.860	0.03	0.20
17	0.694	0.00	0.43	0.717	0.05	0.27
18	0.669	0.00	0.43	0.721	0.05	0.25
19	0.806	0.00	0.42	0.809	0.05	0.22
20	0.806	0.00	0.42	0.811	0.05	0.21
21	0.678	0.00	0.36	0.649	0.00	0.34
22	0.605	0.00	0.38	0.526	0.00	0.38
23	0.527	0.00	0.40	0.504	0.00	0.37
24	0.527	0.00	0.40	0.504	0.00	0.37
25	0.527	0.00	0.42	0.504	0.00	0.39
26	0.642	0.00	0.40	0.622	0.00	0.38
27	0.509	0.00	0.41	0.581	0.01	0.32
28	0.678	0.00	0.35	0.657	0.01	0.32
29	0.652	0.00	0.36	0.650	0.01	0.31
30	0.652	0.00	0.36	0.669	0.01	0.30
31	0.685	0.00	0.37	0.692	0.01	0.32
32	0.590	0.00	0.38	0.640	0.02	0.29
33	0.784	0.00	0.31	0.847	0.01	0.18
34	0.642	0.00	0.36	0.606	0.02	0.32
35	0.620	0.00	0.33	0.592	0.00	0.31

TABLE 12   (concluded)

EFFECTIVE CORPORATE TAX RATE BY TYPE OF ASSET,
SELECTED YEARS: 1973, 1979

	1973			1979		
Asset	Present Value	ITC	Effective Tax Rate	Present Value	ITC	Effective Tax Rate
1	0.813	0.06	0.13	0.773	0.09	0.06
2	0.774	0.06	0.20	0.728	0.09	0.13
3	0.730	0.04	0.29	0.680	0.09	0.19
4	0.883	0.04	0.08	0.849	0.06	0.05
5	0.813	0.06	0.11	0.773	0.09	0.06
6	0.810	0.06	0.19	0.773	0.09	0.08
7	0.818	0.06	0.14	0.780	0.09	0.06
8	0.776	0.06	0.20	0.724	0.09	0.16
9	0.776	0.06	0.18	0.724	0.09	0.15
10	0.813	0.06	0.15	0.773	0.09	0.06
11	0.805	0.06	0.25	0.751	0.09	0.19
12	0.810	0.06	0.18	0.767	0.09	0.09
13	0.781	0.05	0.24	0.730	0.09	0.15
14	0.889	0.03	0.18	0.865	0.05	0.13
15	0.929	0.02	0.14	0.908	0.03	0.12
16	0.860	0.06	0.07	0.819	0.08	0.00
17	0.694	0.06	0.26	0.644	0.09	0.23
18	0.739	0.06	0.20	0.686	0.09	0.17
19	0.805	0.06	0.19	0.763	0.09	0.10
20	0.813	0.06	0.15	0.769	0.09	0.08
21	0.514	0.00	0.42	0.437	0.00	0.43
22	0.372	0.00	0.45	0.304	0.00	0.45
23	0.370	0.00	0.43	0.302	0.00	0.44
24	0.370	0.00	0.43	0.302	0.00	0.44
25	0.370	0.00	0.45	0.302	0.00	0.45
26	0.495	0.00	0.45	0.421	0.00	0.46
27	0.504	0.02	0.35	0.428	0.09	0.29
28	0.534	0.02	0.38	0.458	0.09	0.31
29	0.534	0.02	0.37	0.458	0.09	0.30
30	0.566	0.02	0.35	0.491	0.09	0.28
31	0.593	0.02	0.37	0.518	0.09	0.30
32	0.558	0.04	0.31	0.482	0.09	0.27
33	0.841	0.03	0.15	0.793	0.06	0.11
34	0.528	0.04	0.34	0.447	0.09	0.31
35	0.503	0.00	0.36	0.446	0.00	0.36

only 21 percent. By 1973 the minimum effective tax rate, 7 percent had shifted to aircraft. The gap between effective tax rates for aircraft and for hospital buildings was 38 percent. The maximum gap rose to 46 percent in 1979, when the effective tax rate on aircraft dropped to zero and the rate on other nonfarm buildings rose to 46 percent.

A difference between effective tax rates of 46 percent in 1979 corresponds to a difference between social rates of return of 5.16 percent. As before, it is useful to put the gap between social rates of return that existed in 1979 in perspective by considering the value of an investment at this rate of return beginning in 1946. The investment would have been worth $1.65 in 1956 and $2.74 in 1966, both corrected for inflation. By 1976 the value of the investment would have grown to $3.93, and by 1981 the investment would have grown to $4.94, again corrected for inflation. We conclude that the loss in efficiency of capital allocation due to differences in effective tax rates among assets in 1979 was very large. It is important to emphasize that gaps among social rates of return would increase with a decrease in the rate of inflation.

To measure the burden of taxation on individual industries and differences in tax burdens among industries we have calculated effective tax rates by industry for the 44 industries listed in table 13. For each industry we have compiled data on the composition of investment by type of asset for each year of the postwar period 1946–1980.[8] Using the relative proportions of investment among assets as weights we have calculated effective tax rates for equipment, structures, and total investment in each industry in each year. We present the results in table 14 for the business cycle peaks 1953, 1957, 1960, 1966, 1973, and 1979. Differences in effective tax rates among industries given in table 14 are less than differences in these rates among assets given in table 12. Effective tax rates for individual industries are essentially averages of rates for all assets with weights that differ among industries.

The maximum gap between effective tax rates for different industries in 1953 was between street railway, bus lines, and taxicab service, with an effective tax rate of 56 percent and crude petroleum and natural gas extraction with a rate of 32 percent. The gap between effective tax rates for these two industries was also a maximum for 1957 and 1960 at 19 percent in each year. By 1966 the maximum effective tax rate for any industry had shifted to finance, insurance, and real estate at 33 percent while the minimum rate had shifted to air transportation at 20 percent. By 1973 the maximum effective tax rate was for pipelines, except natural gas at 36 percent; the minimum was for air transportation at 8 percent. By 1979 the ef-

TABLE 13

INDUSTRIES

1. Food and kindred products
2. Tobacco manufacturers
3. Textile mill products
4. Apparel and other fabricated textile products
5. Paper and allied products
6. Printing, publishing, and allied industries
7. Chemicals and allied products
8. Petroleum and coal products
9. Rubber and miscellaneous plastic products
10. Leather and leather products
11. Lumber and wood products, except furniture
12. Furniture and fixtures
13. Stone, clay, and glass products
14. Primary metal industries
15. Fabricated metal industries
16. Machinery except electrical
17. Electrical machinery, equipment, and supplies
18. Transportation equipment, except motor vehicles, and ordnance
19. Motor vehicles, and motor vehicle equipment
20. Professional photographic equipment and watches
21. Miscellaneous manufacturing industries
22. Agricultural production
23. Agricultural services, horticultural services, forestry and fisheries
24. Metal mining
25. Coal mining
26. Crude petroleum and natural gas extraction
27. Nonmetallic mining and quarrying, except fuel
28. Construction
29. Railroads and railway express service
30. Street railway, bus lines and taxicab service
31. Trucking service, warehousing and storage
32. Water transportation
33. Air transportation
34. Pipelines, except natural gas
35. Services incidental to transportation
36. Telephone, telegraph, and miscellaneous communication services
37. Radio broadcasting and television
38. Electric utilities
39. Gas utilities
40. Water supply, sanitary services, and other utilities
41. Wholesale trade
42. Retail trade
43. Finance, insurance and real estate
44. Services

TABLE 14

EFFECTIVE CORPORATE TAX RATE BY INDUSTRY, SELECTED YEARS

Industry	1953[a]			1957[a]		
	Total	Equipment	Structures	Total	Equipment	Structures
1	0.43	0.46	0.36	0.41	0.43	0.34
2	0.43	0.45	0.37	0.41	0.42	0.34
3	0.42	0.44	0.36	0.40	0.42	0.34
4	0.44	0.46	0.36	0.42	0.43	0.34
5	0.42	0.44	0.35	0.40	0.42	0.34
6	0.42	0.45	0.36	0.40	0.43	0.34
7	0.42	0.45	0.35	0.40	0.42	0.34
8	0.39	0.45	0.35	0.37	0.42	0.34
9	0.44	0.46	0.35	0.41	0.43	0.34
10	0.43	0.45	0.36	0.41	0.42	0.34
11	0.43	0.46	0.35	0.42	0.44	0.34
12	0.43	0.47	0.35	0.40	0.44	0.34
13	0.43	0.46	0.36	0.40	0.43	0.34
14	0.42	0.45	0.35	0.40	0.42	0.34
15	0.43	0.46	0.35	0.41	0.43	0.34
16	0.43	0.47	0.36	0.40	0.43	0.34
17	0.43	0.46	0.36	0.40	0.43	0.34
18	0.42	0.47	0.36	0.39	0.43	0.34
19	0.45	0.47	0.36	0.42	0.43	0.34

20	0.43	0.47	0.35	0.40	0.44	0.34
21	0.44	0.47	0.36	0.40	0.43	0.34
22	0.46	0.47	0.38	0.43	0.43	0.36
23	0.46	0.47	0.38	0.43	0.43	0.36
24	0.42	0.44	0.41	0.38	0.41	0.37
25	0.44	0.44	0.38	0.40	0.41	0.35
26	0.32	0.45	0.29	0.33	0.42	0.31
27	0.44	0.44	0.39	0.41	0.42	0.36
28	0.45	0.45	0.39	0.43	0.43	0.36
29	0.43	0.44	0.41	0.41	0.41	0.39
30	0.56	0.56		0.52	0.52	
31	0.50	0.50		0.47	0.47	
32	0.44	0.44		0.41	0.41	
33	0.45	0.45		0.42	0.42	
34	0.38	0.43	0.37	0.35	0.41	0.35
35	0.49	0.49	0.38	0.46	0.46	0.36
36	0.40	0.43	0.35	0.38	0.41	0.33
37	0.43	0.43	0.41	0.40	0.41	0.37
38	0.39	0.44	0.36	0.37	0.41	0.34
39	0.37	0.44	0.36	0.34	0.41	0.34
40	0.37	0.44	0.37	0.35	0.41	0.35
41	0.46	0.47	0.38	0.43	0.44	0.36
42	0.46	0.47	0.38	0.43	0.44	0.36
43	0.38	0.49	0.38	0.36	0.46	0.36
44	0.46	0.48	0.39	0.43	0.44	0.37

TABLE 14 (continued)
EFFECTIVE CORPORATE TAX RATE BY INDUSTRY, SELECTED YEARS

Industry	1960[a]			1966[a]		
	Total	Equipment	Structures	Total	Equipment	Structures
1	0.43	0.45	0.36	0.27	0.24	0.34
2	0.41	0.44	0.36	0.26	0.22	0.34
3	0.42	0.43	0.36	0.26	0.24	0.34
4	0.42	0.44	0.36	0.27	0.24	0.34
5	0.42	0.43	0.36	0.25	0.24	0.34
6	0.41	0.44	0.36	0.28	0.24	0.34
7	0.42	0.43	0.36	0.26	0.24	0.34
8	0.38	0.44	0.36	0.30	0.25	0.34
9	0.43	0.45	0.36	0.26	0.25	0.34
10	0.42	0.44	0.36	0.27	0.24	0.34
11	0.43	0.45	0.36	0.28	0.26	0.34
12	0.42	0.45	0.36	0.28	0.25	0.34
13	0.42	0.44	0.36	0.27	0.25	0.34
14	0.42	0.44	0.36	0.26	0.24	0.34
15	0.43	0.45	0.36	0.27	0.25	0.34
16	0.43	0.45	0.36	0.28	0.26	0.34
17	0.42	0.44	0.36	0.27	0.25	0.34
18	0.42	0.45	0.36	0.28	0.25	0.34
19	0.43	0.45	0.36	0.27	0.25	0.34

20	0.43	0.45	0.36	0.29	0.26	0.34
21	0.43	0.45	0.36	0.28	0.25	0.34
22	0.44	0.44	0.38	0.26	0.26	0.29
23	0.44	0.44	0.38	0.26	0.26	0.29
24	0.40	0.42	0.39	0.32	0.22	0.35
25	0.41	0.42	0.36	0.23	0.22	0.32
26	0.35	0.43	0.34	0.26	0.22	0.26
27	0.42	0.43	0.38	0.24	0.22	0.36
28	0.44	0.44	0.38	0.24	0.24	0.38
29	0.43	0.43	0.41	0.25	0.25	0.32
30	0.54	0.54	0.36	0.29	0.29	0.34
31	0.47	0.47	0.36	0.27	0.27	0.34
32	0.43	0.43		0.27	0.27	
33	0.43	0.43	0.38	0.20	0.20	0.38
34	0.37	0.42	0.37	0.32	0.27	0.32
35	0.47	0.47	0.38	0.27	0.26	0.38
36	0.39	0.42	0.35	0.27	0.25	0.32
37	0.41	0.42	0.40	0.30	0.25	0.38
38	0.38	0.42	0.36	0.29	0.25	0.31
39	0.36	0.42	0.36	0.30	0.25	0.30
40	0.36	0.42	0.36	0.32	0.25	0.32
41	0.44	0.45	0.38	0.26	0.24	0.38
42	0.43	0.45	0.38	0.28	0.24	0.38
43	0.38	0.47	0.38	0.34	0.26	0.37
44	0.43	0.45	0.38	0.28	0.24	0.38

TABLE 14   (concluded)

EFFECTIVE CORPORATE TAX RATE BY INDUSTRY, SELECTED YEARS

Industry	1973[a]			1979		
	Total	Equipment	Structures	Total	Equipment	Structures
1	0.24	0.18	0.42	0.20	0.12	0.43
2	0.26	0.16	0.42	0.15	0.09	0.43
3	0.23	0.19	0.42	0.19	0.14	0.43
4	0.26	0.19	0.42	0.23	0.14	0.43
5	0.22	0.19	0.42	0.16	0.13	0.43
6	0.23	0.18	0.42	0.19	0.14	0.43
7	0.23	0.19	0.42	0.17	0.12	0.43
8	0.29	0.20	0.42	0.26	0.13	0.43
9	0.24	0.19	0.42	0.20	0.14	0.43
10	0.26	0.19	0.42	0.24	0.15	0.43
11	0.23	0.18	0.42	0.18	0.12	0.43
12	0.28	0.18	0.42	0.24	0.13	0.43
13	0.23	0.18	0.42	0.18	0.12	0.43
14	0.23	0.19	0.42	0.18	0.13	0.43
15	0.24	0.19	0.42	0.21	0.14	0.43
16	0.25	0.20	0.42	0.22	0.15	0.43
17	0.25	0.21	0.42	0.20	0.14	0.43
18	0.26	0.19	0.42	0.21	0.13	0.43
19	0.22	0.19	0.42	0.16	0.13	0.43

20	0.27	0.20	0.42	0.22	0.15	0.43
21	0.26	0.19	0.42	0.22	0.14	0.43
22	0.14	0.12	0.31	0.08	0.07	0.27
23	0.13	0.12	0.31	0.08	0.07	0.27
24	0.34	0.18	0.43	0.30	0.07	0.42
25	0.20	0.17	0.35	0.10	0.07	0.32
26	0.28	0.17	0.28	0.12	0.07	0.13
27	0.19	0.17	0.44	0.09	0.07	0.44
28	0.19	0.18	0.45	0.10	0.08	0.44
29	0.21	0.20	0.35	0.18	0.17	0.29
30	0.16	0.16	0.42	0.13	0.12	0.43
31	0.18	0.18	0.42	0.13	0.13	0.43
32	0.26	0.26		0.23	0.23	0.43
33	0.08	0.08	0.45	0.00	0.00	0.45
34	0.36	0.22	0.37	0.29	0.13	0.30
35	0.19	0.18	0.45	0.13	0.12	0.45
36	0.28	0.23	0.38	0.19	0.15	0.31
37	0.32	0.24	0.45	0.25	0.15	0.46
38	0.32	0.22	0.37	0.23	0.13	0.30
39	0.34	0.22	0.35	0.25	0.13	0.28
40	0.34	0.22	0.34	0.30	0.13	0.31
41	0.21	0.17	0.45	0.15	0.11	0.45
42	0.28	0.17	0.45	0.23	0.11	0.45
43	0.31	0.20	0.44	0.24	0.13	0.44
44	0.26	0.18	0.45	0.18	0.10	0.45

a. Absence of effective tax rates for structures implies that there was no investment in structures in the corresponding industry.

fective tax rate for air transportation had dropped to zero, while the effective tax rate for metal mining and water supply, sanitary services, and other utilities was a maximum among industries at 30 percent.

Our analysis of effective tax rates by type of asset and by industry corroborates the conclusions we reached on the basis of effective tax rates for U.S. corporations as a whole. Only one industry—street railways, bus lines, and taxicab service in 1953 and 1960—has had effective tax rates in excess of the statutory tax rate for any year in the postwar period. Similarly, only one asset—autos in 1953, 1957, and 1960—had an effective tax rate in excess of the statutory rate. For all other industries and all other assets the effective tax rates under U.S. law have been below the statutory tax rate throughout the postwar period. The impact of tax revisions has been to reduce effective tax rates very dramatically for all assets and all industries. However, effective tax rates under current law increase with a decrease in the rate of inflation.

Our analysis of differences in effective tax rates among types of assets and among industries reveals larger differences than those between equipment and structures for all U.S. corporations. Differences between effective tax rates correspond to gaps between social rates of return among assets and industries. These gaps present opportunities for costless increases in the national wealth that would be available for consumption or additional investment. The gaps are very large, indicating that there is a substantial loss in efficiency in the allocation of capital under U.S. tax law. It is important to reiterate that differences in effective tax rates among assets and industries would increase with a decrease in the rate of inflation.

V.   Proposed Systems for Capital Recovery

The objective of our analysis of alternative systems for capital recovery under U.S. tax law is to estimate effective tax rates for assets acquired by U.S. corporations in the future. We consider the provisions of current law as a starting point for a comparison between alternative systems. We also consider two specific alternatives under consideration by the Congress— the Reagan administration proposal and the Senate Finance Committee proposal.[9] Finally, we consider expensing of the costs of acquisition of assets and the deduction of economic depreciation from income for tax purposes as possible approaches to capital recovery under U.S. law.

The present value of capital consumption allowances under immediate expensing of acquisition costs of assets is equal to unity for all assets. We have estimated present values of capital consumption allowances for tax purposes for each of the 35 types of assets presented in table 1 under current law and under each of the three alternative proposals we have listed above. We have also estimated the present value of economic depreciation on the basis of data on the rate of depreciation and the after-tax rate of return, corrected for inflation. For current law, for the two alternative proposals, and for economic depreciation, we have weighted the present values of actual investment to obtain average present values for equipment, structures, and total investment. We present the results of our calculations in table 15.

Under present U.S. tax law and under the two alternative proposals for more rapid capital recovery, capital consumption allowances are based on the historical cost of acquisition of an asset. We have calculated present values of these allowances under currently anticipated rates of inflation, based on the term structure for government securities for 1980 given in table 5. Since anticipated rates of inflation may be higher or lower in the future, we have also calculated present values under anticipated rates of inflation for 1960, 1966, and 1973—all of which involved lower anticipated rates of inflation than 1980. We have also added 4 percent to the yields on government securities for 1980 to obtain hypothetical values of anticipated rates of inflation that are higher than those in 1980.

In characterizing provisions for capital recovery under present law we have assumed that asset lifetimes, scrap values, and accounting formulas for tax purposes will remain the same as those for 1980. We find that at currently anticipated rates of inflation, present law provides capital consumption for tax purposes that exceeds economic depreciation by 7.6 percent. The excess over economic depreciation would rise to 22.3 percent at anticipated rates of inflation of 1973, to 31.4 percent at rates for 1966, and to 35.1 percent at rates for 1960. If anticipated rates of inflation were to increase by 4 percent over currently anticipated rates, the present value of capital consumption allowances for tax purposes would drop below economic depreciation by only 2.6 percent. Our first conclusion is that present law provides capital consumption allowances for corporate investment as a whole that are in line with economic depreciation at currently anticipated rates of inflation.

We next compare the two proposals for more rapid capital recovery introduced in Congress with present law. Under currently anticipated rates of inflation we find that present values of capital consumption allowances would be 27.5 percent in excess of economic depreciation under the Sen-

TABLE 15

PRESENT VALUES OF CORPORATE CAPITAL CONSUMPTION ALLOWANCES FOR TAX PURPOSES ON NEW INVESTMENT

Discount Factors	Policy	Present Values Equipment	Structures	Total	Ratio Tax to Economic	Yield on 10-year Security
1960	Current	0.886	0.641	0.801	1.351	4.13
	Reagan	0.941	0.823	0.900	1.518	4.13
	Senate	0.941	0.760	0.879	1.482	4.13
1966	Current	0.867	0.611	0.779	1.314	4.86
	Reagan	0.927	0.803	0.885	1.492	4.86
	Senate	0.927	0.735	0.861	1.452	4.86
1973	Current	0.831	0.525	0.725	1.223	6.73
	Reagan	0.907	0.758	0.855	1.442	6.73
	Senate	0.907	0.669	0.825	1.391	6.73
1980	Current	0.754	0.418	0.638	1.076	11.16
	Reagan	0.856	0.672	0.792	1.336	11.16
	Senate	0.857	0.563	0.756	1.275	11.16
1980 Plus Four Percent	Current	0.696	0.352	0.578	0.974	15.16
	Reagan	0.815	0.610	0.745	1.256	15.16
	Senate	0.819	0.492	0.706	1.191	15.16

ate Finance Committee proposal and 33.6 percent in excess under the Reagan administration proposal. Under lower anticipated rates of inflation the excess of capital consumption allowances over economic depreciation would rise substantially, reaching 51.8 percent of economic depreciation under the Reagan proposal for anticipated rates of inflation in 1960. At higher anticipated rates of inflation both proposals would result in capital consumption allowances that are greater than economic depreciation.

To calculate effective tax rates under present law and the two alternative proposals, we combine information on the offset to tax liability provided by the investment tax credit with the value of capital consumption allowances as a deduction from taxable income. The effective tax rate for an asset also depends on the statutory tax rate, the rate of economic depreciation, and the rate of return after taxes, corrected for inflation. We present effective tax rates for equipment, structures, and total investment under current law and each of the two alternative proposals in table 16. At this point it may be useful to recall that the effective tax rate for all assets under economic depreciation is equal to the statutory rate of 46 percent, while the effective tax rate with immediate expensing of the cost of acquisition of assets is equal to zero. As before, we have calculated effective tax rates under alternative assumptions about anticipated future rates of inflation.

At currently anticipated rates of inflation the effective tax rate under present law for corporate investment as a whole is 24 percent. This is a little over half the statutory tax rate of 46 percent. The Senate Finance Committee proposal would reduce the effective tax rate on corporate investment to 13 percent. This would represent a little over one-fourth of the statutory rate. Finally, the Reagan administration proposal would result in a negative effective tax rate for corporate investment. The combination of very short asset lifetimes for tax purposes and an increase in the investment tax credit for some assets would imply that the corporate income tax would be replaced by a corporate income subsidy for depreciable assets. Tax deductions and credits for these assets would be available to "shelter" income from nondepreciable assets such as land, inventories, and financial claims.

If anticipated inflation rates were to increase as much as 4 percent relative to those that prevail currently, the Reagan administration proposal would result in a slightly positive effective tax rate. The effective tax rate under current law would rise to 32 percent, while the Senate proposal would result in effective tax rates of 20 percent. If anticipated inflation rates were to drop to those prevailing in 1973, the effective tax rate under

TABLE 16
Effective Corporate Tax Rates on New Investment

Discount Factors	Policy	Corporate Tax Rate			Ratio of Effective Rate to Statutory Rate
		Equipment	Structures	Total	
1960	Current	-0.22	0.20	-0.08	-0.172
	Reagan	-0.88	-0.01	-0.58	-1.267
	Senate	-0.25	0.11	-0.13	-0.277
1966	Current	-0.14	0.22	-0.02	-0.033
	Reagan	-0.71	0.02	-0.46	-1.004
	Senate	-0.19	0.13	-0.08	-0.170
1973	Current	-0.01	0.28	0.09	0.200
	Reagan	-0.52	0.07	-0.31	-0.684
	Senate	-0.10	0.19	0.00	-0.006
1980	Current	0.19	0.35	0.24	0.528
	Reagan	-0.20	0.16	-0.07	-0.161
	Senate	0.05	0.28	0.13	0.275
1980 Plus Four Percent	Current	0.29	0.39	0.32	0.702
	Reagan	-0.03	0.22	0.06	0.121
	Senate	0.14	0.32	0.20	0.440

the Reagan administration proposal would be a negative 31 percent. The resulting "shelter" for income from nondepreciable assets could be sufficient to reduce receipts from the corporate income tax to zero. The negative effective tax rate under the Reagan administration proposal would rise to 46 percent at 1966 anticipated rates of inflation and to 58 percent at 1960 anticipated rates of inflation.

Present U.S. corporate income tax law would result in an effective tax rate of 9 percent at 1973 anticipated rates of inflation, a negative 2 percent at rates of 1966 and a negative 8 percent at rates of 1960. The Senate Finance Committee proposal would result in a zero effective tax rate at 1973 anticipated rates of inflation; this would fall to negative levels at 1960 and 1966 rates, reaching a negative 13 percent at 1960 rates. Our overall conclusion is that current law and both alternative proposals would replace the corporate income tax by a corporate income subsidy at anticipated rates of inflation comparable to those that prevailed in 1960 and 1966, while the Reagan administration proposal would replace the corporate income tax by a corporate income subsidy at current inflation rates or at 1973 rates.

The second issue we consider in comparing alternative systems for capital recovery under the corporate income tax is the differences in effective tax rates among assets. Gaps among effective tax rates result in an inefficient allocation of capital among assets. Under present law the difference between effective tax rates on equipment and structures at currently anticipated rates of inflation is 16 percent. Under the Reagan administration proposal this difference would widen to 36 percent. The gap for the Senate Finance Committee proposal would be 23 percent.

The gap between effective tax rates on equipment and structures under present U.S. law would widen to 29 percent at 1973 anticipated rates of inflation, 36 percent at 1966 rates, and 42 percent at 1960 rates. Under the Reagan administration proposal the gap would widen to 59 percent at 1973 anticipated rates of inflation, 73 percent at 1966 rates, and 87 percent at 1960 rates. As before, we find it useful to translate this gap into the corresponding gap between social rates of return. For rates of inflation anticipated in 1960 the Reagan administration proposal would result in a difference in social rates of return to investment in equipment and structures of 2.78 percent. This can be compared with the average private rate of return of 6.06 percent for the postwar period.

Our overall conclusion is that differences in effective tax rates among assets under present U.S. tax law are substantial, even at the very high anticipated rates of inflation prevailing currently. These differences increase with a decrease in anticipated rates of inflation, reducing efficiency in the allocation of capital. The differences in effective tax rates would widen significantly under the Senate Finance Committee proposal and would widen even further under the Reagan administration proposal. Just as under present law, these gaps would increase with a decrease in anticipated rates of inflation.

We next provide additional detail on effective tax rates by type of asset under present law and the two alternative proposals. For this purpose we have calculated effective tax rates for all 35 assets listed in table 1 at currently anticipated rates of inflation. We give the present value of capital consumption allowances, the effective rate of the tax credit, and the effective tax rate for each asset in table 17. Under present law effective tax rates range from 48 percent for other nonfarm buildings to 8 percent for aircraft. Under the Reagan administration proposal the gap ranges from 36 percent for commercial buildings to a negative 32 percent for office, computing, and accounting machinery. The gap for the Senate Finance Committee proposal ranges from 41 percent for other nonfarm buildings to 2 percent for agricultural machinery.

Similarly, we provide additional detail on effective tax rates by industry under present law and the two alternative proposals. For this purpose we have calculated effective tax rates for all 44 industries listed in table 13 at currently anticipated rates of inflation. We give effective tax rates on equipment, structures, and total investment for each industry in table 18. Under present law the effective tax rates range from 35.2 percent for metal mining to 8.8 percent for air transportation. Under the Reagan administration proposal effective tax rates would be negative for 33 industries and small but positive for the remaining 11 industries. Effective subsidy rates range up to 25.4 percent for trucking service, warehousing, and storage. Under the Senate Finance Committee proposal all effective tax rates are positive and less than 27.4 percent.

Our analysis of effective tax rates by type of asset and by industry under present law and under the two alternative proposals corroborates the conclusions we reached on the basis of effective tax rates for all U.S. corporations. At currently anticipated rates of inflation the effective tax rate under present law exceeds the statutory rate of 46 percent only for commercial buildings, hospital buildings, and other nonfarm buildings. Effective tax rates under present law are as low as 8 percent for aircraft. The highest effective tax rate for any industry is 35.2 percent for metal mining. Even at the very high anticipated rates of inflation prevailing currently, liberalization of tax provisions for capital recovery during the postwar

TABLE 17

EFFECTIVE CORPORATE TAX RATES BY ASSET: PRESENT LAW

Asset	Lifetime	Present Discounted Value	Investment Tax Credit	Effective Corporate Tax Rate
1	7.8	0.743	0.09	0.12
2	9.8	0.692	0.09	0.19
3	12.2	0.639	0.09	0.24
4	5.0	0.828	0.06	0.11
5	7.8	0.743	0.09	0.11
6	7.8	0.743	0.09	0.16
7	7.5	0.750	0.09	0.14
8	10.0	0.687	0.09	0.22
9	10.0	0.687	0.09	0.21
10	7.8	0.743	0.09	0.13
11	8.9	0.718	0.09	0.28
12	8.1	0.735	0.09	0.17
13	9.7	0.694	0.09	0.21
14	4.4	0.846	0.05	0.19
15	3.0	0.897	0.03	0.16
16	6.0	0.794	0.08	0.08
17	14.1	0.601	0.09	0.27
18	11.8	0.646	0.09	0.21
19	8.3	0.731	0.09	0.17
20	8.0	0.738	0.09	0.16
21	25.3	0.389	0.00	0.45
22	41.8	0.264	0.00	0.47
23	42.1	0.262	0.00	0.45
24	42.1	0.262	0.00	0.45
25	42.1	0.262	0.00	0.47
26	27.1	0.373	0.00	0.48
27	26.3	0.380	0.09	0.32
28	23.7	0.409	0.09	0.34
29	23.7	0.409	0.09	0.33
30	21.1	0.441	0.09	0.31
31	19.3	0.468	0.09	0.33
32	21.9	0.432	0.09	0.30
33	6.0	0.765	0.06	0.14
34	24.7	0.399	0.09	0.34
35	24.8	0.398	0.00	0.38

TABLE 17   (continued)

EFFECTIVE CORPORATE TAX RATES BY ASSET: REAGAN PROPOSAL

Asset	Lifetime	Present Discounted Value	Investment Tax Credit	Effective Corporate Tax Rate
1	5.0	0.851	0.09	−0.14
2	5.0	0.851	0.09	−0.12
3	5.0	0.851	0.09	−0.11
4	5.0	0.851	0.09	−0.19
5	5.0	0.851	0.09	−0.13
6	5.0	0.851	0.09	−0.20
7	5.0	0.851	0.09	−0.19
8	5.0	0.851	0.09	−0.15
9	5.0	0.851	0.09	−0.13
10	5.0	0.851	0.09	−0.15
11	5.0	0.851	0.09	−0.32
12	5.0	0.851	0.09	−0.19
13	5.0	0.851	0.09	−0.15
14	5.0	0.851	0.09	−0.29
15	3.0	0.913	0.06	−0.23
16	5.0	0.851	0.09	−0.21
17	5.0	0.851	0.09	−0.11
18	5.0	0.851	0.09	−0.10
19	5.0	0.851	0.09	−0.18
20	5.0	0.851	0.09	−0.18
21	10.0	0.727	0.00	0.27
22	15.0	0.529	0.00	0.36
23	10.0	0.727	0.00	0.23
24	10.0	0.727	0.00	0.23
25	10.0	0.727	0.00	0.24
26	10.0	0.727	0.00	0.29
27	10.0	0.727	0.09	0.07
28	10.0	0.727	0.09	0.09
29	10.0	0.727	0.09	0.09
30	10.0	0.727	0.09	0.09
31	10.0	0.727	0.09	0.10
32	10.0	0.727	0.09	0.08
33	5.0	0.851	0.09	−0.09
34	10.0	0.727	0.09	0.08
35	18.0	0.472	0.00	0.35

TABLE 17 (concluded)

EFFECTIVE CORPORATE TAX RATES BY ASSET: SENATE FINANCE
COMMITTEE PROPOSAL

Asset	Lifetime	Present Discounted Value	Investment Tax Credit	Effective Corporate Tax Rate
1	4.0	0.866	0.06	0.03
2	7.0	0.774	0.09	0.05
3	10.0	0.692	0.09	0.17
4	4.0	0.866	0.06	0.04
5	2.0	0.942	0.02	0.02
6	2.0	0.942	0.02	0.03
7	4.0	0.866	0.06	0.04
8	7.0	0.774	0.09	0.06
9	7.0	0.774	0.09	0.06
10	4.0	0.866	0.06	0.03
11	4.0	0.866	0.06	0.06
12	4.0	0.866	0.06	0.04
13	7.0	0.774	0.09	0.06
14	2.0	0.942	0.02	0.04
15	2.0	0.942	0.02	0.04
16	4.0	0.866	0.06	0.05
17	10.0	0.692	0.09	0.17
18	7.0	0.774	0.09	0.04
19	4.0	0.866	0.06	0.04
20	4.0	0.866	0.06	0.04
21	15.0	0.539	0.00	0.39
22	15.0	0.539	0.00	0.36
23	15.0	0.539	0.00	0.34
24	15.0	0.539	0.00	0.34
25	15.0	0.539	0.00	0.35
26	15.0	0.539	0.00	0.41
27	15.0	0.539	0.09	0.22
28	15.8	0.526	0.09	0.27
29	15.8	0.526	0.09	0.26
30	15.8	0.526	0.09	0.26
31	15.8	0.526	0.09	0.29
32	15.0	0.539	0.09	0.24
33	4.0	0.845	0.06	0.05
34	15.0	0.539	0.09	0.25
35	20.0	0.420	0.00	0.37

TABLE 18

EFFECTIVE CORPORATE TAX RATES BY INDUSTRY: PRESENT LAW

Industry	Equipment	Structures	Total
1	0.187	0.450	0.256
2	0.149	0.450	0.207
3	0.204	0.450	0.244
4	0.197	0.450	0.273
5	0.195	0.450	0.223
6	0.197	0.450	0.246
7	0.181	0.450	0.223
8	0.189	0.450	0.302
9	0.206	0.450	0.254
10	0.207	0.450	0.284
11	0.181	0.450	0.235
12	0.191	0.450	0.283
13	0.179	0.450	0.234
14	0.190	0.450	0.235
15	0.200	0.450	0.261
16	0.208	0.450	0.271
17	0.204	0.450	0.255
18	0.183	0.450	0.256
19	0.194	0.450	0.214
20	0.209	0.450	0.269
21	0.198	0.450	0.273
22	0.141	0.300	0.152
23	0.141	0.300	0.152
24	0.163	0.454	0.352
25	0.147	0.351	0.176
26	0.150	0.272	0.264
27	0.152	0.458	0.170
28	0.161	0.464	0.174
29	0.210	0.320	0.219
30	0.172	0.450	0.173
31	0.178	0.450	0.183
32	0.270	0.450	0.270
33	0.087	0.470	0.088
34	0.217	0.330	0.321
35	0.187	0.470	0.195
36	0.209	0.340	0.241
37	0.210	0.478	0.301
38	0.205	0.330	0.281
39	0.205	0.310	0.290
40	0.205	0.340	0.335
41	0.172	0.470	0.212
42	0.172	0.470	0.278
43	0.212	0.458	0.298
44	0.183	0.467	0.248

TABLE 18   (continued)

EFFECTIVE CORPORATE TAX RATES BY INDUSTRY: REAGAN PROPOSAL

Industry	Equipment	Structures	Total
1	−0.167	0.270	−0.051
2	−0.156	0.270	−0.074
3	−0.139	0.270	−0.072
4	−0.146	0.270	−0.021
5	−0.142	0.270	−0.096
6	−0.138	0.270	−0.059
7	−0.148	0.270	−0.083
8	−0.169	0.270	0.021
9	−0.150	0.270	−0.067
10	−0.135	0.270	−0.006
11	−0.217	0.270	−0.121
12	−0.139	0.270	0.006
13	−0.190	0.270	−0.097
14	−0.153	0.270	−0.080
15	−0.149	0.270	−0.047
16	−0.159	0.270	−0.048
17	−0.156	0.270	−0.067
18	−0.148	0.270	−0.033
19	−0.159	0.270	−0.125
20	−0.165	0.270	−0.057
21	−0.158	0.270	−0.032
22	−0.144	0.080	−0.129
23	−0.144	0.080	−0.129
24	−0.180	0.271	0.114
25	−0.190	0.100	−0.150
26	−0.180	0.067	0.052
27	−0.188	0.304	−0.158
28	−0.191	0.329	−0.169
29	−0.100	0.070	−0.086
30	0.054	0.270	0.055
31	−0.263	0.270	−0.254
32	−0.110	0.270	−0.110
33	−0.207	0.360	−0.205
34	−0.142	0.100	0.080
35	−0.256	0.360	−0.239
36	−0.152	0.090	−0.093
37	−0.150	0.298	0.002
38	−0.146	0.090	−0.003
39	−0.146	0.090	0.045
40	−0.146	0.080	0.071
41	−0.140	0.360	−0.073
42	−0.140	0.360	0.037
43	−0.168	0.333	0.007
44	−0.136	0.332	−0.030

TABLE 18   (concluded)

EFFECTIVE CORPORATE TAX RATES BY INDUSTRY: SENATE FINANCE
COMMITTEE PROPOSAL

Industry	Equipment	Structures	Total
1	0.047	0.390	0.138
2	0.035	0.390	0.103
3	0.056	0.390	0.111
4	0.052	0.390	0.154
5	0.055	0.390	0.092
6	0.052	0.390	0.118
7	0.048	0.390	0.101
8	0.051	0.390	0.198
9	0.055	0.390	0.121
10	0.056	0.390	0.162
11	0.044	0.390	0.113
12	0.049	0.390	0.170
13	0.043	0.390	0.113
14	0.050	0.390	0.109
15	0.052	0.390	0.135
16	0.053	0.390	0.141
17	0.053	0.390	0.123
18	0.050	0.390	0.143
19	0.049	0.390	0.076
20	0.052	0.390	0.137
21	0.050	0.390	0.151
22	0.037	0.240	0.051
23	0.037	0.240	0.051
24	0.045	0.385	0.267
25	0.038	0.262	0.069
26	0.041	0.186	0.178
27	0.040	0.374	0.060
28	0.034	0.363	0.048
29	0.040	0.220	0.054
30	0.040	0.390	0.041
31	0.038	0.390	0.044
32	0.170	0.390	0.170
33	0.050	0.360	0.051
34	0.093	0.290	0.274
35	0.041	0.360	0.050
36	0.059	0.270	0.111
37	0.060	0.404	0.177
38	0.070	0.260	0.185
39	0.070	0.260	0.224
40	0.070	0.250	0.243
41	0.042	0.360	0.084
42	0.042	0.360	0.155
43	0.049	0.350	0.154
44	0.047	0.359	0.118

period has been sufficient to keep effective tax rates well below the statutory rate for all industries. Levels of effective tax rates would decrease for all assets and all industries under either of the alternative proposals.

Differences in effective tax rates among assets and among industries are very substantial under current law. As before, these differences correspond to gaps between social rates of return among assets and industries. These gaps represent opportunities to increase national wealth with no sacrifice in consumption either now or in the future. These gaps would widen significantly under the Reagan administration proposal and would narrow slightly under the Senate Finance Committee proposal. We can emphasize the fact that effective tax rates would decrease with a decrease in anticipated rates of inflation, while differences in effective tax rates among assets and among industries would increase with a decrease in the rate of inflation.

VI. Conclusions

Our first major conclusion is that inflation has had a dramatic impact on capital recovery under the U.S. corporate income tax. For a given set of tax provisions, an increase in the rate of inflation reduces the present value of capital consumption allowances as an offset to the cost of acquisition of assets. The effective rate of taxation increases with an increase in the rate of inflation and decreases with a decrease in the rate of inflation. It is important to emphasize both the impact of higher inflation rates and the impact of lower inflation rates. An important objective of current economic policy is to reduce the rate of inflation. If this objective were to be realized, effective tax rates under present U.S. law would decline substantially, reaching the level of only 8 percent for U.S. corporations as a whole at anticipated rates of inflation like those prevailing as recently as 1973.

Our second major conclusion is that a decrease in the rate of inflation under present U.S. law increases the gaps among effective tax rates for different assets and different industries. At currently anticipated rates of inflation these gaps are substantial, but they would widen significantly with a decrease in the rate of inflation. Differences in effective tax rates among assets correspond to differences in social rates of return to investment in these assets. By transferring investment from lightly taxed assets to more heavily taxed assets it is possible to increase the national wealth with no sacrifice in present or future consumption. Opportunities for costless increases in the national wealth would increase considerably with a decrease in the rate of inflation.

While effective tax rates in the United States are currently among the lowest of the postwar period, proposals for further reduction in these rates are under consideration by the Congress. Even with a 4 percent increase in the anticipated rate of inflation over the unprecedented prevailing levels, the Reagan administration proposal would result in replacing the corporate income tax by a corporate income subsidy with a negative effective tax rate for U.S. corporations as a whole. At currently prevailing rates of inflation the Reagan administration proposal would generate huge offsets to the cost of acquisition of depreciable assets through the investment tax credit and deductions of capital consumption allowances for tax purposes. These offsets would be sufficient to exhaust the income generated by investments in depreciable assets and would spill over to provide "shelter" for income from nondepreciable assets such as land, inventories, and financial claims.

A second consequence of the adoption of the Reagan administration proposal for capital recovery under U.S. tax law would be a substantial widening of gaps among effective tax rates for different assets and different industries. This would very significantly worsen the efficiency of capital allocation and would reduce the level of productivity for the U.S. economy. Under current law and under both alternative proposals we have considered, the gaps among effective tax rates would increase as rates of inflation decrease. Under these policies a successful anti-inflation program would worsen the efficiency of capital allocation.

Our analysis of the impact of inflation on capital recovery under U.S. tax law also provides an answer to the obvious question arising from current pressures for more rapid capital recovery. If effective tax rates on new investment have fallen, why are investors and policy makers convinced that they have risen? The first part of the answer to this question is that effective tax rates have risen since the postwar low of 1977, when rates of inflation in asset prices had fallen to 5.6 percent in 1976 and 7.7 percent in 1977. These rates of inflation can be compared with the level of 12.8 percent in 1975 at the time of the most recent change in tax provisions for capital recovery. However, while rates of inflation were at double-digit levels in 1980, the Reagan administration is projecting a rapid decline in rates of inflation.

A second part of the explanation for the perception that effective tax rates are currently high, while our analysis has shown that they are currently low, is the nature of offsets to tax liability. While the taxpayer receives the investment tax credit as an offset to tax liability in the year an asset is acquired, capital consumption allowances are a deduction from income and are distributed over the useful life of the asset by means of accounting formulas. In effect, the taxpayer receives a claim on future tax deductions that is analogous to a government bond. Unfortunately, the value of this claim, like the value of a government bond, drops with increases in anticipated rates of inflation. Anticipated rates of inflation have jumped almost 4 percent since 1975 and holders of depreciable assets, like holders of government bonds, have suffered drastic capital losses.

If the Reagan administration's antiinflation program is successful, both holders of government bonds and holders of claims for future tax deductions on depreciable assets will experience capital gains that will offset capital losses under the Carter administration in the late 1970s. These capital gains will occur even with no changes in tax provisions for capital recovery. Effective tax rates will decline to very modest levels and may even become negative under current U.S. tax law. Unfortunately, this decline will be distributed very unevenly among assets and among industries. As a consequence, the efficiency of capital allocation will fall, undercutting future productivity.

The impact of the Reagan administration tax proposals will depend critically on the success of the administration's anti-inflation policy. Even if anticipated rates of inflation were to increase by 4 percent, the effective tax rate on new investment under the Reagan administration proposal for capital recovery would still be negative. However, substantial gaps in effective tax rates among assets and among industries would remain, resulting in a drag on productivity. If the Reagan anti-inflation program were to have no impact at all, the effective tax rate for the corporate sector would be negative, resulting in the replacement of the corporate income tax by a corporate income subsidy for investment in depreciable assets. If the Reagan anti-inflation program were to achieve its stated objective of reducing rates of inflation below those that prevailed in 1973, holders of depreciable assets would enjoy huge capital gains on capital consumption allowances still to be claimed on their existing assets. They would also receive substantial subsidies on new investments.

Our overall conclusion is that policies for corporate income taxation that deal effectively with the impact of inflation cannot be based on accelerated capital recovery. As we have seen, variations in the rate of inflation are an important part of the problem facing policy makers. Neither the Reagan administration proposal nor the Senate Finance Committee proposal is capable of coping with these variations. The Senate Finance Committee proposal would succeed in lowering the effective tax rates for different assets and different industries. However, the impact of this proposal, like the impact of the Reagan administration proposal, would be strongly dependent on the rate of inflation that actually occurs.

In closing we can briefly outline two possible approaches to the reform of provisions for capital recovery under the U.S. corporate income tax that would deal effectively with the problem of inflation. First, immediate expensing of the cost of acquisition of assets would result in a zero effective tax rate on income from all depreciable assets, whatever the rate of inflation. While immediate expensing would amount to the elimination of the corporate income tax, this proposal is superior to alternative proposals that would replace the tax by a corporate income subsidy. Policy makers who are optimistic about the success of anti-inflation measures and advocate the elimination of the corporate income tax should regard present high rates of inflation as the last great opportunity to shift to immediate expensing. As rates of inflation decline, subsidies to investment in specific assets through the tax structure will arise. Each such subsidy will generate a political constituency that will act as an obstacle to the introduction of immediate expensing.

A second pathway to the reform of capital recovery provisions of U.S. tax law is more closely related to current tax provisions and preserves flexibility in the selection of an appropriate level for the effective tax rate. The first step in tax reform would be to replace existing capital consumption allowances for tax purposes by a first year allowance, as proposed by Auerbach and Jorgenson (1980). This would completely eliminate the problems that result from forcing holders of depreciable assets to hold claims on the government in the form of future tax deductions that can appreciate or depreciate like government bonds. Since this proposal is equivalent to deducting economic depreciation, it has the unfortunate consequence of increasing the effective tax rate to the statutory rate.

The second step in tax reform would be to provide an investment tax credit that is proportional to the difference between the cost of acquisition of an asset and the first year allowance, as proposed by Brown (1981). By varying the proportion between zero and the statutory tax rate, it would be possible to produce any effective tax rate between the statutory rate and zero. Since the Brown investment tax credit, like the Auerbach-Jorgenson first year allowance, would be taken in the same year an asset is acquired, it would create no claims on the government that are subject to capital gains and losses with changes in the rate of inflation. The resulting first year capital recovery system would preserve the existing features of U.S.

tax law—capital consumption allowances as a deduction from taxable income and the investment tax credit as an offset to tax liability.

As an illustration of a system for capital recovery under U.S. tax law based on the first year capital recovery system, we present in table 19 the first year allowances for all 35 types of assets listed in table 1. These first year allowances are based on a discount rate after taxes of 6 percent. We also present tax credits on these assets that would produce effective tax rates on all assets of zero, half the current statutory tax rate of 46 percent, and the statutory tax rate itself. Investment tax credits would range from 35 percent on residential structures to 7 percent on autos at an effective tax rate of zero for all assets. For an effective tax rate of 23 percent, which is comparable to present law at currently anticipated rates of inflation, investment tax credits would range from 19 percent on residential structures to 4 percent on autos.

The first year capital recovery system, as we have outlined it, would preserve the simplicity of the Auerbach-Jorgenson proposal. Existing provisions of the tax code on capital recovery could be replaced by a simple table like table 19, giving the first year allowances and the investment tax credits permitted by law. As under immediate expensing of assets, tax deductions and tax credits would depend only on current transactions in assets and would not require a cumbersome system of vintage accounts for auditing and verification. The main advantage of the first year system over immediate expensing is the possibility of setting effective tax rates at levels other than zero.

Appendix

In this appendix we describe the methodology we have used to simulate practices permitted by the Internal Revenue Service in calculating capital consumption allowances for tax purposes. Our control total is based on capital consumption allowances claimed by U.S. corporations on their income tax returns. Our depreciable base is a time series of corporate investment disaggregated by the types of assets listed in table 1. Our objective is to estimate tax parameters by reconciling the depreciable base with reported depreciation. These parameters allow us to calculate effective tax rates in the historical period covered by our study, as well as to compare tax rates under present practices to those under proposed systems for capital recovery.

TABLE 19

First Year Capital Recovery System

Asset	First Year Allowance	Investment Tax Credit at Various Effective Tax Rates		
		Zero	.23	.46
1	0.645	0.16	0.08	0.00
2	0.602	0.18	0.09	0.00
3	0.565	0.20	0.10	0.00
4	0.729	0.12	0.06	0.00
5	0.616	0.18	0.09	0.00
6	0.740	0.12	0.06	0.00
7	0.731	0.12	0.06	0.00
8	0.669	0.15	0.08	0.00
9	0.630	0.17	0.09	0.00
10	0.669	0.15	0.08	0.00
11	0.818	0.08	0.04	0.00
12	0.731	0.12	0.06	0.00
13	0.660	0.16	0.08	0.00
14	0.807	0.09	0.04	0.00
15	0.846	0.07	0.04	0.00
16	0.752	0.11	0.06	0.00
17	0.553	0.21	0.10	0.00
18	0.521	0.22	0.11	0.00
19	0.712	0.13	0.07	0.00
20	0.712	0.13	0.07	0.00
21	0.373	0.29	0.14	0.00
22	0.290	0.33	0.16	0.00
23	0.237	0.35	0.18	0.00
24	0.237	0.35	0.18	0.00
25	0.278	0.33	0.17	0.00
26	0.428	0.26	0.13	0.00
27	0.225	0.36	0.18	0.00
28	0.355	0.30	0.15	0.00
29	0.331	0.31	0.15	0.00
30	0.331	0.31	0.15	0.00
31	0.426	0.26	0.13	0.00
32	0.281	0.33	0.13	0.00
33	0.482	0.24	0.17	0.00
34	0.324	0.31	0.12	0.00
35	0.173	0.38	0.19	0.00

Our approach parallels an earlier study by Allan Young (1968), but contains additional detail on capital consumption practices. It should be noted that Young's study was not designed for estimating tax parameters, but for calculating capital consumption allowances to measure profits. This does not require the level of detail we have employed. The results of our simulation of reported capital consumption allowances show that we have significantly improved and extended Young's approach. [10]

We use a simulation model based on a system of closed-end vintage accounts. In each year we open a new set of accounts equal to the number of categories of depreciable investment. In general, gross investment in each asset class minus estimated salvage value serves as the depreciable base. [11] Current year investment is used for equipment investment; since capital consumption allowances on an asset are allowed only when it is put in use, structures investment, which is measured as it is put into place, is lagged one-half year to approximate the lag from the emplacement of capital to the beginning of the depreciation period. [12] Each asset account is divided into two subaccounts, one for accelerated depreciation and one for straight-line depreciation.

As a particular vintage of an asset ages, annual depreciation deductions are added together until accumulated depreciation equals the base. At this point the account is terminated and no asset is depreciated below its salvage value. In a model with two depreciation methods 20 categories of investment with an average lifetime of 10 years would result in approximately 400 active vintage accounts in the aggregate calculation.

Straight-line depreciation allowances are calculated by multiplying the straight-line rate of depreciation, that is, the inverse of the assigned lifetime, by the straight-line base. For accelerated depreciation, we multiply the straight-line rate by an appropriate constant and again by the declining base. Unlike the straight-line method, the base is reduced annually by the amount of capital consumption. [13] The constant, sometimes called the declining balance rate, corresponds to the type of declining balance (i.e., 2.0 for double declining balance, 1.5 for 150 percent declining balance).

Our starting point for parameterizing depreciation is the history of tax depreciation regulations promulgated by Congress and administered by the Internal Revenue Service. [14] Depreciation entered the tax code in 1909 in order to calculate income for tax purposes. Straight-line was the accepted method for calculating depreciation, but little is known about tax lifetimes, except that taxpayers were given considerable freedom of choice. This changed abruptly in 1934 with the revenue requirements of the New Deal. To achieve a desired 25 percent reduction in depreciation allowances, Treasury Decision 4422 was issued, shifting the burden of proving reasonableness of depreciation from the IRS to the taxpayer.

Tax lifetimes listed in the third edition of *Bulletin F* (1942) were generally longer than those provided in the 1931 edition and were probably indicative of the tough stance taken by the Treasury after 1934. Nevertheless, shorter lives were permitted under special facts and circumstances. In light of the long lifetimes suggested in *Bulletin F*, it is not surprising that controversy often arose between taxpayers and the IRS. Tax lifetimes are known to have decreased considerably below *Bulletin F* levels by the early 1950s, if not sooner.[15] The burden of proof of reasonableness was shifted from the taxpayer back to the IRS in 1953.

A notable exception to standard depreciation practices during the period was the special provision for 60-month amortization of defense-related facilities. Certificates of necessity for such practices were issued during World War II and the years around the Korean War. This provision had its greatest effect in 1945 when a statute allowed all remaining undepreciated balances to be written off in that year. This increased depreciation allowances an estimated $1.7 billion from a total of $4.3 billion.[16]

In 1954 the more generous double declining balance and sum-of-the-years'-digits methods were made available to all taxpayers for new investments. Although a small, but not negligible, amount of investment had been depreciated with the units-of-production method before 1954 and although 150 percent declining balance had been allowed since 1946, it was not until 1954 that the widespread use of the straight-line method began to decline significantly. The decline was not rapid; even in 1961, 50 percent of all depreciation deductions were calculated by the straight-line formula.[17]

The most far reaching change in the taxation of income from capital occurred in 1962 with the introduction of the investment tax credit for equipment and certain qualifying structures. At the same time the Treasury issued Revenue Proclamation 62-21 which set forth "Guideline" lifetimes which were 30 to 40 percent shorter on average than *Bulletin F* lives.[18] There is considerable evidence that lifetimes on new investment at this time were already at the level prescribed by the Guidelines.[19] The large immediate impact of the Guidelines on the level of depreciation allowances was due to the inclusion of existing as well as new assets under the system. In the long run, the Guidelines increased depreciation allowances through a general relaxation of all depreciation rules:

> A central objective of the new procedure is to facilitate the adoption of depreciable lives even shorter than those set forth in the Guidelines, or even

shorter than those currently in use, provided only that certain standards are met and subsequent replacement practices are reasonably consistent with tax lives claimed.[20]

The "certain standards" took the form of the reserve ratio test. However, after a three year grace period and subsequent extensions, the reserve ratio test was never adopted. Its relative complexity would have made it difficult to administer. However, it was generally believed that the requirements of the test would not be met by a large percentage of taxpayers, suggesting tax lifetimes lower than the Guideline lives.

In 1962 and 1963, the depreciable base of assets was reduced by the amount of the investment tax credit. The repeal of the Long amendment in 1964 removed this requirement and made depreciation allowances even more generous. The only significant reversal in the trend toward greater acceleration of allowances since 1934 occurred with the Tax Reform Act of 1969. This law limited all real estate signed into contract after July 24, 1969, to 150 percent declining balance depreciation.

In 1971, the same year the investment tax credit was reenacted after its suspension of nearly two years, the Asset Depreciation Range (ADR) System was introduced by the Treasury. This new system allowed taxpayers to adopt lifetimes generally 20 percent above or below their Guideline levels. Although most longer-lived assets used the lower limit, some shorter-lived assets moved upward within their range to take better advantage of the graduated rate of the investment tax credit.[21] Like the Guidelines, ADR was intended primarily for equipment, but had provision for special purpose structures.[22]

The ADR was intended to simplify depreciation accounting but actually proved quite complex, and only the largest corporations could comply with its detailed accounting requirements. However, it is believed that smaller firms, less subject to audit, have informally adopted the lower limit ADR lives.[23] The last major change in the tax code occurred in 1975 when the rate of investment tax credit was increased from 4 to 10 percent for public utility property and from 7 to 10 percent for other eligible property.

A striking feature of the history of tax depreciation is the slowly evolving liberalization of actual practices in contrast to the abrupt changes in regulations. In the case of tax lifetimes, the change in practices have to some degree effectively preceded the changes in rules. On the other hand, in the case of depreciation methods, adoption of accelerated depreciation took place gradually after it was first made generally available in 1954.

The tremendous growth of corporate tax depreciation allowances from the approximate figures of $4.6 billion in 1946 to $25.3 billion in 1960 to

$119.8 billion in 1978 is attributable to four factors: (1) the growth of real investment in durable goods; (2) the rising price level of these goods; (3) successive liberalizations of depreciation rules; and (4) the increasing adoption over time by taxpayers of more liberal depreciation practices. We would expect a drift towards shorter lifetimes, more accelerated methods, and lower salvage values as taxpayers became more familiar with the tax code.

In our simulation model, the growth of real investment and the rising price level for investment goods are accounted for by use of a current dollar investment series as the depreciable base. All changes in the tax law mentioned above are incorporated as well. The timing of their adoption into practice, before or after change in IRS regulations as appropriate in each case, is an issue often ignored. This issue is directly addressed by calibrating simulated capital consumption allowances to actual allowances claimed by U.S. corporations.

It should be noted that data on new corporate investment would not adequately describe the depreciable base over the simulation period unless adjustment was made for the sale of used assets at prices higher than their depreciable value. The only significant data available on used asset investment is from the *Census of Manufactures*. We adjust for resale of assets by constructing a used asset investment series based on percentages of used asset investment to total investment reported in the *Census of Manufactures*. For the years 1947, 1954, 1958, 1963, 1967, 1972 and 1977, the respective percentages are 9.6, 4.4, 5.2, 5.8, 4.3, 5.1, and 5.7. These percentages are scaled upward by a factor of 1.4 to take into account the larger proportion of used asset investment in nonmanufacturing industries apparent from *Statistics of Income* data on used asset investment eligible for the investment tax credit.[24] In our simulation, we create a separate set of accounts for used assets and depreciate them according to IRS rules for used assets. We assume that the undepreciated bases of original owners are 30 percent of resale value and accordingly scale down used asset investment by a factor of 0.70.

The results of our simulation are presented in table 3 and show a close fit of simulated to actual allowances. The parameters used to calculate simulated allowances are summarized in table 4. These results are now examined and checked for reasonableness on the basis of available information on capital consumption practices.

Weighted averages of assumed lifetimes of new equipment and plant used in the simulation appear in columns 2 and 3 of table 4. All pre-1962 tax lifetimes for our 35 classes of assets are changed uniformly as percentages of *Bulletin F* lifetimes.[25] Before 1934, all assets are depreciated at two-thirds their *Bulletin F* lifetimes. In 1934, these percentages are increased to 94 percent and then decreased to 84 percent by 1944 and then to 81 percent by 1958.

According to 1962 *Statistics of Income,* $9.2 billion, or 30 percent of all depreciation taken was under the Guidelines. This we approximated by applying the Guidelines to 26 percent of the total depreciable basis. It is assumed that all investment depreciated under the Guidelines applied to new and existing assets. Thus, there is a sharp increase in allowances in 1962 and no corresponding change in depreciation methods or tax lifetimes for new investment. Corcoran (1979) and Vasquez (1974) report in independent studies that no considerable decrease in lifetimes on new assets occurred in 1962. The present simulation achieves a large increase in 1962 allowances by applying the Guidelines to a fraction of all vintages, not just the latest vintage, and thus considerably increases the depreciation rate of older vintages with longer tax lifetimes.

From 1962 to 1971 it was assumed that the amount of the capital stock depreciated under the Guidelines increased in even increments each year from approximately 26 to 100 percent. At the same time, lifetimes on new assets decreased by about 10 percent. For 1971 and after, only Guideline–ADR midpoint lives are used to calculate depreciation. Lifetimes of certain short-lived assets were adjusted upward if they were eligible for a larger investment tax credit by doing so.

Vasquez (1974) reports a 14 percent decrease in tax lifetimes from 1970 to 1971. In our simulation, the decrease was only about 8 percent. This anomaly is probably explained by a survey sample heavily biased with ADR electors who had most to gain by the change in tax rules. Based on our estimates of Guideline–ADR midpoint lives, average lifetimes on new investment decreased sharply from 93.7 percent of their midpoint values in 1971 to 83.5 percent in 1972, to 78.5 percent by 1978.

Our results are consistent with a relatively small population of large corporations electing the ADR system quite early, followed by more gradual elections of lower ADR range lives by smaller corporations. Small corporations could less easily comply with the ADR's complex accounting requirements. In our simulation the average lifetimes of equipment are as low as they effectively can be in the ADR range by 1978, given upward adjustments of certain assets to take full advantage of the investment tax credit.

Our average equipment lifetime in 1976 was equal to 8.43, or 82 percent of our estimate of our average Guideline–ADR midpoint lifetime. Unpublished Treasury data on the amounts of investment in each ADR class in 1976 allow us to obtain an alternative estimate.[26] The Treasury data derived estimate gives a 9.13 ADR midpoint, which translates our figure 8.43 to 92 percent of the ADR midpoint. This suggests our assumed Guideline–ADR is too high, but much of this can be explained by the fact that Guideline–ADR lifetimes are adjusted upward to take advantage of the investment tax credit.[27]

The amount of new investment using accelerated depreciation is reported in column 4 of table 6. In contrast to Young's study, where all pre-1954 vintage investment was assumed to be straight-line, *Statistics of Income* data show that 7 percent of depreciation of pre-1954 vintage investment deducted in 1959 was calculated by accelerated depreciation methods.[28] To approximate depreciation methods before 1954, percentages of 1.5 declining balance were included that allowed us to duplicate the 1959 figure on depreciation of pre-1954 investment.

Following the lead of Young (1968) and Wales (1968), we take advantage of the similarity between double declining balance and sum-of-the-years'-digits methods and assume all accelerated depreciation after 1954 is double declining balance. In order to terminate the accelerated depreciation vintage accounts, an optimal switchover to straight-line is employed. *Statistics of Income* reports percentages of depreciation taken under different methods for the years 1954 to 1961.[29] This is probably our most reliable data source on which to base our parameterization. The close approximation of these figures in our simulation to the actual figures shown in the last two columns of table 5 gives added credibility to the results. In addition, our 1971 estimate of a new investment with accelerated depreciation of 80 percent is compatible with the 81.7 percent figure reported by Vasquez.[30]

Survey results of salvage value as a percentage of original cost on buildings were reported in a Treasury study[31] and were generally found to be about 1 percent; accordingly, this value was used for salvage of structures in our simulation. Unfortunately, data on the salvage value of equipment are not available. However, we do make inferences about salvage values for purposes of our simulation.

Combining the two facts that the double declining balance method of depreciation is more generous than the sum-of-the-years'-digits method only in the case of nonnegligible salvage value[32] and that double declining balance was much more widely used historically than sum-of-the-years'-digits, it is probable that salvage value was significant for some assets. Informal discussions with IRS field agents suggest figures on average between 5 and 10 percent.

Although the IRS code states explicitly that no asset may be depreciated below its salvage value, certain provisions in the code do effectively lower salvage value estimated for tax purposes. For property acquired after October 16, 1962, taxpayers were allowed to decrease salvage values by up to 10 percent. Therefore, a salvage at 15 percent could be lowered to 5 percent, and for assets with salvage values of less than 10 percent, no salvage value need be considered. In 1971, ADR electors were granted an additional 10 percent reduction in salvage value. Our assumed salvage values for equipment presented in column 5 of table 6 reflect these changes in law as well as the shifts in burden of proof of reasonableness to the taxpayer in 1934 and back to the IRS in 1953.

We conclude that the simulated depreciation parameters summarized in table 3 are close approximations of actual practices used by U.S. corporations and can replace more highly simplified assumptions often employed in models of the corporate income tax. Furthermore, by comparing these parameters with those of proposed policy alternatives, more accurate estimates of the likely impact of policy changes can be made.

REFERENCES

Auerbach, Alan J. 1979a. "Inflation and the Choice of Asset Life." *Journal of Political Economy* 89 (June): 621–638.
_____. (1979b). "The Optimal Taxation of Heterogeneous Capital." *Quarterly Journal of Economics* 93, no. 4 (November): 589–612.
_____., and Dale W. Jorgenson. 1980. "Inflation-Proof Depreciation of Assets." *Harvard Business Review* 58, no. 5 (September–October): 113–118.
Bacharach, Michael. 1965. "Estimating Nonnegative Matrices from Marginal Data." *International Economic Review* 6, no. 3 (September): 294–310.
Bischoff, Charles W. 1971. "The Effect of Alternative Lag Distributions." In Gary Fromm, ed. *Tax Incentives and Capital Spending.* Washington, D.C.: The Brookings Institution, pp. 60–130.
Bradford, David F. 1980. "The Economics of Tax Policy Toward Savings." In George von Furstenberg, ed. *The Government and Capital Formation.* Cambridge: Ballinger, pp. 11–71.
_____. 1981. "Issues in the Design of Saving and Investment Incentives." This volume.
Brown, E. Cary. 1980. "The 'Net' Versus the 'Gross' Investment Tax Credit." this volume.
Bureau of the Census. 1972, 1977. *Census of Manufactures.* United States Government Printing Office.
Bureau of Economic Analysis. 1975. *Interindustry Transactions in New Structures and Equipment, 1963 and 1967, Supplement to the Survey of Current Business.* U.S. Department of Commerce.
Bureau of Economic Analysis. 1976. *Fixed Nonresidential Business and Residential Capital*

in the United States, 1925-1975. PB-253 725. U.S. Department of Commerce, National Technical Information Service.

Christensen, Laurits R., and Dale W. Jorgenson. 1978. "U.S. Input, Output, Saving and Wealth, 1929-1977." Cambridge, Mass.: Harvard Institute for Economic Research (December).

Coen, Robert M. 1971. "The Effect of Cash Flow on the Speed of Adjustment." In G. Fromm, ed. *Tax Incentives and Capital Spending.* Washington, D.C.: The Brookings Institution, pp. 131-196.

Commerce Clearing House. 1962. *New Tax Rules on Business Assets.* Chicago: Commerce Clearing House.

_____. 1978. *The 1978 Depreciation Guide.* Chicago: Commerce Clearing House.

Corcoran, Patrick J. 1979. "Inflation, Taxes, and the Composition of Business Investment." *Federal Reserve Bank of New York Quarterly Review* 4, no. 3 (Autumn) pp. 13-24.

Feldstein, Martin S. 1979, "Adjusting Depreciation in an Inflationary Economy: Indexing Versus Acceleration," Cambridge, National Bureau of Economic Research, Working Paper No. 395, December.

_____.; Green, Jerry; and Sheshinski, Eytan. 1978. "Inflation and Taxes in a Growing Economy with Debt and Equity Finance." *Journal of Political Economy* 86, no. 2, part 2 (April): S53-70.

_____., and Summers, Lawrence. 1979. "Inflation and the Taxation of Capital Income in The Corporate Sector." *National Tax Journal,* 32, no. 4 (December): 445-470.

_____. 1980. "Inflation and the Taxation of Capital Income in the Corporate Sector: Reply." *National Tax Journal* 33, no. 4 (December): 485-488.

Gravelle, Jane G. 1979. "The Capital Cost Recovery System and the Corporate Income Tax." Washington, D.C.: Congressional Research Service, report no. 79-230E (November).

_____. 1980. "The Capital Cost Recovery Act: An Economic Analysis of 10-5-3 Depreciation." Washington, D.C.: Congressional Research Service, report no. 80-29E (January).

_____. 1980b. "Depreciation Policy Options." Washington, D.C.: Congressional Research Service, report no. 80-182E (October).

_____. 1980c. "Inflation and the Taxation of Capital Income in the Corporate Sector: A Comment." *National Tax Journal* 33, no. 4, (December): 473-483.

Hall, Robert E. 1977. "Investment, Interest Rates, and the Effects of Stabilization Policies." *Brookings Papers on Economic Activity,* pp. 61-122.

_____., and Jorgenson, Dale W. 1967. "Tax Policy and Investment Behavior." *American Economic Review* 57, no. 3 (June): 391-414.

_____. 1969. "Tax Policy and Investment Behavior: Reply and Further Results." *American Economic Review* 59, no. 3 (June): 388-401.

_____. 1971. "Application of the Theory of Optimal Capital Accumulation." In Gary Fromm, ed., *Tax Incentives and Capital Spending.* Washington, D.C.: The Brookings Institution, pp. 9-60.

Harberger, Arnold C. 1980. "Tax Neutrality in Investment Incentives." In Henry J. Aaron and Michael J. Boskin, eds., *The Economics of Taxation.* Washington, D.C.: The Brookings Institution, pp. 299-316.

Hulten, Charles R., and Wykoff, Frank C. 1980. "Economic Depreciation and the Taxation of Structures in U.S. Manufacturing Industries: Empirical Analysis." *The Measurement of Capital.* Chicago, Ill.: University of Chicago Press, pp. 83-109.

_____. 1981a. "The Estimation of Economic Depreciation Using Vintage Asset Prices: An Application of the Box-Cox Power Transformation." *Journal of Econometrics,* forthcoming.

_____. 1981b. "The Measurement of Economic Depreciation." This volume.

Internal Revenue Service. 1942. *Bulletin F.* Washington, D.C.: U.S. Department of the Treasury.

_____. 1962. "Depreciation Guidelines and Rules." Washington, D.C.: U.S. Department of the Treasury, Publication 456.

_____. *Statistics of Income: Corporation Tax Returns;* various annual issues.
Jeremias, Ronald A. 1979. "Dead-Weight Loss from Tax-Induced Distortion of Capital Mix." Ph.D. thesis, Virginia Polytechnic Institute and State University.
Jorgenson, Dale W. 1963. "Capital Theory and Investment Behavior." *American Economic Review* 53, no. 2 (May): 247–259.
_____. 1965. "Anticipation and Investment Behavior." In J. Duesenberry, G. Fromm, L. R. Klein, and E. Kuh, eds. *The Brookings Quarterly Model of the United States.* Chicago, Ill.: Rand McNally, pp. 35–92.
_____. 1971. "Econometric Studies of Investment Behavior: A Review." *Journal of Economic Literature* 9, no. 4 (December): 1111–1147.
_____. 1973. "The Economic Theory of Replacement and Depreciation." In W. Sellekaerts, ed., *Econometrics and Economic Theory.* New York, N.Y.: MacMillan, pp. 189–221.
Jorgenson, Dale W., and Siebert, C. D. 1968a. "A Comparison of Alternative Theories of Corporate Investment Behavior." *American Economic Review* 58, no. 4 (September): 681–712.
_____. 1968b. "Optimal Capital Accumulation and Corporate Investment Behavior." *Journal of Political Economy* 76, no. 6, (November/December): 1123–1151.
_____. 1972. "An Empirical Evaluation of Alternative Theories of Corporate Investment." In K. Brunner, ed., *Problems and Issues in Current Econometric Practice.* Columbus, Ohio: Ohio State University, pp. 155–218.
Jorgenson, Dale W., and Stephenson, J. A. 1967a. "The Time Structure of Investment Behavior in United States Manufacturing, 1947–60." *Review of Economics and Statistics* 49, no. 1 (February): 16–27.
_____. 1967b, "Investment Behavior in U.S. Manufacturing, 1947–60." *Econometrica* 35, no. 2 (April): 169–220.
_____. 1969. "Anticipations and Investment Behavior in U.S. Manufacturing, 1947–60." *Journal of the American Statistical Association* 64, no. 325 (March): 67–89.
Leape, Jonathan. 1980. "Tax Incentives and Capital Formation." Washington, D.C.: U.S. House of Representatives, Committee on Ways and Means.
Marston, Anson; Winfrey, Robley; and Hempstead, John C. 1953. *Engineering Valuation and Depreciation.* New York, N.Y.: McGraw-Hill.
Mayer, Thomas. 1960. "Plant and Equipment Lead Times." *Journal of Business* 33, no. 2 (April): 127–132.
Myers, John H. 1960. "The Influence of Salvage Value Upon the Choice of Tax Depreciation Methods." *The Accounting Review* 35, no. 4 (October): 598–602.
Office of Industrial Economics. 1975. "Business Building Statistics." Washington, D.C.: U.S. Department of the Treasury (August).
Pechman, Joseph A. 1977. *Federal Tax Policy,* third edition, Washington, D.C.: The Brookings Institution.
Samuelson, Paul A. 1964. "Tax Deductibility of Economic Depreciation to Insure Invariant Valuations." *Journal of Political Economy* 72 (December): 604–606.
Vasquez, Thomas. 1974. "The Effects of the Asset Depreciation Range System on Depreciation Practices." Office of Tax Analysis Paper no. 1. Washington, D.C.: U.S. Department of the Treasury (May).
Wales, Terrence J. 1968. "Estimation of an Accelerated Depreciation Learning Function." *Journal of the American Statistical Association* 61, no. 316 (December): 995–1009.
Young, Allan H. 1968. "Alternative Estimates of Corporate Depreciation and Profits: Part I." *Survey of Current Business* 48, no. 4 (April): 17–28.
_____., and Musgrave, John C. 1980. "Estimation of Capital Stock in the United States." In Dan Usher, ed., *The Measurement of Capital.* Chicago, Ill.: University of Chicago, University of Chicago Press, pp. 23–68.

THE SOCIAL COST OF NONNEUTRAL TAXATION: ESTIMATES FOR NONRESIDENTIAL CAPITAL

Jane G. Gravelle

A conventional result in welfare analysis is that the efficient allocation of the capital stock requires that the social return on investments be equated at the margin (within given risk classes). In the absence of external effects, market forces will tend to equate social returns, as investors choose projects with the highest yields. When taxes are imposed, allocative efficiency can be achieved (under certain conditions) when equal tax rates are applied to all returns, so that those projects which earn the highest private after-tax return will also earn the highest social or pretax return.

If, on the other hand, taxes are imposed at differential rates, the result is a misallocation of the stock of capital. This misallocation occurs because the imposition of the tax creates an incentive to reallocate capital toward the more lightly taxed uses. This reallocation gives rise to a differential in the social rate of return to capital in different uses, and thus to

[Jane G. Gravelle is specialist in Taxation and Fiscal Policy, Congressional Research Service, Library of Congress. The views in this paper are solely those of the author and do not necessarily reflect those of the Congressional Research Service or the Library of Congress. The results are based on research done in partial fulfillment of requirements for the Ph.D. degree at George Washington University. The author thanks Don Fullerton for his helpful comments on an earlier version.]

a deadweight loss. In this situation, a gain to society would occur if a unit of capital could be moved from the lightly taxed alternative to a more heavily taxed one, and such gains would continue until the yields on all investments are equated. The amount of this total gain is a measure of the waste or deadweight loss associated with the differential tax.

The effective tax rates on depreciable assets are dependent not only on the statutory rate of tax but also on the allowances for depreciation and on any other tax allowances or credits. If economic depreciation is allowed, then tax rates across assets are equated (presuming investment subsidies are also neutral with respect to asset durability).[1] The present U.S. tax structure fails to meet this standard in a number of ways. Depreciation rates are based on rules which do not necessarily correspond to economic depreciation. Furthermore, these depreciation allowances are based on the original cost of the asset, resulting in a mismeasurement of real depreciation during inflationary periods. An investment credit is also allowed, which does not correspond to the correct form of a neutral incentive. Both the investment credit and the use of original cost basis have been shown to have differential effects with respect to asset durability, with the investment credit favoring and original cost basis penalizing short lived assets relative to a neutral tax regime.[2] The magnitude of these offsetting effects as well as the effect of tax depreciation methods and the restriction of the investment credit to equipment produce different tax rates—and thus different social returns—across different depreciable assets.

The resulting misallocation of capital is estimated to produce a waste or deadweight loss for nonresidential capital alone equal to $2.5 billion in 1978. Since the overall real pretax return on capital assets is estimated at 8.2 percent, this amount is equivalent to wasting $30.5 billion of capital, as this amount of capital would be required to produce a $2.5 billion return. At 1981 price and output levels, this amount represents a reduction in the effective capital stock on the order of $40 billion. The magnitude of this loss implies that efficiency considerations are important in the design of a tax structure.

This estimated welfare loss captures only part of the distortions induced by the present structure of taxes on capital income—those which favor the use of some assets over others. The overall level of taxes on capital also creates an intertemporal distortion favoring present over future consumption. Furthermore, the distortions which might favor the use of an asset in a given industry or sector are not considered; yet these distortions have typically been the focus of most studies of the dead weight loss from nonneutral taxation of capital income. The final section of this paper considers the issue of intersectoral versus interasset distortions and suggests some theoretical grounds for considering the interasset distortions the more important of the two.

The Measurement of Waste

The measurement of waste from the nonneutral taxation of capital has been most closely associated with Arnold Harberger.[3] Harberger approximated welfare losses by the triangle ½ dp dq where relative prices are affected by taxes, dp is the difference between the distorted and undistorted price, and dq is the difference between the distorted and undistorted quantity. By assuming unitary elasticities of substitution between labor and other inputs and unitary price elasticities, this approach can be applied to any number of sectors (or assets). The total welfare loss is the sum of the absolute values of the triangles for each sector. These studies of waste have generally focused on the distortions between sectors (such as the corporate versus the noncorporate sector) or between different industries and rely on profit data.

Although Harberger's general methodology will be followed, there are several important modifications. First, the distortions measured are based on the differential taxation of assets rather than sectors and arise from the rules for tax depreciation allowances and investment credits. Previous studies have focused on sectoral differences and have measured distortions which were the result, in large part, of differential tax rates. The estimates in this paper ignore sectoral differences and treat all assets as owned by the corporate sector; the final section of this paper, however, provides some justification for this assumption.

The second modification is in the measure of price and tax induced distortions. Most studies define the price of capital as the rate of return (gross of tax). The data used to calculate deadweight losses are profit and tax payments data. Since it can be assumed that profit is the product of the rate of return and the capital stock, these data are used, in conjunction with the elasticity assumptions, to measure rates of return and the size of the capital stocks in the distorted and undistorted equilibria.

This approach is modified in two ways. First, following standard neoclassical theory, the price of capital is measured conceptually as the rental price or user cost of capital, typically denoted as c. This measure captures the notion that the marginal product of capital includes not only the rate of return or cost of funds but also the cost of using up capital, or depreciation. While there is little disagreement that the user cost concept

is the appropriate measure of price, one could calculate the price for purposes of estimating welfare losses as gross product of capital (c) or net product, the pretax return. With unitary elasticities (that is, a Cobb-Douglas
production function if the elasticity is unity at all points), using c implies
that the production function is a measure of gross output, while using the
rate of return implies that the production function is a measure of net output (or gross output minus depreciation allowances). In general, however,
the empirical work which lends support to the assumption of a Cobb-
Douglas production function has been with respect to gross output;[4]
therefore, the price of capital is measured as c. Choosing c tends to reduce
the measure of deadweight loss, as a given change in the rate of return has
a smaller relative effect on price.

With the economic depreciation patterns used in this study, c is equal to
$\rho + \delta$, where ρ is the real pretax return and δ is the economic depreciation
rate. The distorted price of the ith asset is $c_i^* = \rho_i^* + \delta_i$, where ρ_i^* is the
estimated pretax return under existing law and δ_i is the economic
depreciation rate (the unit of capital is normalized to 1). The undistorted
price is $\bar{c}_i = \bar{\rho} + \delta_i$, where $\bar{\rho}$ is a rate of return equal for all assets. The
particular value of $\bar{\rho}$ chosen is a weighted average of the existing pretax
returns under present law for all assets, which keeps the aggregate pretax
and after-tax return on assets (and total gross product of capital) constant.

Modifications are also made in the data used. Data on profits (or, if the
rental cost concept is used, profits plus depreciation allowances) are not
available by asset type, and would be difficult to interpret in any case.
Therefore, the welfare cost estimates rely on direct estimates of the rental
cost and size of capital stock for each type of asset. The rental price is
estimated from a present value approach to determine what price is
necessary to earn a given after-tax return (common to all assets) given tax
rules.

The final modification of the Harberger approach is a minor adjustment in the actual formula used to compute the deadweight loss, which
measures the loss precisely, given the assumption of gross Cobb-Douglas
production functions. If $\dot{c}^*$ is the distorted price, $\bar{c}$ is the undistorted
price, K^* is the distorted quantity and $\bar{K}$ is the undistorted quantity, the
welfare loss approximated by the summation over i assets of the absolute
values $\frac{1}{2}$ dc dK can be measured precisely as

$$W = \sum_i \left| \int_{\bar{K}}^{K^*} dc \, dK \right| \qquad (1)$$

where dc is the difference between the price at any value K and the measured price c*, or c(K) — c*. Since a demand curve with unitary elasticity at every point is described by the function cK = T, where T is a constant, c at any point K is equal to T/K. The function dc is, therefore, equal to (T/K) — c*. If we note that T is equal to c*K*, dc = (c*K*/K) — c*. By substituting this value into (1), solving the integral and simplifying by noting that c*K* = $\overline{c}\overline{K}$ (since both are equal to T), we have

$$W = \sum_i | c^*K^*(\ln(\overline{c}/c^*) - 1 + (\overline{c}/c^*)) | \quad . \tag{2}$$

This general approach to measuring price and welfare loss is also used by Hendershott and Hu.[5] Note in addition that the procedures in this study do not explicitly incorporate an equal yield tax system. Thus the estimates assume that the government spends tax revenue in the same way that private income would be spent.

Empirical Results

In order to estimate the pretax return for each asset type, the current rental price is estimated by the standard formula[6]

$$c = \frac{(r + \delta)(1 - uz - k)}{(1 - u)} \quad , \tag{3}$$

where c is the rental price, r is the real after-tax discount rate, δ is the economic depreciation rate, u is the statutory tax rate, z is the present value of depreciation deductions, and k is the rate of investment tax credit. The present value of depreciation, z, is a function of the method of depreciation, the tax life allowed, and the anticipated rate of inflation, since depreciation deductions are discounted at nominal rather than real rates when historical cost basis is used. Once c is estimated, the pretax return, ρ, is measured as c — δ.

The values of r and the anticipated inflation rate are set .055 and .06, respectively, based on findings of Hendershott and Hu.[7] The tax rate u is set at the marginal corporate statutory rate, .46. These measures are the same across assets. Values of economic depreciation, δ, are based on estimates by Hulten and Wykoff.[8]

Measures of z and k present some difficulties. The investment credit is restricted to equipment (which includes public utility structures for tax purposes) and is generally allowed at a 10 percent rate. For equipment with short tax lives, however, the investment credit rates are lower, and thus investment credits are tied to tax lives.

Guideline lives prescribed in the tax regulations under the asset depreciation range system (ADR) are largely categorized by industry rather than asset type. For those equipment assets where specific lives are not allowed, the following procedure is used. An average tax life by industry (generally two-digit Standard Industrial Classification (SIC) is based on data supplied by the Treasury Department consisting of a distribution of asset purchases and the associated ADR life (generally the minimum life except for cases where longer lives are chosen to obtain a larger investment credit).[9] The average tax life and credit for each class of assets is estimated by weighting these industry tax lives by the share of investment in that category in the capital flow tables.[10] Structures do not qualify for the ADR system, and their tax lives (except for public utilities) are based on a survey of depreciation practices for buildings.[11]

The method of depreciation assumed is the most generous available, a sum-of-the-years'-digits method for equipment (including public utility structures) and a 150 percent declining balance method for structures.[12] Survey data suggest that accelerated methods (sum-of-years'-digits or its close counterpart, declining balance) dominate depreciation practices.[13]

The welfare loss calculation also requires the measurement of the 1978 capital stock for each asset category. The capital stock estimates are constructed from investment data for 1929–1978[14] and the estimated economic depreciation rates. Investment made t years in the past (measured at 1978 prices) has a value of $I(t)e^{-\delta t}$, where δ is the depreciation rate. The total capital stock for each asset is the sum of the depreciated stocks for each year. The value of the 1929 capital stock, which must be added, is estimated by noting that investment is equal to $(g + \delta)K$ where g is the growth rate of the stock and δ is the depreciation rate. The capital stock in 1929 is estimated by dividing 1929 investment (measured at 1978 prices) by $(g + \delta)$, where g is assumed to be .03. While some error may be introduced by assuming an arbitrary growth rate, the 1929 capital stock's contribution to current stocks (measured as $K(1929)e^{-49t}$) is trivial for short-lived assets and represents only a small fraction of the total for long-lived assets.

The assumptions and derived estimates are presented in table 1. An average pretax return of .082 is calculated by weighting pretax returns by shares of the total stock. This average return is added to the depreciation rate for each asset to measure undistorted prices, while the distorted value of c is the sum of the depreciation rate and the pretax return for the asset class. Welfare losses are calculated according to the formula in (2).

The results indicate substantial divergence in pretax returns for different assets, with equipment taxed more lightly than structures. The welfare loss is measured at \$2.46 billion for 1978. At the average pretax return of .082, an increase in the capital stock of \$30 billion (\$2.46 billion/.082) would be required to offset this loss. Measured at 1981 price and output levels, this reduction in the effective capital stock is on the order of \$40 billion.

The total size of the capital stock increases slightly with these calculations, a result which derives from the measure of price, the constraints of a Cobb-Douglas production function, and the choice of average pretax return. These assumptions constrain total gross product to a constant value which is equal to average c times the total capital stock. The movement to an undistorted equilibrium shifts the capital stock towards longer lived assets and lowers the average value of δ. Since average c is the sum of average pretax return and average δ, the fall in average δ results in a fall in c and requires a rise in K for the product of average c and total K to be constant. The effects measured would be expected if the supply of funds to the nonresidential sector were assumed to be perfectly elastic (so that an increase in demand would not drive up after-tax returns to suppliers) implying that the welfare loss measure captures some reallocation of resources to the nonresidential capital stock.

This problem does not occur with welfare losses calculated when the price is measured by pretax return and the depreciation rate does not enter. In this case keeping the average pretax return constant also keeps the total capital stock constant. An alternative procedure would keep capital stock constant rather than the pretax return in these computations, by finding the value of the pretax return which combined with the change in δ would keep average c constant. This calculation, which requires an increase in pretax return to .087 results in a slightly smaller deadweight loss of \$2.3 billion.

Estimated welfare costs will be altered by changes in inflation as well as by any changes in tax rules. Increases in anticipated inflation rates would narrow the differential between equipment and structures while decreases would widen the differentials, since the use of historical cost basis tends to penalize less durable assets. Several proposals for depreciation reform appear likely to magnify distortions between structures and equipment; an

TABLE 1

Welfare Loss: Nonresidential Capital

Asset Type	Economic Depreciation Rate	Tax Life (years)	Investment Credit Rate	Capital Stock ($billions)	Pretax Return (percent)	Welfare Loss ($million)
Equipment						
1. Autos	.3333	3.0	.033	50.0	6.7	14.2
2. Office, computing, and accounting equipment	.2729	7.0	.10	43.9	5.6	40.8
3. Trucks, buses, and trailers	.2537	5.0	.066	80.6	6.1	79.1
4. Aircraft	.1818	9.2	.10	11.5	6.7	4.9
5. Construction machinery	.1722	5.0	.066	27.3	6.0	25.9
6. Mining and oilfield machinery	.1650	9.2	.10	9.6	6.6	5.1
7. Service industry machinery	.1650	9.9	.10	28.9	6.9	9.7
8. Tractors	.1633	7.1	.09	27.4	6.0	26.2
9. Instruments	.1473	10.3	.10	51.4	6.9	17.4
10. Other equipment	.1473	8.8	.10	23.4	6.4	17.0
11. General industrial equipment	.1225	9.9	.091	54.5	6.9	21.4
12. Metalworking machinery	.1225	7.8	.086	45.0	6.3	36.9
13. Electric transmission/distribution equipment	.1179	13.8	.10	42.4	7.8	1.9

14. Communications Equipment	.1179	11.5	.10	85.0	7.1	24.8
15. Other electrical equipment	.1179	9.0	.10	11.3	6.3	10.3
16. Furniture and fixtures	.1100	8.0	.10	39.5	5.9	50.8
17. Special industrial equipment	.1031	9.2	.10	55.8	6.3	67.8
18. Agricultural equipment	.0971	8.0	.10	43.4	5.9	61.7
19. Fabricated metal products	.0917	14.2	.10	21.7	7.5	2.9
20. Engines and turbines	.0786	18.1	.10	15.9	8.1	0.0
21. Ships and boats	.0750	16.0	.10	17.6	7.6	1.7
22. Railroad equipment	.0660	15.0	.10	37.6	7.3	9.8
Structures						
23. Mining exploration, shafts and wells	.0663	na	0	77.9	6.1	114.1
24. Other	.0454	31.0	0	17.8	11.2	58.4
25. Factory ⎱ Industrial structures	.0361	36.0	0 ⎱	205.4	11.0	649.3
26. Warehouse ⎰	.0273	37.0	⎰			
27. Public utilities	.0316	22.0	.10	360.2	7.6	61.8
28. Retail ⎱ Commercial structures	.0247	35.0	0 ⎱	476.5	10.4	1,028.4
29. Office ⎰	.0220	41.0	0 ⎰			
30. Farm	.0237	20.0	0	65.8	9.1	23.4
Total	.0808			2027.3	8.2	2,462.7

exception is the Auerbach-Jorgenson proposal which is a design for a neutral, inflation-proof system.[15]

Distortions between Assets versus Sectors

The deadweight losses measured across assets are in contrast to those measured in previous deadweight loss studies, where distortions across sectors have been measured. While distortions in the use of different assets exist regardless of whether there are distortions across sectors, there are grounds for suggesting that distortions between assets are the more important ones caused by differential taxation of capital income. Previous studies rely on a model of investment where after-tax returns are equated in each sector or industry, as if there were a single individual investor.[16] Since after-tax returns are equated, pretax returns must differ with different taxes. Thus, the higher taxes on corporate equity capital produce a distortion leading to too little capital allocated to the corporate sector.

There are several difficulties with this model. Corporations use debt as well as equity finance; furthermore, they have the option of renting rather than purchasing assets and could presumably increase their profits by renting assets from the noncorporate sector. More importantly, such a model implies that pretax returns on identical assets, held by different sectors, would be different and therefore that the rent for an office building would vary depending on ownership. Thus, the rent for office space in a building owned by a corporation would be higher than that for a building with identical characteristics owned by an individual.

Furthermore, individual investors in the economy are not homogeneous, particularly in that they are subject to differing tax rates under a progressive income tax structure. Thus, after-tax returns in the same investment vary for investors with different marginal tax rates.

These problems with the traditional model have led a number of economists to question the size, or even the existence, of sectoral distortions due to the higher tax rates on corporate equity, mainly by focusing on corporate financial policy and progressive personal tax rates. If taxes on debt financed investment are lighter, and thus the cost of debt cheaper, corporations should rationally choose to finance through debt rather than equity. Some models suggest that new investment *is* financed by debt and existing equity is a holdover from the period prior to the income tax. This view requires some institutional constraints on share repurchases which could be used to eliminate equity capital. If marginal corporate investment is financed by debt which is taxed in the same manner as noncorporate investment, the sectoral distortions between the corporate and noncorporate sectors would disappear. Others have focused on the progressive tax rates in the personal income tax and the fact that retained earnings are not subject to personal tax until realized as capital gains, which are also taxed at lower rates when realized. In the extreme case where all earnings are retained and capital gains deferred indefinitely, all individuals with personal tax rates above the corporate rate would prefer corporate equity to corporate debt. In this case, too, the sectoral distortions would also disappear, since the marginal investor is subject to the same tax rate in each sector.

Other economists have focused on the additional risk of bankruptcy induced by incremental increases in the debt-equity ratios of corporations. Gordon and Malkiel,[17] for example, review a number of earlier studies and suggest that those studies which rely on the use of debt or marginal tax rate calculations are counterfactual since some new equity is issued and since dividend payments are a substantial share of corporate earnings. They suggest that bankruptcy is the primary explanation. They also indicate that sectoral distortions still exist but are much smaller due both to partial debt finance and to lower personal tax rates on returns to corporate equity. The authors do find a significant social cost due to the bankruptcy risk factor, but this social cost acts like an extra burden on capital and is a form of intertemporal distortion rather than a distortion in the allocation of capital.

By contrast, little attention has been focused on the equally puzzling question why corporations do not rent capital from the noncorporate sector. If the rate of return before tax and the implicit rent on such capital assets is less than that on assets which are purchased, corporations could increase their profits by renting rather than owning assets. Furthermore, both corporations and individuals rent certain assets, particularly structures, to third parties and competitive markets would suggest that the same rentals would be charged regardless of ownership. Martin Bailey[18] has, in fact, extended the marginal progressive tax rate analysis to investment by individuals in physical assets, although he does not explore the implication of such a model for sectoral distortions.

One can extend to the corporate and noncorporate sector the marginal tax rate analysis. As a simple illustration suppose the pretax return on corporate investment financed by equity is $r_e/(1 - u)$ where u is the corporate tax rate and r_e is the after-tax earnings, and assume that this pretax return is equated to that in the noncorporate sector, r_n. If the noncorporate return is taxed as the personal tax rate t and the corporate return is taxed at the personal tax rate αt, $\alpha < 1$ to reflect treatment of retained earnings, the tax rate at which an investor would be indifferent occurs when $r_n(1 - t) = r_e(1 - \alpha t)$. By noting that $r_n = r_e/(1 - u)$, one can solve for t which is $u/(1 - (1 - u)\alpha)$. For example, if α is .5 and u is .46, investors with marginal tax rates about 63 percent would prefer corporate equity.

This example is extremely simplified. Even in the two asset model different after-tax returns might be expected for a given investor in the two sectors due to risk and liquidity. In particular, noncorporate investment might require a higher after-tax return to the same investor because it may be viewed as more risky and less liquid than corporate equity, an effect which would drive down the marginal tax rate at which the investor is indifferent. The implications of a model which presumes that pretax returns on assets are equated in a competitive equilibrium are significant. In the extreme case, they imply that the corporate tax does not induce distortions in the *allocation* of capital (although it may magnify intertemporal distortions). If corporations face a common cost of funds and if tax rates are applied equally across physical assets, there would be no rate of return differentials across assets and no deadweight loss. If corporations face different effective tax rates across physical assets due to tax provisions such as the investment credit and depreciation allowances, there *is* a misallocation of capital. Furthermore, since estimated pretax returns derived from investment decisions of corporations are also the pretax returns on noncorporate capital, the fact that some individuals own assets can be ignored in calculating the deadweight loss.

No simple model can capture all of the complexities of investment choice particularly because financial and rental markets are imperfect. Yet, if these types of models are reasonably representative they suggest a different focus to the study of tax induced distortions in the allocation of capital.

PITFALLS IN THE CONSTRUCTION AND USE OF EFFECTIVE TAX RATES

David F. Bradford and Don Fullerton

I. Introduction

The easiest and most common approach to estimating effective tax rates on investment has been to calculate actual taxes paid as a proportion of capital income. This "flow of funds" approach is particularly useful for income effects to capital owners, revenue effects to government, or generally for discussing the relative size of the public sector.[1] Some have also used this approach to capture the different incentive effects for using capital in different industries. The implicit assumption is that marginal tax rates in a given industry are not far from the ratio of actual taxes to capital income in that industry. Harberger (1966) estimated the efficiency cost of differential capital income taxation using this approach, as did

[David Bradford is professor of economics and public affairs, Princeton University and director of the program on taxation at the National Bureau of Economic Research (NBER). Don Fullerton is assistant professor of economics and public affairs, Princeton University and research fellow at NBER. This material is based upon work supported by NBER, Princeton University, and the National Science Foundation under grant SES 8025404. The authors are grateful to Thomas Kronmiller for research assistance. For general discussions on these issues, the authors are grateful to Robert E. Hall, Dale W. Jorgenson, and Mervyn A. King. The research reported here is part of the NBER's research program in taxation. Any opinions expressed are those of the authors and not those of the NBER or the National Science Foundation.]

Shoven in his (1976) correction to Harberger. The approach is still used in recent general equilibrium estimates by Fullerton, King, Shoven, and Whalley (1981).

A new approach is now emerging, based on the pioneering work of Hall and Jorgenson (1967). Their cost of capital formulas have long been used to analyze investment and the incentive effects of tax policy changes. More recently, the formulas have been used to estimate effective marginal tax rates, as in Hall (1981) and Jorgenson and Sullivan (1981). Tax rates based on the cost of capital approach have been used to recalculate Harberger-type efficiency costs, as in Gravelle (1981), and to recompute general equilibrium effects, as in Fullerton and Gordon (1981).

This newer approach considers a "hypothetical project" of a dollar invested in a particular asset to be used in a particular industry. (Some versions of the approach also assume that the investment is maintained in real or nominal terms by subsequent reinvestment.) The view of taxes is prospective in the sense that the cost of capital formula looks at the expected change in future tax liabilities, usually discounted to the time that the original investment takes place. The method can simultaneously incorporate actual depreciation rates, type of finance, eligibility for investment tax credit, accelerated depreciation rules, and depreciation at historical cost. It is greatly facilitated by the availability of estimates for depreciation rates of different assets, such as those in Hulten and Wykoff (1981).

The prospective nature of the cost of capital (hypothetical project) approach implies that it is probably more useful for investigating incentive effects. It measures the expected tax consequences if a given investment is undertaken. It also concentrates on marginal effects by considering a particular unit of investment. Though we see many potential benefits of using this approach, the purpose of this paper is to investigate some of its dangers. In particular, we shall illustrate three points that should be considered by any study which uses the cost of capital approach.

First, as mentioned, the cost of capital method considers the expected future tax liabilities associated with a hypothetical project, discounted to the time that the original investment takes place. Though the investment tax credit has immediate consequences, other features of tax systems do not. Accelerated depreciation, for example, has the effect of delaying some tax liability. As a result, effective tax rate estimates will necessarily depend upon the after-tax interest rate or other rate used for discounting. We shall show this sensitivity below by plotting a tax rate estimate against the interest rate used to obtain it.

Second, the tax law allows some assets to be depreciated at rates faster than their values decline. With investment tax credits and with the deductibility of nominal interest payments, the asset need not earn a positive marginal product for the investor to receive a normal return. Though the implied subsidy might be measured in a meaningful way, the rate of subsidy might not be. When the investment's return in the denominator of an effective tax rate formula approaches zero, the rate of subsidy can be arbitrarily high. Similarly, on an asset with a low real return, a positive tax can be an arbitrarily high portion of it. This problem can be dealt with by using the numerators of these tax rate estimates alone to describe the effective tax wedge on a particular asset in a particular industry.

Third, effective tax rate estimates depend on assumptions about how inflation affects nominal interest rates. Hall (1981) and Jorgenson-Sullivan (1981) effectively assume that nominal interest rates increase by the inflation rate over one minus the corporate tax rate. This increase is just enough to keep the real after-tax interest rate constant for corporations. If all taxpayers faced the same tax rate as corporations, and if the rules for measuring the income from real investments were perfectly indexed for inflation, then a strong a priori case could be made for this behavior of interest rates. The real consequences of given decisions to borrow, lend, and invest would then be independent of inflation rates. However, historical cost depreciation, nonuniform tax rates, and other tax features tend to weaken this a priori case. Indeed, Feldstein (1980) has argued that the monetary authorities have acted so as to impose Fisher's Law, keeping the real before-tax interest rate invariant with respect to inflation. We show below how tax rate estimates differ according to whether nominal interest rates increase by just the rate of inflation, or by enough to keep real after-tax rates constant.

This paper does not seek to estimate new or better effective tax rates. It only seeks to investigate the sensitivity of existing estimates to some of the issues just described. These can be clarified adequately within the context of fairly simple and straightforward cost of capital formulas such as those used by Hall (1981) and Jorgenson-Sullivan (1981). In order to be particularly careful about the assumptions used in this procedure, we rederive the cost of capital in section II.1. In order to be particularly careful about what is being estimated, we describe an array of possible tax rate definitions in section II.2. Then in section II.3, we state the parameters of the investment and tax systems, chosen for comparability with Hall (1981). We also display the possible outcomes for savers and investment returns. These constitute the components of effective tax rates.

In the three parts of section III, we elaborate on each of the three issues raised above. Tax rate estimates are shown to be sensitive to the interest rate in section III.1. The fact that tax rate definitions are very nonlinear relationships is illustrated in section III.2. The effect of inflation on nominal interest rates also significantly affects the estimates, as shown in section III.3. It should be clear by the end of this paper that the sensitivity of tax rate estimates implies that one can obtain a wide variety of tax rate estimates with different choices of parameter values and other assumptions.

The problems emphasized in this paper involve primarily mechanical features of the analysis. That is, they concern potential misunderstanding of the tax rate formulas and of the assumptions often encountered. We also touch on some underlying modeling problems through the course of the paper. Foremost among these is the question of the true relationship between inflation and the interest rate. There are, however, several additional aspects of the use of effective tax rate estimates which deserve attention. In the concluding remarks of section IV, we allude to further work we are doing on these problems.

II. Analytical Framework

Because we feel that previous studies have not been explicit enough about what they were estimating, we devote considerable attention at the outset to deriving and defining different sorts of tax rates. Any of these might be estimated by a particular study.

II.1. THE COST OF CAPITAL

We begin with a simple expression for the cost of capital, that is, the annual market rental price of a unit of capital, predicted to obtain in a competitive market equilibrium. Although a similar derivation has been exposited many times, it will be helpful to have a restatement of the underlying assumptions and the interpretations of different variables.

Define ρ to be the expected real rate of return to the hypothetical project, net of economic depreciation at the exponential rate δ.[2] In light of our introductory comments, we require a model incorporating the dependence of ρ on the nominal interest rate i and on the rate of inflation π. However, many complexities can be safely ignored. Hall (1981), for example, considers (but does not really use) the possibility that a proportion of accrued capital gains are taxable at the statutory corporate tax rate u. Jorgenson and Sullivan (1981), on the other hand, allow for (but then abstract from) the possibility that the acquisition cost q and the rental price c of the asset are arbitrary functions of time, rather than assuming only that they increase with inflation. Jorgenson and Sullivan also consider the possibility that the rate of economic depreciation is an arbitrary function of time, rather than using our simpler assumption that true depreciation is at constant exponential rate δ. They allow depreciation deductions as an arbitrary function of time, while we assume the tax law allows depreciation deductions on a historical cost basis at constant exponential rate δ'.

An investment tax credit at rate k completes the description of our hypothetical real investment project and its tax consequences. A corporate purchaser of a unit of real capital incurs an immediate after-tax-credit expense of $(1 - k)q$, and subsequently obtains a cash inflow, expressed as a function of τ, the time since acquisition of the asset. This cash inflow includes rental at a rate that starts at c and grows at the rate of inflation π. The quantity of capital embodied in the investment declines at the depreciation rate δ. At time τ the rental receipts thus equal $(1 - u)ce^{(\pi - \delta)\tau}$ after the corporate income tax. The cash inflow also includes tax reductions due to depreciation allowances, which at time τ equal $uq\delta'e^{-\delta'\tau}$ (depreciation at rate δ' is allowed on the remaining basis $qe^{-\delta'\tau}$).[3] By changing k, u, and δ', the tax authorities change the attractiveness of these net-of-tax cash flows, given q, c, and π. Since (at least) q and c are endogenous to the system, changes in the tax rules will ultimately be reflected in changes in the values of q, c, or both.

The power of the analysis is based upon the valuation of such cash flows. More specifically, it is based on valuation relative to available alternatives. Prominent among these alternatives is the purchase or sale of debt. The analogue of buying a machine is buying debt, or lending. If the market interest rate i is constant, for an initial outlay of \$1, a corporation can accummulate $e^{(1-u)i\tau}$ dollars by time τ, where the factor $(1 - u)$ in the exponent reflects the taxation of interest receipts. Of course, most non-financial corporations are sellers of debt, not buyers. The emphasis therefore is usually on the deduction of interest outlays and not the taxation of interest receipts. Note that this deduction is a logical extension of the taxation of interest receipts. It is not, as sometimes made to appear, an explicit subsidy of corporate borrowing.

If borrowing and lending are unconstrained, and if real investment is riskless, it is possible for a corporation to undertake offsetting transactions, by selling debt and buying an equal amount of real capital. Explicitly or implicitly, most analyses depend upon the elimination of any possible pure surpluses from such transactions to determine the equilibrium relationship among i, q, and c (given π and the tax rules). More prosaically, most analyses represent the corporation as discounting nominal cash flows at the "after-tax nominal interest rate," $(1 - u)i$.

In equilibrium, then, the present value of the nominal cash flow from a unit of capital, as summarized above, must just equal the initial outlay. This implies

$$(1 - k)q = \int_0^\infty (1 - u)ce^{(\pi - \delta)\tau}e^{-(1-u)i\tau}d\tau$$
$$+ \int_0^\infty uq\delta'e^{-\delta'\tau}e^{-(1-u)i\tau}d\tau \quad . \quad (1)$$

Explicit integration leads to a relatively simple relationship between the gross of depreciation rental rate, c/q, and the interest and inflation rates:

$$\frac{c}{q} = \frac{\delta + (1 - u)i - \pi}{1 - u}\left[1 - k - \frac{u\delta'}{\delta' - (1 - u)i}\right] \quad . \quad (2)$$

This is our basic equation for later computations. Note that this equilibrium condition is *independent* of the actual financing method of the corporation; it does not matter whether the source of the investment funds is debt or equity. The *option* of arbitrage between debt and real capital implies equation (2).[4]

Since the original Hall and Jorgenson treatment of this subject (1967), the notation z has been the conventional symbol for the discounted sum of depreciation deductions on a one dollar investment. Therefore (2) can also be written as

$$\frac{c}{q} = \frac{\delta + (1 - u)i - \pi}{1 - u}(1 - k - uz) \quad , \quad (3)$$

where it must be remembered that z depends upon i and u.

For changes in the tax parameters u, k, and δ', it is conceptually straightforward to calculate the effect on the equilibrium social rate of return, ρ, which equals $c/q - \delta$. This can be done for different combinations of i and π. Commonly, though, a further simplification is adopted, namely, an assumed relationship between i and π. This reduces the number of cases to consider, for the whole system described by (2) then has a single exogenous parameter, π.[5] While a number of relationships are possible, two particular assumptions about inflation and the nominal interest rate are often encountered. The first is a strict version of Fisher's Law. If we let i_o represent the interest rate presumed to prevail in the absence of inflation, Strict Fisher's Law says that

$$i = i_o + \pi \quad . \tag{4a}$$

The argument for this result is simply that this adjustment leaves all real borrowing and lending opportunities independent of the rate of inflation. Implicit is the absence of taxes on interest. With a tax at a flat rate u on net interest receipts (which implies a deduction for interest payments), the same argument predicts what might be called Modified Fisher's Law:[6]

$$i = i_o + \frac{\pi}{1 - u} \quad . \tag{4b}$$

Theory does not give us firm predictions about the relationship between i and π in a world of imperfect income measurement rules, diverse marginal tax rates, nonlinearities, noise, and other considerations. Feldstein and Summers (1978) estimate that i has varied slightly less than point for point with π in the U.S. since World War II. On the other hand, Hall (1981) explicitly assumes Modified Fisher's Law. Jorgenson and Sullivan (1981) postulate constancy of the real rate of return on investment after the corporate tax, citing empirical work by Fraumeni and Jorgenson (1981). This procedure is equivalent to assuming Modified Fisher's Law when arbitrage with corporate bonds is encompassed by the model.[7]

Later we consider the choice between (4a) and (4b). For our illustrative calculations, we consider three situations: no inflation, 10 percent inflation with equation (4a), and 10 percent inflation with equation (4b). The real interest rate to a bond holder with no tax is the same in the first two scenarios, but the real interest rate after tax at rate u differs. In the first and third scenarios, the real after-corporate-tax interest rate $(1 - u)i - \pi$ is the same, but the real interest rate for a nonprofit (nontaxable) institution differs. There is no real interest rate which is the same in all three cases, and so we studiously avoid defining any parameter as the real after-tax interest rate. Instead, we take as a basis of comparison the interest rate i_o that would prevail with no inflation.

II.2. EFFECTIVE TAX RATES

The concept of an effective tax rate on capital refers to some measure of the difference between ρ, the real social rate of return earned on a real asset, and s, defined as the rate of return received by the person or institution financing its purchase. Then we can define the tax "wedge," t^w, as

$$t^w = \rho - s. \tag{5}$$

This wedge can be thought of as an annual levy on the specified financer with respect to a dollar's worth of the asset in question. It may be either positive or negative.

It is usual to express t^w as a ratio to either the social return or the saver's return. The first is a tax rate on a base that includes the tax: a "tax inclusive" rate in the language of the Meade Report (1978). Since the base is gross-of-tax, we refer to it as a "gross tax rate" t^g. The other tax rate is on a "tax exclusive" or net-of-tax basis, and is referred to here as a "net tax rate," t^n. These rates are related to ρ and s by

$$t^g = \frac{\rho - s}{\rho}, \tag{6}$$

$$t^n = \frac{\rho - s}{s}. \tag{7}$$

Notice that these rates are nonlinear functions of s and ρ and may behave rather erratically in some circumstances. Particular care must be used where the denominator of one of these formulas approaches zero, or passes from positive to negative. In later sections we shall see examples of the practical relevance of this erratic behavior.

Different values of ρ and s can be derived for

    (a) assets with different depreciation rates δ,
    (b) assets with different tax rules (δ' and k),
    (c) savers with different tax circumstances (u, m),
    (d) different types of finance (bonds, stock, direct ownership), and
    (e) different i and π combinations.

In particular, we shall focus on an "effective corporate tax rate," a "total effective rate of tax on bond financed corporate investment," and a "total effective rate of tax on equity financed investment."

In performing this analysis however, there is some question as to what should be taken as constant. Since the interest rate i is a price established on a market in which all can trade, it is arguably the natural fixed point. Given this interest rate and a single tax rate u for all traders, the social return ρ would be determined by the equilibrium condition (2) for arbitrage between bonds and real capital. In concluding remarks we touch upon the possibility of corporate and noncorporate arbitragers with different tax rates. For now, however, we make the customary assumption that the market is dominated by corporations with tax rate u. Because the corporation arbitrages between real capital and bonds yielding $(1 - u)i - \pi$, it is either a borrower or lender at that real after-tax interest rate. In this sense, we can take $(1 - u)i - \pi$ as the net return to savings of the corporation, s_c.

Thus, the corporate tax wedge, the effective gross rate, and the effective net rate are given by

$$t_c^w = \rho - s_c = \rho - [(1 - u)i - \pi] \quad ,$$

$$t_c^g = \frac{\rho - s_c}{\rho} = \frac{\rho - [(1 - u)i - \pi]}{\rho} \quad , \tag{8}$$

$$t_c^n = \frac{\rho - s_c}{s_c} = \frac{\rho - [(1 - u)i - \pi]}{(1 - u)i - \pi} \quad .$$

Note that the model developed in the previous section implies ρ and i are functionally related to each other, and i is functionally related to π. Hence the model implies values for the corporate tax wedge and the corporate effective tax rates as functions of π.

If we imagine a corporation choosing to purchase a dollar's worth of real assets with some funds it has in the bank, the net of tax real return must be $(1 - u)i - \pi$; otherwise (2) would not be satisfied. This can be thought of as income to the stockholders, who are taxed on it at marginal rate m_e. This personal rate is designed to capture the effective personal tax on these earnings when part may be paid as dividends and part retained. It should also account for the low effective personal rate on accrued capital gains resulting from retentions. The net return to stockholders on equity is thus $s_e = (1 - m_e)[(1 - u)i - \pi]$. The tax wedge on equity, the effective gross rate, and the effective net rate are given by

$$t_e^w = \rho - s_e = \rho - (1 - m_e)[(1 - u)i - \pi] \quad ,$$

$$t_e^g = \frac{\rho - s_e}{\rho} = \frac{\rho - (1 - m_e)[(1 - u)i - \pi]}{\rho} \quad , \tag{9}$$

$$t_e^n = \frac{\rho - s_e}{s_e} = \frac{\rho - (1 - m_e)[(1 - u)i - \pi]}{(1 - m_e)[(1 - u)i - \pi]} \quad .$$

An individual debt holder with marginal tax rate m_d receives a real return on bonds of $(1 - m_d)i - \pi$ after taxes. Call this return s_d.[8] We are entitled to compare s_d to the social return on corporate investment, and the difference is customarily referred to as the effective tax on corporate investment financed by debt. Thus the tax wedge on debt, the effective gross rate, and the effective net rate are given by

$$t_d^w = \rho - s_d = \rho - [(1 - m_d)i - \pi] \quad ,$$

$$t_d^g = \frac{\rho - s_d}{\rho} = \frac{\rho - [(1 - m_d)i - \pi]}{\rho} \quad , \tag{10}$$

$$t_d^n = \frac{\rho - s_d}{s_d} = \frac{\rho - [(1 - m_d)i - \pi]}{[(1 - m_d)i - \pi]} \quad .$$

In two senses, these effective tax rates have nothing to do with whether the investment is actually financed by issue of debt. First, because i is a market interest rate, any debt holder with tax rate m_d will earn s_d. The corporation earns ρ on a particular investment. The values ρ and s_d are all that is required to define the effective tax rates, independently of any connection between the two. Second, when the corporation makes its real investment decisions by comparing the returns on capital and debt, there is a connection between ρ and i. This relationship depends on potential and not actual arbitrage, however. Thus the t_d expressions are not only defined, but relevant for analysis regardless of whether debt finance is actually used.

Two points may be noted from these formulas before we proceed to illustrate them. First, if the personal rate m_d happens to equal the corporate rate u, then the total tax on debt (equation 10) is equivalent to the corporate rate alone (equation 8). When Hall or Jorgenson and Sullivan report effective corporate tax rates t_c^g, we can reinterpret them as total tax rates t_d^g on a debt financed investment where the lender has a tax rate m_d equal to u.

Second, if m_d is zero, then equation (10) implies

$$t_d^g = \frac{\rho - (i - \pi)}{\rho} = \frac{(c/q - \delta) - (i - \pi)}{(c/q - \delta)} \quad . \tag{11}$$

If we use equations (2) and (4b) to obtain ρ, this is exactly the tax rate on debt calculated by Hall (1981). Thus Hall's tax rates on debt can be thought of as the lowest extremes of a spectrum from $m_d = 0$ to $m_d = u$. For the other extreme, we can simply look at the effective corporate tax rate t_c^g. Below, we reproduce Hall's results and then recalculate them for different real net of tax interest rates and for different assumptions about how inflation affects nominal interest rates.

The various effective tax rate expressions are drawn together and summarized in table 1.

II.3. PARAMETER VALUES

Having specified the mechanisms determining the social rate of return and the saver's rate of return, we can explore the behavior of the various effective tax rates under different assumptions about parameters. Hall (1981) has chosen a particular classification of investment types and saver types; it will facilitate our discussion to adopt the same parameter values.

First, take u to be .46, the marginal tax rate for corporations where nearly all corporate investment takes place. For m_d, Hall uses a value of zero, on the assumption that all bonds are held by tax-exempt institutions. As we have mentioned, we can also consider the case of $m_d = u =$

TABLE 1

DEFINITION OF DIFFERENT EFFECTIVE TAX RATES

	SUPERSCRIPTS		
SUBSCRIPTS	w Wedge	g Gross	n Net
c Corporate	$t_c^w = \rho - s_c$	$t_c^g = \dfrac{\rho - s_c}{\rho}$	$t_c^n = \dfrac{\rho - s_c}{s_c}$
e Equity	$t_e^w = \rho - s_e$	$t_e^g = \dfrac{\rho - s_e}{\rho}$	$t_e^n = \dfrac{\rho - s_e}{s_e}$
d Debt	$t_d^w = \rho - s_d$	$t_d^g = \dfrac{\rho - s_d}{\rho}$	$t_d^n = \dfrac{\rho - s_d}{s_d}$

where $s_c = (1 - u)i - \pi$
$s_e = (1 - m_e)[(1 - u)i - \pi]$
$s_d = (1 - m_d)i - \pi$

.46 with no extra calculations or table space. Thirdly, let m_e equal .28, the value chosen by Hall. He assumes that the typical stockholder is in the 40 percent bracket, receiving one-half of corporate equity income as fully taxable dividends and the other half as capital gains. Only 40 percent of the latter are included in the individual income tax base. We regard the figure of .28 as somewhat high. The value of deferral and of the write-up of capital gains basis at death probably cut the effective proportion of accrued gains included in taxable income to something like 20 percent.[9] With this assumption, m_e would be .24. For purposes of illustrating the characteristics of the tax system, however, the difference is not of much importance.

Hall identifies three real assets. "Equipment" depreciates at 10 percent per year, receives a 10 percent investment tax credit, and is allowed depreciation deductions at 15 percent per year. "Structures" depreciate at an annual rate of 3 percent, receive no investment tax credit, but are allowed accelerated depreciation deductions at 6 percent per year. Finally, "intangibles" (e.g. advertising or R&D) are assumed to depreciate at 10 percent, receive no tax credit, but may be written off immediately. These asset characteristics are summarized in table 2. Tax rate estimates will be sensitive to these assumed parameters, but they do represent plausible examples of real asset characteristics. Notice that equipment and intangibles are technologically identical (have the same depreciation rate). We can thus attribute their different results purely to differences in tax treatment.

It remains to specify the interest rate. Hall chooses as his starting point an assumed real after-corporate-tax interest rate of .04. In the absence of inflation, this is our $(1 - u)i_o$. We also consider .02 and .06 as alternative

TABLE 2

PARAMETERS FOR THREE ASSET CATEGORIES

		1	2	3
Definition	Parameter	Equipment	Structures	Intangibles
Effective investment tax credit rate	k	.1	0	0
Economic depreciation rate	δ	.1	.03	.1
Tax depreciation rate	δ'	.15	.06	∞

assumed values of $(1 - u)i_o$. Whereas Hall takes Modified Fisher's Law (4b) as given, we want to look at the effect of varying this assumption. We take Strict Fisher's Law (4a) as an alternative. In each case we display the results for $(1 - u)i_o$ equal to .02, .04, and .06.

As mentioned above, we consider 10 percent inflation with (4a), 10 percent inflation with (4b), and zero inflation, a rate at which the two versions of Fisher's Law imply the same interest. We thus consider three inflation assumptions, three distinct saver types, three asset types, and three values of $(1 - u)i_o$. Any single interest-inflation combination can be used in one direction to determine the social return on each investment, ρ, or in the other direction to determine the return to each saver, s. The values of ρ and s for all of these combinations are displayed in table 3.

Readers are advised to spend a few minutes absorbing table 3. Notice, for example, that because intangibles are expensed, this form of investment is effectively untaxed at the corporate level ($\rho = s_c$). The column of real returns on intangibles just shows the behavior of the real after-corporate-tax interest rate under the various assumptions. With Strict Fisher's Law and low values of $(1 - u)i_o$, this interest rate is negative. The column of real returns to tax-exempt debt holding savers, s_d, shows what happens to $i - \pi$ under the various assumptions. With Modified Fisher's Law, the real rate of return to tax-exempt debt holders rises sharply with inflation.

Readers can now construct their own effective tax rates. First, choose a row of table 3. Second, subtract from any real social rate of return ρ, any saver's real return s in that row. Third, decide whether to divide by the former, the latter, or not at all. In the remainder of this paper, we discuss some of the issues to keep in mind during this exercise.

III. Three Caveats

III.1. TAX RATES ARE SENSITIVE TO THE INTEREST RATE

The first of our three points is very simple, now that the apparatus of section II is available: effective tax rate estimates depend on the assumed interest rate. Given π, the interest rate determines ρ. Thus each tax rate, such as t_c^g, t_e^g, or t_d^g, is a function of the interest rate. Different tax estimates will result from different interest rates used as input.

Later, we shall develop the point that tax rates are also sensitive to how inflation affects nominal interest rates. To abstract from that point here, consider the simple case with no inflation. Table 4, part A, displays the various gross tax rates under these circumstances.

TABLE 3

SOCIAL RATE OF RETURN AND RETURN TO SAVERS UNDER VARIOUS ASSUMPTIONS

	$(1 - u)i_o$	REAL SOCIAL RATE OF RETURN, ρ (in %)			REAL RATE OF RETURN TO SAVERS, s (in %)		
		Equip.	Struc.	Intang.	Corporations alone, or Debt Holders with $m_d = .46$ s_c	Equity Holders with $m_e = .28$ s_e	Debt Holders with $m_d = 0$ s_d
A. With no inflation	.02	1.0	3.1	2.0	2.0	1.4	3.7
	.04	3.9	6.4	4.0	4.0	2.9	7.4
	.06	6.9	9.8	6.0	6.0	4.3	11.1
B. With 10% inflation and Modified Fisher's Law (eq. 4b)	.02	4.3	4.8	2.0	2.0	1.4	12.2
	.04	7.2	8.2	4.0	4.0	2.9	15.9
	.06	10.1	11.6	6.0	6.0	4.3	19.6
C. With 10% inflation and Strict Fisher's Law (eq. 4a)	.02	−1.9	−2.4	−2.6	−2.6	−1.9	3.7
	.04	0.7	0.6	−0.6	−0.6	−0.4	7.4
	.06	3.5	3.9	1.4	1.4	1.0	11.1

Let us pause to study the numbers in table 4A. Looking across any row, say for $(1 - u)i_o = .04$, we see the expected wide range of effective rates applicable to different holders of different types of claims on different forms of real capital. The effective corporate tax rate on intangibles is zero, because this asset receives immediate expensing, which is equivalent to eliminating the tax. The corporation equates ρ on this investment to the after-tax return it can earn on other assets, $(1 - u)i$. Since i is the rate of return received by tax-exempt bondholders, their implied effective tax rate is negative: $t_d{}^g = (\rho - i)/\rho = -u/(1 - u) = -85$ percent. The holder of equity, on the other hand, pays a tax of 28 percent (the assumed value of m_e) on $\rho = (1 - u)i$.

Still for $(1 - u)i_o = .04$, the effective corporate rate on structures is 37 percent, below the statutory rate of 46 percent. This difference reflects depreciation allowances in excess of economic depreciation. The higher 55 percent total tax rate on equity simply reflects the "double taxation" of corporate income. Finally for structures, the rate on debt is -16 percent. This subsidy is less than the subsidy for intangibles because structures do not receive immediate expensing. This asset has a higher marginal social rate of return while the return to debt-holding savers is the same.

The three tax rates for equipment follow a similar pattern. Investment tax credits and accelerated depreciation imply a near zero corporate rate, while the rate on equity is higher and debt is lower.

Now we turn to examination of the columns of table 4A, that is, to the effect of varying the assumed interest rate. We note immediately that the effective taxes on intangibles are unaffected while those on equipment move rather dramatically. The former result follows from the fact that the various tax rates are simple multiples of $(1 - u)$, independent of i. Put another way, there are no delayed taxes or benefits with immediate expensing, so the discount rate does not matter.

The behavior of the effective taxes on equipment can be understood by reexamining three aspects of equation (2). First, the return on the investment is indeed taxed at rate u. Second, it receives investment tax credit at rate k. Third, it receives accelerated depreciation since $\delta' > \delta$ (we can ignore historical cost problems here since π is zero). When the discount rate $(1 - u)i_o$ is low, the future depreciation advantages are relatively more important. Together with the investment tax credit, they outweigh the corporate tax, and a net subsidy results. As the discount rate increases, accelerated depreciation becomes less and less important until the corporate tax outweighs the credits and deductions, so a net tax results.

The effective tax rates for structures turn out to be less sensitive to the

TABLE 4

EFFECTIVE TAX RATES AS PERCENT OF CAPITAL INCOME GROSS OF TAX

A. EFFECTIVE TAX RATES WITH NO INFLATION

$(1-u)i_o$	t_c^g = Corporate Rate only, or Total Rate on Debt if m_d = .46			t_e^g = Total Rate on Equity if m_e = .28			t_d^g = Total Rate on Debt if m_d = 0		
	Equip.	Struc.	Intang.	Equip.	Struc.	Intang.	Equip.	Struc.	Intang.
.02	−104	35	0	−47	53	28	−278	−21	−85
.04	−2	37	0	26	55	28	−89	−16	−85
.06	13	39	0	38	56	28	−60	−13	−85

B. WITH π = .1 AND EQUATION (4b): INFLATION ADDS MORE THAN POINT-FOR-POINT TO NOMINAL INTEREST.

$(i-u)i_o$	t_c^g = Corporate Rate only, or Total Rate on Debt if m_d = .46			t_e^g = Total Rate on Equity if m_e = .28			t_d^g = Total Rate on Debt if m_d = 0		
	Equip.	Struc.	Intang.	Equip.	Struc.	Intang.	Equip.	Struc.	Intang.
.02	54	59	0	67	70	28	−183	−153	−511
.04	44	51	0	60	65	28	−122	−95	−298
.06	40	48	0	57	63	28	−95	−70	−227

C. With $\pi = .1$ and Equation (4a): Inflation Adds Point-for-Point to Nominal Interest.

$(i - u)i_o$	t_c^g = Corporate Rate only, or Total Rate on Debt if m_d = .46			t_e^g = Total Rate on Equity if m_e = .28			t_d^g = Total Rate on Debt if m_d = 0		
	Equip.	Struc.	Intang.	Equip.	Struc.	Intang.	Equip.	Struc.	Intang.
.02	−38*	−8*	0	1*	22*	28*	296*	254*	242*
.04	181	193	0	158	167	28*	−896	−1043	1335*
.06	60	64	0	71	74	28	−219	−188	−694

* denotes tax rates with anomalous signs as described in the text.

interest rates in the range considered here. Because structures do not qualify for the investment credit, the effective corporate tax rate must be at least zero.

The sensitivity to the interest rate remains when there is inflation. Let us continue to delay the issue of how inflation affects nominal interest rates. For now, just consider the case of equation (4b), where the real after-corporate-tax interest rate $(1 - u)i - \pi$ is constant. The nominal interest rate starts with no inflation at $i = i_0$ and increases to $i = i_0 + \pi/(1 - u)$ with inflation at rate π of 10 percent. Resulting effective tax rate estimates are shown in table 4B.

Again the tax rates with $(1 - u)i_0 = .04$ reproduce estimates from Hall's paper. Again the tax rates on intangibles are insensitive to this interest rate, except for $t_d{}^g$. The insensitive tax rates result from the fact that the real after-tax interest rate is constant. For tax-exempt bondholders, however, the real return rises because the equilibrium market interest rate increases by more than the inflation rate. The higher is the inflation rate (relative to the rate of return) the larger is this subsidy.

Tax rates for equipment and structures in table 4B may appear to be fairly stable, but only because of the range for i_0. Hall reports a 44 percent tax rate at $(1 - u)i_0 = .04$, while the table shows a lower rate (40 percent)

FIGURE 1

CORPORATE TAX RATE ON EQUIPMENT WITH $\pi = .1$ AND EQUATION (4b)
(INFLATION ADDS MORE THAN POINT-FOR-POINT TO NOMINAL
INTEREST.)

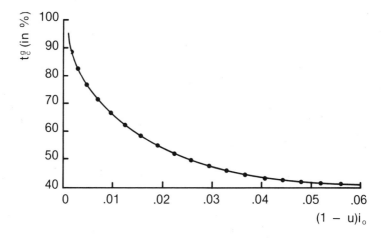

at .06 and a higher rate (54 percent) at .02. In fact, as $(1 - u)i_o$ is reduced further, the tax rate gets even higher. This sensitivity is displayed dramatically in figure 1, which plots t_c^g for equipment against the real after-tax interest rate $(1 - u)i_o = (1 - u)i - \pi$ with 10 percent inflation. With $(1 - u)i_o$ between zero and .06, one obtains tax rates anywhere between 40 percent and 100 percent.

III.2. THE DENOMINATOR CAN BE ZERO

Our second caveat concerns the manner in which a given tax wedge is expressed. Even if we agree on an interest rate (in order to set aside the problems of the previous section), the resulting tax rate estimate might imply that the entire return to investors is financed by government through investment tax credits and accelerated depreciation allowances that outweigh the corporate tax. The required return on the investment, ρ, may be zero. In this case the rate of tax $t^g = (\rho - s)/\rho$ is not defined. If the saver obtains a positive rate of return, it is paid entirely by a tax subsidy. While the gross tax rate is undefined, the net tax rate is defined and equals -100 percent. However, there is no insurance against s going to zero either. The real net of tax return of savers has even been negative in riskless terms with inflation. The remaining alternative is merely to report the total wedge $t^w = \rho - s$. This value can be interpreted as a "property tax" rate, the percentage of asset-value paid in tax each year.

To illustrate the relevance of this problem, consider the corporate tax rates t_c^g on equipment without inflation. These tax rates are reported for selected interest rates on the left side of table 4A. They are also reproduced in figure 2 for all interest rates between zero and $(1 - u)i_o = .06$. With high interest rates (.06), accelerated depreciation has a low present value, and a small net tax results. At $(1 - u)i_o = .04$, as reported in Hall, tax credit and depreciation advantages just about balance the tax at rate u, with an effective corporate tax rate of nearly zero. With lower interest rates, the depreciation advantage is more important, ρ is always less than $(1 - u)i_o$, and t_c^w (the numerator of t_c^g) is always negative. Near $(1 - u)i_o = .014$, the subsidy rate can be as high as desired, since ρ approaches zero. With interest rates below .014, however, ρ in the denominator is *also* negative, with the anomalous result that t_c^g is positive. In no sense is there a positive tax rate in this region, since $\rho < (1 - u)i_o$, yet t_c^g will be positive.

Table 5 summarizes the possibilities for this example of the effective corporate tax on equipment with no inflation. The use of t_c^g is not really acceptable, because the subsidy at .01 appears as a $+322$ percent tax.

FIGURE 2

Corporate Tax Rate on Equipment With No Inflation

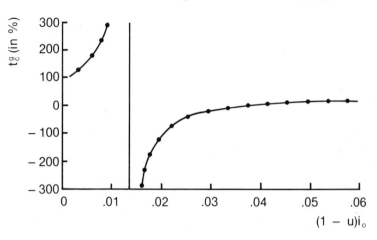

TABLE 5

Alternative Expressions for the Effective Corporate
Rate (Equipment, No Inflation)

$(1 - u)i_o$	$t_c^w = \rho - s_c$	$t_c^g = t_c^w/\rho$	$t_c^n = t_c^w/s_c$
.01	−1.45	322	−145
.02	−1.02	−104	− 51
.04	−.08	−2	0
.06	.93	13	16
.08	2.00	20	25

Note: t_c^w is a percent of asset-value paid in tax each year. The other
tax rates are expressed as a percent of the capital income flow.

The net rate t_c^n seems to make more sense, since the sign is correct here.
However, table 3 reveals that s_c could also be negative in the denominator
of t_c^n. In such a case, a subsidy would again appear as a positive net tax
rate. Furthermore, both gross and net tax rates are subject to misleadingly
wide variation when their denominators are close to zero.

These considerations seem to point toward the use of t^w alone; we do not
need a denominator. This effective tax always has the right sign and is not

so sensitive to small changes in the assumption about interest rates. However, the problem of the assumed interest rate does not vanish. The tax wedge t^w does become larger as the rate of return increases, even though the *rate* of tax levels off as seen in figure 2.

The moral seems to be that analysts should report the underlying components ρ and s, as well as summary figures such as tax wedges, gross tax rates, or net tax rates. They should also include a discussion of the sensitivity of these figures to the underlying assumptions. To follow our own advice, we report tax wedges in table 6 for each asset and inflation scenario. This table has the same format as table 4.

III.3. THE INFLATION ASSUMPTION MATTERS

Fisher's original law predicted that i would increase by π in a world with no taxes. Since most investment takes place in corporations with tax rate u, however, one is tempted to adopt the modified view that i should increase by $\pi/(1 - u)$, keeping constant the real interest rate after corporate taxes. This is the basis for Hall's assumption.

There are, however, influences which weaken the a priori case for this outcome. First, not all investors have the same marginal rate. If the system is dominated by nonprofit institutions with $m_d = 0$, then the argument behind Fisher's Law would imply that i increase only by π, to keep *their* real (nontaxed) interest rate constant. Second, even if all tax rates did equal u, historical cost depreciation and taxation of nominal capital gains will tend to reduce the real net return on investments when there is inflation. These features imply that the interest rate would tend to rise by less than $\pi/(1 - u)$ with inflation.

Feldstein and Summers (1978) have estimated that inflation adds approximately point-for-point to nominal interest rates. This is not the result of a simple Fisher's Law without taxes. Rather, it is the result of two countervailing forces within the tax system: taxation of nominal interest at some average rate, call it m, tends to raise i by $\pi/(1 - m)$, while historical cost depreciation and taxation of nominal capital gains tend to pull the adjustment below this level.

Jorgenson and Sullivan also use empirical work to support their assumption of a constant real after-tax rate of return on corporate investment. This estimated constancy would appear to contradict the results of Feldstein and Summers. The difference can be reconciled by a limitation on arbitrage between bonds and real capital, implicitly invoked by Jorgenson and Sullivan. With such a limitation, real after-tax interest rates could fall with inflation (Feldstein and Summers), while real after-tax

TABLE 6

Effective Tax Rates as Percentage of Asset-Value Per Year

A. Effective Tax Rates With No Inflation

$(1-u)i_o$	t_c^w = Corporate Rate only, or Total Rate on Debt if m_d = .46			t_e^w = Total Rate on Equity if m_e = .28			t_d^w = Total Rate on Debt if m_d = 0		
	Equip.	Struc.	Intang.	Equip.	Struc.	Intang.	Equip.	Struc.	Intang.
.02	−1.02	1.06	0.00	−.46	1.62	.56	−2.72	−.64	−1.70
.04	−.08	2.39	0.00	1.04	3.51	1.12	−3.49	−1.02	−3.41
.06	.93	3.83	0.00	2.61	5.51	1.68	−4.18	−1.28	−5.11

B. With π = .1 and Equation (4b): Inflation Adds More Than Point-for-Point to Nominal Interest.

$(1-u)i_o$	t_c^w = Corporate Rate only, or Total Rate on Debt if m_d = .46			t_e^w = Total Rate on Equity if m_e = .28			t_d^w = Total Rate on Debt if m_d = 0		
	Equip.	Struc.	Intang.	Equip.	Struc.	Intang.	Equip.	Struc.	Intang.
.02	2.32	2.84	0.00	2.88	3.40	.56	−7.90	−7.38	−10.22
.04	3.16	4.17	0.00	4.28	5.29	1.12	−8.76	−7.75	−11.93
.06	4.07	5.58	0.00	5.75	7.26	1.68	−9.56	−8.05	−13.63

C. WITH $\pi = .1$ AND EQUATION (4a): INFLATION ADDS POINT-FOR-POINT TO NOMINAL INTEREST

$(1 - u)i_o$	t_c^w = Corporate Rate only, or Total Rate on Debt if $m_d = .46$			t_e^w = Total Rate on Equity if $m_e = .28$			t_d^w = Total Rate on Debt if $m_d = 0$		
	Equip.	Struc.	Intang.	Equip.	Struc.	Intang.	Equip.	Struc.	Intang.
.02	.71	.19	0.00	−.02	−.54	−.73	−5.60	−6.12	−6.30
.04	1.34	1.25	0.00	1.18	1.08	−.17	−6.67	−6.76	−8.01
.06	2.08	2.46	0.00	2.47	2.85	.39	−7.63	−7.26	−9.71

rates of return are constant (Jorgenson and Sullivan). In terms of our analysis, the Jorgenson and Sullivan procedure is equivalent to assuming Modified Fisher's Law, as far as effective corporate and equity tax rates are concerned. Calculating effective tax rates applicable to bond holders would require a separate model of interest determination.

The choice between Strict and Modified Fisher's Laws does affect tax rate estimates. As is clear from table 3, the required real social returns on investment, ρ, and the real net return to savers, s, depend critically on how inflation affects the nominal interest rate.

Consider first the Strict Fisher's Law of equation (4a). With 10 percent inflation, table 3 shows low and even negative required real rates of return on investment. If the demand for capital is inversely related to this required return, (4a) implies an *increased* capital stock. At the same time, table 3 shows lower real rewards to saving under Strict Fisher's Law. If the supply of savings is positively related to its real net return, this would imply a *decreased* capital stock. The nominal interest rate would have to increase by more than π to encourage savers to supply enough capital to meet investment demand. The figures in table 3 by themselves cannot represent an equilibrium.

Now consider Modified Fisher's Law (4b). The large nominal interest increase associated with inflation implies a higher required real return on two of the three illustrative asset categories of table 3. The higher required ρ would suggest lower incentives to invest. At the same time, however, most savers are receiving higher real returns with inflation. These table 3 figures cannot be in equilibrium, either. Only if interest rates increased by something less than $\pi/(1 - u)$ would savers' desired wealth match the producers' desired capital.

Thus equations (4a) and (4b) represent two logical possibilities for an unknown relationship: the truth is likely to lie somewhere in between. If the assumption of Hall and Jorgenson and Sullivan is correct, then gross tax rates with $\pi = .1$ will look like part B of table 4. If, on the other hand, estimates from Feldstein and Summers (1978) are correct, gross tax rates with $\pi = .1$ will look like part C of table 4.

Table 4C illustrates some of the difficulties to which effective tax rates are subject. The corporate rates on equipment and structures are negative when $(1 - u)i_o$ is .02. As can be confirmed by reference to table 3, these are cases of negative social rates of return. Since the return received by a 46 percent bond holder is even more negative, these negative numbers in 4C reflect a positive tax. At higher values of $(1 - u)i_o$, relatively large positive corporate tax rates are shown. If we compare the tax rates here to those with no inflation in 4A, we might draw the conclusion that inflation effects a disincentive to invest. Again, a glance at the social rates of return in table 3 will confirm that ρ is sharply lower with inflation and Strict Fisher's Law. This can only be the result of *increased* investment, which pushes down the marginal rate of return. Such an outcome is to be expected, since inflation lowers real corporate borrowing costs under this assumption. The relative increase in effective tax rates is simply the result of much smaller denominators in the gross tax rate formula.

One last anomaly will complete the catalog of illustrations. Look at intangibles in the bottom right-hand corner of table 4. We now have outrageous $t_d{}^g$ tax rates between -694 percent and $+1335$ percent. Table 3 or 6 reveals that the wedge $(\rho - s_d)$ is in fact negative for all three values of $(1 - u)i_o$. For .02 and .04, however, this subsidy is larger than the saver's return, and ρ is negative in the denominator. We thus have negative numbers in table 4 reflecting positive taxes, and positive numbers in the table reflecting negative taxes.

IV. Concluding Remarks

Table 4 exemplifies three separate conclusions. Tax rates are sensitive to the interest rate (.02, .04, .06), tax rates are sensitive to the assumed effect of inflation on nominal interest (part B vs. part C), and tax rates are not best expressed as a percent of gross capital income ρ.

Beyond the three major caveats discussed in this paper, there exist other more subtle problems. We are forced by the limits of this paper to abstract from them, as have other studies. However, we might take a few paragraphs to outline these problems for future work.

Different effective tax rates are useful for different purposes. First, one may want an average tax rate or "flow of funds" rate to capture income effects, as described in our introduction. Second, there are different types of marginal tax rates. Capital income can increase because of higher rates of return *or* because of more investment. Since only the latter induces an investment credit, for example, the effect on taxes is not the same. Feldstein and Summers (1979) are not interested in the additional tax associated with another unit of investment. Instead, they seek to measure the effects of inflation on taxes. They need to specify the effect of inflation on nominal interest rates as well as the effect of nominal interest rates on real taxes paid.

Third, even if we agreed on marginal tax rates for additional investment, we might want an effective corporate rate, an effective personal rate, or the total effective wedge between the marginal product and the saver's rate of time preference. Consider for a moment the use of each such rate. The assumptions of our investment model rely heavily on a single market interest rate. Given this baseline for all corporate investment, the "effective corporate tax rates" can be used to measure the misallocations of capital among assets in the corporate sector. They cannot be used, for example, to capture misallocations between the corporate and noncorporate sectors. Given the same market interest rate as a baseline, different savers earn different net of tax returns. Thus "personal effective tax rates" can be used to measure a "misallocation" of savings in the personal sector: not all marginal rates of time preference are identical. Finally, only the total effective wedge between the marginal social rate of return ρ (averaged over different assets), and the marginal rate of time preference s (averaged over different savers), can be used to measure the misallocation of consumption between present and future periods, as caused by capital income taxation.

Analyses of allocative and distributive effects are hampered by the questionable consistency of the tax rates estimated with the assumption of overall equilibrium in capital markets.[10] Condition (2) expresses the requirement that the corporation should have maximized its profits in equilibrium. There can then be no potential for the corporation to gain by arbitrage between bonds and real capital. There are, however, other conditions one might wish to hold. For example, it might be required that profits of noncorporate investors from the same sort of arbitrage be eliminated. Equilibrium would then call for the analogue of condition (2), but with the proprietor's marginal rate m replacing the corporate marginal rate u. But (2) cannot hold for both m and u (unless they are equal).

For the model to tell a consistent story about the effect of taxes, it is necessary to find a way for corporations, individuals, and tax-exempt institutions to be in equilibrium simultaneously. There are two basic ways such a reconciliation might be accomplished. The first is to adopt assumptions that constrain the agents of the model. For example, it seems natural to impose borrowing limits on individuals, and to limit negative positions in (short sales of) real capital. One might simultaneously assume that corporate and noncorporate technologies are distinct, so that investment opportunities available to corporations are not available to other firms.

By a careful combination of such restrictions, a consistent model should be feasible. At this stage, the point to emphasize is that the particular constraints imposed are likely to have a significant bearing on the distorting consequences attributable to taxes. Take as an example the constraint that tax-exempt savings by individuals are subject to fixed ceilings. This assumption is likely to eliminate any allocative effects of the sort of subsidy to zero bracket bond holders that is apparent from table 4 or table 6.

The method of imposing constraints is likely to imply extreme specialization of portfolios. Individuals will hold only stock or bonds, for example, not both. The rates of return in the analysis above are treated as certain, and hence no one would hold assets generating different yields. Actual assets, however, are risky. Thus a second approach to resolving the problem of inconsistency is to attempt an explicit treatment of risk.

This undertaking would clearly be difficult, but it is important to explore. The effect of taxing the return to saving may be quite different from the effects of taxing risk premia. As shown in Gordon (1981), and as estimated in Fullerton and Gordon (1981), a tax on risk premia may constitute a simple risk sharing by government, with no distorting effect at all.

Pending modeling advances along the lines described here, we would urge those who construct and use effective tax rates to exercise appropriate caution.

REFERENCES

Bailey, Martin J. 1969. "Capital Prices and Income Taxation." In Arnold C. Harberger and Martin J. Bailey (eds.) *The Taxation of Income from Capital*. Washington, D.C.: The Brookings Institution.

Bradford, David F. 1980. "The Economics of Tax Policy Toward Savings." In George von Furstenberg, ed. *The Government and Capital Formation*. Cambridge: Ballinger, pp. 11–71.

_____. 1981. "Issues in the Design of Savings and Investment Incentives." In Charles R. Hulten, ed. *Depreciation, Inflation, and the Taxation of Income from Capital*. The Urban Institute Press. Washington, D.C.

Feldstein, Martin. December 1976. "Inflation, Income Taxes, and the Rate of Interest: A Theoretical Analysis." *American Economic Review* 66: 809–820.

_____. May 1980. "Tax Rules and the Mismanagement of Monetary Policy." *American Economic Review* 70: 182–186.

_____. and Lawrence Summers. 1978. "Inflation, Tax Rules, and the Long-Term Interest Rate." *Brookings Papers on Economic Activity* 1, pp. 61–109.

_____. December 1979. "Inflation and the Taxation of Capital Income in the Corporate Sector." *National Tax Journal* 32: 445–470.

Fiekowsky, Seymour. 1977. "Pitfalls in the Computation of 'Effective Tax Rates' Paid by Corporations." OTA Paper 23. Department of the Treasury. Washington, D.C.

Fraumeni, Barbara M., and Dale W. Jorgenson. 1980. "The Role of Capital in U.S. Economic Growth, 1948-1976." In George von Furstenberg, ed. *Capital, Efficiency and Growth*. Cambridge: Ballinger. pp. 9-250.

Fullerton, Don, and Roger H. Gordon. 1981. "A Re-examination of Tax Distortions in General Equilibrium Models." forthcoming in a National Bureau of Economic Research conference volume on tax simulations.

_____., Thomas King, John B. Shoven, and John Whalley. 1981. "Corporate Tax Integration in the United States: A General Equilibrium Approach." *American Economic Review*. forthcoming.

Gordon, Roger H. 1981. "Taxation of Corporate Capital Income: Tax Revenues vs. Tax Distortions." Mimeo. Bell Labs, Murray Hill, N.J.

Gravelle, Jane G. 1981. "The Social Cost of Nonneutral Taxation: Estimates for Non-Residential Capital." In Charles R. Hulten, ed. *Depreciation, Inflation, and the Taxation of Income from Capital*. Washington, D.C.: The Urban Institute Press.

Hall, Robert E. 1981. "Tax Treatment of Depreciation, Capital Gains and Interest in an Inflationary Economy." In Charles R. Hulten ed. *Depreciation, Inflation, and the Taxation of Income from Capital*. Washington, D.C.: The Urban Institute Press.

_____., and Dale W. Jorgenson June 1967. "Tax Policy and Investment Behavior." *American Economic Review* 57: 391-414.

Harberger, Arnold C. 1966. "Efficiency Effects of Taxes on Income from Capital." In M. Krzyzaniak, ed. *Effects of Corporation Income Tax*. Detroit: Wayne State University Press.

Hulten, Charles R., and Frank C. Wykoff. 1981. "The Measurement of Economic Depreciation." In Charles R. Hulten, ed. *Depreciation, Inflation, and Taxation of Income from Capital*. Washington, D.C.: The Urban Institute Press.

Jorgenson, Dale W., and Martin A. Sullivan. 1981. "Inflation and Capital Recovery in the United States." In Charles R. Hulten, ed. *Depreciation, Inflation, and the Taxation of Income from Capital*. Washington, D.C.: The Urban Institute Press.

King, Mervyn A. 1977. *Public Policy and the Corporation*. London: Chapman and Hall.

Meade, James E. 1978. *The Structure and Reform of Direct Taxation: Report of a Committee Chaired by Professor J. E. Meade*. London: Allen and Unwin for the Institute for Fiscal Studies.

Shoven, John B. December 1976. "Incidence and Efficiency Effects of Taxes on Income from Capital." *Journal of Political Economy* 84: 1261-1283.

Stiglitz, Joseph E. 1980. "On the Almost Neutrality of Inflation: Notes on Taxation and the Welfare Costs of Inflation." National Bureau of Economic Research Working Paper 499, Cambridge, Mass.

ROUNDTABLE DISCUSSION ON POLICY INITIATIVES TO STIMULATE PRODUCTIVITY

Mr. Brown: The first speaker will be Bruce Davie. I was asked especially to point out the fact that he is listed on the conference program as being from the Ways and Beans Committee of the U.S. House of Representatives. [Ed. note: Bruce Davie is, of course, from Ways and Means Committee.]

Mr. Davie: I gather that our job this afternoon is to gaze a bit beyond depreciation problems and proposals and look broadly at the question of what can be done through the tax system to enhance productivity.

I will adopt the stance of the moral majority and accept as an absolute article of faith that increasing the rate of productivity growth is a good and desirable thing. I will put aside as irrelevant theology any discussion of conceptual problems involved in measuring productivity and simply plow ahead with this question of what can be done through the tax system to enhance the rate of growth of productivity.

I want to emphasize the "can," because I will be talking in terms, not of a tax system which we might devise if we were to start from scratch, but in terms of the political process through which tax policy is determined.

That process starts with proposals being made, usually to reduce taxes for particular groups. The Auerbach-Jorgenson depreciation proposal is virtually unique in the sense of being a serious proposal that, on further analysis, would in the long run actually increase some people's taxes. The typical proposal is one that would reduce the taxes for some particular activity or group of taxpayers or perhaps grant a positive subsidy through the tax system.

279

If productivity increases become the rhetorical objective of tax policy for 1981 or the 97th Congress, then there are many clever people around who can turn practically any proposal into a proposal which, they will argue, will increase the rate of productivity growth. The new administration will come forth with a set of proposals, and I can assure you that the words "productivity growth" will appear several times in the written and verbal testimony of the new Secretary of the Treasury.

Those administration proposals are likely to be of two types—those that we call Treasury proposals and those that will come from other agencies. Agencies besides the Treasury have vested interests in the tax system. They are always looking for proposals that will help their clientele. Outgoing secretaries will leave memoranda for incoming secretaries saying: "If you ever get a chance to run around Treasury, here is a list of tax gimmicks that are desired by the industries and people our agency wants to help. By the way, this year call them proposals to increase the rate of productivity growth and you are sure to get them incorporated into an overall administration package."

There will also be proposals put forth by members of the tax-writing committees of the Congress. Those will in some cases reflect constituent interests. You can certainly understand that a representative from "Silicone Valley" will want to push a tax credit for research and development. A representative from Detroit will suggest refundable tax credits. But, a number of proposals coming from members will be made for purposes of differentiating the political product. Members of the tax-writing committees will feel that they ought to have their own proposals to put forward and will come up with some not easily explained in terms of constituent interests.

The list of likely proposals is quite extensive. We have been talking here about the kinds of depreciation proposals that are likely to be on the agenda for the next Congress, but there will be many more: the refundability of the investment tax credit; research and development credits; further liberalization of capital gains; a whole potpourri of proposals to "enhance productivity" in the small business sector; dividend reinvestment; perhaps the integration of the corporate and individual income tax; various savings incentives; and expanded job credits. Just a word about including job credits on this list. Even congressional staffers have read Denison's work and know that a lot of the increase in productivity is associated with human capital. It will be argued that we ought to be doing more to assure that young and disadvantaged workers get attached to the labor force early on, and more job credits are needed for that purpose. As the process of differentiating the political product goes on, some junior member of the tax-writing committees may find all the good proposals taken up by senior members and will, in a rash moment, suggest a simple rate reduction.

After all proposals are on the table, at some point, beginning in the Ways and Means Committee and then in the Senate Finance Committee, a package of proposals will emerge. The discipline of putting a package together tends to exclude some items at the expense of others. That whole package might be called the Productivity Enhancing Tax Act of 1981.

The size of that package is related to inflation in the following sense. The Congress periodically makes ad hoc adjustments to the tax system that one may view as a way to adjust, in very rough ways, for impact of inflation. The effect has been to keep the ratio of Federal income taxes to GNP about constant. That process is a rough approximation of what has happened over the last 10 to 20 years.

With the rapid inflation experienced recently, the package of ad hoc adjustments can be relatively large. That tends to break down the discipline of the political process I have just described. With a bigger package surely there is room for this senator's proposal, that congressman's favorite idea, a suggestion that has come from the Department of Housing and Urban Development or the Commerce Department. All of these can be accommodated in addition to what might be called traditional Treasury proposals.

There is, then, this important connection between inflation and what might be done through the tax system to promote productivity growth. The fact that inflation requires a large ad hoc adjustment means that many more tax proposals can be considered. Some undersirable provisions, undoubtedly, will be enacted simply because their revenue loss can be accommodated in a bigger package.

Contrast this, if you will, with a noninflationary world where government expenditures are held to a constant proportion of Gross National Product. Suppose further that the rate of productivity growth is low and tax policies are sought to increase that rate of growth. In that world there would be a much tighter discipline on the kinds of tax proposals considered. It would be very obvious that special tax breaks for this group, or that kind of economic activity, would be at the expense of other taxpayers.

When tax changes are made that in part adjust for inflation, it is not very obvious whose relative tax burdens are being increased when others are having theirs decreased in the name of productivity growth.

It may be possible to improve the package that ultimately emerges through this political process if some proposals are laid on the table that repeal, or at least limit, existing tax provisions which work against increases in the rate of productivity.

Let me just suggest a few: tax preferences for owner-occupied housing; tax-exempt financing of various private sector activities; and casualty loss deductions that encourage investment in noninsurable assets. The casualty loss provision encourages houses to be built on unstable beach fronts and in Malibu canyons which burn every few years. Owners know that the tax system is a way to insure those properties. We can add to this list the tax treatment of employer contributions to health insurance. Those provisions tend to devote too many resources to the health industry.

If proposals to repeal or limit existing tax code provisions which work against productivity improvements are to be considered, let me assure you that the politics are very difficult indeed. We have just been through an agonizing two years trying to reduce the use of tax-exempt bonds to finance owner-occupied housing. That has been an excruciating issue for the Congress to deal with. A favorable outcome of that issue was only possible because of the pressure imposed on the formation of tax policy by the congressional budget process. In the budget process this year the first concurrent resolution mandated a reconciliation process. Various committees were instructed to cut spending and the tax-writing committees directed to raise a bit of additional revenue. It was that instruction which, politically, made the limitation on the use of tax-exempt mortgage bonds possible.

This recent experience illustrates the important role that the congressional budget process has on the formation of tax policy, either through the reconciliation process or a limitation on the size of the tax cut package. Limitations imposed for budgetary reasons can instill some discipline on the political process of selecting from among the great panoply of productivity growth proposals that will be put before the tax-writing committees.

Mr. Brown: Thank you, Bruce (Davie).

Our next speaker is Bob Eisner of Northwestern University. We have had many conversations about accelerated depreciation and investment tax credits over the years.

Mr. Eisner: I guess that I should go way back. I was exposed early in graduate school days to Böhm-Bawerk and the advantages of round-about production. The way I learned it, round-about methods of production were more efficient and more productive, but not necessarily all of the time.

The essential notion was that there was some scarcity of capital or saving which normally prevented us from getting more capital to the point where its marginal net product was negative. But I would like to suggest the possibility that, if you have a pick-and-shovel society and every person has one pick and one shovel to dig his ditches, you are not going to make the society more productive by giving every person two picks and two shovels.

I also, as was suggested by Dale (Jorgenson), have come full circle and united with the extreme right, although I had no idea that at one time I was that left. I am united with what I think should be the extreme right position. That is that you should not intervene in the economy or interfere in capital formation or anything else unless you have good reasons. I will frequently have good reasons, and I will try in the next few minutes to say where I would intervene. It is not in the ways that are usually suggested.

David Bradford begins his paper with a sentence that there is broad agreement that capital accumulation in the United States is too low. I do not challenge him on that statement, but I think that the statement has become a part of the conventional wisdom which has little to do, that I can make out, with reality or meaningful economic analysis.

I think what is true is what comes out in the paper of Hall. It was talked about a good bit in the Auerbach-Jorgenson paper, and in a way it comes out implicitly in the Hulten-Wykoff paper, which compares tax depreciation rates with economic depreciation. If the taxation of capital is very uneven, we are probably sacrificing a great deal in productivity, not by taxing capital too heavily but all too frequently by taxing it too little and by taxing it at such different rates that we push some capital formation up too far and do not push other forms of capital formation far enough.

This is related to the current rate of productivity, a subject to which, as the title of this roundtable discussion suggests, we might address ourselves. I might just raise a question that we should keep clearly in mind. What do we mean by productivity and what should our objectives really be? In particular: are we trying to add to product per unit of labor or to product per capita? You have two quite different solutions.

I think the appropriate focus would be on product per capita. One way to increase product per capita would be to encourage the employment of women, to see to it that the black kids in the ghettos get jobs, to see to it that frictional and other unemployment is reduced, let alone demand-shortage unemployment. That would very considerably increase the output per capita.

Very likely, as good economic theory would suggest, it would also decrease the output per man-hour or person-hour worked. That is nothing to be deplored. I think, if you have idle resources of labor, you put them to work and develop them; then you will very likely be decreasing your capital-labor ratio and decreasing the output per person or per worker-hour employed, but not output per capita in the population.

On the matter, before we go further on depreciation, as to whether capital accumulation is really lagging, I could give you a long catalogue of the utterly misleading figures and comparisons with other countries and the like. I am fond of pointing out that, if you look at recent history, the ratio of gross private domestic investment—let us take nonresidential fixed investment—to gross national product in this country in current dollars, you will find that until the recent recession it was about as high in the last few years as it has ever been, running around 12 percent.

When I point that out to people like Marty Feldstein, he says—I think David (Bradford) may have this in mind in his figures—"You have to look at net investment and take a look at the capital consumption allowance."

That, I submit, is nonsense. Unless you really believe that durability is changing, the gross capital formation to GNP ratio or output ratio will for any given rate of growth in the labor force give you a unique capital-output ratio. To then say that the ratio of capital formation to output is at a peak is to say that we are heading for a peak in the capital-output ratio and also in the capital-labor ratio, except to the extent that your labor force is growing more rapidly. That relates to other considerations of what you want to be aiming at—output per worker or output per person.

I might add that I am sort of amused and delighted. I do not know if I should write this note now or wait a couple of weeks, because the scuttlebutt is, although no one will confirm it officially—we got the No Comment—that that 12-percent figure I am throwing out may be quite low and that actually capital formation has been considerably higher than we have been measuring it.

The capital formation, I should say carefully, as we have been measuring it means business fixed investment or business nonresidential fixed investment.

On depreciation, I hate to sound that critical of Dale (Jorgenson). I have had my differences with him on various issues. However, concerning his paper with Alan Auerbach, I heard a number of people say how wonderful it was and I figured that perhaps here was something that I could agree with enthusiastically, but I had to react in my usual critical manner. The reservations I have are something that I think should be generally kept in mind.

We focused this conference, perhaps unfortunately, although that is what many of us are interested in, on amending depreciation. That is, what we can do about tax depreciation as well as measuring depreciation in order to reach some kind of an optimum. Given the distorting effects of inflation on the crazy tax structure, it is hardly clear that we can improve matters by changing only one thing.

My objection to indexing depreciation, to which the Auerbach-Jorgenson proposal has been likened without corresponding treatment of capital gains and interest deductibility, is that it is very likely to bring us farther from an optimum, particularly I suspect in the way of actually giving an even greater encouragement to the acquisition of certain kinds of capital than we have.

I do not know if all of us as economists live enough in the dirty world to see what is going on. Talk to your tax expert, and I guess the people in the Office of Tax Analysis, (OTA) know.

I was kidding with the person with whom I came in on the plane yesterday a tax lawyer who, I should indicate, was also busy recruiting for the new administration. He was telling me how he had not paid any taxes in the last two years. He said his trick was that, under the technical corrections of 1979, there is a new category of special use properties—hotels, motels, and flophouses. He bought into them and gets a full investment credit, he insists. He said he gets a full investment credit which eliminates his taxes. I even gave the guy's name to the people at OTA, which I guess was dirty pool.

We talk about capital shortages and tax discouragements of savings and investment, but there are hugh opportunities in office buildings, shopping centers, housing, and all kinds of equipment as well, lease deals, various tax dodges. I am not the tax lawyer to give them to you. To sit around and accept the notion that capital is heavily taxed and we have to amend our depreciation to remedy it is, as I suggested very likely to aggravate matters, particularly if you take something like the Auerbach-Jorgenson proposal, which had in a way many reservations that made it unpalatable to Congress, like doing away with the investment credit.

If Congress ever understood that the present values applied to real economic depreciation, which would be a much lower rate than what we have to begin with, they would certainly not touch the Auerbach-Jorgenson proposal. If, in the course of political struggle, Dale and Alan discover that Congress will not buy their proposal as it is, and let them have the investment credit and maybe the Bureau of Economic Analysis (BEA) depreciation, we will have thrown out the bath water and the baby, as well as everything else.

Perhaps finally, I think we tend to miss the boat on all of the discussions of productivity and investment. In other work I have done I have been fond of pointing out (and this may come as a surprise to some of you) that business taxed capital investment in plant and equipment comes, do you know to what percent of total capital formation broadly defined to include human capital, research and development, government fixed capital, household fixed capital? It comes by my estimate, which you could quarrel with even to an order of 100 percent, to about 15 percent of total capital formation.

Therefore, when you talk about encouraging business plant and equipment spending, you are talking about encouraging one small portion very possibly, or inevitably, at the expense of something else. I do not find an automobile acquired by Hertz, which is investment, necessarily any more beneficial to productivity than an automobile acquired by a city, or state, or school district government, which would be government capital expenditures—take a school bus—or an automobile acquired by a household, which is consumption.

Yet, in focusing on tax depreciation for business, we are focusing on one small portion of total capital formation. Indeed, the much more substantial parts go to what was just alluded to by Bruce (Davie) in passing a moment ago, namely, investment in human capital, investment in research and development, investment in software, investment in the job experience that prevents a significant part of a generation from being unemployed or underutilized.

Here I would like to quarrel with Bob's (Hall) assertion that his charming wife is a real beneficiary with her software and computer programs which she sells. She may be, but she is then quite atypical of most investment in human capital.

I think the big point is that, because we are not a slave economy, all of these great capital gains which make so much of a difference on taxation of capital generally are not available to the prospective investor in human capital, while the firm that wants to buy a piece of machinery or build a new building in the suburbs knows that it will get all of those tax advantages of high interest deductibility, no taxation of capital gains, and the like.

On the other hand, if the firm wants to hire a kid from the ghetto, it figures he is a bad risk, because his marginal product is probably negative. There is a chance he will be a success and will not wreck the place, but if he is and does turn out to be a productive worker and does gain from six months' or a year's experience, that firm cannot say that it will make a capital gain on him. That gain will be to the society, because people do not stay in jobs forever and he will move on.

Regarding software, Bronwyn Hall can probably hold onto her software package. I do not know whether other people are cheating on her, but it is not true of a great deal of investment in human capital including, I suspect, investment in research and development.

Therefore, if you are looking for tax subsidies and places to raise productivity, those are the places I would look and not in the subsidization of business plant and equipment spending.

Let me close by trying out something on you. Perhaps I have not thought it through. I am not an advocate of taxing business. I have no illusions that taxing business is the way to equalize the distribution of income. I think it contributes to inefficiencies and to inflation.

How about eliminating all business taxation, corporate and as far as you can handle it single proprietorships and partnerships, and then tax all of the receipts of individuals plus the accrued capital gains?

I suppose that ideally you would want complete indexing on all of the capital gains. If you did this, it seems to me that my proposal would get us away from all of the problems of depreciation, and much of the distortions.

The argument that you cannot tax accrued capital gains efficiently I find to be rather silly. There are problems, but God knows the people from the OTA can tell us about all of the problems on the income tax. It seems to me it would be fairly simple. On all lists of securities you simply list the value at the beginning and on December 31 of successive years. On anything else, where you do not have market value established, the taxpayer would have to declare the value, declare the gain, and to the extent that he cheats you would catch up with him in two ways. Eventually, whenever the thing is disposed of you simply charge him if he has not declared it properly. And you would have a formula for charging him the accrued interest from the point where he misdeclared it. I suppose you could even have penalties of law for obvious cheating.

With that thought, I leave you.

Mr. Brown: Thank you. The moral is: Do not talk to Bob Eisner on an airplane.

Our next speaker is Dale Jorgenson from Harvard University.

Mr. Jorgenson: I realize that this is unfair, but I am going to use the blackboard. First of all, to make the idea of productivity more precise—

and I think Bruce Davie has given us a very good indication of reasons why we ought to try to be precise—you have to have our basic productivity growth equation as follows:

$$\Delta \ell n Q = w_L \Delta \ell n L + w_k \Delta \ell n K + w_T \Rightarrow \Delta \ell n Q - \Delta \ell n L$$
$$= w_K [\Delta \ell n K - \Delta \ell n L] + w_T$$

The growth rate of output Q is the share of labor times the growth rate of labor, the change in the logarithm of labor, plus the share of capital times the growth rate of capital, plus the productivity growth rate.

I am now going to define productivity, as I did there implicitly, as essentially the growth rate of output minus the weighted average of the growth of the inputs, in other words, total factor productivity, the term that John Kendrick has made famous.

A way of rewriting this equation which would be useful for our purposes is to take the output-labor ratio and compute its growth rate and express that as the capital share times the growth rate in the capital-labor ratio plus productivity growth. In Bob Eisner's terms, when we think about the growth rate of output per unit of labor input, it would be expressible, if this relationship holds, as the capital share (around .42) multiplied by the growth rate in the capital-output ratio plus productivity growth.

When I talk about productivity, I will be referring to the productivity growth rate, in other words, what is left over in terms of the growth of output if you take the input given. The productivity growth rate for the whole post-War period in the United States, by measures that I published elsewhere, is .0114, for the period 1948 to 1976, which I think is a relatively low number as these things go.

I think it would be very instructive to look at a few figures for some sub-periods, which I am now going to do. The period 1957 to 1959 is just about average, .0013. Measured against the template provided by the whole post-War average, it is a period of low productivity growth. The next period in my analysis, 1960 to 1966, is a period of very rapid productivity growth, almost twice the size of the productivity growth rate on the average, that is .0211. The period 1966 to 1969 is very much below that, .0004, a hardly noticeable productivity growth. For 1969 to 1973—and these numbers are very familiar to some people in this room—it is .0095, again around the average. Then, from 1973 to 1976 it is −.0070.

I submit by lowering the effective tax rate on capital, it is possible to stimulate the growth of the capital-labor ratio. That was news back in the early 60s; it is not news anymore. What is really news, and this is news in the 80s, is that productivity growth itself, what is left over after you take into account the substitution of capital for labor that is associated with a reduction in the effective tax rate on capital, is itself responsive to relative prices. Those relative prices turn out to include the same price of capital versus labor that we have in our story about substitution of capital for labor.

In fact, in general as the effective tax rate on capital falls, productivity growth rate goes up and vice versa. When the effective tax rate on capital rises, the productivity growth rate falls.

The answer to the question which was posed in the title for this session—What do we do about productivity growth—measured and defined in the way that I have described here, is that we have to figure out some way to reduce the effective tax rate on capital.

To convince you that productivity has something to do with the effective tax rate on capital over and above the long disputed argument about whether the effective tax rate on capital can affect the capital-labor ratio, let me just give you a few effective tax rates for the relevant periods. In 1960 a typical effective tax rate for equipment was around .58. The statutory rate then was around 52 percent, whereas, for structures it was around 51 or 50 percent, something like that. That was the situation in 1960.

Those of you who have been around the tax scene for some time know that between 1960 and, let us say, 1966, our end point there for this period, there were substantial changes in the effective taxation of capital income associated with the adoption of the investment tax credit and the acceleration of depreciation on equipment. In fact, typical rates for equipment dropped from the 60s down into the 30s. In 1965 they were about half of what they were in 1960.

In 1966 there was a slight uptick, but the corresponding rates were in the neighborhood of 38 percent, by comparison with 58 in 1960.

What did that do to productivity growth? As you can see, the productivity growth rate from 1960 to 1966, when there was a tremendous decrease in the effective tax rate on capital, boomed to unprecedented heights, at least in terms of American experience. Then, from 1966 to 1969 there was the Vietnam escalation, the associated inflation, and most importantly the election of Richard Nixon. You may recall that one of his first efforts—again the convergence of the right and the left—was to drop the investment tax credit as a discredited Democratic idea.

The investment tax credit was dropped at a time when accelerated depreciation had been largely undone by inflation, so that effective tax rates in 1969 were at or above the level in 1960. Once again, we can see from the numbers here that that was essentially death for productivity. If you average these two numbers, what you find is a number that is very close to the post-War average. The explanation of the difference between the three subperiods, 1957 to 1960, 1960 to 1966, and 1966 to 1969, is simply changes in the effective tax rates.

After 1969 effective tax rates changed again, because this same Richard Nixon reinstituted the investment tax credit and the inflation rates dipped a little bit after the worst of the Vietnam escalation, although they rose toward the end of the period. Effective tax rates on equipment because of the reinstitution of the tax credit dipped substantially from the middle 50s down into the 40s. Structures, which were not affected by the investment tax credit, remained essentially unchanged.

The effective tax rate was reduced again and again you see from 1969 to 1973 a restoration of productivity growth to more or less the post-War average levels.

After 1973 we went over Niagara Falls in a barrel, so to speak, as far as productivity growth is concerned. That has to do with the effect of energy prices that I will not discuss here.

In any case, the effective tax rates between 1973 and 1976 did not change and the relative price that was relevant to the productivity decline was the energy price, but that is part of another story.

The conclusion is that, in order to deal with a real productivity crisis, and I believe that this productivity crisis is a real one, we have a vast amount of historical experience on which to draw. First, we have the historical experience of the analysis of the effect of tax incentives on the capital-labor ratio. That is a story which will go on forever, as long as Bob Eisner is in the field. It is something that the rest of us have concluded is a fact about the real world, namely, reducing the effective tax rate on capital induces the substitution of capital for labor.

There is a summary of what I take to be pretty close to a consensus position summarizing all of the studies up to that point in a paper that Roger Gordon and I published in the middle 1970s. He will shortly report on some work of his own.

The second point that I want to make is that, not only did the reduction in the effective tax rate have the impact of increasing the growth rate of the capital-labor ratio, but also it has a direct impact on the unknown residual. That is the new fact which is part of a new theory on endogenous productivity growth which I developed in a paper with Barbara Fraumeni that is available from the Harvard Institute of Economic Research or from me. You can simply write to me in Cambridge and get a copy. The conclusion is that the central issue to offset the impact and higher energy prices that occurred in 1973 and again in 1979, and which could occur again in 1981, is to reduce the effective tax rate on capital.

The difficulty with the original form of the proposal that Alan Auerbach and I put forward is that, contrary to what Bob Eisner suggested that it was another sop to the business lobbying interests and another giveaway to the business community, it was in fact an increase in the effective tax rate on capital. That increase is something which could be offset by combining it with things like a graduated investment tax credit.

However, if we follow Eisner's basic idea—integrating the personal with the corporate income tax—then we have to have some way of measuring depreciation. That, fortunately, has been provided for us by Hulten and Wykoff. If we go Eisner's route of carrying out an effective tax rate reduction within the framework of the income tax, then it seems to me that what we ought to do is to adopt something like the Auerbach-Jorgenson scheme plus some kind of graduated investment tax credit.

Thank You.

Mr. Brown: Thank you, Dale (Jorgenson).
Our next speaker will be Emil Sunley.

Mr. Sunley: This morning I concluded by asking whether current law favors or discriminates against real estate. Should the tax laws tilt more toward real estate, let us say commercial and industrial real estate, vis-à-vis machinery and equipment, or the other way around?

During the discussion today some have suggested that the effective tax rates on real estate investments are higher than the effective tax rates on machinery and equipment. Other have suggested that the real estate investments are tax-favored.

I suspect that the current law favors real estate. I take as my evidence the amount of tax shelter activity in the real estate area. Real estate clearly is an investment that appeals to high bracket taxpayers. It throws off tax losses that can be used to shelter other sources of income.

This has both efficiency and equity effects. In the long run for the marginal investor the average rate of return on investments in real estate is probably no higher than after-tax rates of return earned on alternative investments. However, in the upsidedown world of tax shelters, the intramarginal investor, as I think Jane Gravelle pointed out this morning, is getting an above average rate of return.

In 1969 Congress, by taking away the investment tax credit and increasing the recapture rules on real estate, tilted the tax system more toward real estate than it had been prior to the 1969 act. Congress also preserved the more rapid methods of depreciation for residential rental real estate while becoming more restrictive on the depreciation methods allowed commercial and industrial real estate.

This year there is a feeling that we should tilt away from residential real estate and toward commercial and industrial real estate.

The last comment I would like to make relates to recapture of depreciation. It is generally believed that real estate tax shelters encourage the churning of buildings. Investors hold properties for a few years, depreciate them down, and then sell them. The subsequent owner then gets to start depreciation all over again, and this magnifies the tax benefits associated with real estate, or so the argument goes.

I think, on careful analysis one should conclude that the tax treatment of real estate does not encourage churning. When a building is sold, two things happen. First, the seller pays a capital gains tax on the difference between the adjusted basis of the building and the selling price. The subsequent owners get increased depreciation deductions on the step-up in basis which are equal to the gain recognized by the seller. If those increased depreciation deductions are spread over a long period of time, the present value of the tax savings from the deductions will be less than the capital gains tax paid on the sale. If that is true, then every time a building turns over, the government comes out ahead. Put another way, the government gets the capital gains tax at the time the building is sold and gives up the tax savings from increased depreciation deductions spread over the future.

Obviously, as the capital gains rate is cut, it will become more advantageous to churn buildings.

Mr. Brown: Thank You.
Our last speaker is Jim Wetzler of the Joint Committee on Taxation.

Mr. Wetzler: Let me commend both the organizers of this conference for being so topical and the participants for presenting such provocative papers. Congress will soon address the issue of depreciation reform, and the staff of the Joint Committee on Taxation will do its best to make the tax-writing committees aware of the work of the conference.

The overwhelming consensus in the business community, the press, and the Congress is that the tax system imposes a heavy burden on income from depreciable assets and that this burden should be alleviated through greater acceleration of depreciation deductions. Perhaps the most surprising outcome of the conference is that some serious questions have been raised about whether this consensus is correct.

Let me start with the work of Hulten and Wykoff, Jorgenson and Auerbach, and Hall. We are all indebted to Hulten and Wykoff, whose diligent work greatly advances our knowledge about how rapidly depreciable assets really decline in value. Building on these results, Jorgenson and Auerbach computed what they called "effective tax rates" on income from depreciable assets. To do this, they had to make assumptions about the rate of inflation and about the real after-tax rate of return, which they assume is enforced by competition. They also assumed that all assets are financed with equity capital.

During the recent congressional recess, I did some calculations using a slight variation of the Jorgenson-Auerbach formula for effective corporate tax rates. I got the result that the present effective corporate tax_rate on equipment is significantly below the 46-percent statutory corporate tax rate if one assumes an inflation rate of around 8 percent, a real after-tax rate of return of 4 or 5 percent, and economic depreciation at roughly the rates measured by Hulten and Wykoff.

Furthermore, Hall has revised the Jorgenson-Auerbach formulation to take into account the possibility of debt finance. This reduces effective tax rates even further because of the deductibility of interest and leads to large negative effective tax rates for assets financed largely by debt.

I am somewhat perplexed by the large gap between these measurements of effective tax rates and the widespread perception in the business community that the tax system is a major factor in discouraging investment. Businessmen seem to be talking as if their effective tax rates are much higher than those measured by Jorgenson and Auerbach, myself or Hall; and as long as businessmen are the ones making investment decisions, it behooves us to take account of their perceptions.

One possible explanation for the gap is the point made earlier today by Larry Dildine that the rate at which businessmen expect equipment to become obsolete is increasing because of wider fluctuations in energy prices and a more rapid pace of technological change in a world where the United States is no longer overwhelmingly dominant in research and development. More rapid obsolescence would mean that the empirical estimates of Hulten and Wykoff, which assume that there has been a constant rate of depreciation over time, are not accurate.

A second possible explanation is that businesses use a real discount rate much higher than the 4 percent assumed by Jorgenson and Auerbach and also by Hall. In their recent paper, Jorgenson and Fraumeni concluded that historically the real after-tax rate of return on corporate assets has stayed roughly constant at about 4 percent. If it is assumed that competition drives the after-tax rate of return down to the cost of capital, then the Jorgenson-Fraumeni result implies that the corporate real cost of capital is also 4 percent and that profit-maximizing businesses use this rate in discounting real cash flows when they evaluate potential investment projects.

However, when I talk to businessmen about the way they evaluate potential investment projects, I frequently get the answer that they use real discount rates much higher than 4 percent, sometimes as high as 15 percent. I suppose that this risk premium is the operational definition of that elusive "business confidence" that we are always trying to encourage with the appropriate legislation and public statements. At a 15 percent assumed real cost of capital, existing depreciation allowances are a good deal less generous than at 4 percent, and effective tax rates are correspondingly higher.

Neither of these two explanations, however, seems to me to be entirely adequate, and the large gap in perceptions between the business community and the participants in this conference remains a puzzle to me.

Another basic question raised by the conference is whether, in a period of high, variable, and unpredictable inflation, we can have an income capital that is both reasonably equitable and reasonably free from distortions, at least in comparison with other progressive taxes. One recommended change that has been widely discussed is to adjust the definition of taxable income from capital for inflation. Depreciation deductions could either be indexed directly or through the first-year deduction proposed by Jorgenson and Auerbach. A third alternative would be an ad hoc system, such as the 2-4-7-10 proposal developed by the Senate Finance Committee or the 10-5-3 proposal, which attempts to reach the correct result under an assumed rate of inflation and which presumably can be adjusted if the "underlying" inflation rate changes significantly. The definition of taxable capital gains can also be adjusted for inflation, a proposal which passed the House of Representatives in 1978. These changes in depreciation and capital gains might be called "partial indexing."

Complete indexing would require excluding from a lender's income that part of interest which merely offsets inflation and denying a borrower a deduction for that same amount. In view of the mortgage interest deduction's status as a political sacred cow, I'm going to make the ex cathedra judgment that indexing debt is a nonstarter and that, in practice, the only realistic option is partial indexing.

As Bradford pointed out earlier, if all borrowers and lenders had the same tax rate and all inflation were anticipated, under partial indexing interest rates would rise in response to expected inflation by enough to compensate borrowers for both the inflation itself and the tax on that inflation premium. Thus the after-tax real rate of return would be the same as with complete indexing. However, when borrowers and lenders have different tax rates, partial indexing would cause an increase in nominal interest rates which overcompensates borrowers in high brackets and lenders in low brackets, undercompensates borrowers in low brackets and lenders in high brackets, and creates incentives for high bracket taxpayers to own real assets and for low bracket taxpayers to own financial assets.

A second problem with partial indexing is that the required increase in nominal interest rates would impose large capital losses on the owners of the existing stock of debt. This would not be equitable.

I am still agnostic about how serious are these problems with partial adjustment for inflation. If it proves impossible to make the income tax on income from capital reasonably equitable and nondistortionary, Congress is going to have to give some serious thought to alternative possibilities.

The notion of converting the corporate income tax into a tax on cash flow, which was made by the Meade Commission in England and by Robert Hall here, is an idea worthy of study. It would be useful to look into how to make a transition from a corporate income tax to a corporate cash flow tax, which could be a serious problem. For example, in the initial years of a cash flow tax, little if any revenue would be raised if corporations are allowed to deduct both the cost of their new investments and the leftover depreciation on the capital in existence when the transition was made.

Converting the individual income tax into an expenditure tax has received a lot of discussion in American academic circles. There is currently virtually no congressional interest in this proposal, although there is a lot of interest in moving towards an expenditure tax in an ad hoc way with various savings incentives. Bradford's paper was particularly useful in pointing out the possibilities for tax arbitrage with such an ad hoc approach.

Another alternative is simply to reduce individual and corporate income tax rates, thereby reducing all of the problems associated with income taxes. Indirect taxes, such as energy consumption taxes, a value-added tax, or payroll taxes, could make up whatever lost revenue could not be accounted for by spending reductions.

To sum up, then, the conference has been useful for me in raising some difficult questions about the taxation of income from capital. I hope it has been equally helpful to everyone else.

Mr. Brown: Thank You, Jim (Wetzler).

Let us throw the session open to the floor for questions or comments.

I should have asked our speakers first whether they have any further comments.

Mr. Davie: I have a comment about the popularity of depreciation proposals in the business community, an aspect not mentioned today. If we were an audience of lawyers and accountants rather than economists, we surely would have heard about the complexity of the existing depreciation system and the attendant problems that taxpayers have with the Internal Revenue Service. Many controversies between taxpayers and the IRS arise over the useful life of particular assets. Certainly some of the steam behind 10-5-3 is an attempt to get rid of the whole concept of useful lives and to introduce a more arbitrary system simply to get rid of some of the complexity of the current system and the hassles with the IRS.

Mr. Brown: Bob (Eisner), you had your hand up.

Mr. Eisner: Yes. I am a bit surprised by some of Dale's (Jorgenson) remarks. It would seem to me that his paper with Auerbach demonstrated very nicely the fact that many kinds of investment are actually getting tax subsidies. Also, Hall's paper was particularly persuasive. In fact, if you remember, where the rate of taxation that he calculates is less than minus 100 percent, the government is actually paying for projects with a negative real marginal product and that would include, if you look at the Hall paper, three of the five categories—leveraged buildings purchased by corporations, and equipment and buildings purchased by individuals. [This refers to an unrevised version of the Hall paper, Ed.]

The point is that there is no easy acceptance of the notion that Dale propounds and tries to make me the dissident minority of one on, that all capital expenditures add to productivity.

In fact, his very figures in a way hide something. It is rather curious that he tells us that suspending the investment tax credit in 1969 reduced productivity growth. If I read those figures correctly they went up some from 1969 to 1973.

Also, I recall that Denison finds it very difficult to find much effect of changing rates of capital expenditure on the rate of growth of productivity, particularly in this last period when we have a big decline.

The important thing to note—aside from all of the other assumptions underlying that positive marginal product of all capital, which he lumps together, saying that all capital should be subsidized—is that he is apparently ready now to tell the Congress to please take his proposal and take the investment credit and a few other crumbs too—they may not be just crumbs but big pieces of cake—to make it palatable.

You should note that he has gross output, as I just confirmed with him. It may well be that, if you have more investment, you have more output per unit of labor, but just imagine an economy that was diverting 90 percent of its gross output to capital expenditures. You would probably have a higher amount of output per unit of labor than you would have otherwise, but you would have much less net output, because most of that output would be to produce capital goods which are replacing the capital goods wearing out.

There is hardly any relevance to a concept of productivity that you are trying to increase if it increases only *gross* output per unit of labor by simply adding more investment.

Mr. Brown: Dale (Jorgenson), you had your hand up.

Mr. Jorgenson: Yes. I have a couple of comments. I think, just to supplement what Jim Wetzler said about why businessmen think that they are so badly off, it is, as are many things in life, a relative matter, namely, that in 1965 they were beautifully situated. They had effective tax rates which were approximately half the statutory rates for both structures and equipment. Things have been going down hill steadily since then because of inflation and the late, lamented President Nixon and his tax machinations.

The general fact is that tax rates have gone up. Some people feel, and I feel this is where I would part company with the Feldstein-Summers analysis to which various people here have alluded, that that is something which has continued right up to the present. Actually, I think a careful look at the effective tax rates reveals that the process of increase in effective tax rates stopped just about in the period here where the recovery occurred, in 1973. From 1973 to the present effective tax rates have not contributed a great deal either to slowdown in the growth of the capital-output ratio, which has continued at a modest rate during this period, or to the growth of productivity, which has been negative. I think that is largely an issue of energy prices.

The most important thing on which to focus is that, relative to where businesses were in 1965, effective tax rates have increased enormously. I think that is what accounts for the tremendous steam behind the receptivity of the Congress to some relatively bizarre ideas like 10-5-3. Concerning the gross versus the net issue that Bob (Eisner) has raised here and has raised in another context, the answer to that has to do with whether the marginal product of capital is positive. As Böhm-Bawerk and other noted figures on the subject have observed, the relevant question is what the real rate of return is. That is, after all, taking into account the depreciation, what the net marginal product is. That has been very constant over the whole post-War period at about 4 or 5 percent. Therefore, if we add an additional unit to the capital stock and thereby increase the capital-labor ratio by that unit, we will at the margin get something like a 4 or 5 percent rate of return. That has been constant over the whole post-War period. I regard the gross-net argument here, as in many other contexts, to be a red herring.

Mr. Eisner: I have just a brief observation. I think we should keep separate the question of whether business income is too heavily taxed and has become more heavily taxed from the question of whether capital income is more heavily taxed.

There seems to be a loose notion, if not among economists, although they may slip into it, certainly in the business community, that taxing business income is taxing capital. Businesses get income from capital only in sort of a broad Marxian sense, where labor is "variable capital" and income is earned on all capital including labor.

What we are taxing in a business income tax is the difference between business costs, including all costs, and business revenues.

What you get with complaints that business should be allowed to adjust for inventory appreciation the way the Department of Commerce does is a notion that business is really being taxed too heavily but that does not imply that it is investment, least of all plant and equipment, that is being taxed heavily.

I would like to ask the panel one question. I think I know the answer. That is, I have not heard today any adverse comment on the study that Hulten and Wykoff have performed. Is that a consensus on everybody's part, subject to many of the qualifications such as Frank de Leeuw and others have made? Is it the consensus that this is a useful piece of research that will be useful in many ways or could be useful in many ways in the administration of tax, the concept of taxable income, and so forth? Jim (Wetzler)?

Mr. Wetzler: I do not think that is quite the right question to ask. I think it is agreed that Hulten and Wykoff have made an important advance on the rather meager amount of knowledge we had on this question before they started work.

The question is: Has their work advanced to the point where it is useful for public policy? For depreciation the question will concern the fact that you have had a system wherein the Treasury has had discretion to set useful lives for many years. After all these years, they came up with the ADR system. A lot of people in the business are unhappy with what Treasury has done and want that discretion taken away from Treasury, away from apolitical experts, and put into the hands of Congress.

The question is: Can the experts do a better job than Congress or at least a sufficiently better job so that it is worthwhile to push hard to tell congressmen that they are not as good as the experts?

I see that Hulten and Wykoff have gotten very careful estimates about some categories of investment, like autos, and construction machinery. There are other large categories of investment for which they do not present results. In order to use their method for policy, they not only have to demonstrate that they can get results for a few classes of assets, but they have to demonstrate that they can get results for everything, or at least for most assets.

I do not think that the work has advanced to the point where I will be able to go to one of my bosses and say, "No, no. You guys do not need to get control of depreciation from the Treasury Department, because they have just determined a new way to do it." I think all I could say is, "They are in the process of trying to work out a new way to do it. They have gotten some interesting results."

Mr. Davie: I think that the Hulten and Wykoff work, if it were applied in the tax system, would certainly require facing up to the provision that is in the tax code now that allows a taxpayer to justify depreciation on the basis of individual facts and circumstances. Are we going to move depreciation to a system which denies the taxpayer the opportunity to make a claim that, in his particular circumstances, depreciation for his particular asset is significantly different from what it is for a general class of assets? Many of the proposals that have been before the Congress raise that issue, and at some point in the legislative process, that will be battled out. The existing proposals in the equipment area take away that discretion. In the structures area, under the Bentsen proposal, the facts and circumstances claim is allowed as an option.

Mr. Jorgenson: However, 10-5-3 takes it away.

Mr. Davie: Yes.

Mr. Eisner: I think there has been general enthusiasm for the Hulten-Wykoff paper, but one should recognize certain reservations about where they point.

One thing I mentioned earlier. I think it is significant to note, and none of us should forget it, that their estimates indicate a very considerably slower rate of economic depreciation than tax depreciation. Anybody having to testify before Congress or to advise a congressman or senator should remember that.

I would add that, as I view it, the Hulten-Wykoff estimates establish upper bounds to the rate of economic depreciation. All of the caveats that I have, at least suggested that the depreciation may actually be lower. As I noted, the three main caveats relate to the lemons problem and the associated problems of putty-clay and transfer costs. Second, the fact of the accelerated tax depreciation itself tends to accelerate the speed of depreciation. The third point was the assignment of zero salvage costs and the point that actually depreciation will be tied in anticipation, when you are buying an asset, to what you can get out of it. If the asset or the building is going to be torn down because the land has become more valuable, how will we dissuade you from investing in a building because you know you will make a capital gain on the land associated with the building if you buy the building and the land, even with the expectation that some buildings may be retired prematurely?

Mr. Brown: Dale (Jorgenson), you had a comment.

Mr. Jorgenson: Yes. It seems to me that there are three contending parties struggling for control of this very interesting policy area. On one hand, there are the congressional people, or more precisely their staffs, who would have to determine precisely what the depreciation rates ought to be. Secondly, there are the engineers, if you like, the people who have been traditionally in charge of this, and people who are interested in how many telephone poles are replaced every year and what their average lifetimes are, which is part of the Hulten-Wykoff story but not all of it. The third is ourselves, namely economists.

I would say that the Treasury Department, in the form of the Office of Tax Analysis, has done economics a tremendous service, not only in the sense of providing valuable data and information, which as Bob Eisner says is really rather surprising, given what we might have expected from something like that, but also that they have provided economists with a wedge which over the years, I think they can use to get greater leverage over the process.

I feel that we ought to do whatever we can to stimulate the Treasury Department and the Office of Industrial Economics and the Congress to continue to extend this research. As Hulten and Wykoff have emphasized in their own work, this is only the beginning. There is a problem about scope, which is illustrated most dramatically by the fact that office equipment is something in which the only asset they were able to deal with was typewriters, whereas the main assets in that area are computers and data processing equipment. With all of that said, I think it is a very, very promising approach, the econometrics are very impressive.

Let me say that I do feel that the initial reception of this is something which has now been shown to be deficient in a number of respects. First of all, there was the argument that the tax effects—this is something that Marty Feldstein laid a great deal of emphasis upon—on the prices themselves would be very substantial. That, on the basis of our discussion here, is true only for the difference between the first year and other years because of the role of the investment tax credit. As Hulten and Wykoff point out in their paper, they did not use the data for new assets. Therefore, their data on used assets is not affected by that particular point. I think that they have managed to counter that point very effectively.

Whether the a priori argument about lemons is convincing or not, I do not know. I find the argument that there are experts in used assets and they know how to look under the hood of a car, inside a typewriter, and so on, pretty convincing. That is something that, I think, will only be hashed out over time.

As far as the assumption that the pattern is constant is concerned and is therefore independent of changes in not only tax policy but also, say, energy prices, I think that is an issue that is going to be with us for some time. There are obiviously ways of making that more or less precise, and so far we only have a rough cut at it. Nevertheless, it is really pretty convincing that the constant pattern model seems to survive.

Back to Bruce Davie's point, I think that on the facts and circumstances, if you laid out a scenario in which the Office of Industrial Economics is captured by the economists, then I think the facts and circumstances part of that legislation ought to be abolished. In fact, a great deal of emphasis ought to be placed on the fact that everybody has to transact in the same markets for this used equipment. Whether you are Hertz or somebody who is trying to buy a used Hertz truck in order to do a construction job, you have to face the same profile of used equipment prices.

Bob Eisner's point about the used equipment price and the cost of moving is well taken. Nonetheless, I think that that would lead away from the facts and circumstances approach and toward an approach in which something was decided by experts, and the taxpayers would have to live with it.

Mr. Hulten: I would like to say a thing or two about the applicability of my study with Frank (Wykoff). I think that we would be the last people to say that our estimates are written on stone tablets and should immediately be implemented for policy purposes.

What we have shown is that there is a technique for estimating rates of economic depreciation that is defensible, and while it certainly does have problems, there are ways to try to correct these problems.

It is true that we studied only a very limited class of assets, but it must be emphasized that this limit was partly imposed by a limited amount of research time. We did find a considerable amount of other price data that we could have analyzed, if we just had the time to do it. Time and budget limitations also precluded us from using data on market rental prices to infer rates of economic depreciation. There is a tremendous volume of information on market rental price that could be analyzed in a way similar to that described in our paper.

Robert Coen's study of the manufacturing industry provides still another means of inferring the rates of economic depreciation. He fitted a neoclassical investment model using various types of depreciation, and lo and behold, he found geometric-like depreciation in 14 of 21 industries that he studied. That is for both structures and equipment. The interesting thing about Coen's study is that it had nothing to do with prices, yet it comes out with findings close to what Frank (Wykoff) and I came up with.

Mr. Dildine: I think it is worth pointing out that, while the Treasury does now have nominal responsibility to revise a parameter from time to time, that parameter is not the same one that Chuck (Hulten) and Frank (Wykoff) were looking for. All we have the responsibility to revise is a number called the useful life.

One of the things that did seem to come from this research is that useful life is not a particularly reliable measure of anything called depreciation.

The engineers are still in charge, as it were, when it comes to the discretion that the Treasury has over depreciation charges. It is against the law of the Office of Industrial Economics to go out and try to change guidelines based upon estimates of depreciation. They can go out and change them only on the basis of how long assets are held.

To the extent that estimates of depreciation are made and believed, we still need a substantial change in the law to be able to use them, whether that is to be done by the congressional staff or the Treasury staff or somebody else's staff.

NOTES

NOTES TO "ISSUES IN THE DESIGN OF SAVINGS AND INVESTMENT INCENTIVES," DAVID F. BRADFORD

1. I have addressed these larger issues in Bradford [1980]. Readers may also find helpful the discussion there of the problems created by inconsistent treatment of different forms of savings. For further discussion of the general issues see King [1980]. For empirical analysis of the U.S. experience see, for example, Boskin [1978], Eisner [1977], Feldstein [1977a,b; 1980], Malkiel [1979].

2. For an examination of selected investment incentive proposals under consideration recently in the United States see Hendershott and Hu [1980].

3. For further discussion of this issue see Bradford and Toder [1976].

4. For analyses stressing this efficiency problem see Gordon [1980] and Gordon and Malkiel [1980].

5. See, for example, Jorgenson [1963], Hall and Jorgenson [1967].

6. This has been shown by, among others, Samuelson [1964].

7. For an example see Bradford [1980; pp. 42-50].

8. Auerbach [1979a] confirms this point for the case of exponential depreciation.

9. This was one of the methods proposed by the Meade Committee for implementing a consumption tax in the U.K., where the income tax is imposed at essentially a single flat rate for the great bulk of taxpayers. [Institute for Fiscal Studies, 1978; ch. 8].

10. An early treatment of this is found in Brown [1962]; for further details see Bradford [1979].

11. E. Cary Brown [1962] shows that one way to achieve the correct calibration of the credit is to structure it as a flat "net credit," that is, a fixed percentage of the difference between the cost of the machine and the present value (at the net of tax interest for that investor) of economic depreciation allowances. Since this is equivalent to calibration of the "gross credit" to asset durability, it is subject to the same problems.

12. For examples of the formulas applicable to other patterns of depreciation see Bradford [1979].

13. For a general treatment see Stiglitz [1980].

14. This required adjustment in i to compensate savers for inflation has been stressed by Feldstein [1976]. For an attempt to rationalize the fact that interest rates have moved with inflation at most according to Fisher's law (point for point) in the U.S. in recent years see Feldstein and Summers [1978]. Feldstein, Green, and Sheshinski [1978] explore models of interest determination under conditions of inflation. Stiglitz [1980] has emphasized that with imperfect indexing the incidence of inflation depends upon the measures taken to maintain adherence to the government's budget constraint. General conclusions about the effect of inflation thus require modeling the government's reaction.

15. This is only in apparent disagreement with Auerbach's [1979a] view that inflation biases the choice of asset life toward assets with greater durability and to Feldstein's [1980] view that inflation biases the pattern of investment in favor of short-lived assets. Consider first Feldstein's analysis. The basis for his conclusion is the behavior of what he terms the "net cost" of a dollar of investment, defined to be one minus the sum of the investment credit and the present value of real depreciation allowances, where a constant real discount rate is employed in the evaluation. If we let ρ stand for the latter rate, $k(\delta)$, the investment credit

305

allowed for a machine of durability δ, and C_H the net cost per dollar of investment under historical cost depreciation,

$$C_H = 1 - \int_0^\infty m\delta e^{-(\delta+\rho+\pi)s}\, ds - k(\delta) = 1 - \frac{m\delta}{\delta + \rho + \pi} - k(\delta) \quad .$$

Note that if we define analogously a "net of tax real receipts" variable,

$$R = \int_0^\infty (1 - m)ce^{-(\delta+\rho)s}\, ds = \frac{(1 - m)c}{\delta + \rho}$$

the equilibrium condition is $R = C_H$. If in turn the real discount rate, ρ, is determined by arbitrage with bonds to be $(1 - m)i - \pi$, equilibrium in Feldstein's system is described by (21) in the text. The two approaches, being thus equivalent must have the same implications.

By inspection of the expression for C_H we see that the net cost of neither an infinitely durable asset ($\delta = 0$), nor an instantaneously depreciating asset ($\delta = \infty$), is affected by inflation (provided ρ is constant). In between, an increase in π increases C_H, with the relative increase rising and then falling with δ. The range of parameter values considered by Feldstein was drawn mostly from the rising segment of this relationship; hence his conclusion. But if the initial situation is one of equilibrium, the new one is not and adjustment will call for constriction of the middle durabilities, expansion of the extremes and decline in ρ, along the lines described in the text. Note that it may well be the case that quantitatively the bias toward short lives is the more significant.

Auerbach's result is related to his particular modeling of the choice of asset lives whereby there is at any time a single profit-maximizing durability. It is the single durability that increases with inflation in his model. As we just noted the net cost of an asset is increased by inflation (neglecting $\delta = 0$ and ∞) to a degree varying with δ. Auerbach's conclusion concerns the location of the peak of that relationship with δ and is thus compatible with Feldstein's and mine.

This is a rather remarkable example of how verbal descriptions of results may conceal their essential nature.

16.   For detailed discussions of the problems of indexing the income tax for inflation see Aaron [1976], Shoven and Bulow [1975; 1976], Fabricant [1978].

17.   According to Joseph Pechman [1980] the Auerbach-Jorgenson proposal is a rediscovery of an idea of Nicholas Kaldor.

18.   Different depreciation patterns would also require different "recapture rules" applicable to sale of assets, a subject we shall not pursue here.

19.   There is a frequently overlooked but practically highly significant condition in this statement: the investor must have sufficient taxable income gross of the depreciation deduction to make use of it.

20.   This is thus a "net credit," as discussed in ftn. 11. I would like to thank E. Cary Brown for pointing out to me the natural adaptivity of the net credit to the Auerbach-Jorgenson proposal.

NOTES TO "ON MEASURING THE LOSS OF OUTPUT DUE TO NONNEUTRAL BUSINESS TAXATION," W. E. DIEWERT

1.   Many definitions of neutrality occur in the literature. See for example Smith (1963), Samuelson (1964), Hall and Jorgenson (1967, 1971), Stiglitz (1973, 1976), Sandmo (1974),

King (1974, 1975), Boadway (1978, 1980), Auerbach (1978), Schworm (1979), Hall (1980) and many other papers referred to in the above papers.

2. An equilibrium is Pareto optimal if no consumer's welfare can be increased without decreasing some other consumer's welfare.

3. We also impose the condition that the equilibrium in the resource deflated economy be Pareto optimal.

4. If the production sector is not the entire economy, investment goods purchases from other sectors are treated as variable inputs which are transformed into capital stocks.

5. The resulting loss measure is only the producer surplus component of a full blown general equilibrium loss measure such as the Debreu measure referred to earlier. See Diewert (1981) for an analysis of how the Debreu loss measure is related (at least locally) to the other general equilibrium loss measures suggested by Hotelling (1938), Boiteux (1951) and Harberger (1964, 1971).

6. St. Hilaire and Whalley (1981) provide a nice summary of the existing literature.

7. x^T denotes the transpose of the (column) vector x, $x^T y$ or $x \cdot y$ denotes the inner product of the vector x and y, 0_N denotes an N-dimensional vector of zeros, $x \geq 0_M$ means each component of x is nonnegative, $x \gg 0_M$ means such component of x is positive and $x > 0_M$ means $x \geq 0_M$ but $x \neq 0_M$.

8. This way of modeling variable depreciation and utilization rates appeared in Diewert (1977), but it is a straightforward adaptation of the intertemporal production models of Hicks (1946) and Malinvaud (1953). For empirical applications of this model, see Epstein (1977) and Epstein and Denny (1980).

9. This is Diewert's (1973, 1974) term. The concept is due to Samuelson (1953-54, p. 20), who uses the term "gross national product function." Gorman (1968) uses the term "gross profit function," while McFadden (1978) and Lau (1976) use the term "restricted profit function." See these references for proofs of the properties of π.

10. This means: if $(x, y^1, z^1) \in S$, $y^2 \geq y^1 \geq 0_M$, $z^1 \geq z^2 \geq 0_M$, then $(x, y^2, z^2) \in S$.

11. This means: if $(x^1, y^1, z^1) \in S$, $(x^2, y^2, z^2) \in S$, $0 \leq \lambda \leq 1$, then
$$(\lambda x^1 + (1 - \lambda)x^2, \lambda y^1 + (1 - \lambda)y^2, \lambda z^1 + (1 - \lambda)z^2) \in S.$$

12. This means: if $\lambda \geq 0$, $(x, y, z) \in S$, then $(\lambda x, \lambda y, \lambda z) \in S$.

13. This means: for $0 \leq \lambda \leq 1$, $\pi(p, \lambda s^{0*} + (1 - \lambda)s^{0**}, \lambda s^{1*} + (1 - \lambda)s^{1**}) \geq \lambda \pi(p, s^{0*}, s^{1*}) + (1 - \lambda)\pi(p, s^{0**}, s^{1**})$.

14. This means: for $\lambda \geq 0$, $\pi(p, \lambda s^0, \lambda s^1) = \lambda \pi(p, s^0, s^1)$.

15. See Smith (1963; 86).

16. This terminology was used by King (1975).

17. Complications arise if there are output taxes or subsidies on investment goods.

18. This point was fully appreciated by Brown (1948), Sandmo (1974) and King (1975) among others.

19. See Gorman (1968), Diewert (1974, p. 140) and Lau (1976) for additional material on interpreting the partial derivatives of variable profit functions.

20. It will be a reduction in cash flow because some variable outputs will have to be decreased or some inputs increased in order to generate the extra unit of next period's stock.

21. Recall that q_n^{T+1} is the exogenously given scrap value of a unit of stock n in period $T + 1$. However, the endogenously generated period T investment good price for stock n, q_n^T, satisfies $q_n^T (1 + r) = q_n^{T+1}$.

22. Of course, if the sector is an entire economy, there will be certain nonreproducible stocks such as land and natural resources that cannot be varied, and hence these fixed stocks will not appear in the list of N reproducible or variable stocks that are in the s^t vectors. Under these conditions, there will usually be diminishing returns with respect to (s^{t-1}, s^t) and period t rents R^t will usually be positive.

23. For example see Sandmo (1974, p. 291). Moreover, the flow of tax revenues that such a business tax would yield would not necessarily diminish as time went on. Growth of the reproducible stock would increase the scarcity value of the nonreproducible fixed stocks in the economy, leading to increased rents over time. Finally, recalling (14) and (15), it can be seen that w^1 has two interpretations and we have chosen the second.

24.   The period t deduction could be a linear function of s^{t-1} as well as of s^t; i.e., the deduction in period t could be $\beta'^t \cdot s^{t-1} + \beta''^t \cdot s^t$. In this case, set $\beta^t \equiv \beta''^t + (1 + r)^{-1} \beta''^{t+1}$; i.e., consolidate all of the deductions associated with s^t into a single vector.

25.   More precisely, we assume that the following objective function is locally valid for s near s* where s* solves (9) when all stock taxes are zero.

26.   For example, see Smith (1963), Sandmo (1974, p. 301), King (1975), Boadway (1978, 1980) and Schworm (1979).

27.   This case is somewhat unrealistic in that it ignores the role of fixed factors. A diminishing returns to scale case would be more realistic, but more complicated as well.

28.   We need to assume that $(1 + \alpha)(1 + \Theta)/(1 + r) < 1$ so that the growth rate α is sufficiently small for $V(s^0)$ to be finite.

29.   We also use the assumption that A^{-1} exists.

30.   This definition follows Diewert (1974, p. 144).

31.   See for example, Harberger (1974). The relevant literature is nicely summarized in St.-Hilaire and Whalley (1981).

32.   See Hall (1980) for example.

33.   However, Epstein and Denny (1980) have estimated such a model for the U.S. Manufacturing sector, and we expect σ to be close to zero.

34.   Recall that Harberger (1974) considers two sectors (the corporate and noncorporate sectors), but his model is static in contrast to our one sector dynamic model.

35.   Another paper which strongly advocates the Brown-Smith cash-flow taxation policy we have advocated in this paper is Boadway, Bruce, and Mintz (1980).

NOTES TO "THE MEASUREMENT OF ECONOMIC DEPRECIATION," CHARLES R. HULTEN AND FRANK C. WYKOFF

1.   Much of our research on the measurement of depreciation has been supported financially by the Office of Tax Analysis of the U.S. Department of the Treasury. We particularly wish to thank Emil Sunley, Harvey Galper, and Larry Dildine of OTA for their encouragement and intellectual input. We also thank Janice McCallum for research assistance. The opinions and results presented in this paper are, however, our own and should not be attributed either to the Treasury or to The Urban Institute.

2.   The depreciation method for each Conable-Jones class is accelerated relative to straight-line depreciation.

3.   See, for example, the comments of Young and Musgrave (1980) on this point.

4.   See, for example, Musgrave (1976).

5.   Jorgenson (1973) presents a comprehensive mathematical statement of the theory of economic depreciation. See also Hotelling (1925), Hall (1968), Taubman and Rasche (1971), and Feldstein and Rothschild (1974).

6.   Let q(s,t) represent the price of an asset of age s at time t, c(s,t) the rental price or quasi-rent, and r the rate of discount (assumed constant for simplicity of exposition). Under perfect foresight, equilibrium in the asset market requires that the cost of acquiring the asset, q(s,t) just equals the present value of the rents:

$$q(s, t) = \sum_{k=0}^{T} \frac{c(s + k,\ t + k)}{(1 + r)^k}$$

where T is the length of the asset's productive life.

7.   The term 'inflation' is actually a misnomer for the process that causes asset prices to rise over time. A general inflation will indeed have this effect, but it can also occur if relative prices change because of a shift in asset supply or asset demand. For this reason, what we have termed 'inflation' is frequently called 'revaluation.' We will, however, continue to use the term 'inflation' because it aids in the intuitive exposition of the theoretical model, although we will mean it to include both general and relative price changes.

8.   This qualification is necessary because the effects shown in figure 2 refer to discrete changes in age and date. The issue does not arise in continuous time formulation of the problem. If the asset price q(s,t) defined in footnote (6) is differentiable, the age effect *ab* (or *cd*) is the partial derivative $\partial q/\partial s$ and the inflation effect *bd* (or *ac*) is the partial derivative $\partial q/\partial t$.

9.   This relationship is developed in detail in Jorgenson (1973).

10.   The marginal rate of substitution between a new asset and an s year old is defined by the ratio of the respective marginal products. If the marginal productivity of a five-year old asset is, say, only half that of a new asset, the marginal rate of substitution is also one half. If we assign a value of one to the efficiency index of the new asset, the efficiency index of the five-year old asset is one half.

11.   Alternative methods for dealing with censored sample bias are discussed by Heckman (1976). See, also, Tobin (1958), Amemiya (1973), and Hausman and Wise (1977).

12.   For a more complete description of our data sources, see Hulten and Wykoff (1979, 1981), as well as Beidleman (1976), and the U.S. Treasury publication *Business Building Statistics* (1975).

13.   The Winfrey retirement distributions and *Bulletin F* lives are also used in the BEA capital stock studies described in section IV.

14.   Our sample of nonresidential structures contained approximately 7,000 observations, whereas the machine tool sample contained only 50 to 100 observations for each type of tool. Sample sizes and characteristics are discussed in Hulten and Wykoff (1979, 1981).

15.   This model, which was developed by Box and Cox (1964) is explained in detail in Hulten and Wykoff (1981). We will present only a general outline of the Box-Cox model and refer the reader to these references for a discussion of technical details.

16.   Note that equation (1) relates the asset price q(s,t) directly to age s and year t, while the equation shown in footnote (6) relates q(s,t) to the flow of rentals. The two expressions are not inconsistent, since q(s,t) will vary with s and t as c(s,t) changes. However, (1) is more general, since asset prices may not be determined by a present value calculation but still vary with age and year. The generality of (1) is an attractive feature of the Box-Cox model, because the used asset market is more or less left to 'speak for itself.' On the other hand, if the present value formulation of footnote (6) does happen to be correct, then changes in economic variables (c(s,t), r) may cause q(s,t) to vary in such a way that no stable relationship exists between q(s,t), s, and t (as implied by (1)). This issue is dealt with at the end of section III.b.

17.   The semi-log form of the regression is equivalent to geometric depreciation because ln q $= \alpha + \beta$s implies that

$$q = e^{\beta s}$$

The parameter β is, in this case, the rate of depreciation because it indicates the percentage change in asset price resulting from an increase in age (which is our definition of depreciation).

18.   Recall, here, the discussion of footnote (17). In Hulten and Wykoff (1979), the average geometric rate calculated by this method is called the 'best geometric approximation.'

19.   The investment data for this calculation were taken from the *Survey of Current Business.*

20.   The average rates for plant and equipment were calculated using equation (7) of section III. Stocks of capital were estimated using BEA data and equation (6). The stocks were then summed to the level of total plant and equipment, and (7) was then used to estimate an

implicit aggregate rate of depreciation. A different result would have been obtained if investment weights were used in the aggregation. Investment weights would assign a larger share to the most rapidly depreciating assets and would then result in larger average rates for plant and equipment. Our averaging procedure is equivalent to using individual capital stocks as weights and is conceptually superior to the investment weight method because it is the entire stock which depreciates, and not just the annual increments.

21. The Lemons Model was developed by Ackerlof (1970) and applied to the analysis of the used car market. See, also, Heal (1976).

22. One piece of evidence which is frequently raised in favor of the lemons hypothesis is the Taubman and Rasche analysis of office buildings. Taubman and Rasche use a method which is free from the lemons problem and find a one-horse-shay, age-price profile (curve III in figure 5). This finding suggests that the geometric depreciation results obtained using the used market price approach are the result of lemons bias. This issue will be discussed in detail in section V.A. We note here, however, that the Taubman-Rasche findings may be the result of another type of bias, and another study which is free from that bias does not confirm their result.

23. Recall, here, the discussion of note 16.

24. Our stability analysis is presented in Hulten and Wykoff (1981).

25. An excellent statement of the BEA methodology is given in Young and Musgrave (1980).

26. See Young (1975) for further discussion.

27. Our use of the Winfrey distribution and *Bulletin F* lives actually differs slightly from the BEA procedures for certain assets (like structures). The specific differences are discussed in Hulten-Wykoff (1979, 1981). Furthermore, the Winfrey distribution is used by BEA to take into account the heterogeneity of assets in a given group, as well as their retirement from service.

28. Our method for aggregating the BEA depreciation rates to the level of plant and equipment is identical to the method used to aggregate the table 1 depreciation rates. This method is described in footnote (20).

29. Capital stock estimates for the individual types of assets are given in table A.2 of the Appendix.

30. It may be useful to recall, here, the discussion of footnote (10). The efficiency index $\Phi(s)$ is the marginal rate of substitution (or ratio of marginal products) between a new asset and an s year old asset. Equation (9) is simply an equilibrium condition which states that a cost minimizing producer will equate the ratio of marginal products to relative factor costs.

31. Recall, here, the comments of footnote (22).

32. See Faucett (1973).

33. Jorgenson (1971) provides a survey of literature on the neoclassical theory of investment (see also Hall and Jorgenson (1967)). A large amount of research has been devoted to the question of which investment model best explains investment flows. Coen assumes that one of these models (the neoclassical) is correct and proceeds to estimate which pattern of depreciation is correct relative to that model.

34. The lack of suitable capital benchmark data is, unfortunately, one factor which limits the general applicability of this approach.

NOTES TO "ACCELERATION OF TAX DEPRECIATION: BASIC ISSUES AND MAJOR ALTERNATIVES," EMIL M. SUNLEY

1. Existing assets that have not been fully depreciated could be made eligible for any liberalized depreciation. This was done in 1962. Making existing assets eligible would permit

greater simplification of depreciation since taxpayers would not have to operate two depreciation systems at the same time. The major proposals currently under consideration would only apply to new investments.

2. This is strictly true for a taxpayer subject to a given marginal tax rate. Taxpayers subject to a lower marginal tax rate will prefer the investment tax credit and vice versa.

3. Accelerated depreciation involves interest-free loans whereas the investment tax credit is similar to direct grants. Since the interest free loans have to be repaid, the initial size of the loan must be greater than the grants if the loans are to have the same present value of tax savings. Some have argued that the government does or should have a lower discount rate than business and, therefore, should prefer accelerated depreciation to the investment credit. However, any one who has gone through the budget cycle would probably conclude that the government has a very high discount rate given the popularity of proposals for shifting revenue forward or delaying outlays.

4. Given the half year convention that would be permitted under the 10-5-3 proposal, the 10-5-3 proposal might more accurately be described as permitting taxpayers to write off investments in 9.5 years for buildings, in 4.5 years for most machinery, and in 2.5 years for cars and light trucks.

5. For example, if the ADR guideline period is 12.0 to 16.5 years, then the machinery and equipment goes into the 7-year asset class. The 10-year asset class applies if the ADR guideline period is more than 16.5 years.

6. The 10-5-3 proposal would permit taxpayers to "bank" allowable depreciation deductions. Compared to the 10-5-3 proposal, the elections under the finance bill would reduce the flexibility taxpayers would have in delaying depreciation deductions.

7. Under the finance committee bill the elections would have to be made when the tax return is filed. Elections for prior years could not be altered when subsequently it turns out that a different election would have been better. If taxpayers could alter their elections, many taxpayers would file amended returns each year for all open years.

8. The calculations here assume that taxpayers can currently use all depreciation deductions and investment tax credits. The discount rate is 12 percent.

9. Senator Bentsen described his proposal as a 40 percent shortening of guideline lives. If N is the guideline life then the double declining balance rate permitted under Bentsen would be $2/.6N$ or $3.33N$. The president's proposal which was described as a 40 percent increase in the most favorable depreciation rate permitted under present law, would increase the current depreciation rate from $2/.8N$ to $2.8/.8N$ or $3.5N$, slightly greater than that permitted under the Senate Finance Committee bill.

10. See, for example, Alan J. Auerbach and Dale W. Jorgenson, 1980, "Inflation-Proof Depreciation of Assets," *Harvard Business Review,* Vol. 58, no. 5, September-October, pp. 113–118; and Auerbach and Jorgenson, statement and testimony before the House Budget Committee, January 30, 1980.

11. At the lower limit of the ADR range, the Hulten-Wykoff result would translate into 112 percent declining balance depreciation.

NOTES TO "INFLATION AND CAPITAL RECOVERY IN THE UNITED STATES," DALE W. JORGENSON AND MARTIN A. SULLIVAN

1. The rental value of capital is employed in econometric studies of corporate investment behavior by Jorgenson and Siebert (1968a, 1968b, 1972). This concept is also used in econometric studies by Jorgenson and Stephenson (1967a, 1967b, 1969) and by Hall and Jorgenson (1969, 1971). See also: Bischoff (1971) and Coen (1971). Econometric studies of investment behavior are surveyed by Jorgenson (1971) and Hall (1977).

2. A history of provisions for capital recovery is given by Pechman (1977), Gravelle (1979), and Jeremias (1979). See the appendix for a detailed discussion of our methodology for incorporating these provisions into the rental price of capital services.

3. For detailed discussion of the geometric approximation, see Hulten and Wykoff (1980, 1981a, 1981b). References to the literature are given by Hulten and Wykoff (1981b). Additional details on the economic theory of depreciation are provided by Jorgenson (1973).

4. Taxation and efficient capital allocation is discussed by Samuelson (1964), Auerbach (1979a, 1979b), Bradford (1980, 1981) and Hall (1981).

5. Combinations of expensing and economic depreciation are analyzed by Auerbach (1979a), Harberger (1980), and Bradford (1981).

6. Estimates of economic depreciation employed in the U.S. national accounts are discussed by Young and Musgrave (1980). These estimates are employed in a study of the U.S. corporate income tax by Feldstein and Summers (1979). See Gravelle (1980c) for a detailed critique of the Feldstein-Summers study and the reply by Feldstein and Summers (1980).

7. We are indebted to Jerry Silverstein of the Bureau of Economic Analysis for preparing these estimates for this study.

8. For each industry composition of investment by type of asset for each year was determined by a biproportional matrix model described by Bacharach (1965). Elements of the initial matrix are based on asset weights reported in Bureau of Economic Analysis (1975).

9. Alternative legislative proposals have been analyzed by Feldstein (1979), Gravelle (1980a, 1980b), and Leape (1980).

10. Depreciation practices are known to differ significantly across industries. This is illustrated in tables 16 and 17 of a report for the U.S. Treasury by Vasquez (1974), and also in a statistical study by Wales (1966) that estimates rates of adoption of accelerated depreciation for two-digit manufacturing industries. Estimates of practices by industries, similar to our aggregate simulation, could be made with more disaggregated IRS-based data and the corresponding investment series.

11. There are some exceptions. Salvage value is removed from the depreciable base when determining allowances with the straight-line and sum-of-the-years' digits methods, but not in the case of the declining balance method, although the account still may not be reduced below its salvage value. The Long amendment, effective in 1962 and 1963, removed the amount of the investment tax credit from the depreciable base.

12. An extensive survey study by Thomas Mayer (1960) examined lags between the start of construction and completion and found the weighted average to be 15 months. If capital is installed evenly during this lag, the average lag between installment and starting depreciation is seven and one-half months.

13. Throughout our simulation we use a half-year convention which embodies the assumption that taxpayers begin taking depreciation on their new assets at midyear. This is implemented by dividing our depreciation rates in half in the first year of an asset's life.

14. The following history of depreciation practices summarizes relevant details found in Gravelle (1979), Pechman (1977), Young (1968), and various issues of the *Statistics of Income: Corporation Income Tax Returns*.

15. See Young (1968), p. 20.

16. Young (1968) pp. 20, 23.

17. *Statistics of Income: Corporation Income Tax Returns*, 1961-62, p. 6, table E.

18. Although it is widely believed that the new Guidelines as well as the investment tax credit applied only to equipment, there was allowance for certain structures. The Guidelines include "special-purpose structures which are an integral part of the production process and which, under normal practices, are replaced contemporaneously, with the equipment they house. . . . Special-purpose structure shall be classified with the equipment they house, support, or serve." (U.S. Treasury Dept. (1962), p. 12.) A considerable amount of investment classified as structures in NIPA falls into this category. Probably an increasing share of NIPA structures investment adopted considerably shorter tax lifetimes under this provision, as is evidenced by an increasing share of structures investment qualified for the investment tax credit, which has a similar eligibility rule.

19. Corcoran (1979) and Vasquez (1974) reach this conclusion independently.

20. U.S. Treasury Department (1962), p. 1.

21. Since 1971, the investment tax credit has been fully effective for assets with lifetimes over 6 years, two-thirds effective with lifetimes of 5 to 6, and one-third effective with lifetimes of 3 to 4. The movements within the range for shorter-lived assets are illustrated in an internal Office of Industrial Economics memo kindly provided by Dennis Cox, deputy director of the Office of Industrial Economics. From a nonrandom sample of approximately 2000 taxpayers in 1973, we find, for example, that 90 percent of investment in automobiles were depreciated at the ADR midpoint and, therefore, become eligible for an investment tax credit. With aircraft, 76 percent were assigned 7 year lifetimes, the upper limit of the ADR, making such investments eligible for the full tax credit.

22. For instance, under ADR nuclear power plants were allowed to shorten their lifetimes from 20 to 16 years.

23. This was brought to our attention by Dennis Cox.

24. *Statistics of Income: Corporation Income Tax Returns,* 1974, p. 128, table 19, and 1975, p. 118, table 16.

25. *Bulletin F* and Guideline-ADR midpoint lifetimes are shown in table 4.

26. Kindly provided by William Sutton on the staff of Joint Committee on Taxation.

27. Tax lifetimes for asset categories 4, 15, 16, and 17, which make up 19 percent of corporate investment were adjusted upward to take advantage of the investment of tax credit.

28. *Statistics of Income: Corporation Income Tax Returns,* 1959-1960, p. 7, table F.

29. *Statistics of Income: Corporation Income Tax Returns,* 1959-1960, p. 7, table E and 1961-62, p. 6, table E.

30. Vasquez (1974), p. 36, table 16.

31. U.S. Treasury Department (1975), tables 23A, 23B.

32. For elaboration, see Myers (1960).

NOTES TO "THE SOCIAL COST OF NONNEUTRAL TAXATION," JANE G. GRAVELLE

1. The basic form of a neutral subsidy is described by Arnold Harberger, "Tax Neutrality in Investment Incentives," in *The Economics of Taxation,* ed. Henry J. Aaron and Michael J. Boskin (Washington, D.C.: The Brookings Institution, 1980) pp. 299-313.

2. See David F. Bradford, "Tax Neutrality and the Investment Credit," in *The Economics of Taxation,* ed. Henry J. Aaron and Michael J. Boskin (Washington, D.C.: The Brookings Institution, 1980) pp. 281-298 and Alan J. Auerbach, "Inflation and the Choice of Asset Life," *Journal of Political Economy* 87 (June 1979): 621-638.

3. Harberger's initial contribution was "The Corporation Income Tax: an Empirical Appraisal," in *Tax Revision Compendium,* House Ways and Means Committee (Washington, D.C.: Government Printing Office, 1959) pp. 231-236.

4. A review of a number of these studies may be found in Dale W. Jorgenson, "Investment and Production: A Review," in *Frontiers of Quantitative Economics,* ed. M. Intrilligator and D. Kendrick (Amsterdam: North-Holland, 1974) pp. 341-375.

5. Patric H. Hendershott and Sheng-Cheng Hu, "Government-Induced Biases in the Allocation of the Stock of Fixed Capital in the United States," in *Capital, Efficiency and Growth,* ed. George M. von Furstenberg (Cambridge, Mass.: Ballinger Publishing Co, 1980) pp. 323-360. The authors measure price and calculate the welfare loss using similar formulae, and present a diagrammatic as well as a mathematical exposition.

6. This formula is given in Robert E. Hall and Dale W. Jorgenson, "Tax Policy and Investment Behavior," *American Economic Review* 57 (June 1967): 391-414.

7.   Patric H. Hendershott and Sheng-Cheng Hu, "Investment in Producer's Durable Equipment," in *How Taxes Affect Economic Behavior,* ed. Henry J. Aaron and Joseph A. Pechman (Washington, D.C.: The Brookings Institution, 1981), pp. 85-126.

8.   Charles R. Hulten and Frank C. Wykoff, "The Measurement of Economic Depreciation," this volume.

9.   Supplied by Larry Dildine, Office of Tax Analysis, and Dennis Cox, Office of Industrial Economics, U.S. Department of Treasury.

10.   U.S. Department of Commerce, Bureau of Economic Analysis, "New Structures and Equipment by Using Industries," *Survey of Current Business* (July 1980): 45-55.

11.   U.S. Department of Treasury, Office of Industrial Economics, *Business Building Statistics* (Washington, D.C.: Government Printing Office, 1976). The structures category mining exploration, shafts and wells does not receive typical depreciation treatment. Present value of depreciation for these assets is based on expensing of 91 percent of cost and economic depreciation rates on the remainder. For a discussion of these rules, see Library of Congress, Congressional Research Service, "Tax Provisions and Effective Tax Rates in the Oil and Gas Industry," by Jane G. Gravelle, Report No. 77-328E, November 3, 1977.

12.   These formulas are given in Dale W. Jorgenson, "The Theory of Investment Behavior," in *Determinants of Investment Behavior,* ed. Robert Ferber, (New York: National Bureau of Economic Research, 1967) pp. 129-155. The optimal period to switch to straight line under 150 percent declining balance is at one-third of the tax life.

13.   U.S. Department of Treasury, Office of Tax Analysis, "The Effects of the Asset Depreciation Range System on Depreciation Practices," by Thomas Vasquez, Paper No. 1, May, 1974.

14.   Investment data are reported in two historical volumes, U.S. Department of Commerce, Bureau of Economic Analysis, *The National Income and Product Accounts: Statistical Tables,* 1929-1965 and 1929-1974; and in July issues of the *Survey of Current Business.*

15.   For a more complete discussion, see Dale W. Jorgenson and Martin A. Sullivan, "Inflation and Capital Recovery in the United States," this volume.

16.   Hendershott and Hu in "Government Induced Biases in the Allocation of the Stock of Fixed Capital in the United States," where they consider a mix of broad asset and sectoral distortions.

17.   Roger H. Gordon and Burton G. Malkiel, "Corporate Finance," in *How Taxes Affect Economic Behavior,* (Washington, D.C.: The Brookings Institution, 1981) pp. 131-192.

18.   Martin J. Bailey, "Progressivity and Investment Yields under U.S. Income Taxation," *Journal of Political Economy* 82 (November/December 1974): 1157-1175.

NOTES TO "PITFALLS IN THE CONSTRUCTION AND USE OF EFFECTIVE TAX RATES," DAVID F. BRADFORD AND DON FULLERTON

1.   For a stimulating treatment of the problems of measuring both the numerator and denominator in such an approach, see Fiekowsky (1977). We recalled Fiekowsky's paper after completing our own but should probably acknowledge an unconscious debt to him for our title.

2.   By the real rate of return ρ we mean the internal rate of return of the project's real cash flow, gross of taxes and subsidies. Because we confine our attention to simple cases, this rate is always well defined.

3.   Note we have assumed that the corporation will actually manage to use its investment credit and that it will benefit from the subsequent depreciation allowances. This assumption

is far from innocuous because the actual income tax is nonlinear. This nonlinearity is obvious for the case of most individuals, but it also holds for corporations risking low or negative taxable income. We have also assumed that depreciation allowances are based on the historical cost of the asset gross of the investment credit. Finally, note that the cash flow to an individual asset owner with marginal tax rate m is obtained by substituting m for u in these expressions.

4. One way of modeling the imperfect substitutability of debt and real capital is to regard the corporation as subject to constraints on this arbitrage, e.g., the outstanding debt cannot exceed some fraction of the value of real assets owned. In this case the relationship (1) will not generally hold for firms where the constraint binds. Other relationships must then determine c/q. See, for example, King (1977). However, the assumption (if only implicit) of unconstrained debt-real capital arbitrage is frequently encountered.

5. Stiglitz [1980] has emphasized that if we really did the analysis "right," π and i would be simultaneously determined as endogenous variables.

6. To our knowledge the first published appearance of Modified Fisher's Law was in Feldstein (1976).

7. If we use Modified Fisher's Law (4b) to eliminate the current interest rate from equilibrium conditions (2) and (3), we obtain

$$\frac{c}{q} = \frac{\delta + (1 - u)i_o}{(1 - u)} \left[1 - k - \frac{u\delta'}{\delta' + (1 - u)i_o + \pi} \right] \quad , \tag{2b}$$

and

$$\frac{c}{q} = \frac{\delta + (1 - u)i_o}{(1 - u)} (1 - k - uz) \quad . \tag{3b}$$

Equation (2b) is equivalent to Hall's crucial equation, except for notational differences. Hall's d and d' correspond to our δ and δ', and his taxable proportion of capital gains, g, is set to zero. Hall's "real after-tax interest rate," r (assumed constant) is what we have called $(1 - u)i_o$. Equation (3b) is the basic equilibrium condition of Jorgenson-Sullivan, with their "rate of return," r (assumed constant) equal to our i_o.

8. There is a question of consistency or existence of equilibrium if the same taxpayer were to earn different after-tax rates of return on different assets. The concluding section of this paper touches on possible resolutions of this problem.

9. See Bailey (1969) for more discussion on this point.

10. For analyses stressing this problem, see Bradford (1980, 1981).

Index

317